CATCHING HELL IN
THE CITY OF ANGELS

Critical American Studies Series
George Lipsitz, University of California–Santa Barbara, series editor

CATCHING HELL IN THE CITY OF ANGELS

*Life and Meanings of Blackness in
South Central Los Angeles*

JOÃO H. COSTA VARGAS

FOREWORD BY
ROBIN D.G. KELLEY

Critical American Studies Series

UNIVERSITY OF MINNESOTA PRESS
MINNEAPOLIS • LONDON

Published by the University of Minnesota Press
111 Third Avenue South, Suite 290
Minneapolis, MN 55401-2520
http://www.upress.umn.edu

Library of Congress Cataloging-in-Publication Data

Costa Vargas, João H.
Catching hell in the city of angels : life and meanings of Blackness in
South Central Los Angeles / João H. Costa Vargas ; foreword by Robin D.G. Kelley.
p. cm. — (Critical American studies series)
Includes bibliographical references and index.
I BN -13: 978-0-8166-4168-0 (hardcover : alk. paper)
I BN -10: 0-8166-4168-4 (hardcover : alk. paper)
I BN -13: 978-0-8166-4169-7 (pbk. : alk. paper)
I BN -10: 0-8166-4169-2 (pbk. : alk. paper)
1. African Americans—Race identity—California—Los Angeles.
2. African Americans—California—Los Angeles—Social conditions.
3. Los Angeles (Calif.)—Race relations. 4. Los Angeles (Calif.)—
Social conditions. I. Title. II. Series.
F869.L89N4 2006
305.896′073079494—dc22
2006008727

Printed in the United States of America on acid-free paper

The University of Minnesota is an equal-opportunity educator and employer.

18 17 16 15 14 13 12 11   10 9 8 7 6 5 4 3 2

CONTENTS

Foreword   ROBIN D.G. KELLEY   ix

Introduction: Looking Forward to Looking Forward   1

1. Blackness as Exclusion and Isolation: The Making of
    Inequalities in South Central   35

2. Blackness as Sorrow and Solidarity: Women and the
    Ethics of Caring   63

3. Blackness as Liability and Powerlessness: Community under
    Siege and the Welfare State   87

4. Blackness as Mobilization and Movement: The Coalition
    Against Police Abuse and the Panther Legacy   109

5. Blackness as Artistry and Affirmation: Leimert Park and the
    Idioms of Jazz   141

6. Blackness as Self-Help and Social Critique: The Community in
    Support of the Gang Truce   177

    Conclusion: Blackness as Blueprint for Social Transformation   215

Acknowledgments   225

Appendix: CAPA's Community Organizing Manual   233

Notes   249

Index   289

FOREWORD

ROBIN D. G. KELLEY

Catching Hell in the City of Angels . . . the title says it all and more. João Costa Vargas has given us an extraordinary book about black poor and working-class communities in South Central Los Angeles during a period of tumultuous economic change. It is a book about displacement and job-lessness, violence and the drug trade, the police and gangs. It is an honest account of the very world that has become grist for the media mill, from voyeuristic news reports on the Crips and the Bloods to cinematic tales from the dark side by maverick filmmakers such as John Singleton and the Hughes Brothers.

But *Catching Hell* is not simply another mind-numbing story of victim-ization, nor is it another social science treatise about what has happened to the past couple of generations of inner-city black youth. And it is a far cry from what has become a kind of gang-book genre depicting young black men as violent, out-of-control predators whose behavior defines the social crisis of contemporary urban life. Instead, this is a book about lib-eration, about the struggle to transform lives and entire communities that have become refugees from the war on drugs. First and foremost, Vargas wants to document and understand struggles for social transformation—what black urban communities, especially the youth, have been doing in terms of "capturing" this hell we know as Watts and turning it into a site of revolutionary change. Writing from inside movements such as the Coalition Against Police Abuse (CAPA) and the Community in Support of the Gang Truce (CSGT), Vargas reveals that overthrowing the status quo is a real possibility, but one that must be understood in the context of numerous internal tensions.

How is it that Vargas can find movements and spaces devoted to social transformation whereas most ethnographers find only violence, materialism, hopelessness, and nihilism? Because he radically shifts his site of "ethnographic observation" away from the street corners and prisons to spaces of creativity and political organization. Just consider what it means to explore the jazz jam sessions in L.A.'s Leimert Park, organized by poet Kamau Daaood and the late drummer Billy Higgins. Here Vargas reveals how these spaces reinforce aspects of the dominant structure and class tensions between poor/working-class and middle-class blacks and at the same time offer what he calls "a truly utopian, transcendental model of social relations." By looking at movements formed by former gang members, he locates emergent "utopian, transcendental" visions of freedom in CAPA and CSGT. It is precisely through the relationships among these various modes of resistance against class and race oppression and the work of community artists that Vargas is able to explore the expansive and flexible meanings of community.

Community is a word the author takes very seriously. He resists nostalgic depictions of community as cohesive sites of unity and resistance, and instead acknowledges the fault lines, the sharp divisions by class and gender. He recognizes, for example, the prominence of masculinism/male centeredness as a fundamental feature of most liberatory movements emerging in urban, dispossessed communities. What he finds in the 1990s, of course, has direct historical precedents in earlier black liberation struggles. Thus, as most scholars hoping to make sense of post-Rebellion L.A. insisted on focusing on the gang truce and acknowledging the gang roots in the Black Panther Party and the Community Alert Patrol in the late 1960s, virtually no one considered the possibility that autonomous women's organizations might spring up in the "public squares" of Nickerson Gardens, Jordan Downs, and Imperial Gardens. Yet, just prior to the Watts rebellion of 1965, women did the most organizing, in groups such as the Watts Women's Association, the Avalon-Carver Community Center, the Mothers of Watts Community Action Council, Mothers Anonymous, the Welfare Recipients Union, the Welfare Rights Organization, the Central City Community Mental Health Center, the Neighborhood Organizations of Watts, the South Central Volunteer Bureau of Los Angeles, to name but a few. But in the aftermath of the Watts rebellion, most of these women-led organizations were undermined by a Black Power ideology that emphasized male supremacy and male leadership roles.

Vargas understands that unless we confront and critique a politics that privileges black masculinity, we are destined to see the same thing: the silencing of black women. He goes out of his way to find articulations of black feminist thought within the contemporary organizations he studies, while always paying attention to black women's autonomous networks in the community. While this is not the primary focus of *Catching Hell in the City of Angels*, Vargas reminds us that in L.A. and elsewhere, working-class black and Latino women built and sustained community organizations that have registered voters, patrolled the streets, challenged neighborhood drug dealers, defended the rights of prisoners, and fought vigorously for improvements in housing, city services, health care, and public assistance. Examples of these movements include Mothers ROC (Reclaiming Our Children) and Mothers of East Los Angeles (MELA). Mothers ROC was founded in 1992 by Theresa Allison, the mother of Dewayne Holmes, who helped engineer the historic gang truce in the aftermath of the L.A. rebellion but was falsely convicted on trumped-up charges soon thereafter. Her efforts to overturn his conviction convinced her to form a movement that could challenge the racist and sexist criminal justice system. Mothers ROC has called for an immediate end to the War on Drugs (recognizing it for what it is: a war on black and Latino youth); the repeal of the "three strikes" law; more funding for public defenders; an end to mandatory minimum laws; and an end to indiscriminate stops, warrantless searches, and the use of electronic databases to identify alleged gang members.

Fundamentally, *Catching Hell in the City of Angels* is a study of blackness as a mode of struggle and social transformation. *Blackness* is a key word here. Vargas sees blackness as solidarity and sorrow; as mobilization and movement; as artistry and affirmation; and as self-help and social critique. During an era when much of the so-called Left is calling on movements to "transcend" race and identity politics (a position, incidentally, that is becoming increasingly popular among contemporary mainstream black leadership), Vargas argues boldly that "if an ethical commitment to liberatory politics is the energizer of self-making, blackness is *absolutely necessary* as a source of knowledge of the social world, survival, resistance, and community maintenance." Not that he advocates some kind of essentialist politics or a narrow nationalism; he recognizes that a politics rooted in blackness is not inherently closed but rather is open to broader alliances and to dynamic change. Blackness, in other words, has always had the capacity to be remade. Blackness, in real historical and political practice, is expansive, flexible, multiple, and contradictory, and thus can be the potential for revolutionary political vision. And, as we have already seen with regard to gender, conceptions of blackness can also exclude!

For those who see black urban youth as only apolitical, misinformed nihilists, the emancipatory possibilities described in this book might easily be dismissed as wishful thinking. But read carefully, listen to the voices of folks like Michael Zinzun and Kamau Daaood, and remember that moment of possibility when the black and Latino poor were seizing property and destroying what many regarded as symbols of domination. If it is true—that the men and women of Watts and Oakland, Harlem and the South Bronx, Detroit and West Philly, and all the ghettos of North America can really "capture" hell—perhaps the inner cities really are the logical place for a new radical movement in post–Cold War America.

LOOKING FORWARD TO
LOOKING FORWARD

When Kody first saw me, he thought I was a paper collector. Through his metal security door, all he could see was someone bringing piles of paper into the apartment opposite to his. I was moving in and, indeed, most of my belongings were books and loose paper. I had borrowed a small wooden cart in which I was carrying my objects, and the combination of papers and cart pulled by a long-haired, bearded, and brown-skinned stranger allowed for Kody's first guess.

I had not noticed anybody looking at me. I could hear different music coming from various apartments, occasional laughter, shouts, and, as soon as I finished unloading and tried to regain my breath, the sounds of heli-copter rotors and gunshots filled the evening. My apartment's electricity was not hooked up. In the dark, and among vaguely distinguishable debris left behind by the former tenants, the foreign loud noises, gunfire, and police movements in the air were not announcing a pleasant first night in the neighborhood. When the gunfire got closer and the helicopters' flood-lights invaded my apartment, I decided to go back to my former residence and check if I had left anything behind.

The next day was Monday. The building in which I had chosen to live did not look as welcoming as it had before. A "For Rent" sign hung from the second floor of the motel-like construction. (It would be almost another year before the first "Se Renta" was put up, following most of the build-ings in the neighborhood.) Garbage overflowed the containers. Squalid dogs sniffed for food and ran as I walked toward my apartment. Car oil, leftovers and murky waters made the cracked cement patio slippery.

While I was trying to match one of the six new keys to my security door, Kody shouted from behind his metal screen, "Hey man, do you have a smoke?"

I could not see him. He opened his door and introduced himself. I told him I had some cigarettes inside. He went back to his apartment, grabbed his little boy, Jordan, and came back. Black slacks, black sneakers, dark blue sweatshirt: he was approximately 5′6″, dark, sharp-minded, and friendly. Although he looked much older, he was only twenty-seven. His missing teeth, a forehead constantly wrinkled in a frown, and a preoccupied, tired gaze added another ten years to his apparent age. When I pointed to the packet of Drum rolling tobacco, Kody said that was the one he used to have in prison. He had been out for less than a month, trying to get his life back together. He was living with Shannon, with whom he had had Jordan, and two other kids Shannon had from previous relationships, Joshua and Florence. The kids were four, five, and six, respectively.

We sat around a little table that I had set among the jumble and rolled our cigarettes. Kody looked around and, pointing to the burn marks on the dark brown carpet, told me that my apartment used to be a crack house. I wasn't very surprised. I had also noticed similar marks in the bathroom and, from what I remember, the kitchen floor was also badly marked before being replaced. He quickly added that the bungalow next door was now the street's crack house, and that the people running it were friends with everybody in our building. He told me the name of the Crip set that controlled it, a combination of letters and numbers from which Kody drew visible pleasure in reciting, and we contemplated the smoke filling the room.

Our daily conversations usually took place in the early evenings. Since coming out of prison, and having two strikes on his record—both connected to crack cocaine—Kody was trying to find a job outside the narcotics economy. He left early in the mornings, and sometimes I gave him a ride to his interviews. Openings for cleaning personnel, janitors, cooks, mechanics, dishwashers, security guards, clerks: Kody would pursue all of them. We first tried eight, then seven, then six in the morning: no matter how early we arrived at the job selection places, there was always a small group of people waiting in line. Most of them were Latina/os, chatting in Spanish, wet hair, neatly dressed and, despite the frequent "se habla espanol" sign, visibly intimidated by the situation. Kody and most of the

Blacks there, on the other hand, although anxious to get hired, did not dress especially for the occasion.[1] Nobody flew their colors, that is, no evident gang signs were displayed, but the tension was there. Vendettas happened not so much between Crips and Bloods as they did among different Crip sets. Kody carried his loaded 9mm gun all the time, and he would always ask me to drive slowly by the group of people waiting before we got out of the car. He wanted to be sure no recognizable foes were there. His eyes carefully scrutinized the Blacks; Latina/os were mostly ignored, save for the surprise their large numbers caused.

"Damn those Latinos, man! No wonder homeboys aren't getting no jobs! Look at that! Where the hell they come from? They must have slept here, man!"

From what I gathered along our conversations, Kody's name was associated with an extensive and well-known list of enemies he had killed. Kody had a reputation for his shooting accuracy, courage, and mercilessness—characteristics difficult to reconcile with his general friendliness and his will to enter the formal job market and provide for his family. He was desperately trying to put his past aside and start anew. The prospect of getting his third strike and spending the next twenty-five years in jail without the possibility of parole, as he was constantly reminded by his parole officer and by himself, served as a strong encouragement to find work. Yet, erasing his memories and maintaining the self-imposed ostracism from gang life did not depend exclusively on him. Much of what he experienced out of prison only served to sabotage his wishes to assimilate into the poor, less-than-minimum-wage working class. After the first month of job search, he was beginning to consider a $4-an-hour job offer a lucky strike.

As his tattooed arms, neck, and hands symbolized, he was permanently marked by gang life. His will to abandon the set that protected and provided for him, and for which he was once willing to kill and die, was not enough to overcome his past. It was certainly not enough to get a job; it was not enough to end the death threats toward him and his family; it was not enough to deal with the guilt—more pronounced the more he distanced himself from the gang—associated with the deaths he perpetrated and, most of all, it was well short of alleviating his escalating state of anxiety, fear, and depression. Kody was feeling trapped between his difficulties in finding work, the imperatives of providing for his kids and companion, and the constant danger of being attacked by his enemies.

I later learned that Shannon and Kody had chosen our specific building because, having a U-shaped court protected from the streets, it provided a relatively safe playground for the children as well as enabled Kody to have a view of anyone who arrived. From behind the metal screen door, Kody entertained the kids while keeping an eye on the outside movements.

Even though overwhelmed and increasingly discouraged as he was turned down for work again and again, Kody was determined not to give up. This meant, above all, ignoring the seductions of easy money and fast life the gang offered. Shannon made sure he kept to a minimum all contacts with his homies, his fellow set members. Although he considered the gang his kin and missed them, he kept his distance and followed Shannon's instructions. He limited his visits to the times he saw his mother, still living in the area dominated by his expanding and ever-powerful gang. There he socialized with his friends, and was updated on what was happening in the gang war.

Cutting ties with the set was proving to be much more difficult than he had expected. Since joining the gang when he was eleven, Kody found in his new kinship group most of the emotional and material goods that were missing in his other social networks. His father had left home before he could remember. Even though he showed up for birthdays and Thanksgiving when he was not in jail or not too altered by alcohol and heroin, he died of cancer in 1986. According to Kody, his father's problems started when he lost his job at a local tire factory in the early 1980s. Following the layoff, his second wife left, he started collecting public assistance checks, and he fell into a downward spiral of addiction and depression.

Meanwhile, Kody's mother also collected welfare benefits, meaning that Kody and his sisters and brothers lived on a very tight budget. The frequent abuse his mother suffered from her successive volatile companions, in addition to the difficulties she had harmonizing children and adolescents growing up in economic deprivation, generated an atmosphere in the house that became unbearable very early. Both his older sisters dropped out of school to help their mother; upon being caught for small robberies and returning from juvenile camp, one of his brothers, three years his senior, left home—never to be heard of again; and Kody was left to take care of his younger brother and finish school. Education, his mother often repeated, was his only way to make it. Before marrying his father, she had been a telephone operator, and often emphasized that good jobs required good schooling.

But school seemed dull compared to the flashy clothes, jewelry, and cars young people began to display as Kody was growing up. In his recollections, his early adolescence was marked by the fascination successful drug dealers and gang members exerted on him and on most kids in his neighborhood. With the death of his best friend, slain right next to him during a drive-by shooting aimed at some enemy gangster who lived in the area, Kody joined his street's Crip subdivision. He began as a lookout, warning the dealers of police and enemy presence. The days were mostly spent on his ten-speed bicycle, his first one, given to him by the dealer he was working for. He was making between $30 and, exceptionally, up to $100 a day, most of which he gave to his sisters. Kody's mother was extremely upset with her son's new activities, worried that he might be caught by the police or killed. She threatened to kick him out of the house if he did not stop his activities. He did not stop and did not get kicked out of the house: instead, he managed to sneak in money for overdue bills and much needed groceries. As the economic conditions in the house improved, and as the general mood became less tense, Kody's mother stopped asking about his gang involvement and the benefits that came with it.

By the time Kody reached seventeen he had become a runner. The runner is the contact between the cocaine-processing laboratories and the dealers. Kody repeatedly told me how much he loved this occupation. He frequently had to drive long distances and master a series of ever-changing routes throughout the Los Angeles County region and beyond. During our trips to job selections, groceries, and pharmacies, Kody always took pleasure in naming the streets and freeway exits; he drew satisfaction in telling me which way was the fastest at a given time and which regions were to be avoided. He had a complex knowledge not only of our immediate surroundings, but also of greater Los Angeles' arteries and geographical references. He integrated several variables into his assessments of the best routes: time of the day, frequency of stop lights, speed limits, likelihood of traffic, and so on. Of course, he also knew which territories belonged to different sets, and where the police were most likely to be at any given time of the day or night. Above all, Kody appreciated the freedom to ride away from his neighborhood, freedom that was enhanced, during his runner occupation, by the fast and relatively easy money he was making. Around 1986—the year Kody remembers as being the last before his first long term in the penitentiary—he would receive up to $250 a day. By then he was living alone, had his late-model automobile, was spending large amounts of money with women and parties, and was heavily armed.

Yet the easy money came with a price. Compared to the lookout position, doing runs was a much riskier job. Indeed, Kody was first shot during one of those runner operations. Anticipating his route from the laboratory, a group of rival Crips ambushed him and tried to seize his cocaine. He drove a late-model Cadillac and was armed with a shotgun and an automatic pistol. (Kody did not tell me if he was accompanied, but it is safe to assume that he had somebody with him since a lookout is always important during transactions.) Kody was hit in both legs and a forearm, but did not surrender the merchandise. It was while proudly showing the scars that he first told me about his former activities in the drug economy. He was sure that he killed one and seriously wounded another in that four-person assault group. His multiple wounds, although requiring several operations and long hospitalization periods, were relatively simple (so he made them seem). Yet they marked him as a survivor and, most important in terms of his curriculum in the drug trade, as a lucky and skillful killer. The benefits of his acquired reputation quickly followed.

His services were now becoming more valued and requested. Money, clothes, gold, women, and cars were increasingly available. But so were the intense and often deadly struggles with other gangs and with the police. Kody's narrations of his adventures toward notoriety in the gang world are full of violence—imprisonment and death were as part of everyday life, as was the material abundance. He considered himself very fortunate to have survived: "Most don't make it past twenty. I'm really lucky, man." The more he traded, the more he killed, and the more he survived—and the more he became concerned with death. Drive-bys were becoming increasingly frequent. It was at that time that Kody began putting aside some of the merchandise he distributed for his personal use. The psychological strains of having to kill in order to survive were becoming unbearable. He remembered that the majority of lookouts and dealers were high most of the time. If death came, he sometimes said, it would be like just another trip.

With the escalation in the volume of drug trade and the unprecedented levels of currency available throughout the drug networks, disputes between and among sets intensified and became more sophisticated. Kody remembers when, in the mid-1980s, shotguns and automatic pistols became almost obsolete compared to the widespreading use of automatic assault rifles such as the AK-47, Uzi submachine guns, and M16 semiautomatics. The ambush that could have claimed his life served as a wake-up call to acquire more powerful weaponry.

Shortly after the ambush Kody became a dealer, commanding a small group of runners and lookouts while still doing runs for himself and for others in his set. Money came in as fast as ever, and I heard several times from Kody—especially during bursts of frustration with the difficulties finding work and the pressure from Shannon—that during those times he would make up to $2,000, even $3,000 a day.[2] This meant that his work schedule was very flexible and allowed for plenty of diversion time. Women were fundamental indicators of wealth and prestige. Cars, clothes and jewelry were not as meaningful if not enhanced and accompanied by women. Every time Kody talked about his life as a successful dealer, he emphasized the increasing availability of women and how this consolidated his reputation. The "bitches," as he classified them, appear in his recollections as mere pleasure objects, too vain and available to be seriously considered. As objects, they had no voice and were subjected to the man's wishes. In exchange, Kody pointed out, they acquired some notoriety, were given clothes and jewelry, and had access to the best selection of drugs. Nevertheless, monogamous relations were not the norm, and the benefits of being a dealer's sexual "partner" were short-lived, either due to being abandoned for other women or because of the dealer's imprisonment or death.

The extreme derision with which Kody and other dealers related to women became even more salient when he described his relationship with Shannon. Shannon, he often affirmed, was not a dealer's bitch, and submitting to any man was out of the question. They met in 1991, shortly after he completed four years of a sentence resulting from a raid in his house following an undercover agent's lead. Shannon was nine years older than he, and even though she had been a gangster and went through incarceration, during her days gangbanging was less violent and glorious than in Kody's accounts. Her quarrels often resulted in no more than a few knife and fistfights. She had lost one of her front teeth and a scar ran down from her forehead to her chin on one side of her face. Since the beginning, she was the dominating personality in the relationship. Kody had been changing.

By the time he was out of the penitentiary, he had lost his turf and the power that came with it. Many of his friends were incarcerated or dead. And even though a younger generation of gang members respected and accepted him as their natural leader, Kody had become more cautious with business. Having been caught so easily and unexpectedly by the police made him suspicious of most people. Thus, very cautious and surrounded by a few old-timers and even fewer new recruits—"I had never seen so many little homies around, man, where were they coming from?"—Kody lacked the aggressiveness required to start, expand, and maintain a drug-trade territory. He didn't think seriously about leaving the drug business for that was all he knew how to do. But his hesitations were becoming stronger. Then he met Shannon.

In the spring of 1991 Shannon was taking care of two babies: Florence was not quite two years old and Joshua was barely one. As was still the case in 1996, she attended the Shields Program at the Martin Luther King Jr./Drew Hospital for her crack dependency, and received Aid to Families with Dependent Children (AFDC) and food stamps. Shortly after starting the relationship with Kody, she became pregnant. Shannon did not expect Kody to take responsibility for their child. Her other children's fathers had disappeared as soon as she told them about her pregnancy, and she did not count on anything different from Kody. Yet, Kody's long time in prison and his less-than-enthusiastic new beginning in South Central's drug market had made him more sensible. He was genuinely concerned with Shannon and their baby. Moreover, Shannon's strong character and her struggle to overcome crack addiction impressed Kody. When telling me their story, he frequently accentuated Shannon's determination and strength. And because she commanded the income and paid the rent, she dictated the rules. Kody was not allowed to stay there overnight for she feared drive-bys and other attacks. Were they to be together, he had to leave the gangs and the drugs; most important, he had to find a job. "Man, I was so impressed with that lady. In my old days I'd only meet those hollow-headed bitches, you know what I'm saying? I mean, they were around us for the money, and some were hooked really bad on that shit we were selling. They were dirty, man, really dirty! But my ol' lady here, damn, what a woman!"

Even though Kody cared for Shannon and was trying to stay away from the gangs and the dope market, he had by then developed a crack-cocaine addiction. The solution he found for both his addiction and the need to contribute to Shannon's expenses was to do some runs for dealers he knew. This strategy lasted less than a year and a half. During this period his addiction grew more intense and expensive, he became very unreliable, and the relationship with Shannon deteriorated. Jordan was born during this turmoil and before his first birthday Kody was arrested for the second time. Shannon visited Kody whenever she could, and they reconciled while he was serving his sentence. But their future reunion was not the only matter they talked about. Doctors suspected Jordan had developmental problems due to Shannon's crack use.[3] Kody remembers the first two years of prison with great distress since his son's coordination and reactions were developing at a slower pace than expected. But even though Jordan cried incessantly, was very irritable, and took almost three years to walk and pronounce his first words, he grew up to be perfectly normal, save for his relatively smaller size.

During my first four months in South Central, Kody was not able to obtain and maintain a single job, except for a two-day stay at a shoe store in Gardena, about three miles south of where we were. We celebrated his new job with beer and cigarettes he had saved for special occasions. Shannon was visibly happier and, for the first time since I was living there and had known Kody, she did not mind us having our little party. The job offered no benefits, but with the $4.50 per hour, Kody would now be able to substantially contribute to their two-bedroom $550 rent. Monthly, Shannon received $378 in food stamps and $595 in AFDC. To this Kody added $118 in food stamps per month. I eventually learned these numbers by heart since they were repeated to me every time Kody asked to borrow money—usually to buy medication or food for the children, and sometimes for cigarettes. If they paid their rent and bills on time, their money did not last beyond the first week of each month. After that, they depended on family and friends to feed themselves and the kids. Jordan and Joshua felt their money problems in their stomachs, and thus greeted tenants with murmurs of either "do you have a dollar?" or "do you have cookies?"

But Kody was now certain that their financial situation was going to improve. He planned on doing extra hours during evenings and weekends. The kids needed new clothes—they were growing quickly—and Kody was euphoric with the possibility of planning ahead. Simply looking forward to looking forward. He confided that Shannon and he might get married since, not only was he working, but also Shannon seemed to be pregnant.

"Man, homeboy here is gonna make it! He's gonna get this little dough coming every month, feed the kids, have some new furniture, get a stereo, take his ol' lady to the movies, get her some nice clothes, and eventually get a ride—you know, L.A's such a huge place, everything is far away. And my mom's house also needs some things, some work done. . . . I'll make her proud."

On his third day at the shoe store, Kody came back home early. From my apartment, and even though we were not next-door neighbors, I could hear Shannon screaming and venting every possible swear word she could imagine. She said that she could not take that anymore, that the rent was due, the kids were hungry, and that no man was going to live in her apartment doing nothing. There was no way Kody could calm her down until two women and a man who lived in the building came to the scene and told Kody to let them talk to Shannon and take the kids away from the house. Kody came over with Josh and Jordan, leaving Florence with her mother. I asked him what happened.

"Well, that motherfucker parole officer called my boss yesterday."

"Hadn't you told them you had been in jail?"

"You kidding, man? Why do you think I was getting nothing so far? No way, man! Plus, they didn't ask anyways."

Kody told me that something similar had happened before. It was common for parole officers to call employers who hire people under their supervision. The consequence is usually the loss of the recently and arduously acquired work. It is difficult to believe parole officers are not conscious of the effects their actions have on those under their surveillance. In Kody's case, the fact that he had not told his new boss of his parole only made matters worse. His boss felt betrayed and did not accept any explanations. Kody's short-lived punctuality, honesty, and disposition were not enough to counter the stigma of a convicted felon with a history of gangbanging.

The days following his firing, Kody fell back into his melancholic state. He was still searching for jobs, but his enthusiasm had vanished. Being a high-school dropout with his criminal record and displaying gangster demeanor and vernacular did not make matters any better. After a series of unsuccessful searches, and with tension between him and Shannon rising as the useless days followed one another, he became indignant. This time the Latina/os were to blame.

"They always pick up the fucking Latinos, man. Those motherfuckers don't say nothing. $3 an hour my ass! Fuck that!"

Interestingly, Kody had always reiterated that he had no problem with any racial group. If he were to choose, he told me once, he would socialize with non-Blacks. "Blacks are always measuring you up. There's lot of competition, and homeboys are always jealous, always looking for trouble. One of my best friends, back when I was selling that shit, was this White dude from Santa Monica. We were really cool with one another." But now times were different. He found most job openings to be filled with Latina/os. His frustration intensified when he heard that Latina/os were willing to work for less than the minimum wage and that they did not press for any benefits. We did not know any Latina/os, and all the information we had about them came through the grapevine. Their large numbers at job selections and Kody's unsuccessful searches only served as evidence that confirmed the rumors.

Shannon's impatience and Kody's frustration were escalating to the point where every time he arrived home from an unsuccessful job search they started an argument. Following one of those arguments, Kody came over to my apartment and said Shannon had decided to have an abortion. He also asked for a ride to the clinic. He was against the procedure, but he was also very conscious that the difficulties they were already having were only going to get worse with a new baby. They had their last argument the day following the abortion. Kody had suggested, in between Shannon's loud complaints that the kids were hungry and that they had bills to pay, that he was going to start selling drugs again. From my apartment I heard Shannon's explosion of anger and disappointment as she told him to leave. As happened with increasing frequency, neighbors came to their place to cool things down. Kody was sent to my apartment, where he told me what had happened. He decided to stay with his mother until he found work, even though his mother lived in a gang area that made him even more worried. On that same night he requested to be driven to the supermarket where he bought collard greens. According to Kody, the doctor had recommended them for Shannon. It would help in her recovery.

A couple of weeks went by before I heard of Kody again. A police car pulled in the building's driveway. I saw Shannon speaking to one of the officers. She did not seem upset or surprised. As I came out of my apartment to see what was going on, she gave me the news brought by the police.

"You know what happened to your brother Kody? He's in hospital, with this big hole in his head."

"Was he shot?" I asked, waiting to hear the worst.

"I don't know. They say he was run over by a car or something." Kody had been taken to the hospital's intensive care unit.

According to Shannon Kody was doing well, but before he totally recovered he left without notice. Nobody knew where he was. Shannon told me that he might be at his mother's and that, if I wanted to speak to him, she would give me a number where he could be reached.

Kody had probably been the victim of what he had expected for a long time: an assault by one of his many rivals. The story told by the police, namely, that he had been accidentally run over by a car, did not make much sense. As for leaving the hospital as soon as he could walk, it was consistent with the stories he had told me. He had been seriously wounded at least twice before this last incident. He always dreaded hospitals, not so much for the cold environment, but for the vulnerability he felt lying in bed not fully conscious. Several times during our conversations he mentioned it was common practice to finish off gangsters who were in for treatment. Kody feared that as soon as the news of his hospitalization reached the grapevine he would be in serious danger.

☾

Young people in South Central Los Angeles live a complex social and psychological existence in the face of imminent death. Many of those born in poor but formerly working-class families (often broken by the consequences of the absence of work) turn to gangs—or "sets," as they are more commonly called in the inner city—for support and validation.[4] Faced with chronic unemployment and underemployment, they find work in the drug economy, which provides an opportunity for remuneration as well as an entry into a seemingly supportive social world. Because of its children's participation in the drug economy, a household may temporarily have some income other than public-assistance checks or the meager wages of informal work.

Young males are more frequently recruited and more richly rewarded in this work, creating new meanings for old categories of gender and generation. While a young man's contributions may ease the daily struggle to survive, his family and his neighbors may well become unintended targets in the endless vendettas that characterize gang wars. Only by leaving the family can a gang member substantially reduce its vulnerability to death. Imprisonment or assassination often cause the separation. Yet even while the threats and tension diminish, once the remaining family is left without the income provided by illicit activity, it finds itself once more in severe pains to make ends meet.

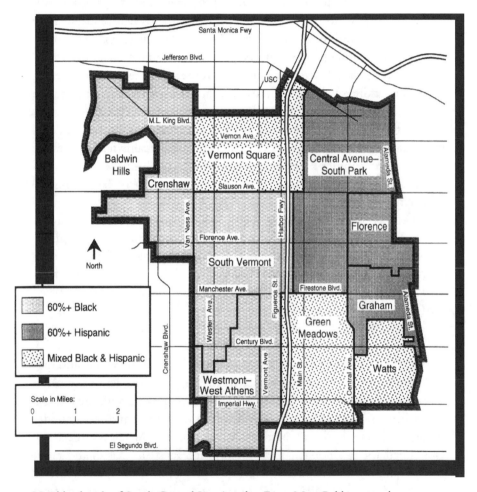

Neighborhoods of South Central Los Angeles. From Marc Baldamare, ed., *The Los Angeles Riots: Lessons for the Urban Future* (Boulder, Colo.: Westview Press, 1994), 21.

If the gang member survives long enough, this cycle is not only repeated, but becomes more intense every time he tries to constitute a family, for the longer one survives, the more work one has to do to maintain and expand territories. This often means having to intimidate and kill. More commonly, poor young men in South Central expect neither to constitute nor settle with a family, spend much time out of prison, or live past their twenties. In spite of desperate attempts to break away, this spiral of death is often a self-fulfilling prophecy. Unemployment leads to gang involvement, which leads to imprisonment (if not death), which renders future employment more difficult, reinforcing gang attachment, which restarts the cycle at a more intense, death-prone pace. In Los Angeles County today, one in three African American men between the ages of twenty and twenty-nine is under the supervision of the criminal justice system, either in prison or in jail, or on probation or parole.[5]

This situation is often attributed to alleged weaknesses in the character, motivation, and morals of inner-city dwellers, but in reality it illustrates the reduced opportunities Black youngsters have in the formal economy and suggests orchestrated institutional efforts to maintain social exclusion. The persistently depressed inner city can only be deciphered once the multiple effects of joblessness, gang involvement, and the justice system are analyzed within the historical framework of institutionalized racism, segregation, massive immigration into the inner city, and income and wealth concentration. In Los Angeles' case, these factors are intensified by a history of fragmentation between the city's neighborhoods *and* within the Black inner city itself.[6]

☙

This study describes and analyzes recent economic, demographic, and spatial transformations in Los Angeles from the point of view of its African American population. How are Blacks coping with multiple assaults on their physical and spiritual well-being in the largest and most rapidly changing city on the West Coast? Since the 1980s Los Angeles has been the most divided city among all U.S. metropoles. Its social classes and racial groups have been increasingly polarized by wealth, income, and place of residence. For people of African descent, such disparities reveal unprecedented depths. The City of Angels today contains both the richest and the poorest Black populations in the country.

By investigating internal dynamics within South Central Los Angeles, this study focuses diachronically and synchronically on the worldviews and practices of those who, by virtue of their perceived race and irrespective of their individual attributes, character, and effort, have been discriminated against so systematically that their sheer collective existence is at risk.

All Blacks in Los Angeles experience subordination and domination, suppression and repression, but not in the same ways. In this study, I explore how different forms of blackness emerge from different experiences, conditions, and spatial settings. The chapter titled "Blackness as Sorrow and Solidarity" characterizes the shared social life and collective identity created among residents of an apartment building in a low-income, drug-ravaged neighborhood. "Blackness as Mobilization and Movement" captures the meaning attributed to shared racial experiences by members of the activist Coalition Against Police Abuse. "Blackness as Artistry and Affirmation" embodies the core concerns and self-concepts prevalent among artists and entrepreneurs associated with a Black cultural center in a South Central neighborhood. "Blackness as Self-Help and Social Critique" encapsulates the contradictory mixture of individualism and collective unity propelling the Community in Support of the Gang Truce (CSGT).

Each of these versions of Black identity reveals how African Americans of various backgrounds are coping with (and at times contributing to) systematic oppression. Each group's experiences elucidate the issues that bind and separate Blacks from diverse social, economic, and cultural backgrounds. Social fault lines in South Central Los Angeles reflect both contemporary social and economic disparities and long-term struggles between and among Blacks of different social groups, genders, sexualities, places of residence, ages, political outlooks, and relations with the state.[7]

Although replete with structural causes and consequences, fissions and fractures within the Black community often coalesce around cultural questions about idealized notions of authentic blackness. Pervasive and unremitting residential segregation causes involuntary proximities among Black people. Wealthy Blacks find it difficult to move away from poor Blacks. Black entrepreneurs rely on Black customers because discriminatory lending and procurement policies impede their access to other communities. Housing segregation makes blackness the banner around which Black politicians rally their supporters. The power of state institutions in their lives compels Black voters to seek assistance from Black politicians. Yet in attending to the inescapably racial dimensions of their experience, Black communities run the risk of allowing blackness to occlude other axes of oppression and suppression like class, gender, sexuality, and citizenship.

Black consciousness serves as a necessary and productive source of solidarity and social critique for tenement residents, activists against police brutality, artists, and organizers of the gang truce. Members of each group go far beyond biology to inscribe political import to their understandings of blackness. Yet exclusive focus on race can obscure how racial identities are inflected by and permeated with other identities, associations, and experiences. No one experiences identity in isolation: race is lived through modalities of class, gender, sexuality, and citizenship.

Social class plays a particularly powerful role in giving parochial inflections to generalized notions of blackness. For African Americans in Los Angeles, the Black class structure is both a divisive force in the community and a markedly compressed entity mandating solidarity. Upward mobility by Blacks is precarious and fragile as inequalities in wealth and property mean that gains in income and occupational status are likely to be lost in the next generation.[8] Moreover, terms such as *middle class* or *working class* are unable to capture the intermediate classifications that are used in everyday conversations among Blacks to convey one's place in society. Class concepts used by Blacks in South Central frequently refer less to empirical social and economic standing than to everyday matters of speech, style, labor, and leisure, to how one walks and talks, where one lives, what and how one eats, how and where one spends free time, and with whom one interacts. The ability to perform specific identities—as well as the ability to switch between different codes depending on the context—reveals one's class position(s) and suggests the relative fluidity of the category. Class is inflected by, and in turn shapes, how race, gender, sexuality, age, place of residence, and political inclinations, among many factors, are experienced.[9]

With all its necessary fluidity, social class remains a perpetual source of tension within Black communities. Because Blacks continue to be segregated, social distance does not produce spatial distance. South Central Los Angeles exemplifies this phenomenon paradigmatically. Clashing notions about politics, public space, and social mores become expressed in vehement ways that would perhaps not be as intense were it not for forced proximity. The social dynamics of South Central Los Angeles revolve around conflicting, necessarily class-related worldviews that define how the inner city is experienced. Blackness in this context is a matter of consensus *and* conflict, solidarity *and* stratification, mutual recognition *and* mutual recrimination.

Social class in South Central serves as a proxy for specific notions of race, geographic space, gender, sexuality, culture, and politics. When people define themselves as working class or as residents of the more affluent areas of South Central, they make statements about income and occupation, but also about notions of blackness, respectability, and political allegiance. Social class absorbs, transforms, and in turn becomes shaped by a gamut of variables. Conversely, notions of race, gender, sexuality, and politics are also indications and determinants of how social class is lived.[10]

I emphasize tensions among African Americans because the seemingly insurmountable obstacles hampering meaningful explanations, effective strategies, and powerful social movements capable of appealing to the varied hearts and minds of Blacks and other aggrieved racialized communities create radical divisiveness as well as radical solidarity. Structural and systematic discrimination, embodied in a plethora of public policies, and institutionalized through a vast array of everyday practices, are not the only adversaries racialized groups face in their struggles for survival and social justice. As daunting as these certainly are, they are only part of the story.

The genocidal suppression of Blacks is essentially a social phenomenon—it is collective, cumulative, and continuing, devastating people regardless of their individual aptitudes and efforts.[11] Resistance and survival require struggle by progressive, grassroots social movements. In the face of collective injury, self-help and its older ideological cousin, individualism, do not work.[12] This does not mean that personal responsibility and individual transformation are not important. They are necessary, but they are certainly not sufficient to combat collectively experienced oppression, much less annihilation. To understand the meaning, importance, and force of everyday practices and political organizations that have the potential to bring about social justice and change, we must also pay attention to the hurdles in the way of constructing effective social movements. We must be aware of political, social, cultural, and generational chasms *within* the communities that bear the disproportionate brunt of structural inequalities and racist policies. We must recognize the contributions that we, as Blacks, make toward facilitating our own genocide. We must address our complicity with the powers that, unchecked, will divide, imprison, and kill all of us. Consequently, if there exist hopes for a better future amid the inner city's routinized chaos, these hopes must be understood vis-à-vis both historically actualized structural inequalities *and* persistent tensions emerging out of varied experiences and outlooks among those living in hypersegregated Black ghettos.[13]

My principal concerns in this work are to locate, describe, and understand critically explanations, strategies, and social movements that have the potential for challenging current ideologies and policies. The ultimate aim of this ethnography, therefore, is to identify and assess political visions that point to projects of social organization whose premises and practices make it possible to survive genocide, achieve justice and freedom, and decolonize ourselves in the process. Yet critical theories and practices are already in place. They are precisely what have made it possible for Blacks to have survived to this day, to transcend slavery, lynchings, police brutality, environmental racism, employment discrimination, residential segregation, and unequal education. Only by an act of infinite ignorance and no less infinite arrogance could I claim any authorship of this Black radical tradition. This book does reflect, however, a small part of that vast political imaginary that is and has been in place for a long time.[14] By translating such imaginary to this written and academic language, I run the risk of impoverishing it. But there is a consolation in that this book may help to raise the curiosity and courage of those interested in thinking about and engaging with decolonization and radical transformation.

Social critique and political practice necessarily imply engagement and commitment. This ethnography, therefore, does not pretend to be impartial. I do not claim to have a detached view toward the society and the many persons and institutions with whom I interacted and studied. Participant observation is always determined by the anthropologist's moral principles. In my case, and especially considering my (many times involuntary) entanglement in my neighbors' everyday problems, my work in unapologetically political institutions such as the Coalition Against Police Abuse (CAPA), and my extensive involvement with the local Muslims and amateur jazz musicians, *observant participation* better describes the ways in which I obtained my data.

The "fly on the wall" approach in anthropology, still taught as an antidote to the influences of one's subjectivity on the research process, only obscures the fact that even those who try to be insects are, at the very least, already influencing the social environment in which they conduct their fieldwork and, more important, are already committing themselves to a very clear moral and political position—that of letting things remain as they are, of leaving the status quo untouched. Neutrality is impossible— or better still, neutrality may work for the maintenance of privileges, but it does not work for all. Many forms of oppression, exclusion, and death continue to be perpetrated in the name of objectivity and detachment.

Still, I do not refrain from criticizing those with whom I interacted, from questioning their representations and behaviors. By contextualizing the events of everyday life within a greater framework of historical and genealogical information about the production and maintenance of racialized inequalities, and by juxtaposing this greater framework with the microphysics of the quotidian, I attempt to present a critical analysis whose form and content, rather than being those of a Cartesian *demonstration,* suggest an *argument.*[15] An argument is more easily permeable to debate than a demonstration. The open-ended character of an argument, moreover, reflects its necessarily partial, localized, historically determined, and dialogical nature. All the phases involved in critical ethnographies—especially the never-ending feedback that is established between those who are part of the study and what the study presents—are necessarily dialogical. More important, the Black radical tradition that is reflected in the following pages is itself dependent on permanent, open-ended dialogue, deconstruction, and reconstruction. This ethnography and its internal logic, therefore, only attempt to follow the oppositional consciousness of those who have no choice but to resist their genocide and live for complete transformation.

❦

Recent anthropological works on U.S. inner cities, while providing important insights into specific experiences of persons living in aggrieved communities, rarely attempt to connect their ethnographic data with an informed analysis of pertinent historical and structural facts.[16] At best, historical structures of discrimination actualized and maintained by institutions and individuals are either mentioned *en passant* or simply alluded to, and the reader is left to imagine the connections between the lives of the persons studied and the wider society. The following excerpts are indicative of this trend. The first one is from the introduction of a celebrated book on East Harlem drug dealers.

> The extreme—perhaps caricatural—responses to poverty and segregation that the dealers and addicts in this book represent, afford insight into processes that may be experienced in one form or another by major sectors of any vulnerable population experiencing rapid structural change in the context of political and ideological oppression.[17]

The next excerpt is from a book on working-class Blacks of Chicago's South Side.

> [T]he problems of ghetto life reflect broader trends in the wider society. What distinguishes the poor from other members of society is not that they are isolated from mainstream values, but that they do not have the standard of living to buffer them from the destructive effect of permissiveness, freedom, and spontaneity of American life. Many pathological social trends in the ghetto are more concentrated reflections of life in the wider society.[18]

Inadvertently, perhaps, the ethnographies that refrain from systematically approaching broader structures of social organization tend to present the lives of those studied as if their lives can be understood in the ethnographer's own terms. Although these ethnographies attempt to trace connections between the Black ghetto and the wider society, such attempts seldom go beyond more or less vague generalities.[19] In spite of the usual claims that segregated Blacks' behaviors reflect behaviors of the wider society, we rarely get a glimpse of what those behaviors of the wider society may be—their precise mechanisms and manifestations, historical backgrounds, and institutional supports. In fact, as soon as the "wider society" problem is announced—if and when it is announced—it usually disappears from the rest of the ethnography. While such works often reveal (at least some aspects of) local everyday dynamics, and therefore, as the ethnographers point out, provide clues to how broader historical structures are actualized by individuals, fundamental problems remain. The absence of specific historical research on crucial issues such as segregation, work opportunities, the role of the police, the ideas and attitudes of the wider society and the relation between these ideas and attitudes and inner-city life—these absences prevent such ethnographies from accessing the full extent to which disadvantaged racialized groups are the object of systemic, unjust, and genocidal practices.

My premise is that the predicament of those confined to the inner city can be better understood through analysis of systematic practices and the manners in which they have been historically actualized. More important, this work is based on the idea that it is only *within* and *relative to* historical forms of oppression that alternatives to these forms of oppression can be detected, comprehended, and evaluated. The critical potential of ethnography, in sum, can only be realized through a serious consideration of the historical factors that are necessarily projected in social life.

At first sight, South Central Los Angeles seems like any other Southern California working-class neighborhood, with two-bedroom and three-bedroom Spanish stucco houses interspersed with apartment buildings, with some well-kept lawns and tree-lined streets. In the poorest parts of South Central, however, you will be hard-pressed to find American flags hoisted in front of homes. Houses are often subdivided, occupied by more than one family. Their outside appearance conceals their many hazards, including precarious electrical and sanitary installations. These seemingly well-kept homes, as well as some of the apartments in the many tenements that punctuate the inner city's skyline, sometimes conceal drug posts, where marijuana, heroin, PCP (phencyclidine, also known as angel dust), and crack cocaine are sold, bought, and distributed. Gang members and drug dealers told me there were at least two crack houses per block in the area where I lived between January 1996 and March 1997. The sounds of desperation associated with the drug trade—the gunshots, police helicopter rotors, and sirens—resound as banal everyday occurrences. These sounds often intensify as the night falls and continue until daylight.

The impoverished Black women who comprised most of those living in my apartment building faced a life shaped by the uncertainties of poverty and unemployment. Their volatile and precarious domestic realms depended on mutual material and affective support for their survival. Such local sociabilities become an antidote, even if only temporary, to often overwhelming personal hardships. Various types of easily maintained addictions express and intensify adversities. It is not only marijuana, angel dust, and crack that affect these women. Just as addictive, fat and sugar in a variety of fast foods provide them with cheap and temporarily satisfying relief to the hunger, anxiety, and depression that they suffer from along with their sons and daughters. Their domestic spheres are also in constant interaction with persons and institutions that do not belong to the immediate everyday circles of sociability. Police officers, landlords, social workers, and health and rehabilitation personnel are prevalent social actors in impoverished Black women's domestic sphere.

Elements of Black feminist thought and praxis clearly emerge from, and indeed are inextricably connected to, the everyday experiences of the African American women living in these besieged conditions. As their racialized gendered and class-inflected perspectives draw on shared social conditions of imposed marginalization, they articulate powerful critiques of society's gendered racism and its ensuing exclusions. In doing so, they show how, as Black women living in poverty, their experiences cannot be reduced to either that of women removed from their social conditions (Black or otherwise), or that of Black men, even those also living in poverty. Their specific angles of vision—their standpoint—project a collective consciousness that works both as a source of insight and also as a reference according to which everyday acts of survival and resistance are crafted. As many authors have noted, it is precisely this already existing body of knowledge that maintains, informs, and transforms a Black radical tradition.[20]

Such elements of Black feminist thought and praxis indeed serve as a key reference according to which I construct a narrative describing and analyzing other life worlds in South Central—the male-centered community organizations CAPA, CGST, and Leimert Park's World Stage sociabilities. While Black women are mostly absent from such Black male-centered spaces, gender is a central aspect of how personal and political identities are interpellated and self-made. By focusing on how race, gender, class, and place of residence, among others, intersect and produce specific—and often conflicting—perspectives on Black experiences, I follow Black and U.S. second/third world feminists' theoretical interventions concerning the centrality of racialized gendered, sexualized, and class-inflected modes of marginalization and the need for organized, coalition-oriented action against the multiple, overlapping, and ever-shifting forms of oppression.

Expressing my engagement with the theoretical/political interventions by progressive and radical U.S. Black and second/third world feminisms is certainly not sufficient to render my analysis any less immersed in and reflexive of my necessarily colonized, patriarchal, and otherwise limited standpoint that derives from social class, gender, color, sexuality, and nationality privileges/blinders, among many others. Such active engagement, however, is a necessary step in both recognizing and challenging the oppressor within while continuing to engage in the hard work of coalitional politics. My narrative is then necessarily hostage of this endless process of decolonization—personal, theoretical, and political—and as such is a frozen snapshot of an ongoing, nonlinear, open-ended liberation-oriented practice inescapably replete with contradictions.[21]

Controlling images, as described by Black feminist scholars and activists, are one of the main ideological instruments utilized in everyday interactions and by societal institutions (schools, prisons, hospitals, for example), policymakers, and hegemonic scholarship to describe and justify (even if unwillingly) the imposed marginalization of communities of color. While images of the mammy, matriarch, welfare mother, and Jezebel conjure up a host of negative stereotypes that dehumanize African American women by emphasizing their purported infra- or superhuman physical, sexual, and psychological characteristics, related images of the hustler, criminal, inner-city youth, and high-school dropout fulfill analogous purposes as they hegemonically categorize African American males, particularly those deemed poor.[22]

If controlling images do in fact actualize and inform systems of social domination against both Black women and men, they however do not work the same way. Black men still benefit from—and indeed are often the paradoxical victims of—patriarchy-informed controlling images insofar as their imposed and often-accepted representations situate them as necessary dominators in hierarchical relationships with others, Black women included.[23] As cultural and political constructs maintained by and reflexive of racialized and gendered social hierarchies, controlling images are part of commonsensical understandings that are often shared across lines of race, class, gender, and sexuality. It is thus not surprising to find controlling images orienting Black institutions, persons, and community organizations. Indeed, such controlling images demarcate imagined communities within hypersegregated Black areas according to clearly drawn boundaries of blackness.[24]

Still less surprising is the influence of controlling images in galvanizing dangerous and misleading stereotypes that often emerge out of academic works concerned with inner-city life. In *Streetwise* Elijah Anderson correctly recognizes that inner-city youths "would work if they could find gainful employment," but most of his ethnography confirms hegemonic clichés about the absence of a work ethic and deficient commitment to family prevalent in contemporary Black urban settings.[25] Following a tradition of urban anthropology concerned with "the ghetto" that consolidated itself in the 1960s and early 1970s, Anderson draws on archetypes to describe expected behavior.[26] Whereas for women "the high life, welfare, prostitution, single parenthood, and crack addiction await," for men the norm is described as follows:

> These emerging figures are in many respects the antithesis of the traditional old heads. The man derides family values and takes little responsibility for the family's financial welfare. He feels hardly any obligation to his string of women and the children he has fathered. In fact he considers it a measure of success if he can get away without being held legally accountable for his out-of-wedlock children. To his hustling mentality, generosity is a weakness. Given his unstable financial situation, he feels used when confronted by the prospect of taking care of someone else.[27]

Although the general contours of this picture can indeed be seen in South Central, they represent, at best, the surface of social relations. The historical and ethnographic data I present question each and every one of Anderson's propositions. If there is a superficial, generalized derision toward "family values," for example, there is also a clear, stronger, often-desperate desire among most Blacks of South Central to break away from their tragic, self-perpetuating horizons of broken families, unemployment, addiction, welfare dependency, and imprisonment. Such generalized desperation among men and women indicates that family values are still a central part of Blacks' worldviews and practices—in fact, as central as generosity, solidarity, and self-imposed obligations toward their children. The question we may want to ask, then, is what type of "family values" are at work? How different are those "family values" from those considered "mainstream"? We shall see that such "values" are in the making, improvised, and while they certainly indicate strong relations to "conventional" family values, they constitute something singular. They are not mere "adaptations" to harsh conditions, as many anthropologists see them; they embody criticisms of society, they express the many pleasures and joys and camaraderies so central to the lives of the people who shape them, and they often project a type of sociability, funded on mutuality, that is the antithesis of the dominant materialistic individualism. Anderson misses fundamental aspects of contemporary life in the Black inner city, aspects that, I argue, provide some of the crucial elements that keep people alive and hoping.

The lacunae in Anderson's work can be explained by a common mistake among students of the urban poor. The lack of family values and work ethic is often interpreted as a direct reflex of the unavailability of work. If work organizes social life, then social life becomes disorganized if there is no work to structure it. Wilson, among others, has made a similar point:

> As Pierre Bourdieu demonstrated, work is not simply a way to make a living and support one's family. It also constitutes a framework for daily behavior and patterns of interaction because it imposes discipline and regularities. Thus, in the absence of regular employment, a person lacks not only a place in which to work and the receipt of regular income but also a coherent organization of the present—that is, a system of concrete expectations and goals. Regular employment provides the anchor for the spatial and temporal aspects of daily life. It determines where you are going to be and when you are going to be there. In the absence of regular employment, life, including family life, becomes less coherent. Persistent unemployment and irregular employment hinder rational planning in daily life, the necessary condition of adaptation to an industrial economy.[28]

The hectic aspects of life in the inner city will no doubt surface in this study. The relations between chronic unemployment and the uncertainties of everyday life will also be evident. Yet rather than interpreting poor Black folks' adaptations to extreme deprivation as a sign of irrational planning of daily life, I attempt to understand those adaptations on their own terms *and* within given historical circumstances.[29] That regular forms of work—work in the formal economy—have disappeared from inner cities such as South Central is beyond doubt. That the disappearance of work also impinges on the unemployed's self-esteem—as Wilson also suggests— is repeatedly exemplified in this ethnography.[30] It is rather problematic,

however, to utilize a set of analytical expectations derived from a form of
social organization that obviously does not apply to most of those in the
Black ghetto—that of regular employment in the formal economy—and
interpret the contemporary predicament of those clearly outside of this
formal economy in relation to the parameters given by this same formal
economy (discipline, regularity, punctuality, and so forth).

Utilizing the parameters of bourgeois sociability derived from work
prevents an understanding of how chronically unemployed communities
deal with their predicaments through new, improvised, sometimes chaotic
but effective actions that necessarily fall outside of "rational" and "expected"
realms. Although there are clear signs that the work ethic and family values as espoused by Anderson and Wilson, for example, are still important
principles among men and women chronically unemployed, without an
openness to the specificity of the nuanced, critical, and varied perspectives
among those trying to survive American apartheid, one will not fully comprehend their condition. As this work will show, many factors are pushing
Black communities to new configurations in which relations between
class, gender, and generation are in the making. Idealizations of, or values
based on the stable, nuclear family, must be revised. They do not help
understand the present conditions defined by hypersegregation. They do
not provide a useful and attainable model of social relations in a context
in which work, and therefore social relations, have been refigured dramatically since (at the very least) the deindustrialization of the 1980s; and,
finally, they project values that inevitably condemn the so-called dysfunc-
tional families to moral and social marginality. Without a fuller, ethno-
graphically informed, historically grounded comprehension, one will not
be able to perceive the inventiveness of their survival strategies, or the
pains and pleasures experienced in extremely difficult social conditions.
Furthermore, without this deeper and broader perspective one will not be
able to understand that grassroots, alternative projects of social organization are being developed within Black communities, in their own terms,
based on their own comprehensions of themselves. Black communities'
own comprehensions of themselves, in turn, have to be understood as
dialogues and struggles with histories, institutions, persons, and ideas that
go well beyond the confines of the imposed ghetto.

Several often-competing comprehensions of Black communities exist.
There are many real and imagined Black communities. In spite of (or

perhaps because of) Wilson's self-professed liberal views, his is still an unmistakably top-down perspective. His long- and short-term policy suggestions completely bypass local attempts to locate and redress shared historical problems. How Blacks have resisted their genocide, and in the process imagined and fought for a just and liberated society, must be put front and center when reflecting on the past, present, and future of Afrodiasporic communities.

❧

Fractures in the Black community reflect differences based on length and place of residence in the city, homeownership, education, occupation, gender, sexuality, and political affinities. The Watts uprisings of 1965 provide a snapshot of the dynamics of Black social, political, and cultural divisions within South Central. The rebellions—as well as the various interpretations of them that appeared in the Black press—dramatized not only the systematic oppression Blacks of all backgrounds experienced, but also the tendencies toward residential, social, and generational differentiation among Blacks of the inner city since at least the 1940s. The Watts uprising thus marked at least two concomitant processes. On the one hand, it was the culmination of a long history of imposed segregation, job discrimination, institutional disrespect and disregard, and police brutality. On the other hand, the uprising exposed the widening divides among African Americans. In the 1960s, in a process that would become even more intense in the following decades, Blacks born in wealthier families had the greatest chances of attaining good jobs, educating their children, and moving to better neighborhoods, while those born in poorer families often became even poorer, found their already difficult-to-obtain jobs even harder to find, witnessed the intensification of police brutality, and became the favored scapegoats of conservative ideologies and policies.[31]

The period that stretches from the stagflation of the 1970s to the Los Angeles uprising of 1992 not only further divided Blacks along lines of wealth, income, occupation, and place of residence, but also added to this already tense configuration new, emerging elements, including the national political shift toward the right (with issues related to race explicitly becoming the main opinion divider), the adoption of new, more specialized, and flexible modes of production (whose main effect in South Central has been an unparalleled wave of deindustrialization), and massive immigration from Mexico and Central America. I explore the effects of these processes in the lives of South Central's Blacks and show how the 1980s staged an unprecedented widening in social inequalities in which wealth was distributed even more unevenly than income. The gap between social classes widened abruptly for all during the Reagan years, but for Blacks the abyss was much more pronounced. The relatively few Blacks who climb the social and occupational ladder only underscore the great gap between them and other African Americans. Social mobility, which for Whites is coterminous with wealth and work, is for most Blacks a defunct American dream. The result of these combined processes is that contemporary Los Angeles has the poorest and the richest Blacks in the United States. As Black middle-class homeowners increasingly migrate to distant areas such as San Bernardino and Ventura, as far away from the ghetto as possible, South Central has been left with deteriorating housing stock, very high levels of poverty, and latent inter- and intraracial conflict. It is quickly becoming the exclusive home of the Brown and Black California version of the *lumpenproletariat,* and as such has become the site for an unprecedented volume of imprisonments and deaths.[32]

❧

Local grassroots organizations challenge injustice and inequality. I worked at the Coalition Against Police Abuse (CAPA) on a daily basis between January 1996 and March 1997. The Coalition's historical genealogy, its symbolic and practical connections with the Black Panthers, as well as its contemporary practices, have set the conditions for the incorporation of ex- and current gang members willing to establish and expand the Watts Gang Truce initiated in 1992.[33] Through an examination of techniques of community organization and responses to concrete cases of police brutality, I present the developments that led to the role CAPA played in the foundation of and its fusion with the Community in Support of the Gang Truce (CSGT). As it questioned centralized power (both within its own ranks and in other institutions), as it attempted to find common political grounds between groups and persons of diverse races, genders, sexual preferences, social classes, places of residence, nationalities, and generations, this fusion marked a qualitative shift in CAPA's original practices and outlooks.

The alliance between CAPA and CSGT registers the dilemmas and possibilities contemporary social movements encounter when operating in historically divided and oppressed contexts such as South Central. Disciplined activities, even those that at first sight suggest conservative tendencies, play a vital role in building radical consciousness. Video and computer classes, silk-screen training, and even Jim Brown's Amer-I-Can program help give youths a greater sense of personal responsibility, discipline, and answerability to others that can be proto-political in ways that have previously been underestimated.

Ethnographic data collected over twenty-six months of continuous observant participation starting January 1996 forms the basis for my explorations in "Blackness as Artistry and Affirmation" in Leimert Park's public norms. I analyze individual experiences and some of the social networks that intersect at the jazz jam sessions of the World Stage—a storefront workshop and performance space founded by poet Kamau Daaood and legendary drummer Billy Higgins. I present a side of the inner city that, due to its social and racial diversity, stands in sharp contrast to the social settings analyzed in other chapters. Leimert Park's public spaces, in spite of their marked heterogeneity, are strongly determined by values that emphasize the nuclear family, work, obeying the law, and bourgeois respectability.

Although the infrapolitics of Leimert Park at times reinforce the present state of fragmentation within Black communities, at other times, however, it suggests and enacts a powerful critique of dominant forms of thought and action. Leimert's art forms are necessarily embedded in—and in dialogue with—the historical structures of discrimination, class, generational and gender tensions among Blacks. They are necessarily part of the racialized gendered politics of everyday life and actualize, on the one hand, seemingly irreconcilable differences, and on the other, a truly utopian, transcendental model of social relations.

Struggles against racialized injustices are producing an array of alternative and radical visions that challenge dominant relations of power. These visions contest ideological constructions of Blacks as individually and collectively weak and isolated. They also reinforce the crucial significance of race, place, class, and generation in the contemporary U.S. urban landscape. While certain tendencies toward particularisms and essentialisms need to be taken seriously and are indeed an important aspect of contemporary inner-city life, it is precisely in relation to such tendencies that the alternative projects of social organization elaborated among Blacks and other aggrieved communities must be evaluated. Particularisms and essentialisms are explicitly overturned when individuals and groups cultivate, reflect upon, and sometimes criticize *both* their specific practices and those of other individuals and groups. It is in this light that we must value South Central's mutualities of everyday life, communitarian programs of grassroots organizations, and transnational, Black diasporic utopias. Such mutualities, programs, and utopias are necessarily grounded in specific and harsh realities, and thus reflect particularized experiences. Yet, they also, at times at least, point to broader political horizons, to everyday and formalized alliances based on more inclusive and expansive notions of community, and thus more effective ways of bringing about social justice and radical change. Up against daunting adversaries and in the brink of extermination, many persons and groups of the inner city fight back. Their imaginings provide fundamental lessons for all of us concerned with and working toward a more just and egalitarian world. They resist their genocide and along the way provide lessons for the remaking of our necessarily fascist selves and the pursuit of freedom.

However, because CAPA, CSGT, and the communities of artists that congeal around the World Stage are markedly male-centered, their visions of social transformation and the everyday praxes that go along with them are inevitably mired by an absence of gender critique. Patriarchal maleness is the default parameter according to which personal and political identities are crafted. As the description and analysis of such communities suggest, while complex understandings of race, social class, segregation, artistic performance, and politics emerge in these contexts, such understandings are nevertheless limited by a gendered bias that most of the time goes unchallenged. Patriarchal expectations and roles remain, highlighting the difficulties in the way of decolonization. Even though I recognize the powerful liberatory political potential of such shared visions, I must also point out that, in order for them to fully actualize their dreams of freedom, they must engage with the inevitable gendered nature of the multiple forms of unjust social hierarchies in which race features prominently, but not solely. Yet, because the potentially radical projects that I analyze are in the making, and because they recognize their necessary unfinished character as one of their main strengths—which allows for dialogue, self-critique, alliance-building, and re-elaboration—the crucial gender analysis is in no way incompatible with their nature. Indeed, I would suggest that, at least in the cases of CAPA and CSGT, the emerging gender-conscious-informed praxes serve as testimony to the ever-evolving nature of such projects of radical social transformation. If only elements of Black feminist thought and praxis that manifest themselves in the lives of the women whose community of struggle I was temporarily a part of, if only these elements could be engaged with and radically incorporated into the potentially revolutionary projects of social transformation, then our freedom dreams would be one giant step closer to actualization.

(

When I began looking for a place to rent in South Central, in December 1995, I found that perceived race was a central factor determining how one was treated. I was well received by managers, most of whom were Black women. When asked what brought me to the neighborhood, I said I was doing community work, and I mentioned the Coalition Against Police Abuse and Michael Zinzun, its coordinator. Although not many people knew the Coalition, most had heard about Zinzun. Being a graduate student from Brazil also helped me because most people with whom I talked valued formal education. While they didn't know much about my country, my non-White appearance—and, I found out later, my accent that did not sound "Latino" as people in South Central understand the term—seemed to be enough to warrant some sympathy.

I had no trouble finding a place to rent. The manager of the building in which I ended up living for the next sixteen months was kind. Although Elen did not tell me that there was a crack house next door (which all the windows in my first-floor apartment directly faced), nor that my apartment used to be the crack house until its former occupants were arrested, she, as did the other women in the building, ended up being my good friend. Being a Brazilian of color spared me the treatment I would have received had I been White or "Mexican" or "Latino," who were all not very well liked by my Black neighbors.

Retrospectively, it is obvious that my perceived racial ambiguity, coupled with the fact that I self-identify as Black, facilitated my relations with other Blacks in South Central. Since race is such a central part in the lives of those who appear in this work, and since my own perceived race was certainly a crucial determinant in the type of ethnographic data I was able to collect, it is necessary to briefly elaborate on my own racial background.

A light-skinned Black Brazilian by birth and nationality who speaks Portuguese as my first language, I have lived in the United States since 1993. While I have maintained close contact with Brazilians and have intensified my visits in the last two years, Brazil has become a familiar but distant place, one that I can hardly claim as home. I was born in a mixed-race family light enough so that our blackness was carefully concealed by middle-classness, yet grew up among overwhelmingly European Whites in the interior of São Paulo state, France, and England; many (although not close to all) of the racial dynamics around whitening, self-hatred, and the impossibilities of the Black condition, as analyzed in connection to colonialism and the African diaspora, were and are first-hand experiences.[34] Although in Brazil darker-skinned Blacks often consider me White, for Whites in Brazil my whiteness is a concession, the nature of which unmistakably emerges in what they consider playful comments concerning their impressions about what they think are my African traits. Nevertheless, as it commonly happens to all of us mixed-race Brazilians who claim blackness, Whites will not seldom engage with such claim by stating, "But you are not Black, you are my friend." At work here is the hyperconsciousness/negation of race dynamics, so prevalent in Brazilian social relations.[35]

The many racial identities to which I can be interpellated are in part a result of the multiple racial and ethnic origins of my ascendants: Black, Indian, Iberian, and European. But this multiplicity, if obvious in my phenotype, is the object of an array of social constructions that work differently in different places. In Brazil, for example, even though my racialized identity is ambiguous, my social class amplifies the White characteristics while defusing the Black ones. If, however, I were to be assumed poor and without education, the reverse would happen and my Black traits would become dominant. This logic is probably behind the various times that, in São Paulo and in Campinas, I have been searched by security personnel while leaving stores, my checks were not accepted, and police officers approached me for no apparent reason.

The relativity of racial classifications is well illustrated in contexts where Brazilian social determinants are not at work. In those situations, my physical traits that are associated with non-White racial groups are often more defining. While in France, where I lived for seven years until I was nine, I was thought to be an Arab or Algerian (but not by Algerians, who saw me as Moroccan); in England, where I resided for three years as a teenager in the late 1970s and early 1980s, daily insults reminded me that a paki I was. In the United States I have been taken as Mexican, Moroccan, Algerian, Italian, Iranian, Indian, Cuban, Egyptian, and Ethiopian, among many others.

This short digression on the relativity of racial constructs across countries and social lines is intended to provide an introduction into the types of conceptions and attitudes I encountered and the negotiations I had to undergo while in South Central. My racial identity was never a stable one. My perceived race was the product of different contexts—it depended on how well I was accepted and the types of expectations I was supposed to fulfill. Even though I presented myself as Black, I am obviously not an American Black, much less do I have physical characteristics that link me unambiguously to my African heritages. But I found that my self-definition served at least to reaffirm, in the eyes of those living in Los Angeles' ghetto, my non-White condition. Although I met White persons who had chosen to live and work in the inner city and who were eventually accepted by Blacks, Whites are seen with a great amount of suspicion and it takes them much more effort and time to be accepted and trusted by Blacks. As well, most Blacks in South Central did not see me as a "Latino." This was just as important, for the tensions between Blacks and those perceived as Latina/o were and still are considerable. I was the only non–African American living in the building in which I had found an apartment, and it didn't take long to perceive that such homogeneity was fiercely enforced by those who lived there and wanted to keep it that way. I didn't really "choose" my apartment—those who were already living in the building gave me permission to be there.

A note on improvised methods and conventions: During my observant participation, I did not take photographs or tape-record any conversations. I wanted to avoid the hazard of having information that could potentially incriminate and identify persons—a possibility that was quite high in a context in which the criminal justice system is ubiquitous as are deadly vendettas. Aside from putting other people at risk, recorded interviews—and the knowledge, by others, that such interviews existed—would also certainly put me in harm's way. I did take notes about conversations and other facts as soon as I could after they happened. I carried a notepad

with me in which I wrote the basic information which I would later com-
plement. Due to the obvious limitations of such recording methods, in
this study I will only use dialogues that happened more than once or that
were typical of the interaction I had with different persons.

As for the names utilized throughout the work, simple, basic rules apply.
To preserve the anonymity of those who were not public figures and requested to be left that way, I have used pseudonyms without surnames—
"Hector" and "Angela," for example. Names that appear in their full
form—for example, Michael Zinzun and Billy Higgins—represent public
persons whose private lives I have attempted to conceal as much as I could.

chapter 1

BLACKNESS AS EXCLUSION AND ISOLATION

The Making of Inequalities in
South Central

The different forms of blackness surveyed in this analysis cannot be understood outside the structural conditions from which they emerge. The tenement dwellers, political activists, and artists whose versions of blackness shape this study have themselves been shaped by macrosocial forces—by residential segregation, employment discrimination, educational inequality, police brutality, environmental racism, and the disproportionate effects of economic restructuring and deindustrialization on communities of color.

The 1965 Watts rebellion marked the full maturation of South Central Los Angeles as a Black ghetto. The next thirty years brought profound transformations to the area's ethnic composition, work patterns, and policing. The period from the stagflation of the 1970s to the Los Angeles Uprisings of 1992 further divided Blacks along lines of wealth, income, occupation, age, gender, and place of residence. In addition, new modes of production and massive immigration from Mexico and Central America exacerbated this already tense configuration.

Systematic deindustrialization hit Los Angeles during the 1970s and 1980s, especially affecting African American blue-collar workers with inadequate formal education and few skills. By 1990 almost 70 percent of young Black men between twenty-five and thirty-four with less than a high school education were unemployed in South Central Los Angeles.

Blacks in Los Angeles and other metropolitan cities bore the brunt of the costs caused by the poor performance of the U.S. manufacturing sector.

By the 1980s more than 1.1 million manufacturing jobs vanished from the economy, mostly in large cities.[1] In 1989 the average U.S. worker put in 138 more hours on the job annually than in 1969.[2] Yet while many blue-collar jobs disappeared, those at the top saw their wealth and privileges soar to unprecedented levels. Intense growth in economic inequality starting in the 1970s stemmed largely from the gains made by the already better off. In 1968, for instance, the poorest 40 percent of the population received 18.1 percent of all family income, while the richest 5 percent received 15.6 percent. That year marked the greatest equality the United States had ever experienced. In tandem with the decline of the American economy since the early 1970s, however, the richest 1 percent of U.S. households saw their income skyrocket: between 1977 and 1991 the more privileged sector of society had its aggregated income rise 100 percent. By 1990 income distribution had been completely reshaped. The richest 5 percent received 17.4 percent of all family income, while the poorest 40 percent shared only 15.4 percent of the total family income.[3] Relative to income, thus, the rich got richer, and the poor got even poorer.

Similar (if not more dramatic) processes, this time relative to *wealth*, also happened during the same years. In times of economic stagnation, declining wages, and threats of job loss, the importance of property in relation to income increases sharply. Inequality, therefore, cannot be fully understood without an awareness of wealth distribution.[4] The concentration of wealth in the United States was more pronounced in 1989 than at any time since 1929. Between 1983 and 1989, the richest half-percent of families received 55 percent of the total increase in household wealth. Meanwhile, the biggest loss in wealth was experienced by the lowest income group (i.e., the poorest one-fifth of American families with incomes, in 1989 dollars, less than $10,000). Between 1983 and 1989 their ratio of average net worth to total average wealth dropped from 0.19 to 0.13.[5] Thus, the 1980s staged an unprecedented widening in social inequalities in which wealth was distributed even more unevenly than income.

Most of the income loss for the poorest one-fifth of U.S. families and most of the greatest increase in income for the richest one-fifth occurred in the 1980s, during the Reagan presidency. In this period the poverty rates in the United States doubled those in European industrial nations, even though unemployment in the United States was lower and economic growth greater.[6] Unemployment for the period oscillated between 6 and 7 percent of the labor force, and even when it reached a low 5.1 percent in February 1989, this figure was still higher than the average unemployment rate for the entire 1950s and 1960s.[7]

In this context, the assaults on welfare programs, civil rights laws, and affirmative action programs intensified high rates of poverty caused by massive layoffs and lack of work opportunities. The welfare programs of the Johnson administration's War on Poverty—which for all their ideological contradictions and practical dilemmas virtually eliminated hunger in the United States in the 1960s and early 1970s—gave way to Reagan's "war on welfare." As a result, an estimated one-third of all poor families, comprising an estimated 1 million individuals, did not receive food stamps in the 1990s, reflecting a cut of 14.3 percent in funds. Moreover, the basic welfare program, Aid to Families with Dependent Children (AFDC), was cut by 17.4 percent, leading to an additional 400,000 families losing their eligibility for government assistance. The Comprehensive Employment and Training Act (CETA), a public-service employment program, was eliminated altogether, while other community-based programs had their funding drastically reduced.[8] In the wake of these government funding cuts, homelessness became more widespread as three-fourths of all the poor families were not eligible for any type of housing assistance.

The Reagan administration's policymaking was based on the idea that the economic ills of the nation were due in great measure to big government and its excessive regulation of industry and private enterprise. Welfare, according to this logic, was not only ineffective, but indeed it exacerbated poverty, crippling the recipient's work ethic and sense of responsibility. Last but not least, civil rights legislation—especially affirmative action—was thought to have gone too far and was now causing what it set out to combat in the first place: discrimination, this time against Whites. In that context affirmative action became equated with "preferential treatment," and expressions such as "reverse discrimination" permeated public debates and everyday conversations.[9] The most immediate result of such policies was that the structure of economic opportunity for racialized groups, especially Blacks—whose hiring depended heavily on the observance and enforcement of fair hiring practices—was dramatically reorganized, even devastated.[10]

Public opinion became increasingly antagonistic to government spending on programs for the poor, revealing deepening gulfs between Blacks and Whites on issues related to the role of the state. Asked whether government should provide jobs or let every person get ahead on his or her own, 70 percent of the Black persons sampled asserted their belief in government intervention against 30 percent who would rather see the state step back on the matter. Whites, on the other hand, while divided in similar proportions, nevertheless chose the opposite remedy: 62 percent contended that government should let "every person get ahead on his own," while 38 percent thought government help necessary.[11] This racial division expressed itself more strongly among those White Democrats who ended up voting for Reagan. Among the so-called Reagan Democrats, 71 percent agreed that Blacks have worse jobs, income, and housing than Whites because "they don't have the motivation or will power to pull themselves out of poverty." Only 24 percent of Reagan Democrats disagreed with this statement.[12]

Yet contrary to what conservative authors and politicians declare, race is a determining factor in the life chances of non-Whites.[13] In 1973 the percentage of Black men with twelve years of schooling with low wages was 27.7 percent as compared to 15.6 percent of Whites with low wages and the same education. This percentage swelled to 44 percent in 1987— a time when the percentage of White men with twelve years of education and low earnings stood at 22.9 percent. The figures for Latinos for the same period were 22.2 percent and 38.2 percent respectively. Blacks and Latinos, generally in this order, have systematically been earning less than Whites at all comparable levels of education. Furthermore, during the eighties this gap widened. The present tendency is for further increases in this earning faultline.

The statistics are unequivocal: Black men and Latinos with high school diplomas were much more likely than White men to be low wage earners in the late 1980s than in the early 1970s.[14] During the eighties, across every race and ethnic group, men and women alike, the percentage of workers earning a wage lower than the real value of the 1979 minimum wage increased sharply. Blacks and Latina/os, nevertheless, were again the most affected. Latina/os of all races experienced almost a threefold increase in the percentage of those earning below the 1979 minimum wage: from 10.7 percent to 31.7 percent. African Americans experienced an increase in those earning below the 1979 minimum wage from 13.8 percent to 36.7 percent. For Whites, this rate augmented from 8.1 percent to 23.3 percent.[15]

Although there have been comparable increases across race in the contingent of people earning below the 1979 minimum wage, it is obvious that Latina/os and Blacks were proportionally much worse off than Whites. Not only were their wages significantly smaller than those received by Whites, but also the wealth of non-White families compared to that of Whites was even more disproportional. In 1989 non-White families averaged less than a fifth (0.19) of White families' wealth; relative to income, the proportion was 0.63.[16]

These inequalities reflect both historical and contemporary racial barriers. As a result, Blacks generally lacked wealth assets "necessary to optimize their children's life chances."[17] Even successful Black families have difficulty passing on their class status to their children because their increased earnings cannot make up for their lack of inherited wealth or the disadvantages they face in accumulating assets that appreciate in value and can be passed on intergenerationally.[18] Nearly a quarter of Blacks from upper white-collar backgrounds see their children fall to lower blue-collar occupations. For Whites, the corresponding figure is 11.6 percent, less than half of that for Blacks.[19] As Oliver and Shapiro argue, "among many Blacks parental status does not signify much. Blacks from professional and self-employed origins possess much less wealth than Whites from lowest status families. So Whites not only command a greater ability to pass along occupational status than Blacks, but they also command a greater ability to pass along wealth, and this may be of even greater importance."[20]

The links between race, on one hand, and transmission of occupational achievement and wealth, on the other, become rather apparent. Table 1 highlights the distinct intergenerational dynamics that separate the fate of Blacks and Whites as far as occupational status goes. For Whites the highest proportion of those who maintained their parents' occupational status is verified among upper white-collar workers (60.8%), but for Blacks the greatest number of workers who follow their parents' status occurs among lower blue-collar workers (39.5%). True, 36.2 percent of Blacks maintained their parents' upper white-collar occupational status, but this number pales in comparison to the proportion of Whites who did so—60.8 percent. Moreover, Blacks were much more likely to descend the status ladder than their White counterparts. Among Black lower blue-collar workers, almost half (46.8%) came from upper blue-collar families; 38.2 percent had parents who were lower white-collar workers, and almost a fourth (23.4%)

of those lower blue-collar workers had parents who were upper white-collar workers.

It is clear that, for Whites, the occurrence of intergenerational status fall is not as pronounced; indeed, Table 1 shows that Whites' chances of maintaining, or improving, their parents' achievement is proportional to their parents' status: the higher the parents' status, the higher chance one has of improving or maintaining it. For Blacks the equation is radically different: with the exception of the upper white-collar families, the lower one's parents' status, the highest one's chance of maintaining (or dropping) the parents' occupational achievements.

Radically distinct generational patterns also emerge when transmission of wealth is considered (see Table 2). Blacks whose parents belonged to upper white-collar occupations possessed less than half (44.8 percent) of their White counterparts' total net worth.

The picture is even more aberrant regarding net financial assets: Blacks coming from upper white-collar families held 2.5 percent of what Whites from the same background did. While the spread of assets among Whites is relatively small, for Blacks, except for the wealthier ones, assets simply

Table 1. Offspring's occupational status relative to parents' occupational status, by race

Offspring's occupational status	Parents' occupational status			
	Upper white collar	Lower white collar	Upper blue collar	Lower blue collar
White offspring				
Upper white collar	60.8%	53.6%	42.2%	36.4%
Lower white collar	17.9	21.8	15.9	16.6
Upper blue collar	9.7	10.6	20.2	17.7
Lower blue collar	11.6	15.0	21.8	29.3
Black offspring				
Upper white collar	36.2	29.4	20.1	28.0
Lower white collar	29.8	26.5	17.8	20.8
Upper blue collar	10.6	5.9	15.4	11.8
Lower blue collar	23.4	38.2	46.8	39.5

SOURCE: Oliver, Shapiro, and Press, "Them That's Got Shall Get," in R. Ratcliff et al., eds., *The Politics of Wealth and Inequality: Research in Politics and Society* 5 (1995): 83. Copyright 1995 Elsevier Science; reprinted with permission of Elsevier Science.

do not exist! Blacks, therefore, not only have much less wealth than Whites, but their riches are also much more unevenly distributed. The gap between social classes widened abruptly for all groups during the 1980s, but for Blacks the abyss became much more pronounced.

In addition to the greater class polarization among Blacks, it is clear that intergenerational transmission of wealth also happens differently among African Americans. Blacks whose parents were professionals or self-employed have less wealth than Whites who come from lower status families. Whites originating from lower blue-collar families had a median wealth of $3,890, while Blacks from similar families had an insubstantial $230. Other, not so "well-off" Black families fared even worse, as we have already seen.

ℂ

Urban spatial arrangements reflect and reinforce these configurations of race, status, wealth, and income. Historical patterns of segregation have defined the human geography of every major city in the United States. The result of "racist attitudes, private behaviors, and institutionalized practices

Table 2. Family background, median wealth, and race

Parents' background	Whites	Blacks
Upper white collar		
Total net worth	$47,854	$21,430
Net financial assets	9,000	230
Lower white collar		
Total net worth	51,864	2,483
Net financial assets	9,500	0
Upper blue collar		
Total net worth	54,172	7,179
Net financial assets	8,774	0
Lower blue collar		
Total net worth	38,850	4,650
Net financial assets	3,890	0

SOURCE: Oliver, Shapiro, and Press, "Them That's Got Shall Get," 87. Copyright 1995 Elsevier Science; reprinted with permission of Elsevier Science.

that disenfranchised the Blacks from urban housing markets and led to the creation of the ghetto," American inner cities exacerbate people of color's (especially Blacks') poverty.[21] Discriminated against by employers and actively avoided by White homeowners, Black residents of the ghetto have been systematically and persistently blocked in their attempts to relocate. The ghetto is thus the result of widespread social forces galvanized against Black spatial mobility.

Although the Fair Housing Act of 1968 outlawed residential racial segregation, not much has changed. Enforcement mechanisms are decentralized and weak. Most people do not know the nature of the law. New forms of mortgage discrimination, insurance redlining, and predatory lending outpace the efforts of the voluntary fair-housing groups who serve as the only serious constituency trying to ensure equal opportunity in housing. White ideals of neighborhood economic and racial homogeneity lead real estate agents to show prospective Black buyers houses solely in areas where a Black majority already lives. In defiance of laws and court decrees, local authorities do not provide affordable housing on a nondiscriminatory basis. Race and class polarizations that divided Blacks and Whites along lines of income, wealth, and occupational mobility only made racial segregation another element in the constellation of the radical shifts that characterized the Reagan and Bush years of the 1980s and early 1990s.

During the 1980s, the semantic connection between race and urbanity became fully accepted by a large proportion of the U.S. public. Dominant political discourses equated, on the one hand, the urban inner cities, and on the other, neighborhood deterioration, people of color—especially Blacks—and purported amorality. Just as key code words in political discourse like "welfare" and "special rights" relied on stereotyped images of lazy and overtly sexual African American mothers, "cities" became an icon for the deleterious effects of government intervention in poor areas. The widespread acceptance of these images was accompanied by the fact that, during the same period, suburban voters and their representatives became a political majority in this country. The politics of suburbia, notes Mike Davis, are not so much Republican as they are antiurban and, indeed, anti-Black.[22] Clinton's 1992 presidential campaign clearly aimed to convince suburbanites of his worth by stressing strong stands on crime and intolerance to welfare, thus striking the subliminal code words that had been successful in previous Republican discourses. Suburbanization, and the economic and political forces it galvanized, thus intensified Black segregation. Persistent discrimination in the real estate market and in financial institutions only exacerbated these trends. [23]

Inner-city electoral politics hardly generate alternatives to segregation. Black communities tend to vote in block for a few Black representatives. Due to the ghetto's spatial and social isolation, building alliances around common interests with other communities is difficult. A mounting fiscal crisis and an intense competition for scarce resources compound this difficulty. As a result of this tendency toward balkanization, Blacks are mostly unable to lobby or extend their political rewards beyond their communities. Their interests, for this reason, remain weakly represented.[24]

Even in cities where Black politicians experienced some relative electoral success from the 1960s on, a myriad of institutional obstacles devised by established White leaders effectively blocked people of color's attempts for political incorporation. In Los Angeles, for example, until the early 1970s, city leaders used unsubtle gerrymandering to fragment the Black vote. As Black leaders expressed in the pages of the *Eagle* and the *Los Angeles Sentinel* throughout the 1940s, '50s, and '60s, the City of Angels kept racialized communities silent and invisible.[25] When a Black politician became mayor, the result was ambiguous. Tom Bradley's ascension to the City Council and then, in 1973, to City Hall, challenged in some ways yet mostly reinforced people of color's disadvantages. Supported by strong community organizations, endorsed by the Black media, and heading a Black-Jewish coalition that would keep him in office for more than twenty years, Bradley left a mixed record concerning Blacks' (and other non-Whites') effective incorporation into the city's power structure, jobs, and housing market. During Bradley's regime, representation by people of color in the council increased rapidly. Between 1973 and 1991 the city's employment progressively reflected the city's ethnic and racial composition, with the White share of the city's workforce dropping from almost 70 percent to less than 50 percent. Bradley also shifted the balance of power, previously concentrated on the real estate and media families, to the upwardly mobile communities of color and to the liberal west side.[26]

Yet even in the early, progressive period of his administration, Bradley's coalition was rather ineffective about matters concerning poorer, historically disadvantaged communities of color. In the area of low-income housing, for example, Bradley's tenure at City Hall did not produce any significant results.[27] Bradley's administration, as well as enhancing the already more privileged sectors within communities of color, also openly supported the status quo in its clear probusiness stance.[28] An African American mayor and a Black middle-class and upper-class alliance with Westside Jews were not enough to even slightly alter the Black majority's everyday living conditions. In Bradley's final years, between 1988 and 1993, South Central systematically received less funds and services than wealthier areas such as West L.A., the Valley, and the North Central area of the city.[29] "It is thus fitting that following his retirement from public office in June 1993, Bradley went to work for Brobeck, Phleger, and Harrison, a corporate law firm specializing in international trade."[30]

℀

Patterns of residential segregation amplify the effects of unemployment and blocked social mobility among the large majority of Blacks. Constantly moving from one tenement to the other—trying to keep one step ahead of the landlord—poorer Blacks in the ghetto see themselves excluded from employment networks. These networks are the main mechanism of information and referral through which jobs can be obtained. Employers always prefer to fill up positions with persons known to older employees. Thus, when most social ties established between dislocations prove to be temporary, the sense of isolation among individuals and families, in itself a source of great affliction, becomes an even greater problem as it noticeably diminishes work opportunities. By the late 1980s the proportion of men who were excluded permanently from the labor force was more than 100 percent higher than it had been in the 1960s.[31] These men are generally in the prime of their productive lives—between twenty-two and fifty-eight years old—and have very limited, if any, marketable skills. They are also the main victims of the reorganization of mass production.

Low-skilled Black inner-city women, although inextricably part of this general state of economic depression, have nevertheless, at least statistically, better chances of obtaining jobs in the service sector. Hospitals, schools, health and rehabilitation centers, as well as social service, have increasingly absorbed less-educated Black women and thus prevented them from joining the swelling mass of inner-city joblessness. From 1979 to 1993, there has been a very significant increase in the proportion of less-educated Black women working in the social services, from 30.5 percent to 40.5

percent.[32] Yet poor, unskilled Black women are trapped in high poverty areas along with Black men.

Even employment and a relatively stable family do not necessarily constitute a warranty out of poverty and desperation. Most jobs available to Black persons are barely enough to make ends meet. The attractions of the illegal economy, not surprisingly, become rather compelling. As a Black woman stated:

> My husband, he's worked in the community. He's 33. He's worked at One Stop since he was 15. And right now, he's one of the highest paid—he's a butcher—he's one of the highest paid butchers in One Stop. For the 15— almost 18—years that he's been there, he's only making nine dollars an hour. And he's begged and fought and scrapped and sued and everything else for the low pay he gets. And he takes so much. Sometimes he come home and he'd sit home and he'd just cry. And he'd say, "If it weren't for my kids and my family, I'd quit." You know, it's bad, 'cuz he won't get into drugs, selling it, you know, he ain't into drug using. He's the kind of man, he want to work hard and feel good about that he came home. He say that it feels bad sometime to see this 15-year-old boy drivin' down the street with a new car. He saying, "I can't even pay my car note. And I worry about them coming to get my car."[33]

What this woman's husband experiences in his work is a direct reflex of the structural phenomena analyzed previously. In particular, the man's difficulty in obtaining a salary raise is in accordance with the general rule verified for the economic opportunities of blue-collar African American workers, namely, systematic obstacles against mobility within and across jobs. We can also affirm without the risk of erring that this family has not received any significant amount of wealth from a previous generation, nor that it is going to be able to transmit some wealth to the next generation. Still, this family's situation is relatively privileged when we consider the general difficulty Black men have in finding and maintaining work.

The attitudes of employers, coupled with the power they bear in determining one's economic fate, is a fundamental element that connects and reinforces the different structural constraints Blacks systematically encounter. Employers' attitudes reflect negative stereotypes, particularly against African Americans, thus perpetuating the cycle of unemployment, segregation, social isolation, and violence. Imbued with commonly held, highly stereotyped knowledge about Blacks' aversion to work and proneness to unacceptable behavior (among which heightened sexuality and dishonesty feature prominently), employers play a central role in the perpetuation of the *idea* and the *facts* of the segregated inner city.

The dominant ideological matrix that emerged with full force in the 1980s resolved apparent contradictions related to poverty and race. On one hand, it affirmed the cultural roots of poverty, at least Black poverty, by blaming it on how Blacks in the inner city perpetuated self-defeating sets of expectations and behavior. On the other hand, however, this ideology ignored the historical and structural forces that produce imposed marginality. By stressing the role of environmental and cultural determinants, this matrix of thought also avoided focusing on race. The dominant ideology about (racialized) poverty concentrated on the primacy of the individual (of color) over society. By claiming that those who fall into poverty are victims of their own character deficiencies, it proposed that individuals could overcome their difficulties by pulling themselves up by their bootstraps.

Even if silently, however, race plays an important integrating function in this matrix. When Black employers join the dominant ideological chorus on poverty and race—even when they negate the racial implications of joblessness—they reveal and reinforce deeply held U.S. values and behaviors. First of all, as the White employers do, they carve a safe, unambiguous, distant social and cultural position from those considered society's underclass. Their statements dig deep into the chasms among Blacks of different social classes. Poor Blacks' predicaments become alien to their experience—at best, poor African Americans' conditions only reveal, by contrast, their superior *individual* moral strength and determination to overcome the inner city's overwhelming *environment*. Through such reasonings, these Black persons in positions of power draw the force of their argument by casting a shade over systematic political and historical discrimination. By focusing on the individual and on superficial notions of what are supposed to be social and cultural conditions in the ghetto, Blacks and Whites sustain, often silently, and in different degrees, deeply held beliefs in racial inferiority.

Spatial apartheid in Los Angeles, albeit the result of specific historical patterns of urban development with roots in both national and local forces, intensified after Reagan's ascension to the presidency. "In effect," Davis summarizes, "these polices have also subsidized White flight and metropolitan resegregation." The majority of Black workers were trapped in the inner city, as almost the totality of the White working class of the older central industrial belt—approximately 200,000 people—relocated to the suburbs during the 1970s and 1980s.[34] In this period, Los Angeles gained more than two million jobs in suburban areas, while more than 50,000 disappeared from the historical center.

Los Angeles, as elsewhere in the country, has thus developed a job machine whose main characteristic is its polarized extremes. On the one hand, this job machine has produced a small niche of well-paying, technology-related occupations, and on the other, an enormous and still swelling sector of low-wage, often below subsistence work. In the 1980s the city and its surroundings seemed to be heading toward occupying a central role as the main corporate and business center of the Pacific Rim. However, "today [1997] the region more resembles the opposite: a production-dominated artisan economy, designing and manufacturing everything from garments to sitcoms to education software."[35] In spite of the high-tech clusters, this artisan economy is mostly supported by cheap immigrant labor. Low-skilled Blacks are mostly excluded from this relatively new sector. Due to labor market polarization, and the prevalence of low-wage work, the Los Angeles region, countering a national trend, has the members of its groups of color earning less today compared to Whites than was the case forty years ago. U.S.-born Mexican Americans were paid 81 percent of the median income of non-Latino White men in 1959. By 1988, however, this figure had dropped to 61 percent. Black men, on the other hand, went from earning 67 percent of what White men were earning in 1959 to about 57 percent in 1989. Most surprisingly, in the same period Black women—who elsewhere in the country have greatly diminished the earning gap with White women—saw their pay compared to White women's drop from nearly 88 percent to 78 percent.[36]

As Los Angeles exacerbated suburbanization with the massive plant closures in the inner city, it also staged a resurgence of sweatshops (especially in the furniture and garment industries) that in the last five years have spread to older, mostly Latina/o, central neighborhoods. The Los Angeles region is thus both a financial and high-tech zone and an emerging open-shop conglomerate, in which working conditions are "often worse

than . . . in South China, Honk Kong and Vietnam, where buildings are
likely to be newer and well ventilated, and workers subsidized with housing and food."[37]

In the resulting spatial arrangements, only 2 percent of the region's total
Black population lives in the suburbs. The other 98 percent of Blacks are
concentrated in the city's central areas whose poorer quarters, in the same
period, witnessed the arrival of 328,000 Mexican immigrants, employed
mostly in nonunionized manufacturing and service jobs.[38] As a result, Los
Angeles became the second-largest Mexican metropolis after Mexico City.
With the arrival of Central Americans, Middle Easterners, and Asians, in
the 1980s the City of Angels lost its Anglo majority and became a metropolis with a majority of minorities: 48 percent of its inhabitants were Anglo,
28 percent Latina/o, 17 percent African American, 7 percent Asian, and
1 percent Native American. By 1990 Latina/os became the largest minority,
and Los Angeles had now the largest Salvadoran, Korean, Iranian, and Fil-
ipino diaspora populations in the Occident. At least half of its population
over the age of five spoke a language other than English at home.[39] Attesting to this demographic dynamism, Los Angeles' population in the beginning of the nineties had the following proportions: 40 percent Latina/o,
37 percent Anglo, 13 percent African American, 9 percent Asian American,
and 1 percent Native American.[40]

While there is an increasing racial/ethnic diversity within the city, such
diversity is arranged throughout the urban space in clear patterns. According to the 1990 census, the Westside is still primarily Anglo.[41] The South
of Los Angeles, by contrast, contains the smallest percentage of Whites
and the only neighborhoods in the city where Blacks are, if not the majority, at least a significant large minority.[42]

Not surprisingly, unemployment rates, income, and percentage of persons below poverty level reflect these racial/ethnic arrangements in the
urban spaces. The areas with the largest incomes are mainly White. The
more Blacks and Latina/os occupy an area, the lower the average incomes
become. The same holds for unemployment and poverty levels.[43] Levels of
segregation between Latina/os and Whites have augmented since the 1970s,
and more complex processes have been taking place between Latina/os and
Asians and Latina/os and Blacks.[44] As we decrease the scale of analysis—
from cities, to tracts, to blocks—ethnic and racial mixing, as well as separation, have recently been happening at unprecedented intensity.

Los Angeles County, for example, displays concentric bands whose ethnic and racial heterogeneity increases the farther they are from the inner
city. Indeed, the most central areas have the greater homogeneity, with
predominantly Latina/o and African American communities. The communities in which Latina/o immigrants first settled, in particular, constitute the most ethnically homogeneous in the whole region. In this respect,
Boyle Heights and East L.A. are among the less ethnically diverse in Los
Angeles County. As we move to the next concentric band surrounding the
highly homogeneous Black and Latina/o core neighborhoods, we encounter
an area whose heterogeneity is already much more accentuated than the
previous one. Compton, Carson, and Watts, still very homogeneous until
the end of the 1970s, are now part of an area whose tracts are very mixed,
especially with Latina/os, Blacks, and, to a smaller extent, Asians. The next
concentric belt, however, has the highest ethnic and racial diversity of the
region, reaching parts of the San Fernando Valley, the San Gabriel Valley,
and the northern part of Orange County. Beyond these latter areas, however, as socioeconomic status augments and reaches its highest point in
the region, diversity diminishes significantly, and the Los Angeles coast,
Palos Verdes, and the Santa Monica mountains are all very homogeneous. In sum, diversity is low at the core, greatly augments and reaches its
maximum magnitude in the intermediate concentric bands, and then
diminishes again in the richer, more peripheral rings.[45]

This is not to say, however, that there is such a thing as real diversity in
Los Angeles. Residential segregation persists and the artificially constrained
housing market for Blacks and Latina/os produces at least two interrelated
effects. First, it keeps them disadvantaged in relation to Whites. Second,
it creates antagonisms between Blacks and Latina/os because, unlike for
Whites, the limited supply of inner-city housing is the only one they can
reasonably expect to draw on.[46]

In Los Angeles County, majoritarian White tracts and, to a greater extent, majoritarian Black tracts, have had their numbers extensively decreased
between 1980 and 1990. Predominantly White tracts with 20 to 40 percent non-White inhabitants—those which, following the concentric rings
model, would be expected to be in the intermediate areas—became less
White. Similarly, tracts that were 20 to 40 percent Black in 1980 became
even less Black in 1990. Overall, tracts that already displayed strong tendencies to diversity—with 50 to 75 percent of Latina/os and/or Asians—

consolidated their heterogeneous character and were the ones that mostly increased their percentages of these racial groups.[47]

The tracts that already had the highest proportion of Whites (located in the most outer rings and therefore the wealthier ones) were those which, in 1990, presented the smaller increase in ethnic and racial diversity.[48] Most of the tract changes involve Blacks and Latina/os, with a large proportion of incoming Latina/os settling in tracts previously dominated by or with large minorities of Blacks. In effect, the two inner concentric bands stage complex and intense racial rearrangements, and it is within these areas that, as we shall see below, Blacks and Latina/os have been struggling for work and habitation. Indeed, when instead of census tracts we analyze census blocks, the tensions emerging from these struggles become clearer.

Census blocks—which correspond to actual neighborhood blocks, especially those located in the inner city—still display a very high degree of racial and ethnic homogeneity.[49] Such clustering indicates persistent levels of segregation and animosity between Blacks and Latina/os. The inner city contains an enormous concentration of African Americans in spite of the recent demographic transformations. My fieldwork was conducted in the heart of South Central, in an area that is at least 75 percent Black but rapidly changing. Thus, inter- as well as intraracial conflicts are of fundamental importance when investigating the everyday life of Blacks in South Central. The Black and White scheme of interpretation, if already questionable for the comprehension of the city's previous history, is definitely inappropriate to understand Los Angeles' most recent transformations and struggles.

The massive arrival of Latina/o and, to a lesser extent, Korean immigrants in the inner city has intensified the local struggles for survival. With these new arrivals, we can speculate that structural and labor-market discrimination against Blacks have become even more critical. Put in another way: the effects of immigration on the life of the inner city have to be understood *within* the broader, historically persistent structure of opportunity that systematically discriminates against Blacks and other racialized groups.[50]

To access the impact of immigration on Blacks in Los Angeles it is necessary to compare their plight with those of Blacks in other metropolitan areas. Sociologists Ong and Valenzuela devised a method through which Los Angeles County can be contrasted with fifty-five other comparable metropolitan statistical areas (MSAs).[51] As Table 3 indicates, the Los Angeles metropolitan area presents an inordinately high ratio of Latino immigrants per Black males, placing it first among all the other metropolitan areas considered. It follows from these facts that, if immigrants do indeed have an impact on Blacks' employment prospects, then such impact must be the more accentuated in Los Angeles.

Ong and Valenzuela were also able to gauge the impact of Latino immigration on Black joblessness by comparing data from the Los Angeles metropolitan area with fifty-five other U.S. metropolitan areas. Adjusted for age and education, and compared with other regions, the difference in the rate of joblessness among both young and less-educated Blacks was found to be almost entirely due to the presence of recently arrived low-skilled workers from Mexico and Central America. Here, thus, resides one of the distinguishing traits of Los Angeles vis-à-vis other metropolitan areas: it not only displays an extravagant ratio of immigrant workers per African Americans, but this ratio is what accounts for the relatively worse job prospects Blacks encounter in the City of Angels.

Now, in spite of the unmistakable negative effects the presence of recent immigrants produce on Blacks' economic opportunities, it should remain absolutely clear that the additional joblessness Latina/os generate is not

Table 3. Labor force ratios: Recent Latino immigrants to black males

	Los Angeles metropolitan statistical area	Metropolitan statistical areas for 55 cities	Relative ranking of Los Angeles
Ratio of recent Latino immigrants to:			
Young black males, 18–24	9.7	0.9	1
Less-educated black males, 18–64	2.7	0.3	1
Ratio of recent less-educated Latino immigrants to:			
Young black males, 18–24	8.5	0.7	1
Less-educated black males, 18–64	2.3	0.2	1

NOTE: "Less-educated black males" do not have education beyond high school.
SOURCE: Paul Ong and Abel Valenzuela Jr., "Labor Force Ratios," in *Ethnic Los Angeles,* ed. Roger Waldinger and Mehdi Bozorgmehr (New York: Russell Sage Foundation, 1996), 173. Copyright 1996 Russell Sage Foundation; reprinted with permission.

more than precisely this: *additional* percentage to already very high rates of unemployment. Thirty-nine percent of young Black males in the L.A. metropolitan area—instead of the 46 percent that shows up in Table 4—would theoretically be jobless if the Latino immigration had no impact on their employment opportunities. Their situation would have been already dismal without the immigrants. The Latino immigration to Los Angeles, in this sense, as it augments the availability of workers, exacerbates discriminatory practices among employers. Faced with a surplus of low-skilled, low-wage workers, employers amass obvious economic advantages by hiring Latinos who frequently are undocumented, nonunionized, and therefore willing to accept lower wages and minimal, if indeed any, benefits. It is in light of both persistent discrimination against Blacks *and* the ample availability of cheap immigrant labor that we must understand the results of empirical studies conducted in Los Angeles showing employers' preference for Latino workers over African Americans.[52]

Kody's increasing frustration with his difficulties in finding work clearly influenced the anger he began to direct toward Latina/os. As accurate as his perceptions that Latina/os were "everywhere," that they were being hired for the very same jobs Blacks were being negated, and that Latina/os were accepting work conditions and remuneration that devalued Blacks' work—as sociologically accurate as his findings were, they missed the fundamental point that immigrant labor and its impacts, rather than being the main *cause* of Black joblessness were in fact another *effect* of persistent, structural forms of discrimination. The tragic irony of Kody's perception is that, as

Table 4. Percentage of black joblessness by metropolitan areas

City	Young black males, 18–24 years old	Less educated black males 18–64 years old
Los Angeles	46%	37%
55 other U.S. metropolitan areas	40	30
Raw difference	+6	+7
Difference adjusted for age and education	+9	+8
Estimated net impact of Latino immigration on blacks in Los Angeles	+7	+5

SOURCE: Ong and Valenzuela, "Black Joblessness by Metropolitan Area," in *Ethnic Los Angeles,* 174. Copyright 1996 Russell Sage Foundation; reprinted with permission.

it correctly sees a connection between his fate and those of immigrants, it nevertheless utilizes a form of reasoning that prevents him from visualizing the larger picture. Latina/os, in his reasoning, become nothing more than another racial group, with innate characteristics that render them more or less acceptable by employers, more or less acceptable as fellow workers and neighbors. Trapped in the circularities that racial thoughts sometimes generate, Kody could only experience resentment.

His resentment, it turns out, is an indication of collectively shared sentiments against immigrants. Almost half of all African American and Asian American voters—47 percent—endorsed the infamous 1994 California Proposition 187. This proposition stated that "illegal aliens are ineligible for public social service, public health care services (unless emergency under federal law), and attendance of public schools." It also made mandatory that state and local agencies "report suspected illegal aliens."[53] Among Blacks, the sentiments behind their support of an obviously discriminatory measure was brewing since the 1980s' great wave of immigration. As a survey conducted by the *Los Angeles Times* in 1984 among South Central residents had already suggested, Blacks' grievances toward Latina/os centered almost exclusively on economic issues. Job competition, in particular, was the main cause of Black antagonism toward immigrants from Mexico and Central America. The younger and less educated Black respondents were, the more they tended to express racial and ethnic resentment through phrases such as "undocumented Mexicans take jobs away from American citizens."[54]

South Central has become, since the 1980s, an area intensely marked by Latina/o immigration, deindustrialization, suburbanization of production, and unprecedented polarization among African Americans. The 1980s mark the transformation of South Central from a mostly Black area into an essentially mixed one, where poor African Americans increasingly compete with Latina/os for jobs and residence. South Central, we may recall, was 80 percent Black in the 1970s. In the 1990s, however, Blacks were down to 50.3 percent, and diminishing. Latina/o immigration accounted for most of the area's demographic mutation. Whereas Latina/os constituted 9 percent of South Central's population in 1970, twenty years later they accounted for a surprising 44 percent of its total inhabitants. Still, Black exodus is also a significant factor in South Central's transformation.

Median earnings for Black women and men increased significantly between 1969 and 1989. Black men experienced an increase of 13.6 percent in their annual earnings, whereas Black women saw theirs increase 61.2 in this twenty-year period. Nevertheless, the percentage of Black families living in poverty diminished almost insignificantly, from 22 percent in 1970 to 18 percent in 1990. These numbers suggest that the gains verified in Blacks' earning happened for those who were already better off. Indeed, during the 1980s, the number of families living in census tracts with poverty rates of 40 percent or higher—what is considered *concentrated* poverty—increased by 15,000. Thus, not only did earning gains benefit disproportionately the wealthier segment of African Americans, but also those Blacks who did not participate in this economic improvement saw themselves closer to one another. Here lies the *impression* that Los Angeles' racial segregation has diminished. The prevalent inner-city Black segregation of previous decades is now Black and Brown which, if on the one hand diminishes the levels of statistical segregation, on the other *concentrates* Black poverty and *amplifies* the *internal* conflicts arising from Black and Brown rivalry for scarce resources.[55]

All this indicates that the most dramatic changes in Blacks' earnings occurred among those families in the poorest and richest segments of the Black population in Los Angeles. The number of Blacks in the poorest earning quintile augmented from less than 30 percent of the total Black population in 1970, to almost 40 percent in 1990. While the number of African Americans pertaining to the highest earning categories augmented from less than 5 percent in 1970 to 20 percent in 1990, the intermediate earning categories were unmistakably compressed. In 1970 the middle three quintiles responded for 70 percent of Black earners; in 1990, however, this number went down to 40 percent.[56] Los Angeles is now home for both the richest and the poorest predominantly Black communities in the United States.[57] Inequality among Blacks is, in the City of Angels, more pronounced than anywhere else in this country.

When we consider how Black women's labor market experiences have evolved between 1970 and 1990, some of the impacts of the recent production transformation and immigration can be seen at work. Surprisingly, Latina/o immigration has had, among Black women, the opposite effect it produced among Black men. In the 1970s, for example, Black women were overrepresented in private household work. Today, household work in Los

Angeles—whose demand has greatly increased in the last years—is mainly done by Latinas, and Black women are now underrepresented in this sector. Indeed, "rather than pushing Black women out of the labor market, as sometimes occurs with Black men, immigrants have pushed them up into better-paying positions in the growing corporate and healthcare sectors."[58] This process of substitution explains some of Black women's earnings growth.

What accounts for the better prospects Black women have in the job market compared to Black men? The question is particularly puzzling since the advantages Black women often have over Latinas, especially foreign-born Latinas—citizenship and English fluency—should also benefit Black men when competing with Latinos. But we have seen that such is not the case. Black women's growing level of education, some authors argue, is the main cause for the difference in their employment trajectories when compared to Black men's fate in the rearranged labor market.[59]

The gains registered by Black women in Los Angeles' labor market reflect a national trend toward greater incorporation of women in the work spheres. Additionally, the growth in the service economy put Black women with communication and basic office-related skills in obvious advantage compared not only to their Latina, especially foreign-born, counterparts, but also to Black men, to whom these positions are traditionally closed. It must also be stressed that, as it happens in other parts of the country, employers are much more likely to hire Black women than to hire Black men—women are thought to be more docile, responsible, and have better language skills than men.[60]

Relative to Latinas, Black women have educational and legal advantages; relative to Black males, they are less discriminated against by employers. Yet despite visible gains in employment between 1970 and 1990, in every category, regardless of education, there has been a *decrease* in the percentage of Black women employed from 1980 to 1990. Those with less than a high school education witnessed their rate of employment fall more dramatically. Whereas 40 percent of young Black women with less than high school were employed in 1970, in 1990 this rate went down to about 25 percent. Among those with some or more than a college education, the decrease in employment registered between 1980 and 1990 was the smallest among all educational categories. Add to this the fact that young Black women with some or more than college education were those with the greatest levels of employment throughout the last three decades, and a familiar configuration comes to mind. The job market for Black women—the 1970s' remarkable improvements notwithstanding—has experienced polarizations similar to those verified among all U.S. workers since the 1980s. Such polarizations reached their zenith among Blacks, resulting in unprecedented inequalities in the City of Angels. Similarly, Black women's labor market participation, while considerably better than that of Latinas, and less hampered by employers' discrimination than young Black men, is also marked by an increasing degree of inequalities. Between 1970 and 1990, managerial and administrative occupations that remunerate better and require the highest levels of education registered an *increase* in Black women's participation of more than 1,200 percent; operative and laborer occupations, meanwhile, witnessed a *decrease* of almost 200 percent; retail trade, clerical and sales yielded decreases or relatively small increases.[61]

The inequalities in job-market participation for Black men in Los Angeles are quite similar, if not worse. We have seen how Latino immigration has intensified less-educated young Black men's difficulties in finding work. These difficulties were amplified by Los Angeles' deindustrialization that, in the few years between 1978 and 1982, generated the loss of 75,000 jobs in the auto, steel, rubber, and aircraft industries. As many as 50,000 of those jobs disappeared from Los Angeles' central area, precisely where they were more accessible to inner-city Blacks. The relocation of firms such as Northrop, Rockwell, and Hughes Aircraft to areas outside Los Angeles County greatly affected Black men's participation in the job market. Needless to say, the closing of manufacturing plants also meant the elimination of an important source of work for less-educated Blacks who historically had found jobs in, or related to, these manufacturing plants. This process is what accounts for the competition between unskilled young Blacks and Latino immigrants in the new sweatshop-like production sites that have been replacing the old plants in and around the inner city.[62]

Compared to their better-educated counterparts, young Black men with at best a high school diploma have had their employment rates deteriorate very quickly. The difference in employment rates between better- and worse-educated Black men in 1970 was about 22 percentage points; by 1990 it had more than doubled to 55 percentage points. Black men with low levels of education who are fortunate enough to find work today have been, since 1990, "overrepresented in occupations such as bus and truck drivers, freight and baggage handlers, and telephone installers."[63]

Attesting to the gargantuan inequalities among African Americans, however, better-educated Black men, that is, those with college education or more, have increasingly found good-paying jobs in occupations in which, prior to the 1970s, Blacks were severely underrepresented. Financial, insurance, and real estate occupations have absorbed Black men at rates greater than the pace of growth of the number of men in the region. Still, the most impressive increase in the proportion of employed Black men is in the top occupational categories in the following sectors: managerial-administrative, professional-technical, sales, and in the public sector. Between 1970 and 1990, for example, the increase of Black men in the managerial administrative sector was approximately 150 percent, whereas for all men it was less than 25 percent. In the public sector, the share of Black persons in high-level administrative occupations rose almost ten times, from 1.3 percent to 10.5 percent during Tom Bradley's tenure as mayor, between 1973 and 1992.[64]

It is thus evident that, when we consider the factors behind the occupational success of Blacks with high levels of education, we arrive at a picture that has the germs of the present enormous inequalities. The city of Los Angeles' administration during the Bradley regime is a case in point. Although it greatly augmented the proportion of well-educated African Americans in its payroll, it did not improve the dismal employment standing of less-educated Blacks.

*

South Central's richer Black families began leaving traditional Black neighborhoods in large numbers in the 1960s.[65] From the 1980s on, however, this process, reflecting the astronomical socioeconomic gaps that developed between Blacks of different educational levels, acquired new, more radical traits. The former destinations of better-off Black families were the nearby gentrified neighborhoods of Baldwin Hills, Crenshaw, and Leimert Park. Their more recent migration has extended beyond the limits of the city and county. Table 5 illustrates how San Bernardino County is the destination of the majority of Blacks leaving Los Angeles. Indeed, it has become the suburban area with the fastest-growing Black population in the country.[66] A closer examination of who these persons are sheds light not only on the motivations behind this very significant increase in African American families in suburban areas, but also on the Black families and the general conditions left behind in the inner city.

The typical Black migrants who leave Los Angeles and settle in San Bernardino and Ventura, unlike the ones who target Orange County, are not part of the wealthiest Black elite. The movers are often between thirty and fifty years old, married, and have children living at home. Most important, they are homeowners (60% of them), looking for safer neighborhoods. [67] They belong to intact, working- and middle-class families, some of which seek to transfer or open new business in areas outside Los Angeles County. Indeed, Black-owned businesses are flourishing, supported by the rapid increase in the African American population and reasonable

Table 5. Black population by county, Los Angeles region, 1970–90

County	Number	Percentage
1970		
Los Angeles	743,700	92.0
Orange	7,600	0.9
Riverside	21,600	2.7
San Bernardino	30,700	3.8
Ventura	5,100	0.6
TOTAL	808,700	100.0
1980		
Los Angeles	927,340	88.8
Orange	23,520	2.3
Riverside	34,060	3.3
San Bernardino	47,220	4.5
Ventura	11,660	1.1
TOTAL	1,043,800	100.0
1990		
Los Angeles	927,328	80.9
Orange	37,331	3.3
Riverside	57,326	5.0
San Bernardino	109,575	9.6
Ventura	14,124	1.2
TOTAL	1,145,684	100.0

SOURCE: David M. Grant, Melvin L. Oliver, and Angela D. James, "African Americans: Social and Economic Bifurcations," in *Ethnic Los Angeles,* 401. Copyright 1996 Russell Sage Foundation; reprinted with permission.

commercial rents. A recent feature story in the *Los Angeles Times* noted, "The number of companies which range from mom-and-pop outfits such as dry cleaners and Creole restaurants to financial planners, dentists, car dealerships and industrial manufacturing, has grown exponentially."[68] As a result of this development, San Bernardino had, in the beginning of the 1990s, 3,366 Black-owned businesses, more than any other county in the region excluding Los Angeles.[69]

As impressive as the number of Blacks leaving Los Angeles County by choice is the number of those who do so involuntarily. The criminal justice system is responsible for more than 14 percent of Black migration out of L.A. County. Between 1985 and 1990 9,243 Black persons, the great majority of whom were males, were transferred to prisons and jails in the outskirts of Los Angeles.[70] In 1991, according to a study of the Los Angeles County Adult Detention Center, almost one-third of all young Black men living in L.A. County, between twenty and twenty-nine, had already been jailed during that year alone. As criminologist Jerome Miller explains, "the figures suggested that the absolute majority of young Black males in Los Angeles could expect to be dragged into one or another of the county's jails, detention centers, camps, or prisons as they traversed the years between adolescence and age 30."[71]

With the increasing incarceration of young Blacks, the high-tech militarization of the Los Angeles Police Department, and the out-migration of middle-class Black homeowners to distant areas, South Central has been left with a deteriorating housing stock, very high levels of poverty, and latent inter- and intraracial conflict. It is quickly becoming the exclusive home of the Brown and Black California version of the *lumpenproletariat*. Undocumented immigrants from Mexico are smuggled and crammed into "safe houses" in the area, hoping to elude the INS and to be properly "delivered" by the "coyotes" who get paid $1,000 for the operation. Sometimes anonymous callers turn them in—neighbors all too familiar with the added difficulties immigrants bring to the area.[72] The arrival of Latina/os into the depressed Black inner-city areas has been far from smooth and conflict-free.

For those Black and Brown young men yet to be definitely incarcerated, killed in the gang wars, or to be given a chance in the formal job market, the drug economy is providing its version of reindustrialization. Shortcuts to the realization of the American dream, as Kody's experience demonstrated, are offered in abundance through the thriving rock-cocaine industry. But as the drug and gang wars escalate—with the fundamental complicity of the local, county, and federal police forces—it further drives better-off Black families away from South Central. In the process, inner-city political power dwindles, for those left behind are too busy trying to survive and too disillusioned by the unfilled promises of yesterday's politics to participate in organizing or even voting. Westside politicians are now more willing to incorporate the electoral base of the richer, White suburban areas. Mike Davis explains, "They have brilliantly appropriated the lessons of the 1970s tax rebellion by capturing, for their own strategic purposes, the antipathy of homeowners to . . . high-density development, totally obscuring in the process such questions of equity and affordable housing, job creation, or the plight of the immigrant working poor."[73] Finally, conservative and neo-liberal efforts to make the state less responsive to people's needs by privatizing public services, downsizing, and transforming social justice issues into technical problems to be managed by bureaucrats make politics less important to inner-city dwellers as they see themselves ever more excluded from its realm and rewards.[74]

Thus the vicious circle continues. With declining political weight, the segregated Black and Brown ghetto remains isolated. Unemployment soars. Immigrants arrive. Homeowners leave. The housing stock deteriorates and increasingly becomes subdivided. Poor Blacks feel trapped. Gangs proliferate. Violence escalates. Police repression intensifies. No wonder then that South Central is today one of the most dangerous places in the world. Martin Luther King, Jr./Drew Hospital in the Watts area treats more than 2,000 cases of gunshot wounds every year, a rate that is compounded by gang and police violence.[75]

Lately, fires have been intensifying. Due to the area's declining political importance, the housing supply is not only deteriorating, but is also well short of fulfilling the demand created by the million-plus immigration of the last decade. No social policy or planning exists to accommodate the demand for low-cost housing. Federal housing assistance has been cut by 70 percent since 1981, and no state or municipal compensation exists. Since the construction of the housing projects in Watts and South Central in the 1940s and 1950s, no public dwellings have been built. Precarious and unsafe transformed buildings have increasingly become the option for poor families. City inspection is almost nonexistent. When a series of fires broke out in converted garages in Watts during the winter of 1996, burning several children to death, there was grief but no surprise.[76]

In a study published in the *Journal of the American Planning Association,* Los Angeles was ranked among the top four most crowded areas in the country. In 1970 living conditions for the poor were already alarming: 37 percent of households with incomes below poverty level were characterized by crowded conditions. By 1980 this rate went up to 47 percent.[77] The Housing Department, furthermore, found that severely overcrowded apartments—those with an average of 1.5 persons per room, doubled to 20 percent between 1980 and 1990.[78] Today, it is safe to estimate that 50,000 converted garages such as the one that burned and trapped its victims are spread throughout Los Angeles, and most of those are in South Central. Rents for such units go as high as $400. And hot bedding, a practice common in the 1940s where rotation schemes are arranged so that several persons take turns to sleep on the same bed, has become commonplace again since at least the early 1980s.[79]

Living in precarious conditions, one step away from becoming homeless, poor Blacks and Latina/os in South Central are thus trapped. Trapped in unsafe homes whose security-enhancer iron bars and steel screens became deadly allies of fires; trapped in a labor market that limits, if not totally shuts down (particularly in the case of unskilled young Black men) their work perspectives; trapped in neighborhoods increasingly isolated from middle- and working-class families; and trapped in increasing high numbers by police sweeps.

- spatial segregation
- effects unemployment and social mobility pg 44

BLACKNESS AS SORROW
AND SOLIDARITY

Women and the Ethics of Caring

The sounds of police helicopters and gunfire no longer disturbed me as much they had during my initial weeks in South Central. Kody had now been gone for more than two months. The apartment building, although invariably tense, was now much quieter. A banging on my door startled me.

"Vargas, come out, check this out!"

All in the building had long given up pronouncing my first name. At nearly 11 p.m. Shannon and Vivian seemed unusually happy, excited by something they wanted to share. They dragged me to the middle of our U-shaped, cement-covered court. Both looked up, still smiling, suggesting that I do the same.

"Isn't this something? It's just beautiful. Look at that," said Vivian.

Vivian's face was lit by her joy. Framed by the square contour of our building, a full moon illuminated the sky. Pollution, humidity, or some other atmospheric element had formed a thick ring around the bright satellite.

"Every time the moon is like that, I tell my kids that's where their brother is, with the stars and angels, way up in the sky," said Shannon.

Vivian spoke next.

"Uh huh, me too. That's where all my nephews are. Every time my kids ask about Charlie or Ron, I say they are in the sky, little angels with the moon and the stars. . . . And that's where all the babies who die go, too.

Isn't that so? Now let me tell you something. I can't say the same about some ol' fools I know. They die and God knows where they end up."

They elbowed each other, smiling. They were also crying.

During those few minutes of contemplation, the gunfire, the smell of rotten food overflowing the trash containers, and the tensions of the day all dissipated. For me, at least, coming out to the patio without worrying about closing my metal security door ("Come on, Vargas, don't worry about this now," urged Shannon) and momentarily forgetting about all the dangers and difficulties surrounding us, made watching the moon a welcome interruption. Both women seemed as lighthearted and relaxed as I had ever seen them. Shannon, in particular, usually looked sad and angry and would announce her state of mind clearly (and loudly) to as many people as she could.

Yet if some of the more common pains vanished momentarily, deeper wounds quickly surfaced. In spite of their apparent happiness, both women reminisced about personal tragedies—Shannon more so than Vivian. Shannon's fifteen-year-old son had died six years earlier. She was still mourning. Vivian mentioned her own nephews, but I understood this to be more a way of identifying, acknowledging, and soothing Shannon's pain.

I had first heard about Shannon's slain son from Kody: fragments of stories which, as I became less Kody's friend and more a fellow dweller in that building, were completed by other fragments told by different people. During that moon watching, however, there was no mention of Shannon's son other than the fact that he was in the sky, together with stars and planets, transformed into an angel. It would be a while before I could grasp the full implications of that discussion.

That particular moon-watching circumstance embodied the sociability and solidarity among women that stood at the center of life in our building. Struggling with poverty, unemployment, institutional power, and overwhelming uncertainty, the women in my building organized their lives around kinship relations and household activities. Their extremely volatile domestic lives required mutual aid and assistance, and the material help and affective support they could give each other. Local sociability functioned as an antidote, even if only temporary, for overwhelming personal hardships.

The lives of impoverished Black women in contemporary Los Angeles lead them into constant interaction with persons and institutions that do

not belong to their immediate everyday circles of sociability. Police officers, landlords, social workers, health and rehabilitation personnel, gang
members, and others impinge constantly on the domestic lives of these
women. The persistence of joblessness, the massive arrival of Latina/o
immigrants, and the ensuing transformations of the inner city's human
geography, coupled with police surveillance and inadequate welfare payments, relentlessly shaped the everyday struggles of women in this South
Central tenement.

Out of seven apartments in that motel-like tenement, mine was the
only one-bedroom. All the others had two bedrooms and rented for $550
a month. Women, none of whom had stable jobs or stable companions,
rented each of them. An older couple also lived in the building, but they
did not participate in the building's everyday interactions, avoided all
opportunities to meet neighbors, and refrained from engaging in the common daily conversation. During the period I lived there, one apartment
remained vacant for the most part, occupied only occasionally by people
who never stayed there more than a full month. All the women in the
building had children, and sometimes their children also raised children
of their own.

From time to time the women's mothers and relatives would come to
help or to be helped. Welfare checks provided their only stable source of
sustenance. They waited for them anxiously every month, only to see the
money vanish quickly in the few days following their arrival. A generalized state of uncertainty pervaded the lives of everyone in the apartment
house.

Despite fleeting moments of happiness, the women led very tense and
melancholic lives. They were friends and helped each other as much as
they could, but they also deeply resented having to live so close to people
in their same situation with so many problems. Moreover, they remained
acutely aware of the injustices they had to endure, especially those perpetrated by Black and White men, by the police, landlords, and those
who represented, or worked for, institutions such as hospitals and welfare
offices. Common struggles and hardships bonded them.

The circles of solidarity that these women forged to combat the circles
of sorrow in their lives inevitably took on a racial dimension. Because race
did so much to determine where they lived, what jobs they could hold, how
the police treated them, and what kinds of health care, transportation, and

education they received, it made sense to them to build solidarity along racial lines, to turn segregation into congregation, to borrow a phrase from historian Earl Lewis.[1] Yet solidarity does not necessarily flow from common grievances. Aggrieved groups suffer from the radical divisiveness that accompanies their powerlessness. They see in each other's eyes a mirror of their own humiliating subordination. They compete with one another for scarce resources. Many of the functionaries who supervise them, police them, overcharge them, and deny them needed services look like them. The radical solidarity that blackness gives to people struggling in poverty requires them to distinguish themselves from other Blacks as well as from people of other races. Their experiences prevent them from assuming that all other Blacks will help them. On the contrary, part of the work of radical Black solidarity is to construct a sense of mutuality that will inspire the solidarity needed to combat not only racism, but poverty, misogyny, and political suppression as well.

For the women in my building, friendship networks and family ties provided the main forms of solidarity in their lives. In the context of pressing deprivations, intense if only temporary friendships mattered. Friendship here means more than material, logistical, and psychological support: it also took the form of resistance against the everyday institutional oppression and the degrading conditions the women shared. Not always conscious and often not even effective, these strategies of resistance nonetheless secured temporary relief from the most immediate and pressing needs and troubles. These localized, improvised, and momentary resistances ultimately left unchecked deeper causes of suffering. Still, the friendships women nurtured in their everyday lives enabled them to endure and constituted their most effective, and potentially subversive, weapon against perceived injustices.

Shannon had three children living with her, each one fathered by a different man. With the exception of Kody—who also ended up leaving, although not by his choosing—all her children's fathers left as soon as they learned about her pregnancies. She had been a gang member in her early teens, but distanced herself from the set as her first son grew up. Willie was killed when he was only fifteen. By then Shannon was almost thirty. Florence, her oldest daughter, was then a newborn. With her arduously acquired high school diploma, Shannon found work as a salesperson for a cosmetic company. She lived with her parents in a trailer in their back-yard and was saving money for an apartment in Watts. Her plans fell apart when Willie was shot following an argument with one of his gang-member friends.

"I never liked those motherfuckers around. They were heavy gang-bangers, you know. But Willie didn't care. . . . My mother warned me. . . . She told me to get him out of the city because he was going to end up like every other kid on the block: high on dope, dead, or in jail. I didn't listen. I didn't think it could happen with my Willie."

Shannon told me part of her son's story as I drove her to a drug-rehabilitation program for parents. The program required her to undergo mandatory counseling. Depending on the client's progress, help with food and clothing for children was provided. Shannon confided that the aid she received for her kids was the main reason she continued to attend the sessions. She had been clean for years, she claimed. I soon learned, how-ever, that while her heavy usage may have been over, she still visited the next-door crack house regularly.

"How are the people over there?" I asked about the drug-rehabilitation program.

"They're all right, I suppose. Don't know anything about kids and what they need, though. I mean, the stuff they give me don't last more than a few days. But I need all the help I can get." Her tone was angry and melancholic at the same time. She returned to her slain son's story.

"When the police came, they told me they could do nothing about it. It was gang related. Gang related? My son was never in a gang, you hear? Never! Just because we are Black and lived where we lived, they think he was one of them knuckleheads. Willie was no crazy nigger. . . . My mother was right. If I'd took him away to another town, he'd be alive now."

The guilt and sadness that followed Willie's death quickly turned into drug consumption. Around that time, Shannon started using crack cocaine, a relatively cheap and widely available drug. She knew some of the area's dealers because they were her ex-gang mates. Shannon's attention to work grew increasingly erratic, and she eventually lost her job. Following her son's death, she moved away from her parents' house, had a string of dif-ferent and unstable jobs, and sought treatment for her addiction. Joshua was born in that period, and it was in this situation that she met Kody.

Shannon kept her apartment (directly across from mine on the ground floor of the building) very neat and clean. Shannon was especially close to her daughter, Florence, who was six years old. Florence helped in the kitchen, vacuumed, and took care of her younger brothers—four and five years old. She hardly smiled and seemed much older than her years. During our frequent shopping trips she always reminded her mother of what they needed to buy. Florence, Joshua, and Jordan were always nicely dressed. Shannon went to great pains to wash their outfits in the building's laundry, often at the cost of not having her own clothes cleaned. Shannon also kept them to very strict schedules. Even if they only had one substantial meal a day, everybody had to shower first, and then eat together. I would hear Shannon shout to them from inside her apartment every late afternoon at the same time.

"Joshua, Jordan, come in! Time to shower! Florence, go get those little devils!"

One meal a day was visibly not enough for the kids. Spaghetti and tomato sauce, and whatever meat was available, if any, constituted the usual dinner. (Soda was never missing.) Still, Joshua and Jordan scrambled for candy and money every way they could. They always shared the product of their luck with Florence, who rarely took the initiative to ask for anything. When neighbors gave them things to eat before dinner—usually cookies, chips, or sometimes cinnamon rolls—Shannon would either return the items or tell the kids to save them until they finished their meal.

Shannon did not have much of a social life outside the domestic realm. Relatives and friends stayed at her place during Thanksgiving, Christmas, and sometimes for her kids' birthdays. Relatives also came when she went through difficult phases after her separation from Kody, during bouts of depression, and recurrence of her crack use. Neighbors called her brother-in-law at times when Shannon's state seemed worse than usual.

Among the building's dwellers, Vivian was Shannon's best friend. Vivian was forty-five years old. She lived in the apartment above mine with her daughter, Sheila, who was eleven, and her companion, Al, whom we rarely saw. Rumors had it that he worked in a factory during the graveyard shift. His relatively well-off status was confirmed by the old Toyota sedan he drove, which Vivian sometimes used. This also meant that others in the tenement could benefit from the car. Al abused Vivian extensively. Several times their fights in the middle of the night woke me up.

During one of their frequent fights, Vivian called the police. Al had hit her so hard in the face that she lost yet another front tooth. Upon arrival, the police officers—a White woman and a Latino—recognized Vivian and did not seem inclined to take any action against Al. They seemed to accept his explanations about Vivian's bloody face and tears. We all watched the 3 a.m. scene in which, sensing the officers' hesitation, Al blamed Vivian for the fight. While she bled, Al shouted that she was a junkie and a prostitute.

"You all know about her. A crack head and a bitch. So what's the big deal, huh? Go mind your own business and let the police here do their work."

Shannon intervened, elbowing her way past the officers, grabbing Vivian, and insulting Al very loudly.

"How can you be such a dog, you motherfucker nigger? Can't you see she's sick? Get out of my face before I have my people kick your sorry Black ass. Do you hear me? Get out of my fucking way!"

Before the police officers did anything, Al grabbed his keys, put on a shirt, and left. He knew better than to take Shannon's threat lightly. Vivian, helped by Shannon and Sheila, put a bag of ice over her bruises and seemed inconsolable, crying and gesturing her distress very vividly. As a police helicopter circled around the spotlight that brightly illuminated our whole yard, the officers told us to go home in a very matter-of-fact manner, that everything was okay. Everyone, except Al, felt very frustrated by the police. It was obviously a case of domestic violence with indisputable, indeed confessed, evidence. I offered to take Vivian to the hospital, but Vivian declined. "They won't do anything anyways. Let's just try to get some sleep." Upon Shannon's request, I gave Vivian Tylenol that I had. Nobody talked about this incident again.[2]

Vivian received $475 in AFDC and $116 in food stamps. Her rent, like everybody else's (except mine, due to my smaller apartment), was $550. Al helped sporadically, but obviously not enough, for she was at least one month behind in her rent, as Elen, her friend and manager, kept reminding all of us. Nobody knew much about Vivian's past life or anything about her family. Other than the building dwellers, she seemed to have no acquaintances. When not too much altered by alcohol, marijuana or crack, she was very amiable—a sharp contrast to Shannon, with whom she could be seen most of the day, looking after children, watching the streets for any sign of drive-bys, waiting for the mailperson, cleaning our yard, and gossiping. Like Shannon, she committed herself to attend a drug-rehab program for the material assistance that was conditional on her participation in it, but she hardly showed up. She had been in jail several times for drug possession, had been abused repeatedly by lovers and by the police, yet none of this had halted her crack addiction. On the contrary. All she had to do was to walk across our yard and knock on the house next door, literally. For five dollars she could have a hit that would give her a few minutes of happiness and long intervals of further depression.

While coming back from the house next door one night, shortly after the incident with Al (her mouth was still swollen from that confrontation), Vivian was arrested. As soon as she saw them coming, she ran and shouted for Sheila with all her lungs. The officers subdued Vivian quickly, but she kept struggling. Sheila rushed down the stairs with her friend, Martha— both teenagers—and while Martha watched, Sheila tried to release her mother from the policemen's grab. Although tall, Sheila was very skinny. The officers shoved her away violently and she crashed head first into our mailboxes.

The noise and the screams woke me up. It was early morning. Sheila had to be rushed to the hospital, where she received several stitches in the back of her head, as well as painkillers and anti-inflammatory drugs for the bruises she had on her head, back, legs, and arms. Vivian, meanwhile, was sent to jail and released two days later.

Following this incident, I told Shannon to call the Coalition Against Police Abuse (CAPA), the organization for which I had been working regularly since my arrival in South Central. All of a sudden my job made sense to her, and to the others in the tenement. From then on, I became identified as the one who worked with Michael Zinzun. Well known among Blacks in the inner city, Zinzun appeared on television news stories and discussion programs frequently, especially in response to the common incidents of police abuse in Los Angeles and elsewhere. The women in the building knew about his past as a Black Panther, although few understood exactly what the principles of the Black Panther Party were. My connection with a community-oriented organization brought me closer to my neighbors. Although they had often seen me wearing a CAPA T-shirt and posting fliers about community meetings on the building walls, I don't think any of it made much sense to them until Shannon called the organization's office and asked for help with Vivian's case. Mentioning my name, and hearing a confirmation that indeed I worked there, not only expedited Shannon's request, but also provided a glimmer of comfort to the apartment dwellers. It seemed I could help them against some of the people they feared and despised the most. Being part of a community-based association that clearly worked with disadvantaged Black people's interests made me an acceptable outsider.

The women derived satisfaction from discovering an institution that assisted "people like us" in matters related to police abuse. They had known very little about community-based organizations and the benefits one could obtain from participating in them or simply utilizing their services. Shannon and Vivian, like almost everybody else in the building, were unaware of their rights with respect to the police. Despite a general idea that the police depended on taxpayers' money and that, therefore, they *should* work *for* communities rather than work *against* citizens, in their eyes the police remained a foreign, uncontrollable, and repressive force. Organizing against police misconduct, however, had never seemed a viable option for these women. The "pigs," as they were called most of the time, were simply hated, a force to be feared and avoided. Yet *everybody* in that building, like the great majority of the people I met in South Central, had been in jail, abused, or simply taken into custody without any charge subsequently filed sometime during her or his life. In moments of desperation, like the one Vivian experienced when Al abused her, they might summon law enforcement. The outcome of that incident, however, and Sheila's unjustifiable beating only reinforced the widespread notion that the police were not there to serve Black folks in general, and Black women in particular. Vivian and Shannon viewed the police the same way they considered other institutions run by the "White man," as uniformly hostile to their interests. Hospitals and several care centers for women existed, but largely as examples of hostile public institutions. Although frequently run by "sisters," by Black women working as receptionists and nurses, public health centers in South Central drew intense criticism from my neighbors, most of which, despite my initial misunderstandings, I eventually found to be justified.

After the police arrested Vivian and brutalized Sheila, Shannon and I took Sheila to the hospital. Shannon prepared us for what was to come.

"Don't play smart ass with those people because they'll never get the girl treated, do you hear?"

"What do you mean?"

"Listen, I've been there several times. Once I complained they took too damn long to look at my baby girl—she was sweating, shaking, and everything—and the more I complained, the longer it took. Then Vivian told me to shut my big fucking mouth up, and they got to us. That's what I mean. You just go there, do what they ask you to do, and mind your own business. Know what I'm saying? Those *sisters* over there think they're the smartest ass around. Fucking oreos is what they are. Black skin, but they sure are White inside. Some of them are real mean fat old bitches. I'm telling you."

Shannon was making sure I did not hamper Sheila's treatment, ordering me to comply, be docile, and talk only when asked. From previous experiences, she had learned that complaints and even small talk were unwelcome in those places. These precautions surprised me. I had been to that very same hospital before with Kody when Jordan was showing symptoms of food poisoning, and at that time the staff did not seem particularly impatient or unpleasant. I had obviously missed nuances Shannon and other women knew all too well.

As it turned out, Sheila was treated rather rapidly. (So I thought, anyway.) Although several other patients waited to be treated—some of them in obvious discomfort—we were in and out in less than three hours. Shannon and I completed the forms and waited for our names to be called through the speakers. Sheila was also put in a room for observation for about an hour. Fortunately nothing else was found. Sheila came out of the observation room still shaken but apparently well. Shannon took her by the hand and they walked slowly out of the emergency room to the hospital's main entrance. Meanwhile, I went to the pharmacy to get Sheila's prescription and brought the car to where they were waiting. Sheila's gaze showed that the pain had subsided and at the same time it revealed how terribly uncomfortable she was to be still there. Her discomfort was obviously related to trauma caused by the earlier police brutality, but it was also indicative of her awareness of what was to come.

Shannon complained and shouted all the way back to the apartments. She was very agitated and her screams every now and then turned into a raged cry.

"Why did they have to do this to this little girl, uh? Damn motherfucker pigs! Damn hospitals. Are you all right, my girl? Sure? It's gonna be all right, baby, don't worry. You'll stay with us tonight until your mama comes back. Don't you worry, you hear? You'll sleep in Florence's bed. She's got it all ready for you."

Sheila listened, still with her shocked gaze. Shannon had one hand on Sheila's head (she now was lying in the back seat, legs awkwardly folded), and with the other she gesticulated energetically to emphasize her disappointment. The nurses were disrespectful and not efficient, the doctors were inexperienced, and the whole place was too dirty. Most of all, she was infuriated by the long time we had spent in the hospital. We heard her impressions in many different forms and in various degrees of intensity. In the same way that she did not feel served and welcomed by the police, she considered the hospital service to be second-class, inefficient. She felt the injustice. "I bet White folks don't put up with this kind of shit," she said as we were arriving home, as if to finalize her torrent of indignation.

Her complaints, I later understood, had less to do with *that* particular episode than with all the countless others she and her friends and relatives had been through. Enduring the bureaucratic procedures and the employers' moods at hospitals, police stations, rehabilitation clinics, and welfare offices only reminded Shannon and other Black women of the multiple and overlapping ways they were marginalized. Only underprivileged Blacks (and, increasingly, poor Latina/os) were clients in those places. They could not openly complain for those were the only options given to them. Experience had taught Shannon to meekly comply with (what were considered to be) institutional rules, even if against one's strongest feelings. There was no other way: it was either compliance or further suffering. Because these services were the only option, they were often taken as impositions. "Fuck that hospital," I heard from Shannon when I tried to say that I thought everything had worked out pretty well, especially when compared to similar situations I had been through in public hospitals in Brazil. Shannon felt visibly angry at the fact that she, and everybody who had to use the only available medical services for poor people, were expected to silently submit to what *they,* the institutions, considered appropriate. She was angry at me, too, for not sharing her indignation.

"Don't you get it? Let me tell it to you real clear, OK?" Her tone was sarcastic. "They didn't ask if my girl had any allergy, they didn't ask what happened, who'd done that to her. They don't really care. All they want is to get it over with, that's all. They care little Sheila's been drinking day in and day out? No! So there you go. That didn't stop them from giving her all that shit [painkiller and anti-inflammatory medication]. What if she had a reaction of some sort, huh? They think it's none of their business. I myself wouldn't take none of that shit they gave her, but you know, Vivian might get mad at me if she finds out I took it away from her girl."

Shannon's sarcasm turned into fury again when she linked the day's events with the death of her son. "It's just like what happened with Willie. Nobody gave a fuck! Nobody! Pigs saying he was a gangbanger, he was this and that. . . . All those stupid questions. Report this and report that. And all that gang-related shit. By the time the ambulance came Willie was already dead. The police got there first, but nobody would touch him. My poor Willie bled till he died. So it's the same shit over and over again."

Her complaints expressed the realization that she was trapped, as were all the others in similar situations: trapped in their history, in their memories, in their grief, in their expectations, in the neighborhood. Shannon wanted more respectful health care, she wanted decent police officers. She wanted a better life and she felt entitled to it, but she was reminded constantly that a better life was very far from her reach.

As I reflected on the context in which such complaints were made, I became aware of their deeper meanings, of their importance as ways both to resist and to cope with very harsh material and psychological conditions. Superimposing my impressions (about the hospital's service, for example) to those of Shannon's only revealed my patriarchal, class-specific, very myopic understanding of the social realities women like her faced. They simply could not afford to relativize, ponder, find amicable, the things that might kill them. I had thought erroneously that Shannon was being short-sighted for not realizing that, after all, the medical attention Sheila received was more than acceptable. I even had the clumsiness to voice these thoughts in a moment when Shannon felt she could express her fury, not only about the day's events, but also about other similar, if not worse, episodes. How arrogant of me. The truth is, Shannon, as certainly other impoverished African American women did, knew better. Her knowledge was built not only on her countless encounters and clashes with bureaucracies such as hospitals and the police, but also on experiences that other acquaintances, friends and relatives, had throughout generational struggles. Shannon stood on too many layers of sedimented oppression and grief to be able to ignore them, to be able to operate as if all the circles and circles of sorrows were suddenly removed from under her feet.[3] Her acute consciousness of being part of a social group systematically discriminated against exacerbated her indignation. To complain meant to affirm this historical and social awareness. To complain implied not accepting a given condition. To complain prepared the complainer and the listener for what probably was to come. To complain helped avoid future surprises, but also expressed protest against heartfelt injustices.

If complaining resulted in certain misrepresentations of the immediate reality—one may, after all, believe in the good intentions of doctors, nurses, and receptionists in the hospital—it nevertheless is consistent with the available historical and sociological information. Black women's complaints recognized the systematic forms of oppression suffered in the inner cities: their experience with hospitals and the police, added to the bad quality (or sheer lack) of public services that were supposed to cover our area, like transportation and garbage collection. Only the worst was given to them and expected by them.

Women, in particular, were more exposed to these realities than men. They had to raise children who were often sick. They did not have access to cars as often as men did. They had to deal with public-assistance bureaucracies and agents. Social workers and those employed by the Food Stamps and AFDC offices—and the misconceptions about Black women based on which they operated—were the objects of frequent complaints and fears.[4] With no exception, all the women in our building depended on welfare money to survive. The loss of public assistance would mean falling into an even greater state of desperation and need. Homelessness loomed as a terrifyingly close reality.

This explains the anxiety caused by welfare agents. Shannon and the others were well aware of the power the "missies" had. "Missies" is how they referred to the welfare agents who were often White, apparently young, well-dressed, calculated, more often polite but distant women. For this reason, they always kept their houses even cleaner around the period the missies were expected, made sure boyfriends and other males were not in sight, and had their sons and daughters as well dressed and groomed as they could be. Last but not least, they had to give no sign whatsoever of drug and alcohol use.

Shannon was very clear about the discipline and control exerted on women like her by social workers and the welfare apparatus. Less than a month after Vivian's arrest, Shannon, as had become routine, was asking me for some money to do her laundry.

"I hate to do this. But I need two dollars. I'll pay you back. Come on, man, the missy is about to come over and the kids don't have no clean clothes to put on."

She went on to affirm, once more, her willingness to work and the unavailability of jobs and daycare centers where she could leave her children. It was clear that her thoughts were motivated by the prospect of meeting social workers who—all women in the building agreed—didn't understand Black women's conditions and needs. Rather the contrary. The social workers who regularly visited the tenement invariably left the impression that they, the Black women living there, did not have any wish to obtain work and leave welfare. The suggestion alone, whether explicit or implicit—I did not have the chance to witness one of those encounters—profoundly irritated Shannon.

"Give me a job and somewhere to leave my kids and I'll show you. I ain't afraid of no work. No sir. I'm afraid of welfare. That's what I'm afraid of. *Welfare people.* Those missies come over and all they be looking for is shit we be doing wrong. You know what I mean? They tell you what your babies should do, the kind of food *they* think is better for them. What do they know? I bet those missies don't even have babies. You know how White people are. . . . But they sure come up with all those rules. . . . It feels just like jail, except you're in your own house. . . . Yesterday a missy came over to Elen, so I'm figuring soon enough another missy is coming over to my place. She told Elen to have her tubes tied. She's got some nerve, hasn't she? Of all people. . . . I mean, telling Elen to get her tubes tied? I'm surprised Elen didn't kick the missy's ass out of the house. . . . So we know already what's coming. I heard it over and over again. It makes me so mad. But then, I can't say nothing."

Dealing with welfare people involved more than going through anxious visits. It was more than hearing how one had to raise children, how one's sexual and reproductive life had to be controlled—indeed, sometimes totally interrupted—and how one had to behave to be worthy of public assistance. The threat of being eliminated from the welfare payroll dictated a considerable part of those women's lives.

The intentions of control by the social workers and the institutions for which they worked were unmistakable. Shannon, as certainly all the other women living in our tenement (and those in other similar conditions), experienced these intentions of control with tactics of resistance that, while (temporarily) effective, nevertheless remained charged with anger and produced plenty of anxiety. Sublimating the anger and anxiety the visits caused, and substituting apparent compliance for those feelings, although a tactic of resistance in itself (resistance to scrutiny, at least), produced a gamut of other contradictory emotions. The dissimulation was obviously difficult and humiliating.

Although dissimulation—most of the time, at least—produced its desired results, it also generated more anger. Elen, usually self-controlled, strong, and serious, cried loudly with anger for many hours after the missy's visit, while Vivian tried to comfort her and her baby. "The bitch, the fucking slimy little White bitch," she kept shouting. Elen paced her shouts with open-handed slaps on the wall as she halfheartedly struggled to disentangle herself from Vivian's hold. I later learned that the visitor had threatened to take custody of Elen's year-old baby. The welfare agent suspected, based on Elen's radical loss of weight, that she had taken up crack cocaine again. The truth was that Elen had gone through a very strict diet. Unlike most women in the tenement, she was slim, looked fit and healthy. She even considered having one of her front teeth reimplanted. (Indicative of how they were excluded from basic health services was that the women in the building, without an exception, had at least one missing front tooth.) The fact that the social worker could not comprehend her appearance as anything but drug use exposed the social worker's predispositions toward Black women living in poverty.

The particular drug-rehabilitation program I had taken Shannon to was one she and other clients (with whom I spoke while waiting for Shannon) considered to be one of the gentler in its treatment of current and ex-drug-addicted mothers on welfare. Still, the institution demanded constant visits, reports, tests, counseling—all in exchange for some extra (but truly very little) help for the parent's children in the form of basic foods. Each time Shannon had to attend a programmed session, she also had to negotiate a ride or borrow money for the bus, find somebody to take care of her children, and cook their food in advance. She never paid Vivian, Nadine, or Elen to look after her children, but she knew that asking for such favors implied paying them back soon. Paying back Nadine and Elen often meant taking care of some of the many children they regularly babysat. This prospect worried her because taking care of extra children implied either hustling ways of obtaining more food—which created more obligations among the persons who helped her—or dividing the already scarce supply among an even greater number of kids. Sometimes she left Florence in charge, but this worried her too much. She knew that her neighbors would come over and help her young daughter as soon as she left, even without her request. So this option did not alleviate her anxiety of having to pay back her neighbors. Shannon became very tormented every time she had to leave her children behind. For this reason, she skipped as many rehabilitation sessions as she could.

Vivian and Elen, clients of different drug-rehabilitation programs linked to the welfare system, had on separate occasions told me how ineffective the counseling and the instructions delivered at those institutions were. As Vivian put it, "They haven't a clue of what it's like to live our lives." The fact that most of the bureaucrats and nurses were Black did not attenuate the women's discomfort. On the contrary, it only reminded the clients of their wretched condition and the abyss that separated them from other African Americans. Vivian and Elen also avoided their appointments as much as they thought they could without losing the small but important benefits that came with their compliance to the programs. Although not as vocal as Shannon on their dislike of bureaucracies that served (mostly) disadvantaged Black women, they nevertheless found ways to avoid what they considered to be unreasonable demands. They resisted institutional controls, perhaps not in a fully conscious and articulated manner, yet according to shared understandings and practices elaborated in a context of intense deprivations, violence, and a keen sense that they were suffering injustice. They felt penalized by the intense surveillance to which they were subjected by various institutions, and penalized, above all, by the wider society that had relegated them to an existence of hardships and sorrows. Most significantly, I never heard any of the women in the building blame themselves for their situation. Although ruminations on personal worth and comparisons between oneself and others were common, those women had a clear perspective on who was to blame for their fate—the "White man" and his institutions.

They viewed drug addiction as a result of imposed poverty. I heard countless times from Shannon, Vivian and Elen that crack cocaine was the only thing poor people had to escape: escape from need, suffering, and sorrows. It had nothing to do with personal weakness. On the contrary, as Vivian once put it, "the person who's on drugs is only trying to cope with things that cannot be coped with. You fight and fight and fight and then you give up because you've got nothing left. But you fight very hard before you give up. Then you're just done. . . . No hope left."

By rejecting institutional knowledge and practices, impoverished Black women resisted institutional control. Such resistance, however, entailed paradoxical results. While it exposed the inadequacy of institutional knowledge and its powers to control clients, the women's resistance remained fragmented, unorganized, and thus easily muted. In the repeated cases of police abuse, their resistance only produced more intense brutality. Especially when dealing with public drug-rehabilitation institutions, resistance often resulted in the loss of potential benefits that could have come from the very organizations they so fiercely criticized and avoided. They could have learned more, for example, not so much about the effects the consumption of drugs had on newborns (as the clinics emphasized) but, more important, about the most adequate diet and habits conducive to a good pregnancy. Elen had a baby with Down's syndrome which she suspected— perhaps incorrectly—was caused by alcohol and crack consumption during her pregnancy. Shannon's son Jordan had had a slower psychomotor development. They could have benefited from some useful knowledge about birth control. Shannon had an abortion just before Kody left; abortions and the distress they cause were rather common.[5]

Most paradoxical, however, was that, by consciously attempting to resist the public agencies' control, the women who did not attend their programmed appointments saw themselves under even more fierce and anxiety-provoking forms of scrutiny. If scheduled appointments were unpleasant, troublesome, and oppressive, surprise visits by social workers were even worse. They generated more uncertainty and their consequences could be disastrous, such as the loss of a child. Once under its gaze, the welfare panopticon could not be avoided. Within its domain, resistance against rules only generated further and even more abhorrent forms of control.

❧

Elen was the manager of our building and the only woman living there who had regular income other than public relief, although welfare checks remained her main source of income. She paid $300 for her two-bedroom apartment, which meant that her work as a manager was worth $250 per month. In her early forties and the mother of five, Elen had her hands full. Her oldest son, Freddy, was eighteen; Bryan Jr. was seventeen, Brigit was fifteen, Martha was twelve, and the baby was less than a year old. After being in juvenile camps and the penitentiary, Freddy was now trying to find work and a rental place for himself and his girlfriend. He lived most of the time at his girlfriend's parents' home, visiting Elen during weekends or when his help was needed. Due to his participation in one of our block's gangs, he avoided visits to his mother as much as he could, and when he did so, he hardly left the apartment. Bryan Jr., on the other hand, had been persuaded to quit gangbanging shortly after his first juvenile camp experience. His father sent him to live with relatives in Texas, and he stayed there for a year. Upon returning to Los Angeles, he was forced to live with his father, which meant, as we will see, moving frequently from one place to another.

Elen's baby had Down's syndrome, which Shannon and Vivian told me had been caused by Elen having "too much crack" while pregnant. The baby was looked after with extreme dedication and affection, especially by Elen, her daughters, and by Vivian. In spite of all the attention given to the baby, she was often ill and had to be taken to the hospital emergency ward frequently.

Bryan, her on-and-off lover for the last twenty years, was the father of Bryan Jr. and Martha. In his mid-forties, Bryan had been in prison recently. Upon his release, he quit his activities in the informal drug economy. He also gave up drinking. Every month, Bryan would come over to my place to give me the rent receipt. Those were the only times we talked at length. He seemed to feel less encumbered by Elen's watchful gaze and demands when behind closed doors in my apartment. From those encounters, I learned that he and Elen had reconciled in 1995, and shortly after that moved in together, encouraged by the offer Elen had to manage the building. On one of those occasions, he asked me for some money, visibly very disconcerted. He had difficulties finding and maintaining a job. Bryan first worked in a warehouse, then secured work as a mechanic's assistant. None of those jobs satisfied him. Low pay, no benefits, and the unlikelihood of any career perspective in those occupations made them dead ends. Bryan had finished high school and thought that with this diploma he should be able to obtain better jobs.

"Elen won't understand this. She wants me to stick to anything. She just wants me to be bringing the bacon home, no matter what, as long as it's clean money. But that's not what I want. I know I can be bringing a lot more bacon than this."

Bryan shared some of the manager's work with Elen. He wrote rent receipts for each tenant, swept the courtyard occasionally, and fixed malfunctioning appliances. His main duty, however, was to accompany and assist Elen in difficult situations like fights between tenants, disputes over payments, and the tense and fragile interaction with the landlords. With the kids, Bryan applied the harsher punishments, imposed restrictions, issued the more severe reprimands, and meted out occasional spankings. Bryan largely did what Elen told him to do. Even though he resisted working in low-paying jobs, he would not dare being unemployed for more than a few days. Bryan did not resent Elen for the conditions she applied to their relationship. He frequently praised her tenacity and ability in administering the building. Bryan also often gave Elen credit for his crack and alcohol rehabilitation following his release from prison. He never talked about the reasons that led him to be imprisoned, and I sensed he did not want me to know. He emphasized his commitment to the new and better life he was leading, insisting that the past was dead and buried.

Less than six months after moving in with Elen, however, Bryan left for his mother's house, taking Bryan Jr. with him, despite his son's vehement protests and the ensuing fights that followed between father, son, and Elen. Bryan continued to see Elen frequently and stay at her home for two or three days at a time, especially as the children began to have difficulties. Martha started drinking with Vivian's daughter, Sheila, and becoming a nuisance to her mother and the neighbors. Brigit had occasional bouts of depression, and when Elen and Vivian could not console her, Bryan was called. According to her mother, Brigit had trouble accepting her physical appearance. She had gained considerable weight and avoided being around people. Bryan could be very harsh with the kids, but he could also be very affectionate. He treated all of Elen's kids as if they were his children, too. Elen and Vivian always praised the fact that he did not make any distinction between those he had actually fathered and those he had not. Brigit was not his biological daughter, but was certainly one of his favorite kids, and she always seemed better after Bryan's visits. Bryan would also come to the building to do small repairs and errands, or simply to stay with Elen at her request. Still, Elen had given up trying to live with him. Bryan would not maintain a job for more than a few weeks, and this irritated Elen too much. Their initially strong and loving relationship deteriorated gradually.

Shortly after Bryan left, Vivian told Shannon that Elen was tired of being with a hustler. "She just wants some peace, you know. She's had enough of not knowing when the checks are coming in, how she's going to pay for her baby's medicines . . . all that shit. She's had it all right. And Bryan don't get it. He's always going to be a hustler, never satisfied with anything. It's just too bad because he's good with the kids and sure cares for Elen. I suppose she'd rather be on her own."

Elen controlled the house budget, took care of her apartment, and dealt with the landlords, the maintenance personnel, and the police who frequently visited our building. She tried to keep the tenement in reasonable working order while taking care of her baby. She shared some of the money she received for managing the building and babysitting, paying Vivian $100 a month for sweeping and hosing the yard every other day. Vivian and Elen also kept the laundry room reasonably clean, sometimes washing Shannon's and Nadine's clothes in exchange for their help in looking after the children

At least three times a week, Elen took care of five and sometimes six or seven children left with her in the morning until early evening. She usually shared this job with Vivian and with her daughters Brigit and Martha. They fed the children, changed diapers, and sat with them watching television. The children ranged from less than a year old to about six. Their parents seemed to be middle-class Blacks who needed daycare and found it sufficiently safe and inexpensive to leave their children with Elen while they worked. Elen did not have a fixed price; she charged according to how wealthy the child's parents seemed to be. Their clothes, their cars, the area they lived in, the way they spoke, and the jobs they had all figured into Elen's price. Her fees ranged from completely free to as high as $30 a day for the "Golden Hills snobs," as Vivian called the Blacks who lived in the more expensive neighborhoods.

Vivian was acutely conscious of prejudice among richer Blacks against people like her. "Hey, Vargas, can you imagine what those snobs would say if they saw their babies now, this close to a crackhead?" she joked, as she fed one of the babies when I walked into Elen's apartment to ask for the laundry-room keys.

"What would they say?"

"Those motherfuckers would totally freak out, I'm telling you. 'O Lord, my poor child!', they'd say [as Vivian imitated what she thought was an affected British accent]. And they'd call the police. I'd get my ass kicked real bad, lose some more teeth, I'd get arrested, and the kid probably would be sent to a shrink as soon as he could talk! Man, don't laugh because this is no joke. I'm telling you. . . . "

Elen and Vivian laughed, evidently drawing considerable amusement from the hypothetical story.

Yet, as exaggerated as Vivian's images were, they resonated with very real resentments the women had at being objects of repugnance to better-off Blacks—perhaps the reason why the images were so funny. They knew of the abyss between their existence and Black people who could afford to pay someone to look after their children, who could afford to live away from the poorer, deteriorated, and dangerous areas of South Central, and who could afford to *not* count on the type of racial solidarity they, the women in the tenement, could not live without. Those Blacks had jobs, most of them did not pay rent, their children would probably go to college, and the circles and circles of sorrow that characterized the lives of the poor remained, at most, stories told by older relatives and friends. Their realities differed radically from the everyday struggles of women coping with multiple layers of imposed marginalization.

Most important, Black women living in poverty perceived that richer Blacks lacked what they considered to be one of the Black condition's central defining traits: the solidarity and friendship without which their struggles would have been unbearable. "Golden Hills snobs" constituted a different type of African American, not so much because they had succeeded at the "White man's" game, but principally because, in doing so, they had cut their deeper ties with a community of suffering.

These perceptions, albeit clearly in accordance with the more general drives that impelled Black families out of the poorer parts of the ghetto, miss subtleties and paradoxes. Historically, Black families seeking to move away from the more deteriorated parts of the inner city tried to reconstitute precisely the positive community spirit that they considered an antidote to the problematic side-effects of poverty through a culture of uplift.

This community spirit, although consciously purified of what upwardly mobile people understood to be the lowly habits of the poor—unstable domestic boundaries, dirt, noise, propensity for crime, and unrestrained sexuality—was nevertheless consciously organized around a type of racial solidarity whose roots were clearly in the Black inner city of previous generations. Notions of the expanded Black family certainly played a central role in the definition of the ideal gentrified Black community. Of course, such notions were constructed against an image of the "dangerous classes," helping shape perceptions among the poor that wealthier Blacks were less friendly and understanding than those like themselves.

These thoughts and anxieties about other Blacks motivated Elen and Vivian to carry on their babysitting jobs as best as they could, to be very careful not to disappoint the parents. Their customers usually left with Elen the food their child was going to consume during the day or some money for the children's meals. She would usually buy chicken wings at a clandestine Korean-owned fish market neatly arranged in the back of a house, pasta and canned tomatoes at a local supermarket, and small packets of chips and candy at a "99 Cent Store" nearby. Finally, she stopped at a liquor store where she would buy a packet of cigarettes and a Lotto ticket.

Elen invited into her home the neighborhood women and children whom she thought needed a good meal the most. Among those who regularly shared these routines, domestic spaces, and duties, Nadine was the last one to be called, not so much because Elen did not like her, but because Nadine herself often looked after other people's children. Nadine, though, never asked for anyone else's help with the kids for whom she cared. Nadine never took care of as many children as did Elen, and Nadine also feared that her customers would not approve of exposing their children to unknown (and probably unwanted) guardians. Elen, on the other hand, often invited Vivian and her daughter Sheila (if she was around) and Shannon, even though Shannon did not have particularly friendly relations with Elen. Clearly, Elen acknowledged Shannon's struggles and Vivian's work.

Tensions first erupted between Elen and Shannon during Shannon's intense arguments with Kody. Elen and Bryan intervened several times, more than once threatening to call the police if Kody did not leave. Although Shannon never complained openly about their interference, it was clear she resented their threats. Several times, Shannon voiced resentment toward Elen and Bryan, resentment that was clearly displayed in the cooler, almost formal way she greeted the managers. Still, Shannon could not afford to fight openly with Elen. Like Vivian, her rent had been systematically at least one month behind, and she understood that only Elen's actions prevented the owner from evicting her. Despite Shannon's animosity and resentment, she did not doubt Elen's allegiances to the tenants. Her occasional unpopular measures and attitudes notwithstanding, Elen functioned as the repository of unconditional trust. For all of its flaws, material and emotional reciprocity organized and maintained the tenements' sociability.

℆

Black women living in conditions of imposed marginality bear the disproportionate brunt of the political and economic processes analyzed in the previous chapters. Increasing social inequality is inflected by and in turn influences how race, gender, and social class are experienced in everyday struggles. Because we tend to share patriarchal views on how society operates, we often overlook how women of color are deeply affected by, challenge, and successfully resist—at least temporarily—how unemployment, mass incarceration, and state disinvestment (in the areas of health, child care, education, and job training, for example) impact their communities. While the warehousing of Black males is undeniably catastrophic in its genocidal dimension, these specific and other related policies—as well as the widespread anti-Black political climate they require and help maintain—impact Black communities in ways that we do not yet grasp. Even though we know Black women are the fastest-growing incarcerated population, we know little about how African American women who are still in their communities make it from one day to the next. It is in this deeply embattled context that gender-specific efforts, focusing on the material, psychological, and spiritual well-being of children, fellow women, and men, attempt to maintain the vital communitarian bonds. In the areas most affected by recent neo-liberal policies, it is Black women, by and large, and not Black men—much less agencies, local organizations, or state institutions—that have to find ways to make ends meet; that have to manage drug addiction; that have to guarantee safe and supportive environments for children; that are faced with the ubiquitous presence of the criminal justice system in everyday life and how this has negatively impacted families and indeed whole communities; and that have to protect their loved ones from the constant threat of random violence by men, gangs, and the police. How long can the survival strategies deployed by marginalized Black women last? Sadly, this question emerges when we consider the intensity and breadth of the concerted institutional assaults on such communities.

read episode on p571

p366 friends
p369 police discredit women
p371 view of police
p379 welfare panopticon

chapter 3

BLACKNESS AS LIABILITY AND POWERLESSNESS

*Community under Siege and the
Welfare State*

The unconditional trust that enabled the women in the building to help each other in the face of overwhelming obstacles began to falter when a series of incidents marked the beginning of the end of their solidarity circle.

When the social worker threatened Elen with the loss of her children because she surmised that her weight loss indicated drug use, the building manager wept and moaned while Vivian attempted to console her. Previously, it had been Elen who comforted or delivered reprimands to other women. Everyone in the tenement was sadly surprised. Later that day, when Shannon asked me for quarters so that she could do her laundry, she revealed that she expected a similar visit soon. Two weeks later, the social worker appeared.

Between Elen's and Shannon's visits, however, another social worker also interviewed Vivian at home. Everything had gone smoothly. The social worker seemed pleased with Vivian's progress in rehabilitation and by her report that Al had not shown up again. Both of the "facts" that pleased the social worker, however, were false. Not only was Vivian seriously hooked on crack again, but she rarely went to the rehab counseling sessions. Furthermore, Al visited frequently. Nighttime generally found Vivian high on crack cocaine or craving the drug. Her addiction infuriated Al, and he hit her and insulted her repeatedly. Perturbed by her mother's sufferings, Sheila started sleeping at Shannon's apartment. Vivian accelerated her frequent visits to the crack house next door and became alternately and increasingly incoherent, aggressive, and depressed. Rumors coming from Shannon, who claimed to have heard them from people living in other tenements, suggested that Vivian sold her body to obtain money for drugs. The fact that Shannon, Vivian's best friend, did not bother to argue against the rumor only augmented its plausibility.

Less than a week after Vivian's interview, Shannon received the dreaded visit from the welfare worker. Soon after the agent left her house, Shannon let all the tenants of our building (and the ones next to us) know what had happened. Shannon had been warned that she had to resume her drug-rehabilitation program immediately, and that she had to find work in the next two months; otherwise, she would lose her public-assistance money. I managed to register some fragments of her complaints. She vented her frustrations to Vivian, but her friend did not seem much attuned to the conversation.

"The missy kept saying it's for my benefit. . . . She told me this new law was coming up and the sooner I got my act straightened up and got a job, the better. . . . Get a job? . . . How do you suppose I'm going to look for a job? Who's going to take care of my kids? Who? . . . And don't you think I've already been looking? Yes siree, I've worked my ass off looking for something to do. Problem is, nobody wants somebody like me. I've got high school and everything, and I've got some experience, but there aren't no jobs for me. . . . I know I can't lie about my rap sheet, so I tell them I've been in the pen. And that does it! No job for me." Shannon was angrily crying and screaming.

The social workers had escalated their demands. Their stance reflected the cuts in benefits for the impoverished approved by the California legislature and Governor Pete Wilson in August 1995, which in turn received legitimacy from the welfare "reform" law that President William Clinton signed on August 22, 1996. Although neither measure had yet been implemented, the women anticipated at the very least that the new laws would limit the total time a person could be on welfare, further restrict enrollment of new beneficiaries, and permit even more intrusive actions by the welfare agencies. Politicians and activists spoke about the needs and dangers of reforms. Television programs promised that "welfare mothers" could succeed in the labor market if only freed from the trap of welfare, hinging everything on the work ethic of the poor with no concern for the opportunity structure and the impediments that people on welfare face in seeking waged work.

A month before the social worker visited Elen, I personally witnessed the end of one of the common "overcoming welfare" television programs at Elen's place. Elen and Vivian shouted for Shannon to watch the last segment of the show with them. Shannon came with her three children. The women reacted to the televised story with an uneasy silence, sad gazes, head-scratching, and obvious preoccupation. The program said there would be a 10 percent cut in AFDC in California starting in January of the coming year.

Shannon sighed at the information. "The motherfuckers want us out in the streets, don't they?"[1]

The stories and debates on welfare reform were chronicles of a disaster foretold for the women. They knew that their very delicate economic situation would become unbearable with even the slightest cut in their benefits. They also knew that work in the formal market remained a very remote possibility. In this context of heightened tension and near desperation, friendships and the strong neighborhood networks of support started to unravel.

Following Shannon's interview with her welfare caseworker, she started to suspect that Elen had told the missy about "her business." The first few times Elen heard this insult, the volume of her voice matched her accuser's, maintaining that she had not said anything, that Shannon was imagining things. "You silly bitch! How can you say that? I've been helping your sorry ass since you came here, and now you come up with this? You tripping real bad, do you know that? O yes! You'd better slow down with that shit."

During Vivian's increasingly rare moments of lucidity, she tried to convince Shannon that Elen had not told the social worker anything about her. Shannon would not listen. Fatigue, desperation, depression, and crack overtook her. Her great-aunt had moved in shortly after the agent's visit, but this did not alleviate her hopelessness. If anything, it made it worse. The older woman paid frequent visits to the house next door. At first I thought she was borrowing food and money—which she probably also did—but when she asked me for money for the first time, I immediately realized that she was also going through an intense phase of addiction.

By the end of summer, the building's communal rhythms deteriorated rapidly. Vivian no longer swept the court or hosed the yard, while trash, flies, and stray dogs roamed where the children formerly played. Requests to me for rides to the supermarkets, fish markets, pharmacies and hospitals diminished. Yet requests for money intensified—for five dollars, ten dollars, twenty dollars. Shannon started behaving uncharacteristically aggressive with Elen and me. She resented it when I refused to lend her money, and she continued to blame Elen for the threats she received from the social worker.

Elen, meanwhile, helped by Sheila and Nadine, started to look after Shannon's children more closely. The two boys, Jordan and Joshua, began sleeping at Nadine's and sometimes at my apartment. Shannon did not notice the absence of her children at night, for that was when she was the most altered by the drugs. Florence, only six, tried to help her mother, but after a few weeks of desperately attempting to get Shannon's attention, became unusually depressed. Nadine took Florence in with her, and she began sleeping and having her meals there. During the day, Shannon's children generally stayed at my apartment while Elen and Nadine came over to check on them and either feed them there or take them to eat with the other children.

During her infrequent moments of clarity, Shannon did not speak to Elen or accept her invitations to have meals with her and Vivian. Shannon and her great-aunt were now in worse shape than Vivian. The great-aunt even came up with the idea of removing a few planks from the fence that separated our yard from the crack house next door, so that the short trips to get the drug dealer would be quicker and safer. She claimed—and in view of Vivian's previous experience, reasonably so—that undercover police officers were parked outside our building waiting to catch the crack-house customers. So the passage through the fence began. The two large Rotweillers that protected the crack house already knew most of the tenants in our building, so their presence did not constitute a problem. Attached to their long leashes, the otherwise fierce and loud dogs happily greeted each new visitor that came through the new opening.

Elen decided to call one of Shannon's brothers-in-law, Jordan's godfather. Given the increasing state of desperation that Shannon and her great-aunt demonstrated, and the extra strain Shannon and her relative imposed on the other tenants who were taking care of her children, she felt something had to be done. Shannon usually listened to her brother-in-law and, according to Elen, he had money. The brother-in-law, together with Shannon's half-sister, immediately responded to Elen's phone call. They stayed at Shannon's overnight, not allowing her or the great-aunt to go out. The children returned home. The brother-in-law thanked us for taking care of the kids and told us that if Shannon did not show any willingness to abandon her habit, he would see that she got interned in a clinic. He spoke with calculated authority and candor. Elen and Vivian seemed relieved by his presence.

Shannon's relatives stayed at her place for almost a week. The brother-in-law left in the morning for work while his wife stayed with Shannon and the children. Neither Shannon nor her half-sister came out of the house during the whole day. The kids played only in the courtyard and visits to neighbors became limited to short intervals. On the second day, the in-laws sent Shannon's great-aunt back to her daughter's house. With Shannon's confinement and the great-aunt gone, the building seemed calmer. Elen tried to keep Vivian under surveillance, and this proved to be helpful as Vivian greatly reduced her visits to the crack house.

After her relatives left, Shannon seemed to be doing better. Contrary to what her brother-in-law thought, however, she had not overcome her crack addiction. Shannon soon resumed her trips to the house next door. During the first two months following her relatives' stay, these trips did not occur with the same frequency as before her confinement, and she seemed composed most of the time. Yet her demeanor had changed radically. No longer a part of the building's activities, she displayed less attentiveness to her children and her apartment, which despite Florence's efforts appeared far less neatly kept than before. Shannon's patience with Jordan and Joshua had become very limited.

I noted Shannon started using the terms "nigger" and "little niggers" to call her sons. This was particularly shocking since everybody in the building remembered how upset she had been with Kody when he used the same words playfully with the kids. Joshua and Jordan, in turn, did not seem to mind their mother's new behavior, and started calling everybody they saw "nigger." Elen, Nadine, and Vivian (who seemed to have reached a stable point of addiction in which she was relatively functional although never fully sober) challenged the boys' new vocabulary by calling it to their attention harshly and threatening to whip them. While the women's disciplining worked some when they were present, it did not stop the boys from using their new word to refer to each other when away from adults. Shannon did not mind it anymore. It was as though all the energy she had to discipline and take care of her children, help her friends, clean the house—all the energy she had to cope with her very adverse conditions—had vanished. She had almost given up.

The irony of Shannon's increasing isolation from the building's sociability is that it originated from her suspicion that Elen had betrayed her. Triggered by the welfare agent's visit, Shannon's suspicion, usually turned toward the agents, this time focused on the woman who, despite her less-than-easygoing nature, helped Shannon (as well as the other women in the tenement) as much as she could. In expressing suspicion, Shannon risked excluding herself from the social network of neighbors and friends who, in times of necessity, effectively and affectionately managed to reduce each others' pains. Betrayal, especially to the "White man," was one of the most serious accusations one could make.

Elen's resilience in helping Shannon, even in the face of Shannon's offensiveness, vividly demonstrates the strong understanding and solidarity characteristic of the tenement's sociability. Measured against their group responsibility—obviously built on personal past experiences of hardships that had eventually been managed collectively—frictions among individuals were insignificant. Reciprocity, in that context, was not so much built upon personal, subjective inclinations, but more as a direct result of being conscious of collectively shared experiences of suffering against which solidarity was the most effective, if not the only, remedy. It did not matter to Elen what Shannon said. She could identify with her pain. She had been through similar situations and had been helped in one way or another by all the women in the tenement. She knew all too well the effects of crack on one's emotions and the fundamental importance of group pressure in order to overcome its more devastating effects. Elen's knowledge led her to contact Shannon's relatives, whose impositions she correctly predicted Shannon would accept. Shannon's brother-in-law, a middle-class lawyer who worked and lived in the very same gentrified black area that women in the tenement despised so much (he was, after all, one of the "Golden Hills snobs"), came to the building as an outsider whose outsider status proved instrumental in achieving what the insiders—the women in the building—considered necessary. The brother-in-law, although obviously ignorant of Elen's motives, and despite the obvious fact that *he* thought himself in charge, in reality, and without knowing it, carried out exactly what the women in the building wanted but, due to Shannon's anger, could not openly do.

Despite the women's perseverance in maintaining their network of support to survive the various pressures to which they were subjected, additional pressures began to make themselves felt. Latino/as attempted to rent a vacant apartment in the building and a new landlord initiated a harsher stance toward the tenants. These seemingly innocuous and un-related events compounded the pressures on the social circle that women in the building had created.

In a particularly good mood one day, Shannon looked after a large group of children that included her own, and some of the youngsters cared for by Elen and Vivian. A small stereo plugged into the long orange extension chord used when one of the apartments had the lights turned off played the Spanish-language international novelty hit song "The Macarena." Shannon coordinated the children's dancing according to her movements. As the music and the children got louder, Bryan Jr., Martha, and Sheila joined in the fun.

As the tape was being rewound, a group of three Latinos, all of whom appeared to be in their mid-twenties, showed up in our courtyard. They seemed very shy. They did not speak English. As soon as they saw me, they started speaking in Spanish. I could understand some of their words, but my difficulty in communicating back clearly disappointed them. Attracted by the large white and red "For Rent" sign hung in front of our tenement, the Latinos had probably seen my name on my apartment's mailbox— the only one that was not an Anglo-Saxon name—and supposed that they would be well accepted by the manager. All of their calculations were wrong. I directed them to the manager's apartment upstairs where Elen was taking care of the children. She came out before they arrived at her door, politely informing them that the vacant apartment needed painting and recarpeting, and that it would be another two weeks or so before it was ready to rent. In reality, there was nothing being done in the vacant apartment. Elen was simply trying to discourage the Latinos from moving into the building. The men did not understand what Elen told them, so she used sign language and a few words in Spanish.

I noticed that Shannon was visibly very upset. She first started with muted words that quickly became full shouts. "I don't want to see no

Latinos in this building, do you hear, you motherfuckers? No Latinos? No sir! I don't want my kids playing with no white kids, do you hear? You don't hear? Well, I'm gonna tell you, motherfucker . . ."

Her complaints drew Elen and Vivian out of the apartment. Vivian had a smile that turned into a laugh. Elen smiled in amusement. The children who were waiting to restart their dance did not know how to react at first, but seeing the adults laugh, began to laugh also.

Nadine came out of her apartment (on the ground floor), and told Vivian to stop laughing. "Cut it out! What kind of people are you? What have they done to you? They haven't done nothing to your fat ass. Cut it out!"

Shannon felt compelled to repeat her shouts. Nadine succeeded in stopping Vivian from laughing, but decided not to confront Shannon. She went back to her apartment, closing the metal screen door behind her, mumbling a few words of discontent.

Nadine lived in the apartment between Shannon's and mine. She rarely displayed emotions in public, hardly shouted or used swear words, and did not seem to have problems with alcohol or drugs. She paid her bills on time—her electricity had never been cut off—and she was yet to have any problems with either Elen or the landlords. Nadine rarely needed help from the other women, removing her from most of the interactions in the building. Despite this position, she always helped others as much as she could, often without being asked. She could be counted on at any time. Although not as close to Elen, Vivian, and Shannon as they were among themselves, the women respected Nadine, and the children particularly liked her.

Nadine was in her mid-forties. She moved into the building with her fifteen-year-old daughter about three months after I did. Her husband had died from complications after surgery the year before she relocated to the tenement. He had been an auto mechanic who co-owned (with Nadine's brother) a small repair garage in the heart of South Central. The brother continued the business and regularly contributed money and groceries to Nadine and her daughter. He also let Nadine use his car for at least a week every month, enabling her to do a large grocery shopping for herself and for the other women in our building, to get her hair done, and to visit her other daughters. Nadine complemented the help she received from her brother and from AFDC checks by babysitting—the occupation she had before moving into our building. Although she claimed that she had lost many clients because potential customers considered her new address far more dangerous than her previous one, she managed to have enough clients to make ends meet at the end of each month.

Nadine's brother often had meals with her and sometimes spent the night. He once stayed for almost two weeks because of a dispute with a gang member over the cost of a repair, during which the gang member threatened to kill him. The gang member, however, discovered Nadine's address, broke her brother's car windshield, damaged the paint on the body of the vehicle, and shot and killed the pit bull Bryan had left behind kept on a leash in our courtyard. The assailant left his gang's initials and death threats spray-painted on walls, windows, and junk cars parked near our building. Nadine's brother later found out that the bungalow he lived in had been broken into, its windows smashed, and its walls covered with graffiti.

Nadine had three daughters, the two older ones in their mid-twenties. Each of the older daughters had three small children. One of them had been married for two years, but she and her husband had constant fights. She often spent the night with Nadine after these fights. It was common for her husband to come the next morning and take her and the children back to their home in Compton. The other older daughter was not married, and she had her three children with the same man. She had problems with alcohol and crack, which Nadine attributed to the fights her daughter had with her children's father and with her difficulties finding a job. She had been a nurse at a private clinic, but lost her job when the clinic relocated and cut its staff. Nadine's younger daughter, meanwhile, was in the last weeks of a pregnancy, and spent most of the day knitting on a couch surrounded by the children left in the care of her mother aided by her sisters when they were around.

Nadine had spent her early adolescence in Germany, where her father was stationed with the army. "I know white people, I've grown up with them, I've been to school with them. They don't scare me like they scare everybody else around here. They're not an inch better than I am, and I know how they think. So if you know what they think, you won't be getting into no trouble and you won't be fooled by them."

Nadine's house was decorated with African masks, portraits of Martin Luther King Jr., Malcolm X, Elijah Muhammad, Bob Marley, photographs taken from magazines of basketball star Kareem Abdul-Jabbar and rapper Tupac Shakur. She had many vinyl records by Black artists issued in the 1960s and 1970s, including Jimi Hendrix, Marvin Gaye, Little Richard, Ray Charles, Duke Ellington, James Brown, Miles Davis, and John Coltrane. She took great care of her records, keeping them locked away from the children. She listened only to the tapes she made from her vinyls, and was visibly happy when I demonstrated interest in having tapes of her collection. On the shelf that covered one of her living-room walls, out of the reach of the children and dividing the space with the television and the stereo, rested several trophies her husband had won playing basketball. She displayed many carefully arranged color photographs of herself with her husband, her mother, her daughters, and her daughters' children. In one of these photographs, Nadine, her husband, and their three daughters with two of their kids were dressed in colorful long gowns and golden and elaborate adornments. Noting my interest, Nadine told me that the picture was taken at a Kwanzaa celebration in South Central.[2] Nadine considered Kwanzaa a celebration of Blacks' common heritage, struggles, and achievements. "People nowadays don't even know where they came from. We live like this for a reason—we're here in South Central for a reason. You know what I'm saying? We need things like Kwanzaa to remind us, to bring us together. Alone and without our history, we haven't nothing at all."

❧

During my stay in South Central, the building had three different owners, one of whom, I believe, was no more than an impostor simply trying to obtain our money by pretending he was the owner. I met the first owner when he showed up to inspect the vacant apartment and talk with Elen. A short white man, he exuded visible discomfort at being there. Elen introduced him to me as she took him to each and every home in the building. "Hey, Vargas, Mr. Goldstein's here, the landlord; come out and say hi to him," she shouted through my metal screen door. I had heard her going through Shannon's and Nadine's apartments, introducing them to Mr. Goldstein, conveniently skipping Vivian's, probably because either liquor or crack left her in no shape to meet him. When I came out, she announced, "He's the owner of this place." Elen was uncharacteristically sociable, had a broad smile, was joking with the landlord, and introduced each tenant as if we were part of a happy family. She described me to the owner in the same tone she had used for the other tenants. She had only compliments for us. "This one here, Mr. Goldstein, pays his rent always on time. Right on time every month! He goes to college in San Diego and works here in the 'hood, some community thing. . . . His place's always clean. . . . Check it out. . . . [She gently pushed him so that he would take a step inside my place.] Real nice. The only thing he's got there is books and books. . . . We keep an eye on him, making sure he isn't skipping no meals. You know how young people are, so busy they haven't got time for nothing."

That would be Mr. Goldstein's last visit to our building. The purpose of his visit was to evaluate the general state of his property because he wanted to sell it. Indeed, about a month later, Elen gave us the news that Mr. Goldstein had sold the tenement.

Shortly after we learned that the building had been sold, Elen gave us some unexpected news. She had been informed by the police that the woman who collected our rent checks from Elen had been shot dead as she was leaving the building. The reasons for the slaying were unknown to the police and also hard for us to grasp—she never had any cash with her and we did not know of any outstanding animosity anyone had with her. Most probably she had been another victim of the random violence so common in our area. Elen instructed us not to pay the rent until we found out the identity of the new owner. Yet a problem remained. All the checks and money orders the woman carried with her were missing. Elen instructed those of us who had paid with checks (Nadine and I) to stop payments with our banks. The other tenants who paid their rent with money orders would have to negotiate their situations with the next owner.

The money collector's death created a situation in which we felt justified not paying any more rent until our checks were canceled or our money orders recovered. This prospect made us content. I was going through a very difficult financial situation at the time for my fellowship had been suddenly cut during that summer. This brought me closer to the women's feelings regarding the prospect of a rent break, even though my situation was far less critical than theirs. My difficulties were temporary, but the women lived *constantly* under the pressure of bills. Most of their everyday anxieties stemmed from their (often unsuccessful) efforts to pay the rent and utilities, and feed their children on their meager food-stamp rations, welfare checks, and the cash they gathered from informal work. Even those who could supplement their incomes with regular activities such as babysitting, barely made ends meet. The extra money any of them made quickly disappeared as it was shared with neighbors (in Elen's case) and relatives (in Nadine's case). Even in the relatively more stable households like Nadine's and Elen's, everyday uncertainties concerning money remained a constant subject of conversations and worries.

None of the building's residents, myself included, attached any meaning at the time to the woman's death except that it gave us a very welcome break with the rent. Violence and death occurred frequently. Only on rare days did my neighbors and I not exchange details on (or actually witness) drive-bys, arrests, beatings, or gun battles. Gunshots rang out only occasionally during the day, but almost always at night. Joshua, Jordan, and Florence, like most of the neighborhood children, judged when it was time to go inside their apartments by assessing the intensity of the gunfire noise. By the time Shannon would sense danger and call her children home, they were already there.[3]

Many times, on my way in or out of our building, I drove through the terribly familiar scene of several police cars blocking most of a street, officers isolating the shooting area with yellow plastic tape, helicopters hovering above, mothers and grandmothers and kin and friends desperately gathered around slain and wounded bodies, people running back and forth across the street, and ambulance sirens screaming louder and louder. Many times it was hard to tell who was wounded and who was not, whose blood was soaking clothes and spreading on the pavement. So the death of the money collector did not mean anything to us. Nothing. We did not know her and we did not care.

As it turned out, Shannon and Vivian had not paid that month's rent. They felt relief when told about the collector's death. Vivian owed money to her dealer and was being pressured to pay it. The dealer's friends and his wife made threatening visits to her at least once a day. Although the people who lived in the crack house remained friendly with the tenants in our building—they often lent money, food, and blankets for overnight visitors, they gave old clothes to children and invited us all for their parties on occasions like their own children's birthdays—they could also be harsh and menacing. A man in his mid-forties, two of his brothers, his companion, and another woman, probably the companion of one of his brothers, ran the crack house. The dealer's companion had two young children who seemed to be the same age as Joshua and Jordan. Although those children were forbidden to play in our yard or in front of their house, the children from our building often played with them in their yard.[4]

The contentment and hopes that derived from the collector's death, however, did not last long. Less than two weeks after we learned she had been murdered, three white men came over to each of our apartments and, for those who answered the door, said that they represented the new owner. It was around noon on a Saturday. They followed the signs to the manager's apartment. Elen did not answer the door nor did Vivian. They usually went to dance clubs together on Friday nights and arrived home at dawn. So the visitors came downstairs and rang Shannon's doorbell. They introduced themselves in a polite way and handed Shannon a laser-printed letter. Shannon had been less depressed the last week, and her visits to the crack house had diminished considerably. Most probably she was sober during her encounter with those men, so the antics that followed seemed the result of calculation rather than the effect of drugs.

After quickly reading the one-paragraph letter, Shannon addressed the visitors, who were all shorter than her. Simulating distress, she talked very loudly and gesticulated nervously. It was a clear attempt to intimidate the men. Those of us who knew Shannon well enough also knew that her performance was nothing more than that. She was not minimally bothered or frightened by the visitors.

"I'm not going to pay shit unless you prove to me, with some legal document—not this piece of shit you showing me, do you hear?—that you, or whoever, is the new owner of this shit here, do you know what I'm saying? Ain't nobody coming here saying they the new owners because I'm not falling for that. Do you know how many people come to my door with this kind of shit? No? Well, let me tell you. I get shit like this *e-ve-ry-day*. Yes sir! Every damn day. So don't give me shit like that. . . . You white people think we stupid or something, don't you? Truth is, we're not stupid. O no! . . . And there ain't no official nothing in this piece of crap. I know what those things look like."

The men's banging on Elen's and Vivian's doors and their heavy walk had awakened me, and I paid close attention to Shannon's conversation, as I suspect everybody else in the building did. I quietly unlocked and swung my main door toward me and sat behind the screen door. Those screen doors permitted a view out, but concealed us from anybody looking inside. The men's body language and their voices betrayed nervousness. They were out of their familiar environment and, although they wanted to establish their authority as the alleged owner's representatives, Shannon instantly perceived their uneasiness. She immediately took advantage of her perception, establishing from the start *her* position of authority. The men's clean cut, office clothes, language, and their alleged power did not intimidate her. They tried to argue, toward the end of the conversation even threatening to have the police evict her if she did not pay her rent immediately, but Shannon went back inside and closed her screen door. "You come back with a real motherfucking contract and we'll talk, do you hear me? Now go away because I've got a lot to do!"

The men spoke to Nadine next, who like me stood behind her screen door, waiting for her turn. Although we all knew what was going on, Nadine politely asked them what they wanted, and they explained again. Nadine's tone and control surprised the men. In sharp contrast to Shannon—although sending the same message—Nadine's stance was very formal, quiet, and controlled. Unlike Shannon, who wore her nightgown, was barefoot, had a net over her hair, and looked as if she had just woken up, Nadine dressed simply but neatly in tennis shoes, jeans, and a fresh T-shirt. She chose her words carefully. She read the letter slowly and, sensing the men's uneasiness, told them that she could not comply with their instructions. "You see, try to put yourself in my position. I just paid my rent. The woman who collected the checks was killed, nobody knows what happened to the checks and money orders, and now you come here and ask us for more money. . . . We don't know what is going on, and this paper here don't prove anything. I mean, I've got a computer and printer inside, and I could have made this letter myself. . . . See what I'm saying? Would you trust a letter like this? I'm not saying you're crooks—nothing like that—but I've got to have more. We've got enough to deal with over here, you know, and it's a lot of money we're talking about." Nadine held with disdain the laser-printed, one-paragraph letter. She excused herself and went back inside her apartment.

After handing me the same letter they had given Nadine and Shannon, and politely telling me that they represented the building's new owner, the men asked me if I was going to pay them the rent. Upon my negative answer, one of the men circled the phone number that appeared at the top of the letter and suggested that I called the new owner's office. I told them I would and they left.

We never saw or heard from the alleged owner again, which led us to conclude that, in fact, he was trying to mislead us to think he held legal rights on the property.

We had news neither of the checks and money orders that were stolen from the slain rent collector, nor of the building's ownership status. Our happiness at the rent break had given way to preoccupation. Would we have to pay the rent that was due? Since none of us had saved money in case we did have to pay past rents, how would we obtain the amount necessary? Would we be evicted if we did not? Where would we live?

This state of uncertainty did not last very long. In the middle of October, a letter informed us that the property was now owned by a Beverly Hills real-estate agent. The letter had six lines in which we were told the terms of our previous tenancy remained the same and that "all the rents due should be paid in check or money order, not cash." It also gave us the name of the Beverly Hills agent to whom the payments should be made, and a telephone number in case, "for any reason," we needed to contact the office. The letter made no mention of Elen as our manager—a detail Nadine perceived—which meant that the new proprietor was planning on changing the way the building had been functioning.

Although we were relieved that the Beverly Hills agent was only charging for the forthcoming month, we were also becoming more skeptical about our chances to stand firm against this new supposed owner. He seemed far more assertive and direct than the previous one. More important—and as proof of his alleged power—he had already made clear that Elen was not going to be the manager anymore. This meant that Elen herself was probably going to leave. Her departure would cause an enormous change in the building's dynamic—it would certainly signal the end of the community of support as we knew it. Elen's role in maintaining a fragile equilibrium amid the chaos of the women's everyday lives was as fundamental as her absence was difficult to imagine. When we began to ponder the possible scenario in which everyone would have to leave the tenement, it was more than a matter of the hassle involved in finding a new place and moving. We knew that our small community was in jeopardy. If we decided to leave, we would most probably not see or be able to depend on each other again.

Four days after we received the "Notice to Pay or Quit," the agent came to the building. He went to Nadine's apartment first. We all came to the courtyard as we heard the conversation. Nadine insisted on seeing the grant deed, while the agent threatened that if she didn't pay immediately he would come back with the police and evict her. Having noticed that Nadine was the most articulate among the women, that she had sought legal advice, and that, moreover, she seemed to be behind the tenants' resistance to pay the rent, the agent decided to confront her first and, in this way, demoralize the rest of us by example. But Nadine stood firm. She did not raise her voice and, once again, carefully chose her words, avoiding colloquialisms as much as she could. All of the tenants, except for Vivian and the older couple, stood around the Beverly Hills agent as he questioned Nadine in front of her apartment. After unsuccessfully arguing for the necessity of our payment, the agent reluctantly agreed to send a copy of the grant deed and, once more, emphasized that if payments were not made immediately after we received the deed the police would evict us.

The agent came back early the next morning and slid under our doors a photocopy of what was supposed to be the grant deed. Except for the words "GRANT DEED," it was impossible to read. He had delivered a bad photocopy of a faxed document. Nadine came to each one of our homes and told us that because it could not be read, the supposed deed was invalid. She repeated several times that the document we were given was ridiculous and that it only showed disrespect toward us. "Who do they think they are? They think they be sending shit nobody can read and get away with it? They think we all stupid niggers, don't they? We gonna show them we ain't." We compared our copies, and we noticed that, even though all were mostly illegible, in one of them, what seemed an official stamp, could barely be read. It said "California Counties Title Co.—recorded/filed in official records—Recorder's office—Los Angeles County, California," with the time and date of the supposed transaction below these words. I contacted the title company and discovered that the Beverly Hills agent indeed had the legal ownership of the building.

Nadine did not seem very disturbed by the news. She decided to pursue the confrontation on the grounds that she had the right to withhold her payment until her apartment's problems were fixed. She suggested that we all do the same, but this time added that the final decision was up to each one of us. "I'm not going to impose nothing on you. I've got an appointment with the paralegal tomorrow, so whoever wants to come, it's fine with me. We're filing a suit against the owner for damage. I've been told not to pay anything until my bathroom gets fixed." Shannon decided to go with her and also not pay her rent, while the rest of us decided to pay. Elen then gave us the news that Vivian was going to leave the building and move to San Diego, where Al had found a better job and was willing to take care of both Vivian and Sheila. Elen also told us that she was already looking for another apartment building where she could be the manager. The older couple also decided to leave, giving a thirty-day notice together with their rent payment.

Vivian moved out a few days later. She did not pay the rent, did not say good-bye to anybody (except Shannon), and did not leave an address or phone number. Shannon said she helped her pack her things in the middle of the night and that Vivian and Sheila seemed excited to be leaving for San Diego. They quickly loaded Al's car with clothes and a few personal objects, kitchen utensils, the television and the stereo, and left everything else behind: a kitchen table, three chairs, a couch, a living-room shelf, a lamp, and two beds—all of which were later removed from the vacant apartment by the owner's aide and left in our yard for a long time before they were taken by new tenants and neighbors.

Meanwhile, Shannon sunk into an unprecedented state of depression and crack use. She constantly and desperately asked me, Nadine, and Elen for money. She had long crying spells in which, among incomprehensible words, she shouted Willie's name and called for Vivian, as if to have her friend console her. Nadine and I tried to help her, but she reacted violently every time we approached her. Elen then called Shannon's brother-in-law who, instead of staying with her and her children, as he had done previously, simply took the kids with him and left his wife, Shannon's half-sister, at Shannon's apartment. It did not work. Shannon escaped her curfew constantly, only to be dragged back hours later by her brother-in-law who had been called by his wife for help. Eventually they took Shannon to the brother-in-law's home, where she stayed for about ten days.

Upon returning with her children, Shannon continued her visits to the crack house and resumed her dates with different men. Joshua and Jordan stayed with Nadine at night, and at my place or Nadine's during the day. Florence still slept at Shannon's apartment, but stayed with Elen during most of the day, helping her with the children and housework. Florence seemed resigned to her mother's state and appeared to be truly content to leave her home and stay with one of us. Her brothers, however, were more irritable than usual. They cried and asked for Shannon constantly and only settled down when they ate and slept. Shannon seemed uncharacteristically oblivious to her children, to her house, and to her appearance.

The impasse with the Beverly Hills agent reached an unexpected turn when we were told that the building was going to be fumigated again. With only one day notice, the pest control company planned to spray our apartments one day before Thanksgiving. This infuriated all of the women, because not only had our homes been treated chemically less than a month ago (without any success, I must say), but the new fumigation required removing all the utensils, clothes, and objects from drawers, cabinets and closets, moving furniture away from the walls, and even worse, interrupting the cooking that had already begun. A big dinner with all the tenants and some of Nadine's relatives had been scheduled for the next day. So we all refused to let the fumigation take place.

Our refusal to have the place fumigated again may have precipitated the owner's willingness to evict those who still had not paid their rent. Early on the following Monday, Sheriff's Department officers brought court eviction notices for Nadine and Shannon. The women, however, had already left. Nadine had come over to my place the previous week to say good-bye. Her daughter had given birth to a baby recently, and the newborn delighted both women. Nadine tried to put in perspective the fact that the building's social networks were quickly deteriorating. The birth of her newest grandchild gave her some renewed energy, even though she knew her life, away from the building, was going to be more difficult. "I've lived in many places before, but here it really felt like family, you know, like when I was growing up. We looked after each other. . . . Now I don't know what's going to happen. We're staying with my brother—he's got a house near Gardena—and then start looking. Problem is, the baby is so young, we don't want to be living in any place, you know what I'm saying? Good thing my brother's cool, so we'll have time to look." We exchanged phone numbers and addresses where we could be reached once we left the building—she knew I would not be there for much longer either.

Shannon left without good-byes. Elen believed Shannon had moved to her great-aunt's home, while the children stayed with her brother-in-law. Elen wanted to keep the children with her. She had talked with Nadine and they had agreed to share the responsibilities. But Shannon, according to Elen, did not want to leave her children behind, not even temporarily. "I tried to tell her it was gonna be only for a while," said Elen, "but the crazy bitch wouldn't listen. So fine, go ahead and fuck your life and your kids' life some more." Even though Shannon was in a terrible state of addiction, she still tried, at least during her few moments of clarity, to keep her family together. Yet Elen felt that once the welfare workers found out about Shannon's desperate condition, they would take legal guardianship away from her. Shannon's intention to keep her kids appeared less and less likely to materialize.

The new owner wished to make a Latino couple managers of the building, and they moved into the apartment Vivian vacated in the beginning of December. The couple had three small children and lived with the woman's father, mother, and two other men whom Elen and I surmised were the woman's brothers. From day one, Elen acted very belligerently toward the Latina/os. She did not speak cordially with them, which raised tensions because the Latina/os occupied the apartment immediately next to hers. Elen also took on some of the traits and behaviors she herself had criticized in Shannon. She shouted constantly as loud as she could in a very caustic manner, airing her disgust with the new "white" tenants. "Look at them, Vargas, look at them! They've got some nerve, haven't they? And they've got an attitude too. Check it out! They won't even look at us black people. . . . Have you got a problem with us, huh?"

The Latina/os seemed unaware of exactly what Elen said, but certainly they must have perceived her anger and contempt. Most of our new neighbors smiled at us, but in this they revealed nervousness more than friendliness. They tried to speak with Elen several times, but Elen did not give them a chance to express themselves. They knew very few words of English and Elen was clearly not willing to make their communication any easier. The fact that I did not speak Spanish clearly disappointed them. They initially saw me as a potential ally—they had surely noticed my surname on the mailboxes—but upon discovering my ineptitude with their language, and because of their recurrent unsuccessful attempts at being sociable with Elen (with whom they saw me talking amicably on various occasions), they eventually gave up establishing any form of friendship with Elen and me.

Our old "For Rent" sign was soon accompanied by a newer, larger, and brighter one that read "Se Renta." Similar events took place in the other tenements in and around our block. Our building appeared among the last ones to adopt the "Se Renta" sign; yet, as soon as it did, Latina/os quickly applied and were accepted for the vacant dwellings. By the end of January 1997, Latina/o households at least as large as the managers' occupied the four previously empty apartments in the building. The new families had at least a married couple and two other adults, as well as three or more children. All of the adult Latina/os hardly spoke any English; the children spoke English fluently, serving as interpreters for their parents and relatives. There seemed little communication between the new Latina/o households: each one had its own dynamics and seemed busy throughout the day. The men worked or were looking for work. They left early in the morning and returned late in the evening. The women who were not mothers also worked, while those who had children stayed home. Unlike the building's previous routine, there was no chatting in the courtyard. Each family took care of its children *inside* the apartments, and each apartment seemed self-sufficient. Old but functioning automobiles replaced the junk cars that filled most of the building's parking spaces. Each household had at least one car.

Not surprisingly, Elen felt increasingly isolated. She complained about the noise the children made and about the dirt in our courtyard—even though the noise and the dirt were considerably less than they used to be when our friends lived there. She also complained that her children, and the ones she was babysitting, could not play in our yard anymore. Elen blamed the Latina/os for this also, even though the people who made our common area unsuited for children were Black. Yet, she had a point. The abandonment of the building's common area—a direct consequence of the Latina/os' more reserved daily routines—transformed it into an attractive hangout area. Our courtyard was in time adopted by young Black men. They sat on the staircase and on the furniture Vivian had left behind, calmly smoking, drinking beer, and occasionally listening to music while they chatted. At first, Elen tried to discourage them, but gave up as they resisted menacingly. The Latina/os did not seem disturbed. The youngsters were there only during the day, when all the Latinos were away, and the Latinas did not consider the yard a space in which to spend much time anyway.

Elen moved out in the end of January. She had found a similar apartment west from where we were. Although she did not secure a manager's position, Bryan had promised to help her as much as he could, and she trusted that he was going to keep his word. Fundamental in Elen's decision to move to that particular place was the fact that only Black families lived there. She complained about how difficult it had been to find such a place, adding that the Latina/os had "invaded" the neighborhood and were everywhere.

❦

Pressured by the police, welfare policies, rehabilitation clinics, immigration, labor shortage, and a tight housing market, the community of struggle founded on mutual recognition and solidarity did not resist. The Black women who valiantly refused to accept their objectification as irrelevant by-products of a political system that is, as bell hooks frequently reminds us, irremediably "imperialist white supremacist capitalist patriarchal," in the end succumbed to it.[5] While their everyday strategies of identifying and combating sources of oppression focused on and were successful at guaranteeing their immediate survival, these same strategies were not effective for long-term structural and institutional transformations.

Still, the principles shared and pragmatically utilized when dealing with landlords, the police, drug addiction, incarceration, and everyday interpersonal conflict suggest, at the very least, the potential for social transformation, a project of liberation in the making. Among these principles, the ethics of caring, so central to their survival, reveal the transformative power of mutuality. When what matters the most is the maintenance of the group, regardless of personal interests, as exemplified by how Elen approached Shannon's problems and mistrust,[6] and when hegemonic individualism is challenged by the sharing of affection, spiritual strength, food, money, and child care, then alternative, ethical, and equalitarian visions are forged in spite of the most intense forms of imposed marginalization and dehumanization. The gender-specific forms of racialized wisdom employed for group survival, while temporarily defeated, point to the need for long-term strategies based on these same ethical principles of mutuality, dignity, and justice.[7]

Nadine - ay
money collector / imposter - 96

powerless women +
survival

mutuality

chapter 4

BLACKNESS AS MOBILIZATION
AND MOVEMENT

*The Coalition Against Police Abuse
and the Panther Legacy*

I contacted the Coalition Against Police Abuse as soon as I moved to South Central in January 1996. I wanted to learn about its history and everyday dynamics and work for the organization. I telephoned Michael Zinzun, who asked me questions aimed at revealing my political convictions. The fact that I had supported and campaigned for the Worker's Party in Brazil (Partido dos Trabalhadores)—a grassroots, democratic, socialist organization—certainly helped Zinzun make his decision to invite me to the office so that we could extend our conversation, and see in which ways, if any, I could work at CAPA. Zinzun had known Brazil since 1993. He had been there less than two months before our first conversation together with a group of thirteen students, professors, ex-gang members, ex-convicts, and community organizers. The purpose of the trip was to "both learn and offer help with the growing consciousness-building that is taking place there among the poor, the disenfranchised and people of color."[1]

An important part of our phone conversation revolved around Brazil's racial composition. According to Zinzun, Brazil was the second largest Black nation on earth, with almost 70 million Black people. Only Nigeria, with a population of 100 million, had more inhabitants of African descent than Brazil. As we extended our discussion, I realized that he was interested in *my* racial identity. I told him that I considered myself Black, even though my phenotype was not obviously so. He then told me about Malcolm X, how light-skinned he was, and how this is a common feature among U.S.

Blacks. Zinzun himself, he confided, was a mixture of several races, including his father's Apache ancestry. All that mattered, for him, however, was for people to understand our history and not become entangled in self-deceptions originating in wishes to be lighter or darker. As a political concept, blackness relates to how we make sense of and change our history, rather than passively accepting our various conditionings—I took this to be his main point.

At the office I was given a series of questionnaires, leaflets, brochures, and papers on CAPA and CSGT. While I completed one questionnaire about my willingness to participate in the organization's events, receive its newsletter, and contribute to its finances, Zinzun explained some of the organization's programs and gave me a brief history of its activities since 1976, the year it was founded. I went on to work with them steadily for two years and read all I could about their aims and accomplishments.

By embracing, supporting, politicizing, and eventually fusing with the gang truce established in 1992, shortly *before* the uprisings of that year, CAPA served as a bridge between the social movements of the late 1960s and the pressing contemporary social problems. CAPA's manual for community organizing, which embodies this political history, was first put together in the late seventies (see appendix). It has no date on it, and no one I asked could not be more precise as to its first emergence. This indetermination, indeed, is one of the main characteristics of the document. Everyday practices and acquired know-how constantly become incorporated in the manual, reflecting expertise gathered through community work, legal disputes, and interactions with law-enforcement agencies that go back at least to the Black Panthers' years. Yet the manual also reflects knowledge and techniques acquired through critiques of the Black Panther Party (BPP), as well as from CAPA's own experiences with incidents of police brutality and community organization.

Regularly updated, the manual is a permanently unfinished document. In itself, this permanent open-endedness is a strong indication of the Coalition's willingness to constantly reflect on its role in organizing social movements. Although the 1960s' vanguardist tones remain, they are now the object of discussion and frequent modification. Indeed, one of my first assignments at the office was to transfer the sixty pages of the manual to a computer word-processor, incorporating the most recent changes.[2] These modifications were not particularly substantial. They included grammatical alterations marked in the margins, new phone numbers, and updated juridical details. Putting the manual on a word-processor file made its adaptability for change even greater.

Following the BPP's principles of community organization, the manual advances two main objectives: to present CAPA's interpretation of historical facts about the systematic police abuse endured by inner-city dwellers, and to suggest strategies to cope with police despotism. Community organization constituted its fundamental strategy.

The manual portrays the police as an occupying force, foreign to the community, and representing social control by the wider society. Influenced by Frantz Fanon's *The Wretched of the Earth,* it describes the police as a colonial force. The police, it maintains "were not placed [in our communities] to 'protect and serve' the people." On the contrary, the police

> are not in reality members of the communities in which they patrol and do not relate to our communities on any other level than as "armed enforcers" of racism, sexism and other forms of oppression; are not sincerely working to help our communities' progress, but are actually in our communities for the purpose of intimidation, confinement and control; place little value on the lives and safety of the people in our communities and do not hesitate to use excessive force and violence.[3]

First drafted in the late 1970s, not too long after the BPP's demise, the manual's perspective and language evoke that era's pained struggle to produce social movement mobilization in the face of repression, assassination, and abuse. Politics here becomes challenging hegemonic power by seizing public spaces and voicing collective concerns. Reflecting similar stances adopted by the BPP, CAPA seeks to infuse oppressed communities with fundamental political knowledge. It emphasizes the need to "politically educate people as to the origins of increasing police terror" as well as "educate people about both our human and constitutional rights and to organize a mass base in the communities."[4]

The political education provided by CAPA starts the minute someone walks into the office. Enlarged photographs arranged on stand-up wooden panels show victims of police brutality. Most of the victims are Black, although there are also Latina/os. Persons with disfigured faces and limbs—some of them dead—remind those at the Coalition of the terror inflicted

by law enforcement. Even for people familiar with the extent of police brutality in South Central, the pictures instill shock. One shows a man with
terrible dog bites on his leg and arms. Another showing a dead man with
a fractured skull causes revulsion. First-timers at the office often turn away
from these images. Another picture of a young man hung dead on a tree
raises curiosity, especially among gang members. Zinzun generally explains
that the photograph is not, as he suspects youngsters think, an old one—
it is not depicting what *used* to happen. He points to the training shoes
the young Black man is wearing—a very well-known contemporary brand
and model—and in this manner links the fate of young Black men today
with those in the past, showing what can happen to anyone who is Black.
According to Zinzun, the young man was harassed, beaten, and killed after
getting lost in an all-White neighborhood. He was later hung by a tree, in
the manner historically deployed to punish rebellious Blacks. The young
victim appeals to gang members who, before coming to the office, usually
have not seen or thought much beyond their gang concerns. The photograph indicates that the real oppressor is outside the community; that gang
fighting misses the larger picture. It shows how young people in communities of color face everyday forms of racism (as the hanging shows) that
reinforce the attitudes and behaviors of the police.[5]

A large mural that Charles Freeman painted in 1981 occupies an entire
wall of the room where the photographs stand. The mural depicts Latinos
and Black men in prison, Ku Klux Klan members burning a cross, Black
men gambling, demonstrators of all races protesting against unemployment
and the welfare system, "blind justice" represented by a blonde woman
who has her eyes covered by the U.S. flag, zoot-suited Pachucos in defiant
poses, Huey Newton carrying a shotgun beside a Black woman with her
clenched fist raised in the air, hungry Black children, enslaved Blacks in
chains, the unmistakable portrait of Abraham Lincoln, and policemen in
contemporary uniforms beating Black men to the ground. Through apparently disconnected sketches, the mural's totality brings together the various
scenes. History provides the galvanizing concept represented by a black
background against which the smaller scapes are plotted. Visitors may
not grasp immediately the particular conception of history informing the
mural, but involvement at CAPA soon exposes them to the institution's
vision of U.S. society as historically racist and violent, and thus renders
the images in the mural comprehensible.

In addition to information transmitted through audio and visual media, short courses and seminars meet frequently to discuss American history, Marxism (Marx's *Capital* was analyzed in a seminar organized by Zinzun not long before I joined the Coalition), and writings about Blacks. CAPA's attempts at providing political education move beyond exposition and explanation of images or discussion of books and theories. Its ultimate goal is to organize as many segments of the Black and Brown communities as possible. The manual states clearly that the Coalition sees itself as an instrument of popular mobilization. As such, it must "give concrete direction to the people of our communities to stand up for their rights against police harassment, beatings, racist insults and murder." This stance seems in full harmony with the outlook of the Panthers, an outlook not unrelated to their eventual failure. By making clear, however, that CAPA members seek "new leadership" and intend to "rely on" the organizations and individuals among which it seeks support, the manual voices the organization members' willingness to try new strategies of social mobilization.[6] These claims reveal true commitments to finding alternatives to older methods, and proceed from the perception that the BPP's reliance on and veneration of its leadership made the party vulnerable and led to its destruction.

As CAPA members struggle to devise new strategies to relate to potential constituencies, the organization has unequivocal, precise instructions about how successful collective actions ought to be conducted and at what goals they should aim. The Coalition advances a highly effective organizing technique applicable to the communities they wish to serve. When incidents of police brutality take place, CAPA advises its followers to:

1. Document the case,
2. Reach the people, and
3. Mobilize the people.

Technique is a key concept in this scheme. CAPA's blueprint for effective organization relies on a specific and clear method. For each of the three steps that constitute CAPA's technique of community organizing, the manual provides essential procedures that need to be taken in order to properly reconstruct a case of police violence.

With regard to the first step—"documenting the case"—the method unfolds in three complementary points. First, the witnesses have to be found and interviewed. The manual explains, "The victims of abuse may be able to supply a list [of witnesses]. If not, visit the scene and seek out witnesses by talking to the people who live and work in the area." More than journalistic inquiry, CAPA pushes for and defines in-depth analysis, something akin to short ethnographic research (8).

The procedure also entails interviewing public officials and contacting the mayor, city council members, police community affairs officers, and representatives of the district attorney to secure helpful statements with information that might be available only in the spheres to which these people have access. CAPA advises interviewers to be especially attentive to possible (sometimes accidental) contradictions between the testimonies they elicit and official public statements concerning the case. Inconsistencies may be useful in an eventual judicial proceeding and, consequently, written notes and tape-recordings are essential.

The manual advises activists to collect as much of the public record of the case as possible from newspapers, magazines, and radio or television programs in order to compare the things that are said publicly to statements taken by the group's own interviewers and again to check for contradictions. After documenting a case of police misconduct, the activists need to consult the victims or their friends, families, or attorneys to determine how to proceed. If the aggrieved parties agree, community action begins.

After "documenting the case," CAPA moves on to the "reach the people" phase by producing fliers, fact sheets, leaflets, and newsletters, holding educational meetings, making face-to-face contacts, and generating media exposure (9–11).

The Coalition devotes careful and meticulous attention to media coverage. They sense that they must harness the power of mass communication for their own ends, that political realities and opportunities have to be *created* and that the media has to be *drawn* to them. Moreover, media space must be secured through appropriate and well-informed strategies. This draws upon the BPP's experience of trial and error. The methods and mechanisms suggested in the CAPA manual reflect the lessons of collective historical experience.

Several appendices have been added to the manual over the years to reflect lessons learned by the group. One addresses the issue of media coverage. During their confrontations with the police and the justice system, the Black Panthers learned that public exposure through television and newspapers could expand support and, in the case of the well-known shootout in South Central Los Angeles, keep them alive. The appendix on media offers advice on how to get media coverage, write a news release, conduct press conferences, and identify and use media resources. It explains how to render a case of police abuse newsworthy by focusing on "an event or revelation, preferably one featuring local community people and institutions." This part of the manual also advises activists that a new story "must describe specific occurrences, quote specific statements and name specific people, places, and actions" (36).

Zinzun serves as CAPA's main press spokesperson, although he shares his duties with other members of the Coalition. His sense of what makes news and the relations he has developed with the media over the years have secured the Coalition an important space in local and national reports. Zinzun's quotes appear frequently in newspapers and on television news almost every time a case of police brutality or related protest becomes publicized. Reporters feel welcome at the CAPA office. The group's success in attracting mainstream media coverage attests to the effectiveness of the techniques outlined in the manual.

From its very beginnings, the Coalition has participated in city council commissions and public debates, and supported candidates running for public office. It uses radio, television, newspaper editorials, letters to the editor, magazine features, articles in local weekly and suburban papers, industry publications, shopping news, direct mail, posters, handbills, and calendar sections of local radio stations and newspapers to publicize and thus politicize relevant local facts. The manual stresses the urgency of reaching varied and large audiences, but it also gives precise instructions on how to access and use these media. Careful explanations about "writing a news release," "body of news release," "typing news release," and "dissemination of news release" appear in detail. The release, for example, "should be written in inverted pyramid style with all of the important information in the lead (first sentence or two). This format enables the editor to pick up the important facts in the first few lines and to edit from the bottom if there is not enough space for the entire release." An extensive list of telephone and fax numbers and addresses of several newspapers in the Los Angeles area accompanies these instructions along with information on wire services, and television and radio stations. The manual lists contacts at television and radio stations, newspapers, and magazines. Despite the constant modifications this list requires, it still serves as a starting point each time the group seeks to publicize information. For those willing to deepen their knowledge on the media, the manual provides a bibliographical list containing directories and guides for public relations, publicity, and advertising (42–46).

The manual remains almost devoid of open criticism of the establishmentarian tone of most American mainstream media.[7] Working at the office, however, enabled me to see that everyday commentaries and conversations supplemented and challenged the seemingly uncritical approach to mass media in the manual. Activists read print journalism and watch or listen to electronic journalism every day at the office, almost always in groups. A large table provides the focus of activity, and at that site activists conduct meetings, place telephone calls, listen to music, operate computers, read, and watch videos and television programs. Except during important meetings, several of these activities happen at the same time. When someone reads the newspaper or watches television news, the information is almost always discussed collectively.

Commentaries pointing to the one-sidedness of news are common. Younger members of the Coalition are encouraged to reflect on what is being presented to them. "You should always be able to understand and criticize what is going on," Zinzun frequently says. He advises activists to gather information *and* reflect on who is presenting it, and consider to whom it is addressed. No information is neutral, he explains, noting that the social groups that own and are represented by the media see that their versions of events prevail. News presentations, old-timers[8] frequently add, are political acts, even (and maybe especially when) they are self-defined as objective.[9] Younger members are encouraged to absorb as many facts and mainstream interpretations of them as possible and through discussions and readings develop a critical perspective on them as well.

Television news hours, starting at 4 P.M., provide part of the Coalition's daily rituals. From that time until the end of the afternoon, the television set at the office airs one of Los Angeles' many news channels. Each member stops, if only for a few minutes, to watch and confer about the latest events. Sometimes, activists videotape news segments related to the police or to gangs, and catalogue them into CAPA's large video library. The audience grows and the intensity increases when a broadcast includes a member of the group. These interactive experiences play an important role in building knowledge and solidarity.

The manual's third step for community action advises "mobilize the people." After the specific incident of police abuse has been extensively documented and publicized, mobilization through community meetings and the formation of "justice committees" move the struggle to the next stage. Justice committees articulate specific demands drawn from the experiences of the group as well as those suggested by the manual.[10]

As community meetings focusing on specific cases of police brutality gain support, they open the door for education about the broader social context in which brutality occurs. CAPA activists use films, invited speakers, directed readings, and discussions to address broader issues related to law-enforcement abuse. A rally or picket line may be used "to show some 'muscle' and boost community interest in your group and your issue." These mobilization techniques are meant to be deployed each time a case of police brutality occurs in order to raise community awareness and to politicize it by rendering it public. Yet the process of politicizing an inner-city community is necessarily long and arduous. The manual counsels organizers to "Take a step-by-step approach, plan short range goals with a high probability of success and seek 'small' victories as a way to build confidence among your members" (11–12).

Block-by-block organizing constitutes the starting point for gathering people and information. By generating a grassroots base in the inner city, block organizing produces a "perfect pipeline: you can spread information as you learn what the community is concerned about and what it thinks of the work you have been doing." Focusing on the blocks in the immediate area of the police incident, organizers assign specific blocks to designated members of the justice committee, who then become block contacts whose function is to go door to door and inform dwellers about the committee's activities. The committee's work expands at the same rate that new block contacts are brought to the cause. CAPA's manual, however, warns that block organizers inevitably encounter not only persons who openly oppose community work, but worse, undercover agents (14, 15, 51).

The Coalition has precise guidelines for redressing law enforcement wrongdoings by working through the justice system. Although the Coalition warns that the "legal system is slanted heavily against you," and that favorable results against the police are very unlikely, it nevertheless considers the legal alternative a necessary part of its strategy. Legal action provides a learning experience. CAPA members active during the Black Panther years have acquired a large amount of legal knowledge from their countless encounters with the system. Michael Zinzun's notoriety outside the circles of community activism rests in large part on his successful lawsuits against the City of Los Angeles and the Pasadena Police Department, which will be analyzed later. The legal knowledge accumulated in many years of struggle has been condensed in the manual. The experience of filing a suit and undergoing a judicial process is considered, at the very least, a medium through which theoretical information provided by the manual and by old-timers can be understood, added to, and reformulated.

In addition, systematic and persistent legal actions against police abuse serve as an example for victims of police abuse who might not otherwise have the knowledge or the courage to present their cases in court. This strategy also fulfills a pre-emptive purpose, making police officers feel encumbered by the possibility that their next victim might seek legal redress. By advocating legal action, the Coalition makes explicit claims for the full citizenship rights of communities of color. The manual advises "as citizens of the United States, we are supposed to be able to address different government institutions with any complaint we have. We should utilize this right!" (15).

Legal actions can accompany, result from, and generate momentum for creating new political understandings. Legal actions provide focal points for mass mobilization and media exposure. Press conferences publicize lawsuits, while demonstrations seek to obtain radio, newspaper and television coverage.

The very *tone* of the CAPA manual performs a symbolic function that cannot be dissociated from its actual implementation and eventual success. Resonating with the BPP's vanguardist style of the late 1960s, the manual's imperative tone speaks of a conscious attempt to empower those who have historically been powerless. It references Blacks' capacity to resist, to organize, to be objective, precise, goal oriented. This tone negates the notion that Blacks are overly emotional, idealistic, and incapable of being pragmatic—a notion that, according to various persons with whom I worked at the office, remains prevalent not only among Whites and the wider society in general, but also, and more problematically, among African Americans.[11] Those dominant assumptions motivate the manual to state, "Do not involve yourself emotionally with the cases of police abuse—stick to the facts!" Statements like this permeate discussions in the office, courses offered by the Coalition's staff, and informal conversations. Carefully constructed in a monological, imperative, scientific, and confident tone, this perspective seeks to challenge dominant cultural stereotypes as well as hegemonic social relations.

&

Specific juridical cases pursued by the Coalition over the years have succeeded in politicizing the unlawfulness of law enforcement and in establishing CAPA as an important, widely recognized voice of the community. The Coalition served as a fundamental base for the emergence of key social movements in the inner city. When the Bloods and the Crips signed the gang truce in 1992, for example, CAPA was one of the main intermediaries for the elaboration and maintenance of the peace terms. CAPA helped found and virtually fused itself with the Community in Support of the Gang Truce (CSGT), an organization dedicated to maintaining, expanding, and politicizing the peace agreement.

One particularly significant legal case the Coalition was involved with happened as follows: After discovering in 1979 that CAPA had been infiltrated by police agents, its members, along with other progressive organizations that had also detected and documented the presence of spies in their headquarters, sued the Los Angeles Police Commission for violation of their constitutional rights to assemble, to privacy, and to associate freely. Assisted by American Civil Liberties Union (ACLU) attorneys and staff persons, the 131 plaintiffs agreed to a $1.8-million settlement in 1981. The plaintiffs also imposed a list of nine constraints against the city bureaucracy and the Los Angeles Police Department. The California Supreme Court administered the settlement to ensure enforcement of its terms and to protect the plaintiffs from future spying.[12]

The case came about unexpectedly. CAPA and other progressive organizations had been pressuring the Los Angeles Police Department, among other matters, to incorporate more persons of color into its staff. In response to these demands, the LAPD issued a press release featuring a list of people of color on its staff. To the surprise of CAPA members, the list contained thirteen names of individuals who had either worked or who were still working at the Coalition. Zinzun's personal secretary at the time was one of the LAPD agents. The thirteen infiltrators had worked with several different progressive organizations and, as Zinzun showed me, they appeared prominently in several photographs of rallies against police brutality.

Spying has long been a major concern of the Coalition. During the Black Panther years, *agents provocateurs* played crucial roles in the wars carried on by the FBI and its Counter-Intelligence Program (COINTELPRO).[13] These illegal counterinsurgent strategies continued when the survivors of those wars joined new organizations. I was confronted with the *effects* of these campaigns during the whole period I worked at the office, at first suspected of being an infiltrator by CAPA members, and then as the object of routine threats originating (so attest Coalition members) from the police. In my first few months working at CAPA, the group made sure that I never worked in the office alone, that I had no access to documents, that certain rooms and drawers remained off limits to me, and that I was never the last one to leave. Old-timers informed me that such precautions were routine and necessary. They told me about the spy cases to contextualize the suspicion new members faced and explained I would get keys to the office only when the staff agreed that my allegiance was beyond doubt. This took a little over three months. In the interim, I performed daily tasks at the office, mainly writing fliers, answering the phone, participating in meetings on strategies of community organization, and acquiring and rearranging the furniture in the office. Staff members gave me several CAPA videos to watch during weekends: videos about the LAPD's racism and violence, the Black Panthers' community programs, and Zinzun's monthly cable-television program. They quizzed me later about them, making it evident that I was being observed carefully and my political allegiances evaluated.

As soon as I got keys to the office, the threatening phone calls started. The distorted, metallic voice told me to "get out of the 'hood," and made several other threats, the least radical of which promised to kick my ass "real bad." I asked Zinzun about the intimidating phone calls, to which he responded, matter-of-factly, that they were common. He was certain they were from the police. They came in the form of recorded messages sent to everyone working at the Coalition and at other community organizations.

Threatening phone calls were not the only signs of police activity clearly aimed at destabilizing the Coalition. The office had been broken into several times since its foundation. One in mid-March 1996, less than three months after I started working there. Another break-in took place the following August. The actions were carried out to resemble robberies—a videocassette recorder and some inexpensive objects were taken, and all the drawers and files were searched.[14] But office members and Zinzun believed the true object of the "robberies" were documents CAPA has been gathering about police brutality over the last twenty years. Psychological intimidation was also an obvious purpose of such break-ins. Yet even though these "burglaries" always caused worry and anger, old-timers downplayed their effectiveness. After all, they had been happening for such a long time that they caused no more surprise.

These facts only underscore the constant presence of surreptitious police activity around those working at the Coalition. In 1996, however, this presence was only a pale reminder of the full-scale spying operation that took place at CAPA before it was discovered and made the object of the lawsuit in the early 1980s. If the specific COINTELPRO operations had ceased, their form, content, and inspiration remained, not only during the years of systematic spying at CAPA, but also during recent events. Zinzun often says the office has been infiltrated from its very first days of existence. In the late 1970s, before the Coalition moved to its present Western Avenue office, members of the Coalition daily ate and held conversations in the small storefront restaurant next door. The amiable woman who owned and managed the place, who seemed particularly fond of the young activists, was years later to be identified as a police undercover agent.

The lawsuit settled by CAPA in 1983 resulted in the dismantling of the Los Angeles Police Department's Public Disorder Intelligence Division, held responsible for the spying strategies. Although it obviously fell short of eliminating spying, the lawsuit settlement constituted a significant achievement for the Coalition and other progressive groups. The case settlement was all the more meaningful when we consider it took place in the midst of the Reagan years—years marked by policies (and a corresponding political climate) obviously hostile to urban, Black-led popular movements.[15] By forcing the LAPD to concede some citizen control of its until-then-impermeable structure, the plaintiffs demonstrated that the appropriate methods could make the justice system work for their benefit, at least on occasion.

Zinzun played a major role in the spy lawsuit, often as the public spokesperson representing the plaintiffs. In that period, his direct and emphatic public persona reached beyond the inner city. His notoriety, however, generated contradictory, if not tragic, results. The spotlight served to heighten police antipathy toward Zinzun and the organization for which he worked. By exposing law enforcement's unlawful strategies, he exposed the corruption and contradictions affecting the conduct of those supposed to combat crime and serve communities.

In 1984, in the middle of the night, Zinzun heard someone screaming in the street and went out to see what was going on. The screams emanated from a man being beaten by two policemen. A small group of people in their nightclothes quickly formed around the incident. They asked the police to stop the beating. Instead, the officers radioed for reinforcement based on their perception that a riot threatened to erupt. Soon more officers arrived and ordered the small crowd to disperse. As Zinzun was heading back to his basement apartment, a policeman stopped him, yelling that Zinzun was the one trying to provoke a riot. Other officers quickly circled Zinzun, sprayed him with mace, shoved him to the ground, and beat him brutally and extensively. Due to the combination of mace and the violence with which his eye was hit, Zinzun lost his sight in one eye.[16] The optic nerve had been damaged irreversibly.

Upon being bailed out of jail the next day, Zinzun immediately called a press conference. In front of the cameras, tape recorders, and notepads, wearing a large eye-patch, he recounted the facts of the incident and announced he was suing the Pasadena Police Department. Consistent with the Coalition's technique of political mobilization, Zinzun sought as much media coverage for the case as he could. He framed this case as an example of only one of many systematic acts of police brutality experienced in Black neighborhoods. His political and legal actions brought success. A little more than a year after he sued the City of Pasadena, Zinzun settled for $1.2 million, reinforcing CAPA's visibility and relevance, at least in the Black and Brown communities. This experience also augmented the Coalition's knowledge of the workings of the justice system, thus refining its techniques of community mobilization.

Zinzun personifies CAPA's causes, its dangers and possibilities. As a victim of police abuse and the beneficiary of a legal settlement, he presents a living reminder of the brutality to which underprivileged persons of color, especially Blacks, are systematically subjected. Since Zinzun is a community organizer, a student of the law, and a public personality, his success in confronting law enforcement incarnates the possibilities contained in collective action. His life is emblematic of the harshness and possibilities of the Black experience.

Conscious of CAPA's importance and of his personal symbolic and practical roles in the organization—all of those heightened by the relative financial comfort the settlement brought him in 1985, Zinzun intensified his work after the case with the Pasadena police. "But you see," he once told me, "the pigs thought I was going to move away, buy myself a nice house in some Caribbean island and stay there. But I didn't. I got the house right next to where I was staying with my kids, bought myself this Timex watch, and then I told my kids: 'you got *one* wish.' 'We want a swimming pool,' they said. Fine, so I got the house, made the pool, and life went on, just as before."

Zinzun ran for a seat on the Pasadena Board of City Directors (the equivalent of Los Angeles' City Council) in 1989, his second attempt at that office. Building his campaign on the community work he pioneered in South Central as well as in Pasadena—where he initiated his participation in the Black Panthers—Zinzun calculated the political momentum he had garnered during the police-beating case, together with the many years of work at CAPA, could translate into electoral success. According to his recollection, opinion polls taken at the time showed that he had good possibilities of being elected.

Zinzun's campaign suffered a heavy blow, however, when the Los Angeles Police Department's second-in-command, Assistant Chief Robert L. Vernon, used the Anti-Terrorist Division Lexis/Nexis computer database to gather and spread information about Zinzun's purported connection to unspecified "terrorist" activities. Zinzun narrowly lost the election to Chris Holden, son of Los Angeles City Councilman Nate Holden. Not surprisingly, Nate Holden was one of the strongest supporters of the LAPD, backing its chief, Daryl Gates, even in the aftermath of the Rodney King beating, when several local and national political and civil leaders were demanding the chief's resignation.

Zinzun filed suit in 1991 against Vernon, charging that the public airing of nonverified claims from police intelligence files violated his civil rights and undermined his campaign for a seat on the Pasadena Board of City Directors. Shortly thereafter, the city attorney's office proposed a $450,000 settlement, but the Los Angeles City Council rejected the suggestion. In a closed session, council members agreed a jury should decide the matter. "'The public interest is best served if this goes to trial and the facts are aired in public,' Councilman Zev Yaroslavsky said. 'Then we can let the chips fall where they may.'" Yaroslavsky chaired the council's budget and finance committee and opposed the settlement on the ground that "if all Chief Vernon did was hand over a bunch of newspaper articles, then why should it cost the taxpayers $450,000?"[17]

The fact that LAPD Chief Daryl Gates was initially a defendant in the suit certainly contributed to the council's decision. Gates had been under great public pressure since the police beating of motorist Rodney G. King on March 3 of that same year. The Police Commission, appointed by Mayor Tom Bradley, had decided in the end of that same month to place the chief on a sixty-day leave. However, in a mixed display of allegiance to the chief and self-aggrandizement with relation to Bradley's Police Commission, the council sought a restraining order against the commission's decision in Superior Court. Superior Court Judge Ronald M. Sohigian, obviously sympathetic to the council and the LAPD, quickly issued a temporary restraining order that blocked the Police Commission's decision. Gates was kept in command. It was in this climate that the council overturned the city attorney's proposal of settlement and the matter was sent to trial by jury in the Superior Court.

The petty internal disputes among officials and between the council and the police commission, coupled with the loud reverberations of the King incident of police brutality, could not have provided more favorable circumstances for Zinzun's attorney as his case began to be adjudicated in the Los Angeles Superior Court. After three weeks of deliberation, on May 4, 1991, the jury awarded Zinzun $3.83 million.[18]

Judge Michael Berg declared that the jury had found "clear and convincing" evidence of malice by Vernon.[19] The jurors strongly distrusted the testimonies given by Vernon and Gates. Deputy City Attorney Mary House, who was later to appeal the judgment, captured, if only through an ironic voice, the main factor in the jury's decision. It reflected, as she was quoted as saying in a *Los Angeles Times* story,

> a diminished public confidence in the Police Department as a result of the March 3 beating of King. "These are interesting times and Mr. Zinzun is the 15-year head of the Coalition Against Police Abuse," said House, who

went to trial after the City Council rejected a settlement offer of $450,000. "When he [Zinzun] sues the chief of police and the assistant chief, you have the makings of a movie script."[20]

According to the *Times,* several jurors had found inconsistencies between the top officials' testimonies. More important, it seems, Gates's court appearance as a defense witness served to quell any doubts among the jurors. Gates showed up in full dress uniform and holstered a 9mm pistol that he had worn during a Police Department awards ceremony earlier that same day. "He looked like he was in a clown suit," one of the jurors said. "I was not impressed." Although jurors emphasized that their decision rested "on the evidence alone," it is obvious that the surrounding context of intense public criticism of the LAPD played a decisive role.[21] The fact that Zinzun himself had become blind in one eye due to police abuse only added to the distrust of law enforcement. It is difficult to imagine that the jurors deliberating on the defamation case could do so without influence from the King incident and, indeed, without linking the infamous videotaped scenes of King being brutalized by the police with images of what must have happened to Zinzun in similar circumstances.

To render the connections between the cases of King and that of his client, Dan Stormer, Zinzun's lawyer, used an ingenious line of argument. He claimed that the abuse Zinzun suffered was psychological, not physical. "Sometimes the impact of a psychological blow is less when you see something like a Rodney King incident," he said. By differentiating the nature of the abuse suffered by his client from that of King, Stormer implied a connection between both occurrences—law enforcement's use of unjustified violence. Furthermore, by comparing and contrasting both cases of police misconduct, Zinzun's lawyer reminded the jury that King's beating was not an isolated incident, that it was part of a methodical predisposition the police had toward persons of color and political adversaries. These predispositions, he argued, often cause intense physical and/or psychological harm. Zinzun's deposition, in which he said that "he was humiliated and fearful after receiving numerous threatening phone calls following news reports about Vernon's action," reiterated these connections. Finally, the testimony given by Dr. Gloria Johnson-Powell, a Harvard University professor of psychiatry, sanctioned the implied connections through her expert's discourse. She told the jury "Zinzun suffered from symptoms similar to those she saw in Vietnam veterans and civil rights demonstrators in the 1960s."[22]

Zinzun considered the verdict "firm, fair and compassionate. They [the jurors] sent a message to the city that enough is enough and they won't be a party to the antics of the LAPD."[23] Gaining unprecedented media exposure, Zinzun and his comrades at CAPA seized the opportunity to expose the police's systematic use of unlawful and brutal means. The timing could not have been better. Following one of the manual's suggestions regarding the necessity to detect potential key political moments and actualize (and build on) them via community support, media exposure, and juridical intervention, Zinzun and those working with him perceived the public climate against the police reaching unprecedented levels in the wake of the Rodney King beating and other high-profile cases, and made their moves accordingly. Blacks had been especially sensitized by the videotape images George Holliday had captured of Rodney King's ordeal with the police. Marches, debates, and local media coverage had been intense well before mainstream television channels and publications caught up with the inner-city events.

The Black-owned *Los Angeles Sentinel* began devoting most of its space to articles and editorials concerned not only with police brutality, but also with race relations, especially between Blacks, Korean immigrants, and Korean Americans. King's beating had occurred within a few weeks of the first anniversary of Latasha Harlins's slaying by a Korean shopkeeper who, suspecting that the teenager had stolen merchandise, shot her in the back of the head, instantly killing the African American girl. The Korean shopkeeper received only a light sentence of community work. On April 17, 1991, when it informed the public about the city council's rejection of Zinzun's offer to settle the lawsuit, the *Sentinel* devoted almost its entire first page to issues of police brutality and race relations. A large photograph captioned "Massive Rally: 'Gates Must Go!'" showed Reverend Jesse Jackson, Congresswoman Maxine Waters, and thousands of marchers demanding Gates's ouster following the King incident. Articles on lawsuits filed against the LAPD by Jamaal Wilkes, "former Los Angeles Lakers great," descriptions of a gathering of 400 community residents and leaders at the African American Community Unity Center where elected officials' accountability was discussed, and accounts of attempts by Blacks and Korean Americans to overcome the differences that had produced a series of deaths on both sides, accompanied the photograph on the paper's front page.[24] The same tone permeated articles in the *Sentinel* for at least six months, with photographs and articles related to police brutality prominently featured on its first page.[25]

Thus, as Zinzun's defamation lawsuit reached mainstream media, it intentionally became part of a wider context of politicization emerging from a concrete event of police brutality. CAPA's original point that police brutality represents only one of the manifestations of a broader history of oppression suffered by persons of color, especially Blacks, became an integral part of public debates. It mobilized Black communities in rallies and marches, and it provoked demands for citizen control of the police. It is not surprising, then, that the jury reached a favorable verdict for Zinzun.

The cases of Rodney King, Michael Zinzun, and the torrent of similar incidents that flooded the news media during the first half of 1991 validated CAPA's *raisons d'être*. These cases activated and reinforced some of the Coalition's techniques of community organizing. Zinzun had documented his case meticulously before bringing it to trial. Coalition members and Zinzun himself held meetings with community members, garnered information, received advice, and more important, disseminated the facts in the inner city. They secured media attention through a series of press releases and press conferences given by Zinzun, his lawyer, and aides. They assessed the political climate accurately.

However, a judge claiming to have found procedural flaws in the case overturned the $3.8-million award in July 1991. Zinzun and his team appealed, and in July 1994 they were awarded $512,500.[26] CAPA had by then become a conspicuous presence in both Black and mainstream media. This exposure attracted new and younger inner-city sympathizers to the office, thus paving the way for CAPA's alliance with the gang peace movement.

In August 1991 CAPA and the Committee for a Civilian Police Review Board launched a ballot campaign for an elected civilian police review board in Los Angeles. In its "Statement to the Media," the committee justified the campaign in simple and straightforward terms. Claiming to represent popular sentiment for community control of the police, the statement contextualized recent events of police brutality with persistent and systematic law enforcement harassment patterns:[27]

Last week's police killing of an unarmed Chicano youth in Ramona Gardens in East L.A. was no "aberration," any more than was the assault on Rodney King last March. Shootings, beatings, racial slurs, stun guns, battering rams, Operations "Hammer" and "Cul-de-Sac," sexual abuse, lesbian and gay bashing, police dog attacks, evidence tampering, attacks on union strikers, spying on political activists, human and civil rights violation, KKK organizing inside police precincts—these are daily occurrences throughout Los Angeles. This is especially true in the Black, Chicano/Latino, Native American, Asian American and immigrant and gay communities. An elected civilian review board, independent of the police and the politicians, will be a giant step in putting a stop to these police-state style actions.[28]

The review board would be elected, not appointed. A special prosecutor, independent of the LAPD, city attorney, and city council, would head its hired staff. The review board would also have full subpoena powers and access to shooting sites. As important, the board would have the power to impose penalties such as suspension and firing, as well as the power to review and modify LAPD policies and procedures. Its terms in office would be limited and each member would be required to hold monthly community meetings, thus encouraging ongoing community control of the board.[29]

The committee also demanded Chief Gates's removal and public hearings conducted by the Congressional Black Caucus to investigate police abuse by the L.A. County Sheriff's Department and police agencies from surrounding cities.[30] Although the civilian review board could not eliminate police abuse, it would be an important step toward community empowerment and the politicization of local social problems. Sponsored by CAPA and allied groups, the committee held meetings in local schools and community centers to inform and discuss its proposals. It also organized training sessions for those willing to assist its petition drive. The committee garnered endorsements from several individuals and organized groups including Councilman Mark Ridley-Thomas, Congressman Mervin Dymally, Americans for Democratic Action, the Mexican American Political Association, and the American Friends Service Committee. The commission had thus created yet another collection of relevant political facts that directed public attention to the inner city's problems.

Zinzun cochaired the committee and CAPA's previous experiences in the political and legal arenas provided the committee with crucial resources.

The ACLU Foundation of Southern California, which had been collaborating with CAPA since at least the early 1980s, served as the group's key source of legal advice. [31] The committee needed 230,000 signatures by December 31, 1991, to get the initiative on the ballot for the June 1992 primary elections. It did not make it, but the campaign only added to CAPA's importance as an inner-city political voice.

In 1996 Zinzun received a subpoena from the U.S. Commission on Civil Rights to participate in a hearing about police abuse in the Los Angeles area. Zinzun and others at the office were skeptical about the commission. They viewed its chairperson, Mary Frances Berry, a Black professor at the University of Pennsylvania, as too detached from issues regarding the inner city, a detachment credited to her middle-class condition and political timidity.[32] The commission lacks any enforcement powers to apply specific remedies to concrete situations. Zinzun read a short and eloquent statement to the commission based on the data about police brutality collected over twenty years at CAPA. He mentioned the increasing harassment and incarceration to which Black and Latina/o youth have been subjected since the early 1980s, the gangster-like tactics of the LAPD and of the County Sheriff's Department, especially the emergence within their ranks of gangs calling themselves the "Wayside Whites" and the "Insane Deputy Gangs" organized to provoke and harass persons of color. Zinzun pointed to the increasing evidence of CIA involvement in the distribution of crack cocaine and assault weapons in disadvantaged Black communities, supporting his claims with several exhibits constituted of tables, graphs, photographs, and videotaped footage.

It was all in vain, however. Berry dismissed Zinzun's intervention on the grounds he was not being clear enough regarding the exact amount of law enforcement brutality. When he tried to reply and show in his tables and graphs the exact figures, Berry sarcastically said that she still did not understand and asked another panelist to present.

CAPA's active involvement in police-related issues, its techniques of community organizing, and its high level of public visibility eventually led to an alliance with key gang members. Since early 1991, these gang members, perceiving that an entire generation of Black and Brown youth had become preferential targets of police repression in the Wilson/Reagan/Bush/Clinton years, worked on a peace treaty between Bloods and Crips. The alliance between CAPA and these gangsters evolved to a *de facto* fusion. At the 1996 U.S. Commission on Civil Rights hearings, for example, three eighteen-year-old ex-gang members accompanied Zinzun. They paid close attention to the proceedings and spoke quietly with the other persons in our group to discuss questions being raised. Although they did not directly participate in the writing of Zinzun's testimony, they were obviously trying to absorb as many aspects of the events surrounding the hearings as they could. As I was typing the final version of Zinzun's text in the computer, one of them expressed his wish to be doing my job in the near future. It will not be long before these younger ex-gang members have a more active voice in the Coalition. The Coalition's program, constituency, and activities have already been unmistakably transformed since its fusion with CSGT. Although Zinzun still plays a central role in the organization, younger leaders with new outlooks have emerged, and relations within the inner-city communities may be in the process of transformation. Actualizing its critiques of the BPP's structure, the Coalition today exists as less centralized and more open to ideologies that do not automatically conform to the Black Power perspectives.

☜

CAPA conceptualizes itself as a diverse political group. One of its documents proclaims that "CAPA's membership draws from the Black and Latino communities, workers' organizations, churches, the gay community, the women's movement and concerned individuals."[33] The building utilized by CAPA houses many other small organizations including the Peace and Freedom Party and the CSGT. Two lawyers also share the house on Western Avenue in the northern fringe of South Central. One of them, Walter Gordon, continues a family tradition that spans at least three generations. He employs his expertise mainly in cases related to the plight of Blacks and other oppressed communities. A typical day at the building involves persons and clients from different organizations, creating a climate of constant information exchange and comradeship.

CAPA is a direct product of the Black Panther Party, and its headquarters provides a site where ex-Panthers gather, reminisce, and discuss present issues. The group's logo features a black panther encircled by the words "All Power to the People," the emblematic phrase that expressed the party's goals in condensed form. Several of CAPA's newsletters and fliers are introduced or conclude with "From the Panthers to the Gang Truce, Linking

Our Struggles Locally, Nationally & Internationally," thus making explicit its affiliation with the historical legacy of the Black Panthers. The group's historical genealogy and its contemporary practices have prepared the ground for the incorporation of ex- and current gang members willing to establish and expand the gang truce initiated in 1992. CAPA played an important role in the foundation of gang truce, and its fusion with CSGT marked a qualitative shift in CAPA's original practices and outlooks. It generated new tools in the fight against the genocide of Black people in South Central, genocide that is even more obvious among the youth.

Much of CAPA's self-definition, activities, and style reflect conscious attempts to continue the tradition of political intervention inspired by the Black Panthers and the Black Power movement.[34] CAPA's beginnings are rooted in the dismantling of the BPP in Los Angeles by FBI COIN-TELPRO.[35] By 1976, when CAPA was founded, the government had succeeded in either killing, imprisoning, or forcing to exile most of the local Panther leadership. The Coalition's older members, supporters, and counselors have either been first-hand witnesses or direct survivors of FBI "secret wars." A considerable part of the outlook and vocabulary present at CAPA reflect conscious attempts by those who lived through the COINTELPRO years to preserve and build on a tradition of organized political action. Signs of the value given to the Black Power legacy can be seen in the CAPA office where several "Free Geronimo" posters—each from distinct epochs of Pratt's case, as their various stages of discoloring attest—adorn the crowded internal walls and front windows of the building.[36] The group shows films about the Panthers, and if old-timers who were part of the LA-BPP are present during such showings, they seldom miss a chance to comment on the events depicted. Videotapes of the 1969 L.A. shootout with the police, of Panther leaders' speeches, as well as images of demonstrations, rallies, and Michael Zinzun's campaigns for the Pasadena City Council, and many other documentaries are played almost daily in the office. In addition, the greetings, verbal expressions, and choices of attire come directly from the 1960s.

Yet the symbolism of the 1960s does not suffice to solve the problems of today. Newcomers, youngsters, and veterans often challenge the videotapes, speeches, newsletters, and the ideas linked to the past. I witnessed several showings of Panther film footage. Each time, someone—often an ex-member of the BPP rank-and-file—made a comment on a leader's subsequent corruption, mental illness, or Uncle Tom–ing. Although the verbal abilities and courage of previous leaders of the Panthers still compel admiration, the videos also incite reflections, discussions, connections with present issues, and criticisms directed at the party's power structure, processes, and practices. Such engaged observers often mention how the 1960s leaders grew increasingly isolated from and ignorant of the concerns of people at the grassroots.

On several occasions, women who participated in the BPP survival programs declared that much of the gun-carrying, black leather attire, and confrontational postures that were then cherished and that have now become one of the distinguishing emblems of the Panthers, in fact symbolized sexist and paternalistic attitudes by men against women.[37] These critiques become more poignant when we recognize that the Black Panthers consciously challenged all forms of patriarchy, theorizing and supposedly practicing alternative modes of gender relations. Granted that "the Panthers [theoretically] understood the particular oppression of women and its relationship to the perpetuation of economic inequality within the capitalist system,"[38] recurrent gender problems related to how women, albeit two-thirds of the party's membership, were practically absent from positions of power.[39]

The leadership's reluctance to recognize the central roles women played in the Black Panther Party reflected differences and distance between the leadership and the rank-and-file. Several ex-BPP members working with CAPA who had not belonged to the leadership group complained about the party's hierarchical structure. That structure greatly impaired the flow of communication and understanding between those who were speaking for the party, occupying the spotlight in the national media, and those who in fact carried out the BPP's programs. Although some degree of jealousy and personal animosity inflected these negative comments, the problem goes far beyond petty interpersonal disputes. The negative comments pointed to deep structural problems.

A rigid, patriarchal vanguardist approach to the role of the revolutionary party and its internal formation accounted for many of the BPP's structural problems. Huey Newton and Bobby Seale, for example, saw themselves imbued with revolutionary knowledge without which the masses of oppressed people could not even understand, much less overcome, their condition. Such postures, the old-timers of the rank-and-file repeatedly said, precluded

for paper

the leadership's ability to learn from those at the grassroots level. As one former Panther exclaimed, "The motherfuckers [the BPP's leaders] didn't have a clue of what was happening, man. I'm telling you. They spent so much time in jail, so much time speaking with lawyers and shit. . . . Some of them went nuts. But we were hanging in there. Serving all those breakfast for the kids."

The old-timers' criticisms suggest reasons for the BPP's collapse. Due to the party's inflexible, male-dominated hierarchical configuration, it depended almost entirely on its leaders for courses of action. This made the BPP highly vulnerable to the fate of its higher cadres. It is no coincidence that the COINTELPRO-FBI interventions focused on the most prominent Panthers. The government's success in pulverizing the Panthers, their racist and criminal tactics notwithstanding, can also be attributed to the party's unyielding pyramidal structure. With its leaders imprisoned or murdered, the BPP became a disoriented and vulnerable organization.

Huey Newton commented on some of the party's mistakes while in prison. He wrote: "We were looked upon as an ad-hoc military group, acting outside the community fabric and too radical to be part of it. We saw ourselves as the 'revolutionary vanguard' and did not fully understand that only the people can create the revolution."[40]

While Huey Newton often touched on the distance the BPP created between itself and the Black communities it supposedly represented, he nevertheless did not seem inclined to discuss the party's *internal* structure.[41] It may well be that Newton and other prominent leaders did not think it wise to expose the party's rigidity and question the party's hierarchies in public. Yet the quarrels among leaders gained intentional publicity. The purges of Cleaver and his supporters, among whom was Geronimo Pratt, were enthusiastically (and indiscriminately) vented through mass media while the BPP's bureaucratic arrangements remained unchallenged, highly verticalized, patriarchal, and thus extremely fragile.

Another point often raised by old-timers in reference to the party's leadership positions, repeatedly emphasized by Newton, was the BPP's growing distance from the nonaffiliated, from those Blacks who constituted the working class and the poor in the ghetto. For example, the BPP cut itself off from many thousands of potential members because of its strict membership requirements. All five thousand members functioned as full-time staff for the party although most were either underpaid or not paid at all.

To join the Black Panther Party one had to be unemployed or willing to give up a job. The Panthers also neglected to involve Black workers in the Party's activities, to reach out meaningfully to Black caucuses in unions and factories, or to attract support from many of the more stable sectors of the community.[42]

The Black Panther Party continues to generate fascination and enthusiasm because of its assertion of positive (mostly male) blackness, radicalism, style, insights, and courage. Yet we have to take seriously the various criticisms that, to this day, still preoccupy many of the very people who constituted its blood and bones. As we understand the BPP as a complex, far-from-unambiguous political entity, we gain an understanding of a key protagonist in Black politics that filled the void left by the deaths of Martin Luther King Jr. and Malcolm X, and as important, we can begin to examine institutions inspired by the Panthers.

CAPA and CSGT were formed from the debris left behind by the COINTELPRO. They still struggle with the dilemmas experienced by their predecessors. The questions posed by the old-timers around the role of the leadership, for example, persist. CAPA is consciously organized around the motto, "We'll work *with* you, not *for* you." This means that CAPA's more regular members, although willing to engage in causes that are consistent with the Coalition's program, insist on active involvement by those who tend to see the institution as an all-powerful problem-solver. CAPA and CSGT provide infrastructure, experience, and advice, but their members decline to lead others. CAPA's coordinator, Michael Zinzun, remains greatly admired, respected, and even expected to define and conduct all sorts of activities (especially by the younger people), but he avoids this role as much as he can. Zinzun sees his job as one of *support* for up-and-coming movements, leaders, and ideas. He provides advice, makes suggestions, and offers his help, but demands the same from those who participate in political activities with him and with the Coalition.

One of CAPA's central dilemmas is that those who arrive at the office sometimes intend to be led and told what to do. Instead the group attempts to incite leadership and initiative in these people. It would not be effective for veteran organizers and activists to exert no leadership, so finding the right tone, keeping the youngsters encouraged while telling them to find their own way, becomes the rather difficult task facing the more experienced members of the Coalition.

Relations between CAPA and the larger Black community present another pressing and persistent problem that remains from the Panther years. For all the impressive successes, participants in the organization frequently note how little support they are able to garner in South Central and elsewhere. They complain about resistance from young people in general, and gang members in particular, especially in respect to thinking about the well-being of the whole community rather than about the prestige and power of their own sets. Activists also note the systematic unwillingness of better educated and financially stable Blacks to aid the poor and marginalized. The exceptions only confirm the rule.

A few middle-class Blacks attend meetings, participate in programs, and go to rallies and demonstrations. They are often the most vocal in decrying the aversion that large numbers of better-off Blacks have toward collective, cross-class protest, and alliances with the poor. The interventions of these middle-class Blacks in meetings and casual conversations often feature accounts of how more privileged Blacks refer to the Black poor in very derogatory terms—"lazy," "pervert," "punks," "niggers." These accounts also mockingly depict richer Blacks as overly preoccupied with maintaining appearances. The stories equate aversion to the poor with petty concerns.

These generalizations about richer Blacks call for analytical prudence. We can neither generalize from a few, obviously inflated stories, nor can we lose sight of the fact that the storytellers, themselves privileged with relation to most of CAPA's and CSGT's participants, try to gain acceptance with their tales of the "Golden Hills snobs." A more precise approach might focus on how the stories reveal the intense and historically persistent degree of polarization between and among Blacks of different social, generational, and political backgrounds. CAPA's appeals to "Black power" rely on understanding Blacks as oppressed, insurgent, and radical. Yet opinion polls in the *Christian Science Monitor* and *U.S. News and World Report* disclose that 30 percent of Blacks designate themselves as conservative, that 48 percent blame Black people themselves rather than racism for their disadvantaged position in U.S. society, that 50 percent favor ending welfare altogether, and that 75 percent favor a constitutional amendment instituting mandatory school prayer.[43] These figures, too, require analysis of how the questions were asked, to what populations, and with what intent, but they demonstrate the futility of imagining a unified and monolithic Black experience.[44]

The difficulty radical organizations such as CAPA have in gaining supporters for their causes among Blacks—not only the privileged, but also members of the contemporary working class and jobless poor, and principally the women in such sectors—reveals important characteristics of both activist groups and the communities they seek to mobilize. Differences among African Americans persist in political groups as powerfully as they do in the practices of low-income tenement dwellers. CAPA faces daunting obstacles in bridging the chasm between its outlooks and those persons belonging to segments in the Black community who desire to distance themselves from radical social causes. Black Power activists view middle-aged, middle-class Blacks who have moved away from the poorer parts of the inner city as prone to disidentify with the rest of the Black community. Middle-class Blacks (let alone non-Blacks of all backgrounds) active in CAPA feel compelled to demonstrate their allegiance to the institution in more intense ways than underprivileged Blacks. As I heard several times, "House niggers take longer to realize they're still niggers, and sometimes they never do."[45]

Such mistrust seems to be reciprocal. A considerable number of the well-to-do consider CAPA the representative of the "lowly," the criminal underclass, the gangsters, in short, the very same people understood by the richer Blacks to be a key source of their shame. Among the poor, young people, and gang members, another kind of resistance to CAPA and the CSGT appears. Community-based organizations only rarely play prominent roles in disadvantaged people's lives. More often, such organizations are ignored or seen as ineffective. In the apartment building where I lived, Shannon made it clear to me several times that she did not believe in the gang peace treaty, and she disdained the efforts by CSGT to keep and expand the truce. CSGT makes strong efforts to link gang activity to social and economic problems affecting most residents of the inner city, but its appeals for peace among and between Crips and Bloods, for the most part, fall on deaf ears.

Albeit recognized by most male activists, patriarchy, so central to the Panther's organizational structure and culture, continues to be a mostly unchallenged, silent concern in the Coalition. Efforts to include women's perspectives in its daily activities and power structures have fallen short of relativizing the still-dominant, Black male–centered approach and climate that characterizes CAPA. Among the male activists there is sincere awareness of past mistakes concerning the objectification of women in Black-organized political efforts. They see the need to include women's voices, as well as those of Black gay, lesbian, and bisexual persons, in such a way that the perspectives of Black men do not dominate. Still, while there is certainly a process among Black male activists that indicates self-critique and openness, the process is incipient. Even though the Coalition's climate is one of profound respect for Black women, the terms of such respect are still defined and actualized by Black men, thus revealing deep-seated patriarchal norms.

CAPA and CSGT members know full well the historical barriers that radical political discourses and practices encounter *and* build among African Americans of diverse and often disparate constituencies. Questions regarding how much CAPA and CSGT should adapt and revise their programs generate heated debates. These debates reveal reluctance to carry out internal reforms that might be seen as accommodating to less-than-radical demands, contrary to the Black Power tradition. The gulf that exists between the Coalition and most inner-city dwellers reflects—at least in part—the organization's own difficulties in reshaping its demands and postures so that they become even more permeable and pliable to a greater number of people.

CAPA's radical stance provides the core of its message and appeal. Marked by Zinzun's direct and confrontational style, the institution appears in public events and in the news media as an extremely dissonant voice. When asked by television news reporters to comment on an incident of police brutality, Zinzun generally makes sure his message is as disturbing to mainstream expectations as possible. Invariably he wears a net over his long hair, and a T-shirt with Panther-inspired motifs or bright colors decorated with expressions of Black and inner-city pride. Most of all, his words are harsh and enunciated through his intense, coarse voice. Given enough time, Zinzun will comment not only on the inherent brutality, arbitrariness, and racism of the police, but will also remind viewers of the structural, historical, and persistent neglect to which communities of color have been subjected. He does not merely make comments on television, he gives passionate speeches, customarily ending his remarks with "all power to the people," accompanied by his closed fist raised above his head.

Zinzun's televised persona purposely provides stark contrast to the usually well-attired and polite commentators and common persons interviewed in the streets. Shortly after the 1992 uprisings, Zinzun appeared repeatedly on local news shows. He debated against, among other people, one of the Los Angeles Police Department's supervising officers at the scene of Rodney King's infamous beating, Sergeant Stacey Koon. They discussed King's decision to speak in schools throughout the country about his experience. Koon opposed this, reminding viewers that King had a criminal record, and echoing the Simi Valley verdicts emphasized that the police officers were only doing their jobs when they beat King savagely. In contrast to Koon's suit and tie, Zinzun wore his customary net over his hair and a bright red-and-yellow T-shirt with "South Central" proudly printed in its center. He gesticulated, interrupted Koon several times, reminded the viewers that the King incident was only one among thousands committed by the "racist and fascist police," and ended his speech—this time ignoring the news host's signal to end the broadcast—smilingly telling Koon, "I'll see you in court! All power to the people!"

Zinzun is recognized and greeted by people almost everywhere he goes, as I witnessed every time we were out on an errand together. Yet the causes and the institution he represents are not so well known or endorsed. Younger leaders, mostly young Black men, who work for CSGT and who are politically and personally close to Zinzun, encounter similar problems. The difficulties Black radicals face gaining community support have a long history. An article in the *Los Angeles Times* speculated about the lack of support Geronimo Pratt and his cause received in the Black communities throughout the twenty-seven years he was in prison. It pointed to contemporary political differences among African Americans and among inner-city dwellers—differences that, although greatly intensified since the 1980s, were already in evidence during the Panthers' period of greater eminence.

. . . [T]he Pratt case has never generated the total public preoccupation in the black community that characterized the Simpson trial.

. . . The explanation is found in history, in the attitudes of the black community and the mainstream media toward the revolutionary organization that Pratt helped lead, the Black Panther Party, and toward the powerful, often undisciplined, sometimes lawless, protests that were sweeping through the United States in the '60s and '70s.

. . . [A]s black writer Karen Grigsby Bates put it, "For the most part, black folks are fairly conservative about law and order and a lot of people in the '60s, particularly of my parents' age, people who were activists but [pro-] integration, equal-rights activists, found the Panthers very off-putting. Some people found them almost anti-American."

Kenneth Thomas, publisher of the [weekly newspaper] *Sentinel,* which serves the Black community, said, "They were given an image that was less than American, and the general feeling in the African American community was they did not want to be associated with that group."[46]

The origins of the "less than American" image the Black Panthers projected can be traced to the party's repudiation of middle-class mores, which in turn is a reflex of Black Power's negation of the "American Creed" and the "American Dilemma."[47] Yet repression also has a great deal to do with this perception. To have supported the Panthers when the government worked to annihilate them meant risking life, limb, property, and person in hopes of a better future.

Today's participants in CAPA and CSGT continue to grapple with their relations with wider sectors of Black communities. They know they tend to be seen with suspicion or skepticism by most Blacks. No matter what the topic of a meeting at the office is, it invariably touches on the difficult question of how to make their claims of social justice meaningful to Blacks and other inner-city communities. As a general tendency, old-timers embrace an alternative, communitarian vision of society where the well-being of the group is of prime importance. Current and ex-gang members favor the pursuit of material consumption and individual success. Yet this rough sketch does not account for the old-timers who shun radical ideas, or for the younger activists who can be far more radical than the old timers. Moreover, the relatively recent incorporation of Latina/os into some of the organizations' activities has intensified discussions about what type of political program the organizations should advance and what elements of dominant American ideology might be incorporated into ensuing activities.

❦

The description and analysis of CAPA's history, struggles, and outlooks were done mostly through the experiences of Michael Zinzun, its coordinator and cofounder. By adopting this strategy, I obviously neglected the important, everyday contributions of the many other activists who have dedicated their lives to the organization and the causes of social justice it promotes. At the same time, by highlighting the centrality Zinzun occupies in the organization, I present a view of the Coalition that owes much of its strengths, perseverance, and dilemmas to his charismatic leadership. Embodying a vital history of organized grassroots struggle, Zinzun personifies the intelligence, commitment, and will that have made it possible for unapologetic organizations to draw and expand on a Black radical tradition. At the same time, however, as Zinzun frequently suggests, his views and perspectives, while necessarily enabling—constituting a base, a bridge— are not enough for achieving social change and liberation. Although he constantly emphasizes the need for nonhierarchical, self-critical, and ever- changing forms of organized struggle, the ongoing project is incomplete. Young people are taking on more responsibilities; women are increasing their participation and sometimes challenge dominant patriarchal principles and practices; and collaboration has been forged with non-Black groups. Yet, because Zinzun is still the central person in the organization, his perspectives—which are necessarily grounded in his race, class, gender, and generational specifics—are often difficult to dissociate from that of the Coalition. Amid Black communities defined as much by their common racialization as by the differences that constitute and distinguish them— differences of class, gender, sexuality, place of residence, age—CAPA struggles to mold a political platform that needs to be both plastic enough to incorporate and transform itself through various standpoints, and bold enough to push ahead with projects of liberation. That CAPA does not shy away from these at times painful, provisory, yet always generative processes only reveals its deep commitment to radical transformation.

gang true - 110
manual - 118
Zinzun - 122-126
COINTELPRO say 120
↓
BPP

chapter 5

BLACKNESS AS ARTISTRY
AND AFFIRMATION

Leimert Park and the Idioms of Jazz

The World Stage storefront workshop and performance space occupies a prominent place in Leimert Park, a gentrified area of north South Central Los Angeles adjacent to the Crenshaw and Baldwin Hills districts. With its tree-lined streets, well-maintained houses, Afrocentric restaurants, galleries, shops, cafés, and clubs, the Village—as Leimert Park is also referred to—is the epicenter of a Black cultural renaissance that has been taking place since the 1980s. Founded by jazz drummer Billy Higgins, the World Stage provides a place for all-night rehearsals, jam sessions, clinics conducted by veteran jazz players, and performance showcases for new bands.[1]

As soon as I moved to Los Angeles, I started participating in the World Stage's jam sessions. I had some experience playing jazz in clubs, cafés, and restaurants in Brazil and in San Diego. When Michael Zinzun discovered this, he suggested that I talk with Richard Fulton, the owner of Fifth Street Dick's. Fulton welcomed me in a friendly way, and informed me of the jam sessions at both Fifth Street Dick's (Saturdays from 12 A.M. to about 4 A.M.) and at the World Stage (Thursdays from 10 P.M. to around 2 A.M.) Although I played occasionally at Fifth Street Dick's sessions, I became a regular at the World Stage, where, for me, the atmosphere was more welcoming.

Fifth Street Dick's and the World Stage are on the same block, less than one hundred yards apart. Customers usually go from one to the other many times during the same night. Several songs have been written and performed in homage to Fifth Street Dick's. The local jazz quintet Black

Note's first album, for example, contains a song named after the venue as well as a picture of the group posed inside the easily recognizable café.

The World Stage functions exclusively as a performance space. Except for the admission fee and the opportunity to purchase a few compact discs by Billy Higgins or other lesser-known artists, nothing else is sold. The seating serves only the musicians and audience—no diners or drinkers. Fifth Street Dick's, on the other hand, occupies a storefront converted into a two-floor café. On the first floor, one can consume several types of coffee and tea, homemade cake (the sweet potato cake is everyone's favorite), juices, and popcorn, while sitting on one of the approximately twenty stools arranged against the walls. Seated or standing in line to purchase the house specialties, the customers read the *L.A. Watts Times* and the *L.A. Weekly*, as well as several local magazines and fliers. Black couples of all ages, as well as a few Whites, Asians, and Latina/os also frequent the establishment. College students may bring in their laptop computers and do assignments in the café. Paintings suffused with strong, contrastive colors cover the walls. Most of them depict Black persons in surreal settings. Black pride mingles with controlled, conscious hipness, with a clear 1960s' twist.[2]

A large part of Fifth Street Dick's clientele consists of chess (and some domino) players and their respective audiences, who gather almost every day in front of the café. The games start at around 7 P.M. and last until approximately 11 P.M. Of about twelve tables set on the sidewalk, half are devoted to the contests. Spectators gather and move around the most interesting matches, making conversation with acquaintances both on the sidewalk and inside.

On a typical Thursday night, at around 10 P.M., Fifth Street Dick's jazz band starts the first set of music that will continue until the early hours of the next day. For a cover charge of $5 (unless a well-known musician is being featured), people venture into the twenty-seat room upstairs where the band plays. The club usually features one or two ensembles for about six months, alternating weeks and days if two bands share the bill. Live music nights are Thursday, Friday, and Saturday. Normally trios or quartets made up of drums, bass, piano, and occasionally another horn, the groups carry the names of their leaders. Saxophonist Dale Fielder and guitarist Roy Mulgrow appear frequently to showcase their respective ensembles. Like most of the musicians who frequently play at Fifth Street Dick's, they are relatively young talented players, who have not acquired enough exposure and recognition to venture into better-known larger venues. Both players have discs for sale (whose tracks are sometimes played by the L.A. area's only jazz radio station, Long Beach's KLON-FM) and employ a mix of seasoned and less experienced sidepersons in their live presentations. Some of these side players, in turn, form the bands around which Fifth Street Dick's jam sessions are organized.

The jam sessions at the World Stage, however, do not employ pre-arranged ensembles or paid groups. Everyone who attends the sessions stands on the same ground. Without the inevitable hierarchy and pressure (particularly on novices) that characterize Fifth Street Dick's jam sessions, the World Stage generates a friendlier atmosphere. Fifth Street Dick's sessions sometimes entail intense conflicts between the musicians working for pay and those who are paying to play and waiting for their turns. Even though the paid musicians depend on the participants in the jam sessions for the continuation of their jobs, they frequently display muted condescension and competitive rivalry toward the nonworking players, especially those who are not part of their social networks or who do not appear regularly in Leimert.

On a Thursday night at about 11 P.M., the weekly jam session at the World Stage starts to heat up. The musicians play well and together, negotiating occasional difficulties with serious enthusiasm and sweaty dedication. The tempo builds from tune to tune, as improvisations become more daring and inspired. The audience follows with foot tapping, syncopated finger snaps, and words of appreciation—"Uh-huh, I hear you, brother . . . tell me more." Some players close their eyes while concentrating on the music, drawing smiles of appreciation from the audience. Warm applause follows each solo.

Attracted by the excitement, a small crowd of about twenty people gathers in front of the performance room's large front windows. The two small plastic tables and chairs set on the sidewalk are quickly taken. People standing outside the club exchange words about the tunes and the players' names, commenting on each improviser's approach. A considerable part of this growing audience consists of musicians who begin negotiating their way to the stage as they talk about the ongoing music. Tentatively, they assemble the group of instrumentalists who will perform next. The rhythm section of piano, bass, and drums is more difficult to put together because trumpet and alto and tenor saxophone players abound in greater numbers.

On a good night, at least six different combinations of players take the stage. Ensembles usually consist of the rhythm section and three different horn players. The management allows each group three songs, but enforces the rule only for less experienced players.

Players of different ages participate in the World Stage jam sessions. A regular bass player in his seventies performs side by side with young men (and a few women, most of them singers) in their late teens.[3] On average, twenty people attend the sessions. Although Blacks make up a majority of those playing, a typical night sees from one to four Whites, and perhaps a few Latina/o or Asian American musicians as well. Players from China, Indonesia, Japan, Sweden, Denmark, England, Canada, Australia, Russia, Brazil, Poland, Israel, South Africa, Mexico, Cuba, Argentina, Italy, Spain, France, Germany, Colombia, Haiti, and from various U.S. states appeared at the venue during the time of this research.

The diversity on display at the World Stage extends beyond age, race, and ethnicity, featuring people with heterogeneous occupations, levels of education, and places of residence. Some of the African American regulars live in the adjoining gentrified Leimert Park, Baldwin Hills, and Crenshaw neighborhoods or in nearby Inglewood. Yet working-class and poor Blacks also participate both in the jam sessions and in chess games set on the sidewalk. They come to see friends, tell stories, and exchange conversation about cars, women, and job opportunities. Some of these less-affluent Blacks live in nearby neighborhoods. One does not have to walk more than a mile east or south to be in the more deteriorated parts of South Central. Others make the trip from Long Beach, Pasadena, or other pockets of Black residences in the greater metropolitan area. They usually carpool or, more commonly, take several buses and/or the train. For the less well off, the $3 door charge at the Stage can be prohibitive, and they either have to borrow money from someone or talk to Don Muhammad—the Stage's director and the person responsible for collecting the money—to see if he will let them pay the following week. Blue-collar workers, clerks, janitors, and the unemployed, young and old, interact with doctors, lawyers, dentists, teachers, and professors. Leimert Park constitutes a unique Black public space in South Central, one marked by social, racial, ethnic, and generational diversity.

During twenty-six months of observant participation in Leimert Park, I explored the form and content of the area's public norms. I focused on some of the area's commercial establishments, paying special attention to the jazz jam sessions at the World Stage. In the process, I encountered a form of blackness that stood in sharp contrast to those that prevailed in the tenement populated by low-income people where I lived and in the highly politicized atmosphere at CAPA where I worked. The social, ethnic, and racial diversity in Leimert Park enabled me to extend my investigation into blackness, class, gender, generations, and race relations in South Central Los Angeles.

Significant differences from the apartment building and the CAPA office distinguished this site. Despite its heterogeneity, specific Black norms of conduct dominated. This version of blackness revolved around the normativity of nuclear male-headed families, clearly delimited gender roles, and a valorization of work, obeying the law, gaining education, owning property, and achieving success. Black middle-class patriarchal norms of respectability, evident in a wide array of conversations and behaviors in the Village's public interactions, became even more obvious because they emerged in direct opposition to images of women, despised Black gangsters, hustlers, the poor and unemployed, and sex workers.

Two forces especially influenced these norms. Pride in particular forms of expressive culture—especially jazz music, visual art, and poetry—worked to build an understanding of Black identity grounded in achievement, artistic innovation, and intellectual complexity. In addition, the presence and popularity of Islamic religion, ideas, and values promoted a culture of dignity, respectability, and mutuality. Within music, these commitments could reinforce class distinctions, privileging jazz over hip-hop and blues. Yet—and in these moments the Black male patriarchal norms of respectability were challenged and relativized—recognized local artists also encouraged, nurtured, and championed artistic expressions emanating from young women and men who lived in the poorer parts of the Black ghetto.

❦

Differences manifested themselves even within seemingly homogenous sites. Several Black male amateur musicians, some of them middle-aged and reasonably experienced players, told me about their frustrations with the musicians conducting the jam sessions at Fifth Street Dick's. They made it tough for newcomers by calling for tunes that were not very well known, playing unconventional chord changes, or setting tempos that made their guests' improvisations more difficult.[4] An experienced amateur drummer asserted, "It's like those cats [at Fifth Street Dick's] don't want you to be kicking their ass, you know what I'm saying? They be all friendly and shit, but they're really worried you might get their gig. . . . It's kinda silly, if you think about it [that is, they are, in fact, good musicians] but that's what happens. They be doing their shit in a way that really puts you off. But that's OK, I'm paying my dues and if that's what it takes, hey, *I* am not giving up."

In contrast to what normally takes place at Fifth Street Dick's, the Stage's sessions feature a greater degree of communication, camaraderie, and social interaction among the participants.[5] Although the Stage's sessions appear less intimidating to beginners, their informality requires musicians to invest a considerable amount of effort in the interpersonal negotiations that precede one's performance. Since there is no sign-up list and no one person coordinating the succession of different groups of players who come up to the stage, musicians have to introduce themselves to others, discuss what songs to play, and negotiate the tempo, the order of solos, and other performance details.

Don Muhammad, the Stage's director, has formal responsibility for coordinating the sessions. Perhaps due to his temperament, and certainly as a result of many years of experience, he rarely intervenes. When he does, it is usually on behalf of a particular player who complains about waiting too long. The player in that situation will likely be a novice with no (or few) acquaintances at the Stage, frequently it is someone who is non-Black. Upon hearing the complaint, Muhammad may signal the performers to remind them of the player waiting. The bands seldom comply with Muhammad's requests promptly, however, especially if the waiting player is neither well known nor respected. The musicians on stage may be immersed in complicated improvisations, enjoying each other's playing. Their willingness to step down and make room for a waiting musician at these times is extremely small. Eventually, however, and ever so subtly, Muhammad finds a way to make room for the waiting musicians. At the end of a particular tune, he takes the stage, opens a microphone, and makes some announcements, usually about the performances that the World Stage will be hosting the next Friday and Saturday, urging the people in the audience to support the "up and coming" group. He may also remind the players and the audience of jam-session etiquette: respect for soloists, which for horn players involves not leaving the stage when not playing; the dress code, which is emphasized if there are too many people (usually youngsters) in attire that looks either unclean or too casual; and the more basic rules (which are known by most but hardly followed) of limits of up to three horn players on the stage and three songs per player. At this point, Muhammad summons the players who have been waiting to come to the stage. The musicians that have been playing over the limit of time stipulated by the rules invariably do not attempt to prolong their performance time and quietly step down.

As the sole authority present during the sessions, Don Muhammad performs a role more symbolic than practical. He collects the money, opens and closes the Stage, sweeps the sidewalk on which he then sets the tables and chairs, makes announcements, and reminds everyone of the rules. But most of the time, he just listens, chats with musicians, passersby, and spectators, and at musicians' requests often prolongs his stay when the session is running well into Friday's wee hours. A devout Muslim, he also engages with other fellow Muslims on religious matters, talking about the Qur'an or last Friday's community prayer. During the weeks of Ramadan, he asks other Muslims about their reading and fasting, and encourages them to support the jam sessions.

Muhammad's role revolves around public relations more than rule enforcement. As far as the jam sessions go, he only intervenes as a last resort in situations that do not seem likely to resolve themselves. By being consciously laid back, he reinforces the need for dialogue and negotiation between the musicians. In order to play, it is necessary to interact, take the initiative, and speak with fellow musicians. It is a process of trial and error, for the regulars' personalities vary and the players belong to various cliques.

Regulars approach music at the World Stage with solemnity and seriousness. As Don Muhammad frequently points out when making his announcements, musicians must consider the event as seriously as a paid gig and should conduct themselves with respectful demeanor, attire, and performance: "When you come out here think of this as your opportunity to learn and play in public. Put some nice clothes on, you know, take a shower. Show some respect and you'll get respect back. . . . Treat this as your own gig."

More than weekly meetings of amateur musicians, more than occasions when individuals have an opportunity to express their musicianship and sentiments, the jam sessions at the Stage quite frequently realize a meta-physical quality that transcends these given, more immediate facts. Many of the Stage's musicians attempt to evoke the mood produced by John Coltrane's latter performances, those where he was accompanied by McCoy Tyner on piano, Jimmy Garrison on bass, and Elvin Jones on drums. This lineup, formed in 1961 and active until 1965—when Jones and Tyner left as the saxophonist insisted on ever more experimental approaches—became the quintessential John Coltrane Quartet.[6]

At the Stage, it is not so much Coltrane's modal approach and his use of Arabic and Indian scales and moods that are emphasized, even though these traits are at times employed with considerable skill by some of the more advanced players. Fundamentally, most musicians try to perform Coltrane's spiritual intensity and musical seriousness through their per-sonal renditions of tunes.[7] These renditions may not immediately connect with Coltrane's playing in terms of tone, melody, tempo, and harmony, but they conjure Coltrane's passion and dedication. Several amateurs confided to me that this kind of intensity served as their main goal and constituted the reason for the importance given to Coltrane's work. A tenor saxo-phonist in his mid-fifties expressed his desires, "Man, if I can have *that* energy, blow my soul out of the horn, I'd be Goddamn happy. . . . I don't have to sound like Trane or anything like that, but just blow with that type of vibe, you know what I'm saying?" This particular person was sometimes rather efficient in invoking a Coltrane-like energy (which was made even more evident when he employed Eastern-inspired scales in his improvisa-tions), and those who listened to his moving renditions would confirm his success by linking his effort with the celebrated musician: "The brother was sounding like Trane tonight, just burning and playing the shit out of his horn."

While the music produced at the Stage may not immediately suggest a technical connection with the more spiritually oriented phase of Coltrane's life and work, the underlying motif of Coltrane's spiritual guidance dom-inates the sessions. It is rather emblematic of the Stage's dominant stance, however, that while songs such as "Wise One," "Acknowledgment," and "Resolution" remain favorites commonly held up as exemplars of Coltrane's spiritual force, they are seldom played during jam sessions. Most of those who take part in the sessions do not know those songs well, making it dif-ficult to perform them regularly. Moreover, it is the spiritual and musical intensity emanating from his famous quartet that matters most for the amateur musicians regarding Coltrane's sounds—especially those he recorded in the last two or three years of his life in albums such as *Crescent* (recorded in April and June 1964) or *A Love Supreme* (recorded in December 1964). It frequently happens that compositions from an earlier period of his life, from a period that is not immediately associated with the spiritual force of Coltrane's latter phase, are performed with the intention of compensating, as it were, for the conspicuous absences. This means playing earlier songs at a fast tempo, allowing for "outside" solos—not being too rigid with chord changes and time—and most of all, evoking pulses, rhythms, and lyricism that are associated with the composer of *A Love Supreme*. It is under these conditions that tunes such as "Impressions," a fast-tempo thirty-two-bar modal song that utilizes two minor scales, and "Blue Train," "Mr. PC," and "Equinox," each a minor twelve-bar blues, can be heard in almost every session.

These evocations, however, may hardly be perceptible to someone who does not know the players' intentions or their personal likings. Even when readily recognizable "Trane licks" are employed—note and articulation clichés and tone idiosyncrasies—they do not automatically transform a song's interpretation into a worthy acknowledgment of Coltrane. One of the most experienced amateur saxophonists at the Stage listened to a particular White piano player and at first agreed with most of those at the session that he sounded good. The piano player's phrasing with fourths chords (instead of the more common triads) and use of his left hand creating low pedal points were clearly based on McCoy Tyner's playing as it appears in several recordings with Coltrane. But on second thought, the amateur saxophonist noted that the young White piano player was lacking something. "You know, the cat's got the theory and shit, but it's not happening. . . . You know why? It's too cute. . . . Yeah, too cute." By this the saxophonist meant that the piano player, in spite of his expertise, was not approaching the songs and transmitting emotions in manners that were compatible with (what he considered to be the legacy and essence of) Coltrane. "He's playing without feeling. Trane wouldn't be happy with this, you know. It sounds too clean, too easy, you know what I'm saying?" The others agreed. The White piano player, after all, knew the techniques—the notes, chords, and some of the articulation tricks that made his playing resemble Tyner's—but he did not produce emotions that gave meaning to such techniques in expected ways. Furthermore, the fact that the piano player seemed to be aloof when performing did not help his case. As a middle-aged drummer added: "He ain't giving it a shit either, check it out. What is he all smiley for, huh? Fuck that shit!"

Belittling comments such as "playing cute" rarely are directed against Black men or women. As well as implying lack of commitment to the music, "playing cute," when directed to Black men, has the effect of questioning not only one's social and racial belonging, but also one's heterosexuality. "Playing cute" can be particularly insulting since it is a quality often associated with children and women—associations that threaten to undermine the prized virility of Black male musicians. Furthermore, "playing White" and "playing cute" are often interchangeable, which makes accusing somebody of "playing cute" an automatic challenge to a person's blackness.

Although the charge of "playing cute" questions a Black man's heterosexual masculinity, it does not do so for a White man; at least it is not stated with this primary purpose. From Black men's perspectives at the Stage, White men are already considered less virile than Black men. Thus, the sexual content of "playing cute," when applied to a White musician by a Black person, can be redundant, only reaffirming what is already known. In the obviously Black patriarchal context of the jam session, therefore, what is important is the "non-Black" quality of "playing cute." When Black men say Black women are "playing cute" they do not consider it as offensive as it would have been if directed to another man—from their perspective, it does not question the woman's sexual orientation. But it also implies a wrong approach to the music.

The sexist and homophobic character of these judgments is evident. Jazz has historically been a Black male–dominated arena where standards of performance and behavior that do not conform to what Black masculinity is supposed to be, or expressed by, are marginal at best. In such male-centric context, where Black men are the overwhelming majority of performers, when not producing satisfactory results, Blacks and non-Blacks, men and women may be charged with "playing White," "not swinging," "not saying nothing," "just going through the [chord] changes," or not "putting feeling into it." These principles are fairly consistent and held by most of the regulars of the Stage. No musician, however, is ever going to specify what constitutes the essence of "swing," "feel," or "happening." It is assumed that jazz musicians who venture to the Stage should be familiar with the basics of swing and consistently express it through their instruments. Still, the expectations go well beyond expression. Fellow musicians and audience members know when, for example, an evocation of Coltrane's spirituality is happening and whether it is worthy of praise.

This process, through which a player's accomplishments are judged, is thoroughly dependent on both technical proficiency and the local context—not only the generalized appreciation of Coltrane, but also the gender-specific shared sentiments that emanate from the consciousness of being part of an oppressed racialized community. Recognizable musical patterns aside, identifiable pleasures, as well as suffering and struggle, must be conveyed in one's playing. Ideally, these sentiments are transmitted effortlessly, and this is the mark of a master, a great musician. Among amateurs, however, it is always better to convey struggle than ease, for ease risks being quickly confused with alienation from shared sentiments, even when these sentiments are happiness and joy.

Shared sentiments provide the ultimate standard by which improvised music is judged. This does not mean that non-Blacks are unable to produce valued, meaningful sounds, but it accentuates the necessary burden they face—to understand, to show willingness to learn, listen, and of course empathize with sentiments that constitute the core of the music. Although specific rhythms, scales, modes, and other technical devices may serve as clues regarding a musician's inclination, these technical facts only become meaningful when used as conduits for the expression of recognizable and cherished emotions.[8]

An unmistakable belief in the irreducible and ultimate superiority of the Black experience is ubiquitous in the Village. "Playing cute" offends precisely because it excludes the accused from the valued universe of blackness—a universe that is decisively grounded in patriarchal gender and sexuality definitions. Yet manifestations of exclusivist postures do not happen unchecked. The notion that the same parameters of evaluation should be applied to all, regardless of social, gender, and racial belonging, functions to counter some of the excluding effects the emphasis on blackness as artistic performance entails. Blacks and non-Blacks, men and women, have their musical efforts evaluated according to the same principles. To be praised, one has to produce aural statements that evoke certain techniques and shared sentiments. Such sentiments are thought to be specific to the Black experience, and it may be argued that this fact alone reinforces the exclusivist stances mentioned earlier. In practice, however, this is not what usually takes place. Non-Blacks, women, and persons who do not feel compelled to subscribe to heterosexual self-presentation can and in fact do produce sounds that are much appreciated by the mainly Black male audience of the Stage. Still, skepticism toward non-Blacks is conspicuous. After all, compared to Blacks, and considering the effects of historically imposed segregation, it is less likely that non-Black musicians will have interest or the ability to express the types of socially shared sentiments in forms that are valued in this imagined Black community. Nevertheless, some non-Blacks effectively cross the line, so to speak. Understanding and performing music, thus, present the possibility of relativizing race barriers. While it is a relativization based on Black gendered and sexualized experiences, it points to the possibility of acquiring socially specific knowledge and sentiments irrespective of one's personal background. In this sense, the meaningful performance of improvised music bears unmistakable kinship with the ethic of openness as it is espoused by most of the local well-known artists.

The male-centric parameters Leimert regulars utilize to evaluate improvisation paradoxically question some of patriarchy's key expectations. By also emphasizing sensitivity and vulnerability—traits that are antithetical to patriarchal expectations of control and confrontation—the appreciation of jazz performance in the Village draws on a set of values that allows for a view of manhood that is not exclusively dependent on hegemonic expectations. While "playing cute" refers to aloofness, "soul" is often associated with a musician's demonstrative involvement in the performance. As well, unexpected renditions of standard themes sometimes build on emotional exposure, which is also greatly valued. Gentleness and understanding are as important to one's profile as a jazz musician as are the most easily discernible and often sexist brashness, resilience, and bravado. Thus, as much as the ethic of openness in Leimert is based on easily discernible patriarchal values, it also depends on elements which, in theory at least, question the very male-centric foundations of such ethic. That is to say, the ethic of openness is energized by forces that have the potential to radically reconfigure how not only art, but belonging and community can be conceptualized and experienced.

Amateur musicians in Leimert find themselves encumbered by jazz in a manner quite distinct from musicians performing in predominantly White amateur settings. When I performed jazz in primarily White venues in San Diego and Los Angeles, musicians and audience members viewed the music largely as a vehicle for one's *personal* emotions and choices. Musicians participated in sociability networks formed around a common interest in music; most of them had formal training that made them aware of elements of a widely accepted, institutionally sanctioned notion of jazz. Those players exuded a sense that they were expressing, through music, their own feelings. When they described music as really "happening," it meant that the members of a group were truly communicating among themselves through their instruments, and producing sounds that expressed each individual's feelings. These (mostly White) musicians judged the quality of a performance according to how well their technical renditions captured these personal emotions. Unlike most jazz musicians performing at the World Stage, the amateur musicians in predominantly White settings seem unencumbered by the necessity to express collectively shared sentiments.[9]

For those readers suspicious of clear-cut distinctions such as the ones suggested in the above paragraph, let me say that there are, for sure, amateur Black musicians who base their performance on exactly the same individual terms that were characteristic of the White amateurs I knew. Similarly, White players were able to appeal to Black listeners' technical standards and sentiments by evoking sounds considered eminently Black.[10] Furthermore, those who try to advise less experienced players strongly emphasize the need to develop one's own "voice," one's individual style of playing.[11] The notion that music serves as a means of personal expression was as crucial among Black amateurs as among Whites. Among musicians who participate in the World Stage jam sessions, however, additional, crucial elements regulate the form and content of musical statements. At the Stage, more experienced players constantly reminded Black and non-Black amateurs of their responsibility to play the music to the best of their ability. This music, they advised, embodies a great deal of suffering, imagination, pride, pleasure, and intelligence. It therefore calls for no less than a corresponding amount of respect and dedication. "This is some real serious shit," more experienced players often remind youngsters and beginners whose demeanor and playing during jam sessions did not seem to do justice to this tradition of Black music.

❦

The Stage's moods depend on aural specificity. When its best drummers perform, they deploy Elvin Jones's approaches and technique as their central style. Jones's polyrhythm, his cymbal work, and his impeccable time, especially in fast tempos, are admired, frequently talked about, and copiously quoted during performances. Rare are the jam sessions in which a drummer doesn't mention or attempt to play one of Jones's patterns, especially with the ride cymbal. Equally central in the amateur drummers' model of excellence is the overwhelming, hypnotically intense energy that Jones is (still) able to transmit when he is playing. Although Jones can be very loud in live presentations (to the point of sometimes rendering other musicians' playing difficult to hear), his accompaniments and solos convey an obstinate dedication to his art. Among the Stage's regulars, four advanced amateur drummers, whose ages vary between the early thirties and late sixties, draw a considerable part of their musical vocabulary from Jones.[12]

It is not only drummers who help define the Stage's dominant aural atmosphere. Pianists, bassists, and, most evidently, several horn players also emulate Coltrane's sounds and approaches. The most technical tenor players attempt to incorporate into their playing the famous musician's tone, uncompromising intensity, and some of his harmonic and melodic idiosyncrasies. Of course, such references to Coltrane take place amid very personalized approaches. Each musician has an easily recognizable individual style. Yet, during conversations most express their wishes to "sound like Trane." This means not only producing sounds that are similar to Coltrane's, playing his compositions or those he used to perform, but also approaching life in ways that would be compatible with the general knowledge about his postures, especially those of his latter years in which his work and existence became more spiritually oriented. Whether or not this general knowledge about Coltrane is precise does not matter here (even though, based on several biographies and first-hand testimonies by persons who knew him, they seem to be, in general, consistently accurate). As the musicians base their behavior on a common set of shared beliefs about their favorite artist, they create, reinforce, and communicate a particular standard of playing and relating to others that, inevitably, influences the Stage's atmosphere.

Paid performances also take place at the Stage, usually on Fridays and Saturdays, but occasionally on Thursdays, much to the disappointment of the amateurs, because this often means the jam session is canceled.

Well-known musicians such as Bobby Watson, Horace Tapscott, and Bobby Hutchinson, among others, were featured when I frequented the establishment. Many amateurs who participate in the jam sessions usually listen to these presentations from the outside because the cover charge of usually $4 or $5 is too much for most of them. Coltrane's compositions are frequently performed, and jam-session regulars see them as the highlights of the show.

During the March 1997 Jazz Caravan, approximately 2,000 residents from all corners of Los Angeles, mostly suburbanites, rode in chartered buses and shuttles to visit nineteen of the town's best-known jazz clubs, including the World Stage and Fifth Street Dick's. As two hundred jazz fans circulated through Leimert's tree-lined sidewalks, fifty crammed in the Stage to listen to an all-star rendition of Coltrane's "Ascension" with Billy Higgins on drums, Richard Reid on bass, Horace Tapscott on piano, and Phil Vieux on saxophone. Vieux started off with a prolonged rubato inspired by, but never entirely reproducing, Coltrane's main theme. After the long introduction, the saxophonist paused, cued the rhythm section, and after a few choruses, Vieux stated the theme and began his improvisation. All the regulars listening attentively through the Stage's windows and walls—there were about ten of us—were deeply impressed by all the musicians' performances. Vieux expressed and stretched musical ideas through his obvious command of Coltrane-inspired techniques and his own vocabulary. Amid inspired and energetic playing, during which he reached several provisional climatic statements—each one through different rhythmic, harmonic, and melodic techniques—Vieux's improvisation culminated with a series of ascending cries until, literally, he was drained of breath and energy. Meanwhile, Higgins, Tapscott, and Reid kept the pulse and dynamics flowing, always attuned to Vieux's incursions, at times anticipating the saxophonist's shifts, at times following them. Each one of their improvisations was as inspired and meaningful as the preceding one.

Although the (mainly White) audience truly appreciated the show, warmly applauding and producing shouts of support as the players improvised, its enthusiasm resounded less than that expressed by some of Leimert's regulars who witnessed the tour-de-force in the cold night. The regulars produced an outpouring of commentaries emphasizing their happiness at seeing Higgins perform again, hearing Tapscott's creative voicings, admiring Reid's reliability and tone, and most of all, witnessing Vieux's expressiveness.[13] One of those regulars, visibly moved by the music, mentioned that the show was "the kind of stuff that makes you go on with the struggle. . . . I'm feeling like I used to feel after church, you know what I'm saying? Damn! That was a motherfucker." The others agreed in silence.

Max, the sixty-year-old drummer who made these comments, was a well-known jam session regular. The "struggle" he mentioned referred to his lifelong pursuit of musical skill, a pursuit closely connected to his other personal difficulties. All of us in that group knew what he was talking about. We all had heard Max's stories of his past addictions, family problems, the death of his wife after many years of suffering, and his enduring desire to become a professional musician.

Earlier in that same night, several other groups had presented well-known jazz songs, but none had garnered so many positive responses from the amateurs. It was no accident that the most appreciated performance included a composition by Coltrane. The amateurs were drawn to the rendition of "Ascension" mainly because the musicians performing the song mobilized a range of techniques and produced sensory experiences that expressed some of the principal ideals held by those participating in the jam sessions. The association Max made between that presentation and religion was significant: it expressed the importance given to the spiritual component of music, accentuating the quality of music as an outlet for sorrows, and emphasizing the redemptive quality of Coltrane's compositions. It pointed to the hopes of a better future in which present—collective—sufferings and conflicts would be resolved.

Leimert's normative public codes attain their substance in relation to historically determined social tensions within the inner city and between the inner city and the wider society. The performances on the World Stage manifested aesthetic brilliance, impressive style, and the collective pleasures of creating and consuming culture. Yet the music and attendant social relations at the venue also expressed perspectives on social conflicts, while embodying alternative modes of social organization in response to them.

❦

Islam pervades Leimert Park as a diffuse sensibility informing public standards of behavior. The Islamic aspects of Leimert Park's public culture do not signal a generalized religious devotion, or even an unambiguous allegiance to its Black nationalist manifestations. Yet the locale's core vocabulary, demeanor, and dress codes display Islam's unmistakable influence. Religious Muslims of various orientations appear more visible in Leimert Park than in many other parts of South Central, but they do not constitute a majority of the population. Black Catholics and Protestants outnumber Muslims in the Village. Those who support aspects of Islam, however, do so here in obvious and proud ways, and even non-Muslims often behave in manners that suggest at least some appreciation of Muslim precepts.

Traces of Muslim influence permeate the area's commercial establishments. A good number of restaurants, cafés, and performance spaces have adopted Islam-inspired rules and décor, even though some of those establishments are neither owned by Muslims nor draw most of their clientele from the faith. Within a few blocks of the World Stage, the Shabazz restaurant specializing in soul food hosts live jazz on Fridays and Saturdays and a jam session on Sundays. The establishment does not sell alcohol or use pork in its recipes. The restaurant's owners are followers of the Nation of Islam, but their support for the Nation reveals little preoccupation with orthodoxy. Photographs of Elijah Muhammad, Malcolm X, and Louis Farrakhan occupy the most visible spots in the one-room eatery. These photographs are accompanied by black-and-white pictures of Muhammad Ali, Martin Luther King Jr., Nelson Mandela, the Million Man March, and many other local, national, and international Black celebrities who do not have much in common except being Black. The display suggests that the people responsible for the restaurant's decoration (and perhaps its patrons) cherish diverse representatives of Black success—of the civil rights movement of the 1960s, athletes, local and international activists, and leaders associated with the Nation of Islam.

The symbols of allegiance to the Nation of Islam (NOI) merit a closer examination for they shed light on the syncretic character of the Muslim influences in Leimert. According to the Holy Qur'an and many Islamic scholars, the religion of Al-Islam, as it is practiced today by an estimated one billion people, including members of a dozen mosques in South Central, was revealed to and systematized by Prophet Muhammad in Arabia about 1,400 years ago. Al-Islam is based on the Sunnah (Way) of the Prophet Ibn Abdullah, believed to be the last messenger of Allah. The Nation of Islam, on the other hand, is a U.S. phenomenon. It was founded in 1930 in Detroit, Michigan, by Wali Fard Muhammad, also known as

W. D. Fard. Fard taught Elijah Poole, who later changed his name to Elijah Muhammad, and made him into his spokesman and representative. For a short period between 1975 and 1977, the Nation of Islam changed its name to World Community of Islam and then to American Muslim Mission. During those two years, led by Elijah Muhammad's son, Iman W. D. Mohammed, the organization embraced the religion of Al-Islam. But except for this short time, the Nation of Islam has been preaching ideas and practices that are quite foreign to those who are devout practitioners of Al-Islam. Re-emerging in 1979 under the leadership of Louis Farrakhan, the Nation of Islam has since taught, for example, that Elijah Muhammad was the last messenger of Allah. Furthermore, while Al-Islam teaches no essential difference exists between people of different races, the Nation of Islam defends a view in which there are two types of human beings of extremely different natures: the Black man, and the Caucasian White man.[14]

The décor at the Shabazz restaurant embodies synthesis of seemingly antagonistic images and ideas. The portrait of Malcolm X stands next to pictures of Elijah Muhammad and Farrakhan, uniting symbolically three men whose severe quarrels and disagreements are well known. The proximity of the pictures does not indicate ignorance on the part of the exhibitor, but rather a desire to pick and choose among available ideas and options, forging a new synthesis based on the best aspects of previously atomized entities. As I performed in jazz ensembles at that restaurant (some of which featured White musicians) I saw no signs of racial animosity by the owners or the patrons of the restaurant; no sign that the Yacub story, oftentimes told by Louis Farrakhan, was taken seriously.[15] More evident was the admiration followers of the NOI had for Malcolm X, despite the ostracism imposed on his ideas by the organization. The powerful support for NOI evident in the restaurant nevertheless did not impede attitudes readily associated with the teachings of Al-Islam.

A no-alcohol policy prevails at key venues in the Village, including Fifth Street Dick's and the World Stage. Several local people told me they attributed these policies to the influence of Islam as espoused by Billy Higgins—jazz drummer, legend, one of the founders of the World Stage, and a devout Muslim. The Stage displays a Qur'an prominently in its front window, together with West African instruments and artworks. Portraits and photographs of Black jazz musicians—John Coltrane, Miles Davis,

Billy Higgins, among others—together with cloth and paintings brought from various African nations, adorn its internal high walls. Fifth Street Dick's owner, Richard Fulton, is not himself a Muslim, but his establishment follows the same no-alcohol rule.

The bookstores in Leimert and the open-air second-hand book sale that takes place on Saturdays on the sidewalks at Degnan Boulevard and 43rd Place—both of which attract a considerable number of locals—specialize in Islam-related literature. The same goes for some of the adjacent area's commerce, especially on Crenshaw Boulevard, where a small mosque is located near Muslim bookstores, clothes boutiques, and food markets.

Given the numerous examples of Islamic influence in Leimert Park, it should not be surprising that people in the area commonly greet each other in Arabic phrases—"Salaamun a'laykun" (Peace be on you), and "Al-Hamdu-lil-laah" (Praise be to Allah). One hears these words from shopkeepers, artists, and friends and acquaintances as they meet. Non-Muslims often utilize these Arabic words and Islamic greetings when interacting with people who, in turn, may not be Muslim either.

From the limited knowledge of Islam I obtained through participation in Friday noon Jumu'ah Prayers at a local mosque (which I attended regularly for approximately six months), from conversations with Black Muslims, and from readings of pertinent Islamic literature suggested by local followers of the religion, I came to see that some of the Islamic concepts and routines that are specific to the sociability of Muslims have impregnated the Village's public life. The local public code stressed the need to take active responsibility for one's personal life and for one's community. It advanced the concept of an international community united by good will rather than race and valorized the practice of solidarity between people of different social classes, ages, and cultural backgrounds.[16] While of course overlapping with influences from many different religions and cultures, these Islamic precepts have been assimilated into the Village's public norms. They have become a constitutive part of the local sociability. They do not exist unchallenged and contain many contradictions, but their very existence gives distinct specificity to Leimert's sociability.

The concepts I claim have "migrated" from Islamic circles to the local public spheres may seem so generic that their origins—and therefore their connection to the Muslim circles—would be difficult to demonstrate. Islamic influences have been fused with other precepts and, in this process, become part of a composite set of norms which, as a whole, has characteristics that cannot immediately be reduced to the characteristics of its parts. The appreciation of Black art, for example, conforms to Islamic understandings, but also originates in long traditions of racial uplift and self-activity in African American life.

Appreciation of Black art manifests itself in the many galleries, studios, and performance spaces in Leimert Park. This Black art, however, is of a specific kind. One can find a few hip-hop venues in the area, and a club on the corner of 42nd Place and Leimert Boulevard played rap music regularly in 1996 and 1997. Yet most of the locals view these forms of cultural expression as less worthy than the jazz, poetry, and visual art that prevails at the Village's other establishments. As one might expect, middle-class male Blacks in their forties and fifties tend to express negative feelings about rap, but so do poorer and younger Blacks who are regulars of the area. Rap tends to be associated with gang life, for which there is very little, if any, tolerance.

The blues, on the other hand, occupy a gray area in the minds and hearts of Leimert Park's regulars. Although some great blues artists including B. B. King, Little Richard, and Ray Charles command much respect, the locals generally view this music with suspicion and are unwilling to attend events featuring unknown performers. At best, the blues is considered one of the genuine expressions of the Black condition and an influence on more sophisticated art forms. The area's jazz enthusiasts frequently assert that the twelve-bar form and the chord progressions that characterize most blues songs constitute one of the fundamentals of jazz, that one cannot appreciate or perform jazz without a deep understanding of the blues—its scales, articulations, changes, and moods. They acknowledge that the blues express a common condition of suffering, solidarity, pleasure, and hope that is central in Black art forms, and that the blues imply a shared, eminently Black worldview.[17]

At worst, however, the blues, especially its contemporary electrified versions, is considered too commercial, sometimes too sexual, and not as sophisticated as jazz. Comments on how the blues have been incorporated and made most profitable by Whites usually take place in tandem with its dismissal. The Leimert Park regulars routinely claim that the blues has lost its soul and has become uncreative mass entertainment. Not surprisingly, some of Leimert's clientele affirm that the blues are, after all, the music of unsophisticated Black folks of times past, a type of music made foreign by history and social distance.[18]

Leimert Park's self-image appears to depend significantly on contrasts and oppositions between different kinds of Black art and culture. The term *high-brow* seems an appropriate description of Leimert's preferred Black art. The sophistication of jazz harmonies, arrangements, and improvisations is often contrasted to the repetitiveness of rap, most popular music, and certain variations of contemporary blues.

Yet this characterization misses important ambiguities that provide a better grasp of Leimert's cultural climate. In spite of the Village's overt signs of intolerance, there are unmistakable efforts, among local artists, to open spaces and orient artistic voices emerging from within the hip-hop world. Respected local artists engage in establishing relationships of esteem and mutual exchange with young men and women involved with hip-hop, even though most regulars classify rap art and artists as of questionable value.

Reaching out to hip-hop culture constituted an important part of the work of local poet (and former professor at California State University, Northridge) Kamau Daaood. At the time of my research, Daaood was in his late forties and had shaped his art in the Underground Musicians and Artists Association (UGMA), made up not only of poets, but also musicians and visual artists, part of a fertile Black arts movement that followed the Watts rebellions of 1965. Poets Wanda Coleman, Odie Hawkins, Eric Priestly, K. Curtis Lyle, Quincy Troupe, Emory Evans, and Ojenke, to name a few, participated in this group and most took part in the work of the Watts Writers Workshop in the late 1960s as well. Jazz pianist Horace Tapscott and his "Pan-Afrikan Peoples Arkestra" (influenced by Sun Ra's "Solar Arkestra") both inspired and participated in this cultural movement.[19]

The Arkestra and the Writers Workshop emphasized the need to showcase artists with no formal training. The Workshop attempted to elaborate verbal, poetic analogies to the musical experiments of local jazz musicians such as Tapscott, Eric Dolphy, and Ornette Coleman, who, in turn, were well attuned to, in dialogue with, and influencing the experiments of John Coltrane, Cecil Taylor, Steve Lacy, Anthony Braxton, Dewey Redman, Pharoah Sanders, and Archie Shepp.[20] By manipulating, stretching, and sometimes abandoning musical structures altogether, they moved toward freer improvisations regarding harmonies and time. These musicians, among many others, explored new possibilities within and beyond the bebop idioms of the 1940s and 1950s best represented by Dizzy Gillespie, Charlie Parker, Bud Powell, and Thelonious Monk. This experimental spirit produced a rich artistic and political culture centered on various informal associations and cafés such as the Watts Happening Coffee House.[21] The fact that martyred Black Panther leader Alprentice "Bunchy" Carter had been an active participant in these local artistic spaces offers a glimpse into the organic attachments and the possibilities connecting poetry, music, and politics. Carter was a street poet and member of the Slausons gang, and later became one of the Los Angeles Black Panther Party leaders, only to be assassinated on the UCLA campus in 1969.

Daaood collaborated with Billy Higgins to open the World Stage in 1989. The cultural revitalization that ensued in Leimert Park largely stems from their work. During the period that followed the Watts uprising of 1965, cafés and youth clubs served as cultural catalysts. In the early 1990s, the Stage had a similar role, quickly becoming a magnet drawing both beginning and established artists. Daaood, according to the locals, was the main inspiration and force behind the Stage's initial period. Although Higgins is better known and at least as charismatic as Daaood, in the beginning of the 1990s he was not seen at the Stage and in the Village as often as Daaood. His busy performance and recording schedule on both coasts and abroad kept him away. Then he developed a life-threatening ailment that eventually forced him to have a liver transplant in 1996. These circumstances made Daaood initially more visible in the area than Higgins.

Daaood not only founded the Stage and coordinated its innovative poetry workshop, but he also conducted his own business in Leimert Park. During the early 1990s, he owned a small record shop, Final Vinyl, close to the Stage, where not only jazz enthusiasts, but also hip-hop connoisseurs and producers gathered, conferred on each other's activities, and established a dialogue between distinct Black artistic genres that had been, and would continue to be, a central feature of Daaood's orientation. Bryan Breye, owner of "Museum in Black," an art gallery that opened inspired by the cultural momentum generated by the inauguration of the World Stage, expressed Leimert's general impression on Daaood, stating, "When he came to the community, he awakened a sleeping giant with the poetry. He was instrumental in helping bring that energy back to the area."[22]

In a spirit similar to that of jazz drummer Max Roach and pianist Horace Tapscott, Daaood perceived in hip-hop rhythms and verses a truly revolutionary art form that expressed the contemporary condition of destitute young Blacks in direct, raging ways.[23] In his verses, Daaood presents an amalgam of Black cultural influences. He fashions a contemporary art that can be cherished, shared, and used to bring about new levels of consciousness. In his poetry he fuses the here and now (best represented by the immediacy of hip-hop) with Black art forms like jazz that stand on thick historical layers to provide a new style, new possibilities for pleasure, and new horizons of hopes—hopes of redemption, hopes of understanding. In Daaood's own words, "the arts have transformative power." In verse, he tells the story this way:

> I stand on the OG corner and tell old school stories with a bebop tongue to the hip-hop future
> I see new rainbows in their eyes as we stand in the puddle of melted chains.[24]

In Daaood's model of cultural appreciation, jazz-derived art (the "bebop tongue") and hip-hop interact and intensify each other's messages. He often incorporates musical accompaniment by jazz musicians in his poetry recitals. Daaood emits his spoken words in a way that immediately relates to hip-hop, although the rage that characterizes a number of the latter's manifestations is not necessarily explicit in Daaood's performances. Daaood became celebrated locally as the "grandfather of rap," an elder greatly respected and admired by young poets who came from all parts of the city to recite, listen, and learn. The weekly poetry sessions that he hosted at the World Stage also attracted significant numbers of hip-hop lyricists. As A. K. Toney, a twenty-year-old hip-hop poet mentored by Daaood at the World Stage, explains: "He [Daaood] is the essence of the community when it comes down to the words that need to be spoken about what Leimert Park means to people."[25]

Daaood's approach to hip-hop and to youths who to many of Leimert's clientele are objects of fear and revulsion confronts the dominant local stance toward the young members of the "dangerous classes." Dialogue and comprehension, rather than fear and revulsion, guide the relations Daaood fashions between Leimert's regulars and the poorer and younger

residents of South Central. Rather than consisting of a closed set of elements, his art is a searching, open, and dynamic process, which despite the
locals' most explicit likings, has the potential to produce self-criticisms
and to suggest possibilities that challenge generational, racial, and social
barriers. Art as a transformative force, in these moments of real dialogue,
attains its fullest realization and gives continuity to the project that dates
back to the days of the Watts Writers Workshop.

One of Daaood's poems expresses with passion the urgency of such
dialogue, and suggests an alternative perspective to the everyday media
images about the inner city and the corresponding stereotypes held by
Blacks and members of the wider society. His alternative perspective also
carries with it a powerful critique of dominant modes of thought and
attitudes according to which a better future can be imagined.

> Vomit up your television set
> take a deep breath and exhale your fears
> scrub the tombstones of those who die young until they become mirrors
> in which to see yourself
> take long stares at your hand until true love returns to your touch
> then touch.[26]

Daaood's artistry and activism exemplified the potential for Leimert's
public norms to bridge class, racial, and generational differences. The obstacles that exist between these possibilities and their realization, however,
remain still considerable. For example, Blacks who live in the so-called
deep confines of the ghetto but participate in the Village's nightlife tend
to corroborate negative impressions about their neighborhoods with their
own stories of violence, prostitution, and drugs. As well, hegemonic gender norms are seldom overtly challenged, thus relegating women, at best,
to objects of benevolent male willingness—if and when they speak, it is
often in the terms set by well-intentioned yet still patriarchal men.

☾

The dominant norms at Leimert Park envision a Black community expanded both in space and in time. The Village's public life incorporates
stories, art, and peoples from a wide range of regions of the United States,
as well as from various countries of the world. It also cultivates a Black

historical legacy through its sociabilities and artistic venues. Leimert's cultivation of an international Black culture stretches back to the political era when Malcolm X and other proponents of Black Power made their call for an international community of solidarity formed by the oppressed of the world.[27] Most of the area's respected artists, restaurateurs, and entrepreneurs—Blacks in their late forties and early fifties—developed their trades and outlooks during the 1960s, and the framework of Pan-Africanism proposed then, coupled with the civil rights movement's claims for social justice and solidarity, certainly made an impact. Those who work, perform, and socialize in the Village share knowledge about a collective experience of oppression that links them to others around the world. In Leimert, more than anywhere else in South Central, a sense of belonging to a community that is larger than the city, the state, and indeed the nation predominates.

The Al-Islamic emphasis on the international character of the Muslim community shapes the appeal of art, clothes, instruments and books from various parts of the world, especially the African continent. In the mosques, Muslim restaurants, and in the streets, men and women can be seen wearing African and Eastern-style clothing. Muslims run many of the shops that import these clothes from various nations on the African and Asian continents, notably Nigeria, Pakistan, Indonesia, and India. Yet not all men and women who dress in African and Asian costumes are Muslims. Nor are the shops scattered throughout the Village that sell such clothes run exclusively by Muslims.

Conjoined with Islamic influences, a generalized gaze that looks outward to transcend the local characterizes the culture of Leimert. A few storefronts away from the World Stage, a small shop specializes in foreign objects, including African tapestry, hats, tunics, vests, shirts, bracelets, and rings. Two men run the shop—a Black Muslim who regularly attends the mosque on Crenshaw Boulevard, and a Black man in his early seventies originally from Louisiana who is a devout Catholic, a drum master, trumpet player, and artisan named Juno Lewis. One of the most charismatic and well-known public figures in Leimert, Lewis is respected partly for his age but mostly for his storytelling and eventful life history. The shop is an almost obligatory meeting point for the area's regulars. Musicians, visual artists, poets, and passersby all gather around Lewis at different times of the day. Some of the participants in jam sessions, myself included, make it a habit of stopping by before going to the World Stage.

Juno, as he is universally called, participates sporadically in the sessions. When the music suits his demanding standards, he will show up with one of his multitude of trumpets—instruments to which he has been dedicating his craftsmanship and musicality for the last ten years or so—and captivate the audience with his mix of improvisational wit and theatrical performance. Juno's presence is greatly treasured at the Stage's larger events, which usually take place on Friday and Saturday nights, when he appears as a guest artist during presentations by professional jazz groups. Juno lends his enthusiastic support to local unknown musicians by being present when they perform at the World Stage or Fifth Street Dick's. Always dressed exquisitely in his own mixture of West African, Creole, and Eastern costumes, warm and friendly even with strangers to the locale, Juno provides a focal point of admiration, recognition, and respect for the locals.

Juno has patented several models of drums he has invented over the years, but he is best known for his musicianship. He played and recorded with John Coltrane, among others. His percussion playing and vocals appear on Coltrane's 1965 record *Kulu Se Mama,* titled after the homologous poem written and performed by Juno in the title track.[28] In *Kulu Se Mama,* Juno sings his verses in Entobes, an Afro-Creole dialect, and plays several types of African drums: the Juolulu, water drums, the Doom Dahka, bells, and a conch shell.

Juno's persona invokes a variety of places within the United States and abroad. The list of instruments he played during the *Kulu Se Mama* sessions speaks of a strong connection to the African continent—a connection that is maintained to this day through his playing, manufacturing, and teaching of drums. He acquired his mastery of Entobes, the Afro-Creole dialect he speaks, during his childhood in Louisiana. As well as reinforcing the links with his African ancestry, the dialect accentuates Juno's more recent roots in this country. Juno often speaks about growing up in New Orleans, the large number of people who migrated from there to Los Angeles in the 1940s, and his unusually large family. He often visits New Orleans and comes back with more stories about the music, the food, women, and feasts. He muses on the many Creole Parades he has attended—the dancing, the rhythms, the music—and delineates for us in rich detail the wonderfully different pulses of New Orleans where brass bands take to the streets at every funeral, and funerals become popular feasts of dance, music, and umbrellas. "It's the Second Line kind of thing, you know what I'm saying?" Standing up, he moves his long arms and hands as if he were gently digging an imaginary hole in front of him: "That's the rhythm. And man, once it starts, you're in it." He starts to move his feet slowly, closes his eyes and, looking up to the sky, draws a smile of nostalgia. "Forget everything else because now you're part of the rhythm. You're part of the crowd."

The multiplicity that pervades Juno's performances and storytelling permeates the Village's public spaces and interactions. Juno both feeds from and decisively contributes to the vitality and range of this collective material. His small shop helps solidify Leimert's practices of expanded community. It contains objects from Saudi Arabia, Morocco, Senegal, Ghana, Benin, and Nigeria. Patrons listen patiently to Juno talking about the artifacts while he works on his drums or his latest musical passion, trumpets. The people who gather in the small shop to listen to him revere his experiences with John Coltrane, Miles Davis, and other famous jazz musicians of the 1950s and 1960s. Juno satisfies part of their curiosity with his first-hand knowledge of celebrated musicians' idiosyncrasies. He directs his storytelling, however, to what he considers more important issues. As he describes Coltrane's mannerisms, dedicated practice sessions (said to have regularly consumed sixteen hours a day), and altruistic spirituality, Juno manages to make statements about the need to preserve and encourage not only jazz but Black art in general. Music, visual art, and poetry have healing powers, he claims: they bring out the best in every individual and unite different people through shared appreciation. Juno emphasizes Coltrane's interests in Eastern religions and music: "Trane had that thing with Eastern scales—you can hear it all the time, especially with the soprano saxophone. I think Miles Davis was the one who gave Trane his first soprano, just before they split. . . . And then in the end Trane was seriously into Hinduism, you know what I'm saying? So all that shows in his music. How many people around the world *heard* what he was saying? A lot, black, white, yellow, blue. . . . So that was Trane. He was like that."

The message Juno delivers establishes that the production, appreciation, and enjoyment of meaningful art ideally requires a higher level of personal and spiritual existence. It requires tolerance, open-mindedness, historical awareness, and goodwill. World Stage founder and drum virtuoso Billy Higgins exemplifies this fusion of technical, personal, and spiritual achievement for Juno.[29] "He wasn't born like that, you know. Billy's worked a lot on all his stuff. You can feel him when he speaks, you feel him when he listens to you. Coltrane was kind of an angel—everybody who met him felt the same—and Billy's got that type of vibe. He's nice to everybody, works a lot with the kids; he even gave one of his drum sets—the one that was at the Stage, remember?—to a young kid, and man, his playing is so fresh, so meaningful." Juno sees Higgins as a spiritual reservoir, a great musician, of course, but most of all, a source of inspiration for life.

As Juno weaves into his stories references from Africa, India, New Orleans, Los Angeles, from the past and the present, he emphasizes the foundations of the expanded community. He considers Black art, especially Afrological music, as having the capacity to connect different peoples and parts of the world through shared appreciation of rhythms, colors, words, harmonies, and emotions. His own personal contacts with artistic icons, coupled with a cultivated knowledge about Black experiences in various parts of the United States, render his anecdotes a repository of values. These values carry a utopian model of public interactions that demand a special type of sensibility, nurtured in and through art.

Although the political aspects of this utopia may not seem evident, they can be grasped most fully in the very fact that the imagined community to which Juno alludes challenges accepted ideals, beliefs, and practices about national borders, racial identity, and cultural purity. Black art is not for Blacks only, Juno often says, adding that there is no room for racism in any artistic expression. The utopian public sphere created by Juno, Daaood, and Higgins, to name only a few of Leimert's central public and artistic figures, challenges hegemonic forms of classification and knowledge, but also deeply ingrained beliefs held by some African Americans about the irreducible character of the Black experience. Juno values, preserves, and transmits the accomplishments of Blacks from various coordinates of time and space, but he also posits hope for a better future to be built from the capacity—indeed, the responsibility—Blacks have to utilize their knowledge, art, and sensibilities to accomplish social and personal betterment. By de-essentializing and, at the same time, cherishing blackness and African diasporic cultures and histories, the utopia that Juno so eloquently (albeit seldom explicitly) narrates and embodies helps define Leimert's public sphere.

This utopia depends upon telling and listening. Juno and other musicians, poets, and artists draw respect, admiration, and emulation from others, indicating the special communicative dimension of this community. Through artistic expression, storytelling, and active listening, Leimert's public sphere enacts a metacommunicative system to build a community of shared sentiment. This includes explicit commentaries about social injustices but proceeds more often through allusions to yearning, mourning, pleasure, joy, and hope, which constitute the community.

Fleeting though it may be, the character of this community of sentiment becomes activated in performances by competent artists and storytellers. It also emerges during the jam sessions at the World Stage, and in the midst of conversations between people in the streets, cafés, mosques, and restaurants. Emotions conveyed through various kinds of social performances cement a shared vision of an alternative future, of communion and comprehension exercised through a learned disposition for openness.

The ephemeral nature of storytelling, music, art, emotions, and openness makes this part of the Village's codes fragile and easily obscured by other, more visible stances. The disposition for openness (in general) co-exists uneasily and often in direct contradiction with intolerance toward difference associated with what is considered gang culture, but also differences attributed to non-Blacks. Employing concepts and predispositions that readily resonate with stereotypes about social outcasts held by Blacks and the wider society, the community becomes susceptible to class prejudice, gender blindness, and racial essentialism.

Racial essentialism here means the tendency among some of Leimert's regulars to associate relevant and aesthetically pleasing cultural production with (and only with) a specific blackness. Because the notion of an exclusive community mingled with Black essentialism is mostly defended by patriarchal (mostly male) persons who see themselves removed from the disadvantaged social segments of South Central, it generates aversion to women as well as to poorer (especially younger) Blacks, and of course non-Black racial groups. The cultivation of connections with Africa through interest in history, travels, and art, and the cosmopolitanism that is associated with Islam—these very same elements that are central to the ethic of openness so vivid in the lives and works of Leimert's public individuals—ironically become instruments through which (what is considered) the true, irreducible essence of blackness is to be found, cherished, and elevated above all else.

These essentialist tendencies often manifest themselves openly in public and confrontational ways. Members of the Nation of Islam organize Saturday rallies in the triangular green area at 42nd Place, Crenshaw Boulevard, and Leimert Boulevard, a location at the very geographical center of the Village. One speaker at a rally attended by about one hundred men wearing business suits and women in partial veils exhorted the audience to take personal responsibility, to support and, if possible, start a Black business, and make donations to poor African countries. The speaker charged that Whites in the United States conspire to oppress Blacks and make them break their ties with their original motherland. The speaker concluded that Whites—especially Jews—were responsible for Blacks' wretchedness and self-hatred, that only by dissociating themselves from the wider society and surpassing the "White man" would Blacks overcome their state of imposed inferiority.[30] Applause and cheers followed. I recognized several people in that audience from the Shabazz restaurant and from jazz presentations at both the World Stage and Fifth Street Dick's.

By being direct and confrontational, the exclusivist attitude demands that its supporters appreciate Black art, history, and sociability while at the same time reject all that falls outside of the ensuing Afrocentric universe. It is a stance that searches and reaches out at first, but then raises walls around the newly found treasures to safeguard their purity. As the followers of the Nation of Islam made clear at the rally, they believe that the economic and cultural survival of Black Americans requires them to define unmistakable boundaries and to purge from those boundaries all that is considered not worthy. While this stance provides clear sense of purpose and pride for Blacks, many of whom are not necessarily members of the Nation, it nevertheless operates on—indeed, it amplifies—historical chasms both within the inner city and between the inner city and the wider society. Black exclusionary stances reaffirm the status quo of separatism based on race, gender, class, age, place of residence, education, and so forth. The solidarity that flows from these exclusivist stances does not entail a willingness to engage in the appreciation—or even consideration—of difference. It is a solidarity marked by strict rules of belonging. In spite of the cosmopolitan components within Islam, this leads to a monologic rather than dialogic existence, to a closed and exclusionary ideology.

The form and content of the ethic of openness, on the other hand, suggest new possibilities. In contrast to the exclusive posture, which seeks difference (i.e., Eastern and African cultural traits) to affirm sameness and cohesiveness, the dialogical stance is characterized by a permanent state of restlessness.[31] Through evocation, storytelling, empathy, and emotions, through media that are almost ethereal compared to the in-your-face exclusivist approach, those espousing the (meta)communicative ethic express their discontent against rigid, stereotyped forms of classification. They affirm that the Black young and poor are not threatening, that non-Blacks need not be despised, feared, or pitied, that cultural diversity is to be prized, and that past and present sufferings can be motives for more than anger. Indeed, the past for them serves as a repository of accumulated knowledge from which insights regarding mutual understanding can be drawn. The ethic informed by these postures, based on claims for the universality of human understanding, is essentially plastic. Thus, nothing could be more appropriate than plastic, malleable forms of expression— forms that are constantly searching, experimenting, questioning—to express, precisely, such plastic ethic.

The tension between exclusivity and openness in Leimert manifests itself in contradictions, rather than in discrete, atomized, opposing camps. In everyday life, most of Leimert's regulars stand somewhere between the postures expressed by Juno, Billy Higgins, and Daaood, on the one hand, and by those emphasized by more radical followers of the Nation of Islam, on the other.

Both stances, however, emphasize Black agency. Both visions assert a crucial need for Black people to determine the form and content of the lives we desire. Historical forms of oppression have systematically rendered Black people *objects* of control, surveillance, and critique. In sharp contrast, the projects that can be observed in Leimert Park radically affirm Blacks as *agents* of our own destiny.

Leimert Park's residents and regulars often mobilize around issues that impinge on their community.[32] One of the first local meetings held to discuss allegations that the federal government participated in the trafficking of crack cocaine in South Central took place in Leimert's Vision Theatre. The influence of Islam in Leimert reflects this collective spirit of self-activity. Most Muslims and sympathizers of Islam in Los Angeles had to *become* believers or sympathizers, after being raised in another religion. They had to make a *choice*. It is rare for Black Angelenos (as I suspect for U.S. Blacks in general) to be born in non-Christian families. Appreciation of Black artistic forms, the cultivation of racial pride, and interest in Black history are all acquired perspectives that demand *action* from individuals. As tense as Leimert's public places, norms, and utopias can be, they nevertheless seem to be invariably rooted in this assertion of Black agency and the active work of individual and collective change.

℀

The musicians who participate in jam sessions at the World Stage are in a process of musical growth and change. Hardly beginners, they have mastered the mechanics of their instruments, know chord changes and melodies of at least half a dozen jazz standards, and command the basics of improvisation. Those who lack familiarity with their instruments stand out as exceptions. Unless they improve their playing substantially and demonstrate progress as time goes by, they will be ostracized and not likely to come back. Some who take part in the Stage's sessions have no intention of performing professionally, not even part-time, but they are exceptions. If a player has aspirations to earn money by performing with other musicians, however, the jam sessions constitute a substantial site for learning, developing, and establishing social connections, all of which are essential for success.

Musicians describe this process as "paying dues," a phrase also utilized in situations outside of music. Just as most of the amateur musicians feel frustrated about not being able to play more often, frustrations with jobs, relationships, families, communities, and the wider society require struggle and learning. "Paying dues," in this sense, suggests awareness of the inevitability of individual and collective predicaments marked by adversity. Many of the jam-session regulars have had, or are still struggling with, alcohol and drug dependency. Unemployment and financial difficulties pose problems constantly. Failed relationships, illnesses, and brushes with law enforcement can have calamitous consequences. These shared conditions permeate conversations at the Stage, but they also emerge in the music. Sensitive renditions of standard jazz tunes can evoke these shared experiences of hardship. Soul, in these instances, expresses what the musician has endured. They convey to the audience the sense that the player shares with them a large range of emotions grounded in Blacks' collective social life. In the context of the jam sessions, soul and paying dues, although not the same, can refer to a set of common experiences and sentiments and are thus sometimes used interchangeably.

Paying dues and soul, however, evoke more than just hardship and joy expressed through particular styles and aesthetics. Soulful renditions of tunes and paying dues also communicate a sense of resiliency and transformation. They demonstrate that the musician, in spite of the technical difficulties related to the music, and in spite of his or her condition as part of a racialized group that has been historically discriminated against, is still able to make a statement and thus persevere. Indeed, it is the trying, the very searching for music expressing group and individual conditions that constitutes the most appreciated element of the jam session for the musicians themselves and for their active listeners. When moved by the sounds they hear, people in the audience talk back to musical phrases, call for dynamics, incite riskier approaches, and applaud the musicians' efforts. Soul, in this case, constitutes sensitive and recognizable effort. It has more to do with how much energy one puts into a performance than with how aesthetically pleasing the result of this effort may actually be, although of course aesthetics and style also loom large. "I feel you, brother," or "I feel you, sister," in the context of improvising thus relates to a shared set of sentiments and styles that links listeners with the musician's efforts.

At the World Stage most musicians strive to find their sound, master scales, memorize chord progressions, comprehend improvisation theories, improve their timing, understand jazz conventions, and become better performers. Yet the idea that what counts the most is the emotional and technical *effort* one puts into music still serves as a powerful incentive to carry on, to find and express pleasure, and to develop one's abilities and overcome musical, personal, and social difficulties.

Paying dues, therefore, involves more than the necessary and arduous learning process that musicianship requires—the so-called wood-shedding. For those participating in the Stage's jam sessions, paying dues also implies being aware of, discussing, and attempting to convey musically constraints and possibilities that are lived by African Americans. The musical and social lives of Leimert can be comprehended as commentaries on each other, and in this way illuminate further aspects of the worldviews of Village regulars.

❧

Intolerance toward race, gender, class, and age differences, as well as marked suspicion toward those who lived in areas considered degraded were some of the most readily observable traits of Leimert's social life. Non-Blacks and poor Blacks were viewed as having personal essences that, in principle, placed them in different and distant worlds across which communication and understanding were, if not impossible, at least very difficult. A social environment conspicuously devoid of significant numbers of women, the Village is also indisputably male-centric and by default patriarchal in how men relate to each other and to women.

While this intolerance is more directly connected to the exclusivist stance, of which a version of Afrocentricity analyzed above plays a central role, it is also manifested in the plastic and apparently more accepting perspective based on the ethic of openness. Both the exclusivist stance and the ethic of openness draw on the politics of respectability that strives to define virtuous blackness. Boundaries of blackness, to use a term developed by Cathy Cohen, thus become the object of such politics of respectability.[33] Seemingly more fluid and permeable according to the ethic of openness, and correspondingly rigid and confrontational in the modes put forward by the exclusivist stance, the resulting boundaries of blackness, however, end up doing the same cultural work: delimiting, enclosing, and guarding more or less stable notions of what blackness is and should be. Whether through confrontational utterances that exclude Whites, women, the poor, and the deemed amoral, or whether via artistic performance that engages audiences and invites participation, excluding boundaries of blackness are consolidated inasmuch as they rely on the valuing of specific social class, urban space, gender, sexuality, and age as respectable and necessary indexes for blackness. Confirming the impressions that disadvantaged Black women living in the most marginalized areas of South Central made abundantly clear, the dominant and shared perspectives among those living or socializing in Leimert Park expressed a clear dividing line.[34] On one side of the line stood the considered respectable middle- or working-class males and their community; on the other side of the line stood those who needed to be policed and whose version of blackness had to be silenced.

Thus in most cases those individuals deemed to be on the outside of "acceptable blackness"—because of their addiction, their sexual identification, their gender, their poor financial status, or their relationship to the state—are often left with two choices: either finds ways to conform to "community standards" of membership or be left on the margins where individual families and friends are expected to take care of their needs. In this case, the shared primary identification of group members, while still active, is mitigated by other identities such as underclass, homosexual, drug addict, or single mother. Further, these intersecting identities are used as signals, imparting judgments about the indigenous worth or authenticity of certain group members. Targeted members of oppressed communities are thus confronted with a *secondary process of marginalization,* this time imposed by members of their own group.[35]

Such intolerance, however, did not occur unchecked. In Leimert Park solidarity emerges from a generalized openness, storytelling, music, visual arts, and a variety of discourses based on a clear sense of belonging to streams of history that both include and extrapolate the confines of the here and now and of one's immediate social networks. This solidarity is actualized in the daily diversity of ethnic, racial, and social backgrounds of those who participate in the jam sessions, and those who can be seen in the streets, mosques, bookstores, the small shops, and restaurants. As it emphasizes histories, agencies, and the various corresponding communities, this solidarity, and the ethic of openness that accompanies it, provide the antithesis to various forms of exclusion and essentialism.

While mostly based on the theorization and practice of Black men belonging to specific economic and cultural cliques—artists, entrepreneurs, professionals—the ethic of openness is nevertheless constantly subjected to self-scrutiny, reformulation, and transformation. The processual nature of the ethic of openness, as it operates via storytelling, poetry, and music, makes it appropriate for the expression of vulnerability. This vulnerability projects the ethic of openness as an enabling conduit through which its problematic reliance on notions of patriarchal middle-class blackness—which excludes from its radius women, the poor, the non-Black, gays and lesbians—can be challenged and overcome. By opposing the certainties and resulting exclusions deriving from patriarchal values, the ethic of openness embraces change, self-reflection, and dialogue.

I stress Leimert's more progressive outlooks because they embody political potentials that are also present in other Black social settings—CAPA and CSGT being cases in point. What takes place in Leimert, thus, offers useful insights into both the present predicament of the inner city and some of its possible futures. Rather than constituting some kind of relief to the hardships of everyday life in the inner city, the jazz and the sociabilities around the jam sessions present us with understandings of our past, present, and, most important, of an undetermined future. Such indeterminacy, open-endedness, and will to engage in dialogue—all grounded in desires for social change and justice—provide a blueprint for social transformation that refuses to accept the already given, the easy solutions. As part of a Black creative tradition that is still in the process of becoming—or, as Graham Lock would put it, "a dance between the moment and the stars"[36]—Leimert's progressive stance points to a utopia whose contours are in permanent negotiation.

BLACKNESS AS SELF-HELP
AND SOCIAL CRITIQUE

*The Community in Support of
the Gang Truce*

The gang truce established in Watts between major factions of the Crips
and Bloods in March of 1992 sought to quell the escalating violence
between young Blacks and mobilize them around specific claims for social
justice. It attempted to offer political explanations for inner-city youth
unemployment, police brutality, and the suspicious availability of crack
cocaine and heavy weaponry in South Central.[1] The truce encouraged
discussion and implementation of community-based programs offering
alternatives to the law-and-order and business-oriented solutions proposed by the city administration and endorsed by a considerable number
of Blacks.

The gang truce incorporates different—and sometimes competing—
notions of blackness into its activities, goals, and ideas. Most of the organizers of the truce previously participated in former football star Jim
Brown's "Amer-I-Can program" as either instructors or students. Brown's
efforts aim at enabling inner-city youths to participate and succeed in the
American mainstream. They give little, if any, attention to political education or historical awareness, attributing poverty to lack of skills and
poor planning by individuals. CSGT incorporated Amer-I-Can teaching
guides into its activities in order to help build self-esteem and teach life-
management skills to young people. At the same time, CSGT had veterans
of the Black Panther Party provide intensive political education from a different perspective. These activists stressed development of a consciousness

and practice grounded in membership in oppressed communities—locally, nationally, and internationally.

Instead of considering the coexistence of self-help and social critique as only a sign of ideological inconsistency, I understand it as an indication of the conflicting forces that define the social condition of young disadvantaged Blacks. Their hedonistic wishes for consumption and their desires for incorporation into the wider society coexist uneasily with their sense of systematic exclusion from that same wider society. This paradox permeates the lives of millions of inner-city youths "whose social locations have allowed them to demystify aspects of the hegemonic ideology while reinforcing their ties to it."[2] In the case of current or ex-gangsters, however, such contradictions can become extreme. They feel pulled toward opposite poles—toward changing this society *and* succeeding within it, rising with their communities *and* escaping from them, ending the hurts they experience *and* hurting others.

Trying to enforce the gang truce imposes difficulties of its own. CSGT organizers face nearly insurmountable barriers as prospects for long-term employment decrease while the lure of drug money increases. They endure the daily uncertainties of gang wars, the consequences of the official war on drugs, and the no-less-intense campaigns waged by better-off Blacks against the "bad elements" in the ghetto. To make matters more complicated, Latina/o gangs are now an important presence in Los Angeles generally and in South Central specifically. While CSGT explicitly seeks to incorporate Latina/os in the peace process there remains plenty of misinformation and resentment between Blacks and Browns. Community activists have worked hard to situate interracial conflict in historical and political perspective, but the process of bridging differences and building a common political platform has just begun.

Although gangs have existed in Los Angeles since at least the 1940s, the contemporary multitude of smaller sets that identify with either Crips or Bloods have their origins in the early 1970s. Prior to that point, Los Angeles had a large number of street organizations that functioned more like social clubs and mutual aid societies than like gangs. Despite the large number of such street organizations—Avenues, Slausons, Businessmen, Ace Deuces, Bishops, Roman 20s, Pirus, Brims, Swans, Gladiators, Rabble Rousers, and others—between 1965 and 1969 relations among them remained peaceful. The small amount of criminal activity connected with these groups primarily revolved around occasional muggings of rich Whites and instances of petty theft. Disputes between groups could be resolved quickly by fistfights. Weapons of any kind seldom appeared.[3]

During the 1965 Watts rebellion and the emergence and expansion of Black Power social movements in its wake, many formerly rival gangsters decided to join forces against the much-hated LAPD and the National Guard to attempt to reclaim the streets. Between 1965 and 1968, public teen posts sprouted in South Central. Sporting and artistic activities assisted by teachers, coaches, and counselors attracted and kept occupied many of the youths who would otherwise be tempted to join a gang. Most of the participants in the teen posts came from poor backgrounds, many from broken families. The posts provided youngsters with social ties and support that frequently could not be obtained from their parents and kin. Ending funding for these posts helped promote the rise of gangs.

The closing of the teen centers, the slaying of a member of the Brims by Crips around 1971, and the demise of Black political organizations like the Black Panthers combined to usher in a new era of violence in the inner city. By the early 1970s the Panthers enjoyed wide popularity among inner-city residents in general, but especially among young men and women in high school. Recruits from gangs constituted a considerable part of the Panthers' rank-and-file, including two of the most active leaders of the Los Angeles chapter—Alprentice "Bunchy" Carter and Jon Huggins. Both were murdered on the UCLA campus by United Slaves' members in 1969. Brother Crook (a/k/a Ron Wilkins), a member of one of South Central's notorious gangs, organized the Community Alert Patrol to oversee police abuse.[4]

Several current and ex-gang members interpret the word "Crip" as an acronym for an organization with clear political views. Big Phil, for example, who in 1971 joined the Four-Tre Gangsters Crips of 43rd Street and Western Avenue, believes that Crip stands for "Community Revolution in Progress." "I heard that it was started to stop gang violence, and it turned into gang violence, and that's where the word Crip came from."[5] Twilight Bey, an ex–Pirus Blood gangster, thinks that "CRIP stands for Community Revolutionary Inter-Party Service. This is a revolutionary organization for the grassroots people. The Crips' and the Pirus' jobs were to protect their neighborhoods, feed the kids, take care of the elders in their community. PIRUS stands for Powerful Intellectual Radical Unit of Soldiers.

This is where the mind-set of the homiez was at, back when the gangs first started."[6]

In spite of disagreements about the meanings of their gangs' names, all the O.G.s confirm that the Panthers and other Black Power–inspired social movements and ideologies were central to gangs in the 1970s.[7] They provided young gang members not old enough to join the Panthers a political view of life that shifted their attention to the power structures of the wider society rather than emphasizing the need to combat other Black organizations as the gangs had. When the Watts rebellions erupted, former rival gangsters smiled at each other and exchanged signals of triumph as they broke through police lines.[8]

Jimel Barnes, who calls himself one of the Godfathers of the Crips, dismisses all of these interpretations. According to Barnes, "Crip" was not an acronym at all. He dates the genesis of the Crips to the time when "Raymond Washington came to me and made me walk up Avalon Boulevard to Avalon Gardens from his house and said 'Jimel, I'm going to create a gang called the Crips,' that was the two Godfathers. That was the beginning of the Crips." Barnes explains the gang's name as a variant of "crib," noting "When he [Washington] came over to me, he pulled out a picture of a baby's crib; he said, 'This is what I'm going to call our gang, Crips—like Cribs. It's from the cradle to the grave, C-RIP, may you rest in peace. Chitty chitty bang bang, nothing but a Crip thang, Eastside Cuz. This is going to be the most notorious gang in the world. It's going to go from generation to generation.'"[9]

In Barnes's account, the gang attracted young men who were looking for fights against established gangs and who wanted to wear leather coats and were willing to rob for them. "We had a macho thing going on," he explains, referring to the group's penchant for bullying the police and moving people out of the way as they walked through South Central's neighborhoods. Barnes, Washington, and later the person known as Tookie Williams, who came in after Washington's death, developed reputations for their gladiator-like bodies, sculpted by daily weightlifting. "Women would just go crazy over seeing our bodies. I believe that's what really glamorized it and glorified it," he remembers. Barnes credits himself for the positive concepts of the gang: "I felt we could unite the youngsters and get all the brothers to come together and get more into a positive Black situation. I wanted to get the youngsters involved in sports: football, boxing, things like that" (152–53).

Barnes does not speak for himself alone. I have heard similar impressions of the origins and present role of gangs from many sources. He does not mention any social movement, let alone the Panthers, as important inspirations for the Crips. Awareness of or interest in engaging in organized social movements were absent from his worldview and actual lived experiences with his Crip set.

For young residents of the inner city like Kody, gang life seemed far removed from social movement mobilization. Like so many young Blacks I met in South Central, he could not link the fate of his set with that of larger social groups in similar conditions. He had not heard of the truce, did not care to learn about community political organizations, and conceived of his homies in kinship terms—a notion held by almost every gang member with whom I have talked. Consequently, Kody considered himself and his friends under siege by other such groups and by the "Whiteman." Although he experienced the "Whiteman" through law enforcement, owners, and employers, all that really mattered to him were his closest friends and family.

Twilight Bey's interpretation of the meaning of "Pirus"—the Blood set in which he made his reputation as a gangbanger—is illustrative of his present-day concern with political issues relative to the inner city.[10] Against Twilight's historical interpretation that "everybody [in the early 1970s] was in a revolutionary mind-set" (329), including his Piru set, however, is the fact that the Pirus, from the start, were subdivided into several smaller sets in Watts and in Compton: the Bounty Hunters, the Avalon Park Boys, the BSVs, to name a few. Adding to the confusion, some O.G.s claim that all Pirus used to be Crips—the Compton Piru Crips (183).[11]

The contested histories of the gangs reveal profound past and present disagreements concerning the nature and practices of gangs. The difficulties the supporters of the truce have in maintaining and expanding the peace among gangsters is well illustrated by the contrasts in the sets' reconstructed histories.

Despite the controversies, all gangsters agree on one point. Gangs are, above all, about bonding—they are about affective and material support not usually found in the families of young men and women residing in the inner city. Q-Bone, a Crip O.G., said about his experience in the set: "As I started getting deeper into it, it meant family. It was people who I could share my problems with outside the home. As the musical recording by

the singer Cherelle says, 'Giving you something that you're missing home'"
(299). Ice-T summarized various similar statements I registered among
gangsters when he told an interviewer:

> What gang-banging really is, is male love pushed to its limits. It's like
> surrogate families and brothers bonding together to the death, because it's
> not all about selling drugs or all about banging, it's about kickin' it with the
> homiez and backing the homiez. It's love. As insane as it may seem, it's all
> based on love. I'm trying to bring it full circle, understanding that it's mad-
> ness, mayhem, and wrong, but there's a lot of honor that goes on in this and
> there's a lot of qualities that these young brothers that you may look down
> on have that you ain't got. . . . It's just the wrong direction and the confu-
> sion in the world that they live in that causes them to strike out at each
> other. To the layman it will look like it's a world based on hate, but it's not,
> it's based on love. It's a love for the hood. Every time you write the name of
> your hood across you back, or all your dead homiez all over your body, that's
> some serious shit. (22, 23)

It is such deep affective bonds that constitute the groundwork for the truce.
While a necessary element in allowing for communication, affection is not
sufficient to maintain and expand the peace.

The strong connection between gangs and the drug market presents
a considerable obstacle to the truce. Around 1982 or 1983, gangsters began
to sell crack cocaine in unprecedented quantities. "Prior to that," Leibo
remembers, "all the brothers that were slangin' were selling 'water,' 'Sher-
man,' angel dust, PCP, or whatever you want to call it." Due to its relatively
low price and highly addictive properties, commerce in crack generated
greater and quicker profits than any other drug. Part of the enormous
amount of cash generated with crack was soon converted into sophisticated firearms. "Around '86, '87, it was on. You name it, you could get it.
You didn't hear much about 9-millimeters, M16s, M14s, and AKs unless
you were hooked up and was high on the echelon, but after 1986 they
were available to anybody" (183). As disputes between sets became increasingly determined by economic motives, as controlling and expanding
territories became increasingly equated with profit, as turf contentions
became increasingly militarized, as violence between gangs became the
pattern in the drug market, peace became increasingly associated with the

prospect of losing very profitable businesses.[12] Not surprisingly, between 1984 and 1985, arguably when the drug trade was about to reach its zenith, almost 70 percent of all registered gang-related homicides were also related to drugs.[13]

The violence of the drug trade has become *modus vivendi* for gangsters. By 1996, estimates suggested that gang-related killings accounted for more than 40 percent of the slayings in the city of Los Angeles. South Central's police stations registered over 150 gang-related homicides between 1990 and 1994, far exceeding comparable data in other areas of the city. Fewer than 50 percent of those murders have been "solved" by the criminal justice system. Research conducted by the *Los Angeles Times* indicated that "other things being equal, gang murders were less likely to be solved by police than other murders and cases were more likely to fall apart before trial."[14] While police officials blame the low rate of convictions on gang pressure on witnesses, the victims' families perceive the justice system's failures to solve murders as yet another facet of institutionalized disregard for African Americans.[15]

Many Blacks, but especially those who are older working-class and middle-class, support drastic antigang measures.[16] Their knowledge of police abuse recedes into the background when they focus on gangsters. Jim Cleaver, a constant presence in the *Los Angeles Sentinel*'s opinion columns, speaks for a large proportion of better-off Blacks when he describes gang members.

> We cannot blame white America for this.
>
> Neither can we blame anyone else for the standards we have set for our children. We have expected very little from them and that is exactly what we have gotten. . . .
>
> These gangsters are a gigantic pain in the butt. They are dangerous and injurious to the health of the community. But they are no accidents. They happened because we did not do our jobs and then wanted to blame someone else.
>
> The only way this can change is by our reaching back into the community and taking charge. It will not be easy and someone may die. But this is our community and if the KKK came in here and did to us what we have allowed our children to do, we would have been up in arms a long time ago.[17]

The editors of the Black-owned *Sentinel* were "delighted" with the early 1997 state Supreme Court decision to uphold the tactics sanctioned by San Jose's antigang law, including rounding up, imprisoning, and banning gang members from a neighborhood by means of "intensive police actions."[18] An editorial in the paper reported that the improvement of everyday life in the area was so dramatic that, for those who were given back their communities, "the theoretical debate about the civil rights of gang members is irrelevant."[19] Yet research demonstrates that rather than pacifying neighborhoods characterized by gangs and drugs, police operations targeting the inner cities and barrios of Los Angeles have intensified the violence. The drug war, ironically, began at precisely the same time when violence among Black gang members was diminishing. As Jerome Miller affirms, the rate of African American male victims of homicide dropped from 70.1 in 1972 to 40.9 in 1983.[20] By 1991, however, when the war on drugs and several other operations in the inner city were gaining support and intensifying their scope, homicide rates among young Black men surpassed the 1934 record of 74.2. "The trends suggested," concluded Miller, "that aggressive war on drugs in the inner cities was not making the communities safer."[21]

Moreover, awareness of being systematically denied justice by those persons and institutions supposed to embody justice is widespread among gangsters and constitutes a considerable obstacle for the cessation of hostilities. Distrust in law enforcement, in the context of gang rivalries, only bolsters the need to bring about justice in the only way known to be effective: by one's own hands.

The truce has benefited, however, from unlikely sources. As large-scale law enforcement operations against suspected gang members intensify, sets and gangs initially skeptical about the truce begin to reconsider their position. One of the major grassroots products of the gang truce, CSGT, shares a building, programs, and is supported by the Coalition Against Police Abuse. This fusion of initially diverse social movements speaks of the strong connections that can be established between the organized efforts to render law enforcement accountable and the attempts to unite gangs.

Photographs of the Million Man March in Washington, D.C., on October 16, 1995, show former enemy gang members from Los Angeles shaking hands and pledging to continue and expand the Watts truce formalized in 1992. The pictures appear in CAPA's permanent exhibition, arranged on panels in the main room of its building, and are obvious counterpoints to the depictions of police racist brutality that occupy nearby space. In the Washington scenes, instead of the horrors of brutality and death, one sees joyful faces and reads colorful banners with words of hope and union. Gang hand signs are displayed, but there are no threats accompanying them. At the office, one not familiar with the meanings of the photographs may hear from a member of CSGT the explanation that one of the key events that made possible the Million Man March was the establishment of the gang truce. There would not have been so many people listening to Louis Farrakhan and other Black public figures were it not for the cessation of hostilities between gangs that started in Los Angeles. The Nation of Islam's "Day of Atonement" was thus also an occasion for gang members of all parts of the country to come together and celebrate the peace efforts. As Twilight Bey, a formerly active gang member and one of CSGT's main spokespersons, stated in a live CNN interview as the march was taking place, the event was an acknowledgment of Blacks' collective claim of agency over their destiny. In the interview—a videotaped version of which is often shown at the office—Twilight also emphasized the idea that Black-on-Black violence was no longer a viable option to settle differences. He and ex-gang members were to take active responsibility toward their families and their communities "to bring about change."[22]

Most O.G.s underline that the current ceasefire between gangs established in March 1992 was preceded by several years of difficult meetings and negotiations. Since at least 1988, a truce had been the object of discussion between the gangs that were based in each of the four main housing projects in Watts: Nickerson Gardens, Jordan Downs, Imperial Courts, and Hacienda Village.[23] In Jordan Downs, for example, deaths among Crips in the same housing project were becoming ever more frequent. Generalized mistrust encouraged older members of the gangs to call meetings to discuss the situation. In this atmosphere, the idea of the ceasefire emerged, first within the Crips of Jordan Downs, and then between the various gangs of Watts. In order to "stop the killings and the drive-bys and all of the negative things that affect our community daily," Crips from the Grape Street Watts gang, mostly residents of Jordan Downs, began to hold meetings with the Crips in Imperial Courts. These groups had a long bloody history of vendettas. Don "Playmate" Gordon, a Grape Street Crip

O.G., recounted that the Crips in Imperial Courts "were the brothers who shot me three times with an AK-47 live. . . . [T]hey left thirty-two bullet holes in my car, and three in me" (91, 94).

Once the beginnings of an accord were set, both Crip groups sought to start a dialogue with the Bloods of the Nickerson Gardens housing projects. The next step was to go over to Hacienda Village, dominated by Pirus Bloods, where a similar agreement was approved. Playmate described the general willingness to support the ceasefire:

> We formed the peace treaty because we said, "We can't just sit back and live like this, we have to start doing something." We started realizing that this is a cage. I've been here [Jordan Downs housing project] all my life, since 1966, and basically nothing has changed. *Nothing.* We still have to bathe in bathtubs because we don't have showers in these projects. So we started addressing these issues, like how the police used to ride through and basically do whatever they wanted. They tell us not to break the law, but they break the law every day. Who knew that the police—I didn't even know that the police weren't supposed to stick their hands in my pocket. . . . So when we started focusing on how we're living, and how we're teaching our kids, that's when we got together, as individuals, it wasn't everybody at once. We got together as individuals and started communicating. (91, 92)

Debates and meetings revealed that most people living in the projects were concerned with the same set of issues: poor infrastructure, police abuse, and the endless gang-related killings.

Younger gang members—those between twelve and sixteen—are the most visible face of gangs. They are the ones who occupy the streets, look out for their groups, and make drug runs. They are the gang members most prone to violence, gunplay, and drive-bys. These youngsters did not always understand, respond, or identify with the truce.[24] Yet peace talks implied discussing and eventually overcoming several years of vendettas and deaths. As Playmate explains:

> We had a lot of problems because some brothers weren't in it. We had people that killed other people's cousins, homeboys, and brothers. There was a lot of animosity in bringing about this peace, because everybody wasn't down with it. It was like "It has been like this, let it stay like this."

We weren't going for that. So slowly, but surely, we started having our meetings, and we started having our ciphers. We learned about a cipher, and how
you say the prayer, and we'd sit back and talk and start communicating with
each other. We had to bond first, because we were so broken apart. So a few
brothers bonded back together, and we started bringing about a change. (92)

As the meetings began to attract more enthusiasts, it became agreed
upon that a document formalizing the armistice was necessary. A public
document would symbolize the gangsters' willingness to make the ceasefire
an official resolution, to which other gangsters could eventually subscribe
and refer. Daude Sherrills, twenty-four years old in 1992 and a lifelong
resident of the Jordan Downs housing project, took the initiative along with
Anthony Perry (a/k/a Brother Tony X), who at that time was thirty and a
former gang member, to write the truce document. Sherrills wrote the first
draft, and Perry gave the peace accord text its final form. Perry came up
with the idea to base the truce on the 1949 ceasefire agreement between
Egypt and Israel endorsed by the United Nations. He translated the pom-
pous diplomatic language of the 1949 document into terms intelligible to
the street gangs of South Central. Perry later wrote his own book about
the elaboration of the truce. He explained that the military style of the
truce was necessary given the dominant mentality among gang members.
"It appears as though America's youth have been conditioned to accept and
display war-like behavior. The desire to kill is bred wrongly right into their
little minds during their pre-childhood development years. . . . [T]o them
life has become a joke. Life is no longer respected."[25]

The truce document, entitled "Multi-Peace Treaty—General Armistice
Agreement," contains four articles and two annexes. Articles I, II, and
IV determined the end of violence between the signing parties, establishing clear rules of nonaggression. The Nation of Islam's security force, the
Fruit of Islam (FOI), agreed to serve as a peace enforcer, and up to this
day, suit-and-bow-tied, well-trained, grave young Muslims are charged
with security responsibilities in events related to the gang truce. Article III
promoted "the return of black business, economic development and ad-
vancement of educational programs." In order to secure free competition
between prospective South Central business establishments, "no favorit-
ism or back-stabbing should be tolerated under the truce." Basic rules of
free-market were the backbone of the truce's economic statement.

Sherrills later added to the truce document an appendix entitled the "United Black Community Code." The code encouraged literacy programs, school attendance, voter registration, investment pools, cultural events, a food bank, and hardship funds created by annual dues of $100 per gang member. This addition intended to clarify the educational guidelines and elaborate on gangsters' responsibilities. The approach is surprisingly uncritical of the educational system. Although several O.G.s mentioned that one of the reasons for their gang affiliation was the lack of educational incentives and overall bad quality of local schools, the armistice document did not demand reforms in those areas.[26] Individuals were encouraged to make the appropriate decisions and educate themselves with the means available.

The appendix also established clear codes of individual conduct. Alcohol and drug use were to be avoided. "Nigger" and "bitch" had to be excluded from one's vocabulary. Hoo-riding—raiding rival turf and displaying gang signs—was also forbidden. The code determined acceptable forms of behavior in minute detail from those supporting the truce. For example: when outside one's own immediate community, gang rags could only be worn three inches out of the rear pants pocket. These details were to be followed as signs of respect. "That's technical language on our level," said Sherrills, commenting in the *Los Angeles Times* on the code of conduct.[27]

On March 27, 1992, representatives of the four housing projects of Watts signed the truce. The armistice negotiations that had been going on since at least the late 1980s were then formalized. The results were almost immediate. The *Los Angeles Times* reported that "gang-related homicides in South Los Angeles have dropped markedly—to two last month, compared with 16 in May, 1991—leading police to give new credit to the truce declared between warring Black gangs, a high ranking police official told the Police Commission on Tuesday." Even international relations experts applauded the effort.[28]

In South Central, while the *Sentinel* closely monitored the truce,[29] various community organizations willing to support and expand the Watts ceasefire were formed, most notably the Community in Support of the Gang Truce (CSGT).[30] Founded in March of 1991—a year before the Watts ceasefire was formalized—CSGT supports the gang truce by "addressing the totality of issues affecting that truce."[31] CSGT is closely linked to CAPA. Both institutions share a building on Western Avenue, on the northern extreme of South Central. Twilight Bey, CSGT's mains spokesperson, works closely with Michael Zinzun, coordinator of CAPA. As is the case for most people working in the building, Twilight and Zinzun are constantly collaborating in each other's projects. In practice, therefore, the lines that separate and define CAPA and CSGT are tenuous, although each organization has its own independent nonprofit legal status.[32] We could consider CSGT the heir to the causes embraced by CAPA and, for that matter, the Black Panthers. CSGT's program suggests much ideological and practical continuity with relation to CAPA's manual of social mobilization.

Yet the reality of the truce is more complex. The younger men and women who regularly participate in CSGT—approximately twenty— while having partial knowledge of the Black Power theses and of the Panthers' history, and indeed embracing similar politics, also hold wishes of participation in the mainstream of the wider society in ways that are far more ambitious than those Panthers ever demonstrated.[33] These wishes of participation have been inflated greatly by the gangster atmosphere of easy money. While not necessarily contradictory with the aims of social justice and community empowerment, they tend to emphasize individual success over social responsibility. Gang members, after all, are also a product of the Reagan years.[34] CSGT consists mostly of young men and women in their late teens and early twenties, and the ideological tensions between the group and CAPA are as much about differences in generational perspectives as they are about politics.

The young members of CSGT do their work in a far more violent and repressive atmosphere than was true for the Black Power groups of the past. These are reflected in CSGT's demands, which include:

Stop the criminalization of our youth!

1. Eliminate the national gang database which currently gives youth a permanent record for simply being detained for *"suspicion of being a gang member,"* even if the youth is later released for lack of evidence. What must happen is changing state legislation to erase the records of any individual unjustly detained or arrested and permanently recorded. This record often prevents them from being employed.

2. Eliminate federal programs such as "Weed and Seed" that target whole

communities as being non-rehabilitatable, subject them to repressive law enforcement programs and place social service monies under the jurisdiction of law enforcement agencies.

3. Eliminate illegal searches and gang sweeps.

4. Stop police abuse and their "Us Against Them" attitude.[35]

These demands stem from an array of law-enforcement measures that are specific to the 1980s. As the organization pleads for an end to the criminalization of inner-city youth, it directly opposes Black middle-class tendencies to support police operations aimed at "gang suspects." The group also addresses problems that have been affecting the inner city since the Reagan years through demands such as:

Community Control of the Police! Provide for a Civilian Police Review Board and an ongoing grassroots campaign against police abuse and killings.

1. The Review Board will judge complaints of unnecessary force, false arrest, harassment, tampering with evidence, abuse of authority, violation of civil rights, illegal surveillance, abusive language, gay bashing, racial or ethnic slurs, etc.

2. The Board will have the power to review and alter police procedures and policies concerning the above areas.

3. The Board will have the power to discipline (ranging from censure to suspension without pay for up to six months) and fire police officers. It will also have the power to recommend criminal prosecutions and to award civil damages up to $50,000.

4. The Board will also have an independent staff of investigators with full subpoena powers, plus immediate and unrestricted access to shooting areas.

5. A special Prosecutor will be elected whose job will be to handle cases of misdemeanor criminal charges against police officers.

6. Any police officer who threatens, harasses or discriminates against another officer of the LAPD who witnesses an act of police abuse and reports it to the Civilian Police Review Board shall be subject to penalties as outlined in the Review Board Initiative.[36]

Demands for a Civilian Police Review Board originated in CAPA's 1991 campaign for police accountability. The incorporation of these demands into CSGT's program accurately illustrates the influence of CAPA on the next generation. Frequent violations of civil rights by law enforcement against "gang suspects" highlight the need for social mobilization demanding police answerability. CAPA's program, as it permeates CSGT's agenda and focuses on the plight of the inner-city youth, thus gains a new vitality while providing the ceasefire movement with organizing knowledge accumulated in thirty years of political activity.[37]

CSGT demands better and more recreational facilities—more parks, arts and sports programs, a "midnight basketball league" for teens supervised by community residents, and more theaters staffed by local residents. It demands better health care, especially for senior citizens, family planning clinics to provide birth control and sex education, free pre- and postnatal care, and abortions. As well, it calls for an end to forced sterilizations. Furthermore, CSGT makes claims for tenants' rights, demanding enforcement of health and safety codes in all residences and public housing, more senior citizens' housing, low-income housing, and to "cease eviction of entire families because of a problem of relatives or a single family member."

Far more critical of the educational system than the original truce document, CSGT demands "our constitutional right to education." It appeals for an end to "racism, sexism and White supremacy in education, in teacher training, in curriculum . . ., and in the classrooms." CSGT also demands access to higher education through stipends, scholarships and academic support for students who are economically disadvantaged.[38]

CSGT subordinates the maintenance and expansion of the ceasefire to the economic improvement of South Central's poorer communities, insisting that "without addressing the conditions in the community which give rise to gangs, any truce will only be temporary."[39] Aware of the lack of economic opportunities for Blacks and Browns subjected to inner-city schools, CSGT's proposals challenge dominant perspectives on the solutions to problems in South Central. The organization's concept of economic development explicitly disavows the "market-driven or corporate-dominated approaches which are often promoted by big business and government."[40]

Initiatives such as Rebuild Los Angeles (RLA) bear the brunt of CSGT's criticism. Launched in May 1992 by then–Mayor Tom Bradley in response to the uprisings of that year, and coordinated by 1984 Olympics organizer Peter Ueberroth, RLA promised jobs and economic revitalization to the city's most devastated communities. RLA believed the corporate sector, rather than government, could produce much-needed jobs in South Central. RLA's role in this scheme was to make inner-city communities "attractive to business" by offering subsidies to firms willing to invest there.[41] In spite of Ueberroth's pledge to bring "good jobs at good wages" to disadvantaged areas of the city, RLA and the corporate interests it represented were truly unsuccessful in the inner city, creating fewer than 5,000 jobs despite massive subsidies. This number pales in significance compared to the 90,000 jobs a consulting firm hired by RLA found to be needed in South Los Angeles.[42]

The main problem stemming from RLA and other similar corporate-centered initiatives is that, even though these initiatives promote and indeed speak for large corporations, the rhetoric that accompanies such initiatives tends to exalt small businesses as the main, if not the only, salvation for dilapidated neighborhoods. The ideological intent of such a rhetorical strategy is, obviously, to attract small businesspersons to identify with the discourses of large corporations. A good example of this rhetoric at work was provided in the aftermath of the 1992 rebellions in South Central when city, state, and national officials, as well as high administrators of major industries, inordinately emphasized in the media the importance of investment by small businesses in disadvantaged communities. This emphasis was all the more curious since RLA, with its promises of attracting major companies back to the inner city, had been inaugurated in the same period of time. The *Sentinel* featured a series of articles and editorials on the need to rebuild the Black community by stimulating Black small businesses.[43] Prominent Black ministers preached the same credo.[44]

According to members of CAPA and CSGT, this rhetoric not only fuels divisions and competition within the inner city, but also diverts attention from the necessity of investments in other areas besides small businesses. Because small businesspersons are usually well organized, they tend to attract large proportions of public funds destined for the inner city.[45] During CSGT meetings it is often pointed out that, by adopting the small-business rhetoric, Black entrepreneurs become comfortable with pursuing their own interests, identifying with corporate perspectives, and reinforcing their special, separate status in Black communities. One activist complained:

These business groups in the community are driving me crazy. Every time we try to pressure elected officials to talk about money for schools, hospitals, public health centers, and transportation they talk about loans for themselves. Every time we talk about curbing police brutality they talk about more police and making the community safer for business. And every time we talk about cleaning up toxins and the environment, they talk about how all the rules are killing them. I want to work *with* these people, but not *for* the business class, black or white.[46]

CSGT thus considers the revitalization projects defended by RLA and by a considerable part of the Black small-business class to be detrimental to the majority of South Central's residents. At the heart of this stance is CSGT's socially oriented utopian notion that economic development, rather than premised on competition between persons and groups of persons, should be based on—indeed, be the result of—collective, community-oriented aspirations.

This utopian position goes far beyond the ceasefire document that pursued a peaceful community where individual business initiatives would find an atmosphere conducive to commercial enterprises and free competition. The initial Watts gang truce, in this sense, represented conceptions that were, at the very least, uncritical of the conflict of interests between small businesses and the community at large.[47] CSGT, on the other hand, clearly influenced by the 1960s' Black Power–inspired conceptions as they are perceived by CAPA's old-timers, defends a radically different concept of economic development. More specifically,

Our concept of progressive economic development centers on meeting people's basic needs, people being able to get a sense of satisfaction from their work, and being able to provide their loved ones with a quality of life in which they have access to and can enjoy all the benefits this society has to offer. . . . We also believe that progressive economic development must be based on a sense of individual and collective responsibility for one's community and the world. Rather than economic development that pits one person against the other, or one group against the other, we believe that economic development should advance the individual *and* the community. . . . So instead of enterprise zones, we call for cooperative zones, which promote social and economic justice, and are free of racism, sexism, and other forms of oppression.[48]

In a manner akin to CAPA's emphasis on the affirmation of the rights of persons of color through participation in the public and legal spheres, CSGT demands fuller citizenship for poor people living in the inner city. Accompanying this claim for full citizenship is a critique of common-sense ideas of economic development premised on notions of individual success and "free competition." This critique embodies an alternative project of economic development and, more generally, of social belonging. CSGT's proposed cooperative zones, as difficult to materialize as they may be, present youngsters that participate in gang-truce-related activities with a perspective that integrates personal and communitarian responsibilities. This perspective acquires its significance and specificity in contrast to concepts and practices that directly impinge on the lives of inner-city youth: the original gang-truce agreement, market-oriented official initiatives such as RLA, and the support community business and repressive law-and-order measures against gangs earn among numerous Blacks. CSGT's alternative perspectives provide foundations for a social movement that politicizes the conditions of the ghetto from its youth's standpoint. It posits strong emphasis on work performed by youngsters that is meaningful as a source of income, personal satisfaction, and communitarian fellowship and solidarity.

Based on these ideals, CSGT members make concrete claims for public financing for their job-training proposals and "economic development projects":

> We demand funding for job training and job skills with federal monies seized through the Drug Forfeiture program that emphasizes the use of public schools and public works. High schools in our community can open their doors in the evening for trade and skills training classes initiated by trade unions. Youth will be taught a trade and educated on organized labor and the need to join organized labor.[49]

A sense of entitlement organizes these demands. The drive to alert oppressed communities of their rights stems from CAPA's political activities. CSGT has incorporated this stance and reframed it in terms of the actual existing conditions for youths of color. Yet while young men and women participating at CSGT are encouraged to seek their rights and explore public infrastructure and funding, the organization does not expect much from government. CSGT has applied for several public grants and asked to use public facilities to conduct its programs, but its demands have been ignored. The group has been more successful with private funding agencies, having received several small sums of money since its inception. One of my jobs while at the office was to write the grants. Liberty Hill, Wellness, and the Streisand Foundation, among others, have awarded CSGT with sums of money—varying from $1,000 to $5,000—which were applied to the organization's activities.

With assistance from these philanthropic organizations, CSGT carries out diverse programs. Video classes teach the use of video cameras and related equipment, but also the utilization of the medium as a tool to record community-related events, police arrests and abuses, and gang-truce activities and ceremonies. This program is most often taught by Michael Zinzun, a strong advocate of video camera use; he also keeps in good order the video library in the office shared by CAPA and CSGT. The use of video cameras to record police arrests and abuses is, in essence, a direct product of the Panthers' first activities in Oakland. The idea is to monitor police activities while asserting persons of color's rights to scrutiny and accountability related to law enforcement. Huey Newton and Bobby Seale used shotguns to do this job; now it is done with video cameras. Although the police beating of Black motorist Rodney King, captured by George Holliday, a White plumbing company manager, put in evidence the potential political power of video cameras, CAPA and CSGT had been utilizing this instrument well before the 1991 incident.

CAPA and CSGT frequently show videotapes of contemporary and historical events. Over the years, a vast number of videotaped documentaries have been compiled. These also serve as incentives for future recordings. The recorded marches, rallies, police beatings, and meetings with gangsters from other cities and countries all provide background knowledge that members interested in documenting events can use to compose their future videos. As new videos are produced, more information about the gang truce is spread. Finally, video sales provide a new means of income for those involved in their production. CSGT and CAPA have for sale videos on police abuse, gang meetings, and documentaries on South Central's youth. Those who become proficient with the use of video cameras and editing and producing techniques can also venture into related activities for private or public organizations. Graduates of the free video classes will have the opportunity to use their knowledge in events run by either CAPA or CSGT. Zinzun has donated several cameras, video-players, and editing equipment to the office. Video-class graduates can be seen at every public event supported by the organization, and when possible, these persons get paid for their work.

The videotaping of events considered relevant to the community plays an important role in sustaining the organization's sense of history and purpose. The videos serve as a repository of information, pride, and inspiration. By affirming the point of view of young Blacks and Latina/os, they oppose the official versions of events. They affirm the agency of persons of color through depictions of organizing, speaking, debating, and protesting, and they demonstrate technical skills held by members of oppressed communities.

In addition to video work, CSGT offers many other opportunities for artistic, vocational, and activist training. Established artisans instruct youngsters how to silk-screen in courses offered by the organization in the office's backyard. Those who graduate the course produce T-shirts for CSGT and CAPA. With the acquired knowledge, some of these graduates run a community business in South Central. Another course instructs youths to use boric acid to kill roaches that are so common in South Central households. The students who obtain these skills are encouraged to initiate their own businesses in the community.

Perhaps the most innovative concept advanced by CSGT has been its pilot project to provide jobs, empowerment, and housing to people of the inner city by manufacturing recycled plastic Omni-Spheres—igloo-shaped shelters approximately ninety feet in diameter. Made up of large plastic pieces, they are easily assembled and are intended to provide temporary housing for homeless people while the campaign for decent and affordable housing goes on. CSGT's silkscreen workshop operates inside one of those domes in the office's backyard. Homeless advocate Ted Hays has already started a homeless dome village in downtown Los Angeles. His project, however, utilizes fiberglass domes, which are expensive and non-recyclable. CSGT's proposal is to use cheaper and recyclable materials. The Omni-Sphere project intends to train youth in the processes involved in manufacturing the plastic pieces that are used in the domes. As one of CSGT's newsletters stated, "[O]ur vision is that youth will run and control both the plastic manufacturing operation and the building of the dome, thus serving as a source of income."[50]

Since June 1996, CSGT has been training young community members in computer software. I designed and taught the first course. Following Zinzun's suggestion, I introduced a group of six ex-gang members to the basics of software with emphasis on word-processing, accounting programs, graphics, and the Internet. Upon completion of the course, each participant is encouraged to use the acquired skills both for personal benefits (education-related activities, services, finding a job) and for community services (teaching and assisting others, participating in the production of newsletters and fliers). This course has evolved into a full-fledged program teaching not only the basics of common software but also sophisticated image and sound manipulation via computers. Graduates have produced fine documentaries on CAPA and CSGT programs, some of which are now used in various learning contexts, including community groups and universities.

A speaker's program encourages, trains, and sometimes pays ex-gang-bangers who support the truce to speak across the country and around the world about the history of the ceasefire and the uprisings of 1992. Several regular speakers draw honoraria for speaking engagements, usually fifty dollars. In 1993 and 1995, funded in part by a grant received from Liberty Hill and by Zinzun's own monetary contributions, some of these speakers traveled to Europe, Africa, and Brazil, where they told concerned audiences about their plight and learned about similar struggles in the host countries. This program deploys techniques of public presentation that were first elaborated in the mid-1970s when CAPA began its activities. Those seeking to become part of the speakers' bureau learn how to communicate effectively in public from a brochure entitled "Preparing Speeches and Presentations."

It may be argued that CSGT's small-scale programs and the communitarian utopia that organizes them present little relief for inner-city joblessness. Studies have shown that "very small businesses"—firms that employ fewer than ten workers—although providing 75 percent of the total of employers only generate 10 percent of all the jobs in Los Angeles County. In larger firms, moreover, there is greater possibility of labor union organization, higher wages, and job protection.[51] It is thus not difficult to defend the idea that key to large-scale job development in areas such as South Central are medium-sized and large firms. The enterprises suggested by CSGT fall into the "very small businesses" category.

CSGT programs, however, are as much about self-activity as they are incentives for economic agency. All of the organization's programs teach skills and encourage the holders of those skills to apply them to their own economic advantage and to the benefit of the community. This emphasis on entrepreneurial agency is all the more significant when we consider that poor and young persons of the inner city are portrayed by society at large—and by a number of Blacks who also reside in South Central— as lacking the will and discipline to engage in such activities. Youngsters from underprivileged backgrounds often suffer from doubts about their capacity. Many of them arrive at the office with very low self-esteem. CSGT's programs—indeed, the entire atmosphere of the building, with its celebrations of Black history, pride, and collective struggles—directly challenge these doubts. While these programs may not be the most suitable for the full economic recovery of the inner city, they provide an alternative project of community that politicizes the aspects of inner-city life that top-down sweeping plans for the revitalization of the ghetto are incapable of addressing. In politicizing the conditions and lives of poor youth, CSGT also establishes a public voice that in itself breaks the silence to which grassroots movements are usually condemned.

In all of CSGT's activities, "mutual respect, peaceful struggle and frank discussions before decisions are made, and collective work and responsibility" function as guiding principles. These principles are explained in a document every new member of CSGT is expected to read and understand before he or she is accepted.

The norms of mutual respect are particularly important when we consider that CSGT's programs involve ex-gang members accustomed to resolving differences, especially with persons who do not belong to one's set, through violence. Furthermore, these apparently trivial rules of respect toward others are fundamental in organizing interpersonal relations in an institution that seeks to bring together people of different ages, genders, races, sexualities, and social classes. In all of the organization's programs there are Latina/os and, occasionally, young Black women.

Although Black women and Latinas are not as common in CSGT, when they participate in the group's programs the men demonstrate marked respect toward them. Here again, the old-timers are responsible for orienting ex-gangbangers on this matter. Misogynist ideas and behavior are typical among Black youth, making the degree of camaraderie between men and women in the office all the more compelling. The fact that young men from different gangs and races can be respectful of women is indicative of success in providing an alternative set of values and conduct. While CSGT is still a male-dominated environment, where women hold few, if any, position of power and responsibility, such rules of respect—which are still emerging out of men's concerns with their overt misogyny rather than the product of women's own views on gender roles—question patriarchal assumptions in political organizing and interpersonal relationships. CSGT, like CAPA, recognizes the political and personal problems generated by male-centric perspectives; yet in their way to finding alternatives to the hegemonic views on gender roles, men and women are building an environment of mutual respect. It is this mutual respect that constitutes the necessary groundwork for honest and constructive dialogue between men and women, which is still embryonic.[52]

☙

A communitarian utopia lies at the heart of CSGT's outlooks. This utopia, whose genealogy can be traced directly to the Black Power movement, shapes activities, bridges racial, gender, and nationality differences, and provides an ethical framework from which youngsters supportive of the gang truce draw moral substance. This communitarian utopia, however, coexists uneasily with market-oriented guidelines that are also championed by CSGT and exemplified in the Amer-I-Can program, adopted by CSGT as part of its "urban life management skills" teachings.

Amer-I-Can represents somewhat of an oddity at CSGT. Unlike the other programs CSGT and CAPA embrace, Amer-I-Can is not a descendant of the 1960s' Black Power experiences. It emphasizes individual initiatives and psychology, rendering it peripheral to a progressive agenda. Nevertheless, Jim Brown's program is considered by most, if not all, of the Watts ex-gangbangers as a crucial catalyst for the gang truce.

Amer-I-Can's influence on the truce is unmistakable. Anthony Perry and Daude Sherrills, architects of the truce document and key articulators of the peace process, were both part of the program. Sherrills served as its chief of staff, and Twilight Bey, cofounder of CSGT and one of the main spokespersons for the gang truce, has also been part of Amer-I-Can since 1990. Don Gordon (a/k/a Playmate) remembered that the Amer-I-Can program was a decisive factor for the first dialogues between residents of the housing projects in Watts:

[In 1990] we started taking these classes up at Jim Brown's house, which is the Amer-I-Can Program, which teaches you responsibility, and self-determination. That alone gave us the knowledge that we didn't get in school. All through school they would tell me about goals, but nobody ever sat down and told me that my goals had to be realistic, they had to be worthwhile, attainable, timely, and manageable. They didn't tell me that my goals had to be accomplished with perseverance, and understanding. They just told me that you need a goal. It's a trip,' because the schools never told me how to respect myself, first. How to use my own mind.[53]

All these ex-gangbangers are still part of Amer-I-Can, either working in its bureaucracy or as hired facilitators. They credit Jim Brown for providing the conceptual foundations for the truce and the encouragement to begin conversations among former enemies. Brown held several meetings at this house at least two years before the final peace agreement.

Twilight Bey taught an Amer-I-Can class in which I participated together with eleven students, three of them women. Two of the women taught school in South Central. One of them was White and had been living in the inner city and participating in CAPA since the late 1970s. A third woman was a visiting Black activist from London, England. The two schoolteachers were in their early forties, while the woman from England was in her mid-twenties. Among the men, five were ex-gangbangers in their late teens and early twenties, two were old-timers in their mid-forties (one of whom worked daily at CAPA, while the other was a former member of Los Angeles' BPP chapter), and a third man was an unemployed artist in his early thirties who lived in Leimert Park and who had participated in one of CSGT's video classes.

The course was held at the office's main room, where we met twice a week, in two-hour sessions, for six weeks. Each participant received a seventy-eight-page manual which was a polished, easy-to-read, well-organized reader. The classes were structured around the printed material and a series of cassette tapes directed the reading. The instructor—the "facilitator"—operated the cassette player, posed questions, and dictated the rhythm of the classes.

We sat in a circle and introduced ourselves. The facilitator did the same and gave us our first instructions. The course, he said, only works if we begin to speak in the first person. We all had to use "I" when making comments and answering questions. Every time someone used "you," "we," or "they," the facilitator intervened, demanding that the point be rephrased with "I." As we introduced ourselves, the facilitator corrected us several times, stressing that it was imperative to use the first person.

The explanation that Twilight gives for the emphasis on "I" is that it constitutes the first step in achieving personal success. Since the program is aimed primarily at those "who society disregards"—persons usually with low self-esteem—it is necessary, first of all, to recognize one's own subjectivity, one's personality, weaknesses, and strengths, and then begin to act rationally toward fulfilling attainable goals. As we were told in the first day of class by the voice in the tape recorder:

> The Amer-I-Can program systematically develops the attitude of the trainee from one of self-doubt to self-determination. We believe that in addition to understanding the goal-setting process, a person must honestly examine the whys and wherefores of past behavior patterns that have negatively affected their lives. Once this understanding has been firmly established, that person will be able to change his/her thinking from I-Can't to I-Can, by accepting the responsibility of determining the direction of his/her life.[54]

The program's overall goal is clear. As Jim Brown states in the preface of the manual, "I feel the Amer-I-Can program is, in many ways, a missing link—empowering those exempted from power to *participation in the mainstream*" (emphasis added; 2). By overcoming "childhood conditioning" that generates self-doubt and self-hatred, the program capacitates its graduates to "break through the blanket of suppression" (9). The empowerment sought by the program is preeminently psychological in nature. It makes no explicit claims for social justice, no mention of social movements. Although the negative psychological conditioning is said to have been placed "upon us by society," the program focuses on the effects of these conditionings on the self, on the effects that prevent individuals' incorporation into the economic, social, and—it is assumed—psychological mainstream.

To induce self-examination, every class starts with students having to choose an emotion from a list of approximately 250 "feeling words" divided in different categories: *happy, sad, angry, doubtful, eager, hurt, fearless, physical, interested, affectionate,* and *miscellaneous.* The facilitator usually starts with his choices and explains his feelings. He then asks for a volunteer. In my group, the schoolteachers usually spoke first, while the younger men were the least likely to talk. The old-timers frequently made their statements after the women. One of them, the ex-Panther, showed his frustration with the need to speak using the "I" in one of the first classes. Explaining his choices of emotion-words, he used "we" to refer to something that had occurred in this family. "Back when I was little, we were always grateful to learn new things," he said. "My parents and my great-aunt and her sons all lived together, and we always listened carefully to what the elders had to say."

He had chosen the word *grateful* from the "happy" column. Twilight interrupted him several times affirming the need to use "I." One of the schoolteachers also pointed to the times "I" had to be used. The ex-Panther was not pleased. "Look, I come from a big family, you know what I'm saying? And we always used 'we' for everything. It was we and them for those who weren't part of the family. There was no 'I' but everyone knew who needed what and when."

Twilight explained that "there is no 'us' if there is no 'I'—it makes you think about things that aren't usually thought about." Twilight went on to explain the benefits of using "I" in the context of the gang truce. He said that, especially when working with younger gangsters, as soon as they start utilizing the first person, the blaming of others stops and self-criticism and personal responsibility begin. Twilight added that the use of the "I" forced persons to dwell on individual experiences, promoting strong bonds between participants of the program. Such bonds are important because the maintenance and expansion of the ceasefire is based on personal trust and understanding. Gang members who participated in the classes confirmed these impressions. According to one O.G.:

> Once we started taking the classes, we got a brother named Aqeela from our hood, he is now the director of education for the Amer-I-Can Program, that's our homeboy. . . . *We had a feelings session every day, that's how we got that bond.* We had so many fights, you wouldn't believe it. The brothers that were in that one room, twelve brothers having a feeling session, talking about respecting somebody's opinion. The bonding process—man, we got kicked out of buildings [starts laughing]. I'm serious, man, it's funny now, but it was a serious process to get to know each other, to get to trust each other, to learn what we're really about, learning to speak a new language.[55]

Twilight's argument for the importance of introspection, and the fundamental role it played in the gang truce as a tool for building a "new language" of trust, did not satisfy the old-timer. Although he continued to participate regularly in some of the activities organized by CAPA and CSGT, he did not come back for the Amer-I-Can classes. Later he told me he did not believe in "collective therapy," as he put it. Nor did he think Amer-I-Can had any use for consequent political education and mobilization. "What do you do with that 'I' thing? Man, we be talking all day about feelings, childhood stuff. . . . It's all right for some people, but not for me. I guess these young people now have different needs. They want to make it big time, you know what I'm saying? Big companies, big cars, big houses and shit like that. So all that talk about feelings, that 'success is there for everybody,' man, that's totally bourgeois shit!"

Although other participants of the program also expressed some concerns over its emphasis on emotions, they were willing to continue with the classes and consider their benefits. When I asked what she thought about the ex-Panther's disappointment with the course, the White schoolteacher, herself an old-timer at CAPA, pondered that her daily first-hand experience with inner-city adolescents made clear their need for emotional support. According to her, those who join gangs and become violent usually do not know how, and do not have the opportunity, to express their emotions. She contended that the large list of words for emotions, and the possibility that participants of the course had in sharing those emotions, were fundamental in providing support for individuals who otherwise would only have recourse to frustration and violence. Twilight, finally, made a similar point when he told us, during one of the classes, that when "feeling sessions" did not compel certain gang members to talk and express their emotions, he asked the persons in the group to talk about their mothers. "It was a trip, seeing all those great gangsters crying like kids. You know, they be going through the program hard as a rock, but then they break down when they start speaking about their moms. It's when you know that something's changing—it's when the person is getting in touch with his feelings."

As the course progresses through the chapters of the manual, even the initially reticent ex-gangbangers start speaking and correcting each other when the first person is not used. Chapters 1 and 2 advance the program's basic philosophy in which self-consciousness and discipline are the keys to personal success. Subsequent chapters reaffirm the same points from different angles. "Life offers us opportunities and choices. Too often when we see these opportunities and choices we do not look inside ourselves and ask if we are prepared to do whatever is required to seize them. Often, we feel that if there is an adjustment to be made for Success, it is not our responsibility to make that adjustment." Success, in other words, is "within us and within our grasp."[56]

A central tenet of the program is that individuals' fates are within their own control. Throughout the course, Jim Brown provides glimpses of his own professional success as a proof of this principle. His recorded voice tells us, for example, that in college he almost gave up on his football career due to the resentment coaches displayed toward him and the self-destructive, negative behavior that he adopted. Fortunately, his high school principal told him he should never give up. He said, "[I]f you keep applying yourself, something good is going to happen because you have the talent" (19). Success is thus also a matter of having discipline and perseverance. These attitudes must be framed according to an efficient, three-step strategy: first, "eliminate the negative," second, "establish the facts," and third, "choose your best option" (12). Indeed, one of the course's main mottos—one that is repeated throughout the fifteen chapters of the program—is "goals must be realistic, worthwhile, and attainable."

In the beginning of chapter 6 we learn that most of the program's maxims, including the motto mentioned above, are part of McDonald's Corporation teachings at Hamburger University, an advanced training facility for store and franchise managers. Ray A. Kroc, founder of the McDonald's Corporation, is given as an example of self-knowledge, discipline, and success. Kroc is quoted saying that "nothing succeeds like success and nothing recedes like success." Brown explains that what he meant by that "was that the practice of established processes for success will ensure success; and conversely, abandoning the practice of established processes for success will ensure failure" (32). Among these "processes for success" is the rational setting of goals ("we should use our reasoning powers to control our lives") and the commitment everyone has to make in his or her effort to achieve the desired goals. These desired goals, as discussed in class, could be anything from dieting to furthering one's education and looking for a job.

McDonald's success is Amer-I-Can's main inspiration. The fast-food business is successful because, we are told, it tells its employees that it is their responsibility to become the most knowledgeable about their occupation. The company's success seems to be directly linked to the fact that it encourages and rewards individual initiative:

> When you visit a McDonald's restaurant, you will see various people in different forms of managerial clothing. Each person's garb represents a plateau of accomplishment. Even the crew people have badges with insignias that indicate they have mastered different forms of tasks and are being recognized for their Achievement. All of these Achievements begin with the employee saying that he or she wishes more responsibility, more training and more satisfaction in his or her job. As they become more proficient, they are given more responsibilities, more recognition and more money. *This process evidently works, as all McDonald's managers are promoted from within the corporation; and almost all of the top operations executives started their careers as crew members.* (Emphasis added; 51)

We are also told that McDonald's merits stem from its emphasis on how workers should relate to customers and other staff members. Pleasant attitudes, "selling or giving some of your personality to the customer when you greet the customer with a genuine smile and a courteous attitude": these behaviors, according to Amer-I-Can, guarantee successes such as McDonald's and should be made the norm of conduct for those wishing to be accomplished.[57]

Several debates about "acting positively in order to achieve success" took place in our class. Twilight set the tone by mentioning his decision to leave gangbanging and to become a responsible man. He mentioned how important it had been for him to conduct an honest self-examination. He said his days as an active gang member were marked by profound negative feelings about his family, his community, and, most of all, about himself. Once he recognized this hatred and perceived how it was directing him to self-destruction, he started to set small, attainable goals to change. He stopped drinking, quit drugs, and became concerned with his young daughter and his community.

The other gang members in the group, certainly encouraged by Twilight's narrative, gave examples of how they had overcome their need for violence. One of them mentioned he decided to lose weight. He had been eating not for nutrition, but to express frustration with himself. He wanted to look ugly and fat because he was ashamed of the harm he was inflicting on others. This testimony was quite impressive for, up to that point, this particular ex-gangbanger was very reluctant to speak out, only doing so when asked by Twilight.

The Black schoolteacher spoke next, saying she felt similar self-hatred when she found herself utilizing several credit cards and not planning on how to pay her debts. She suggested that credit-card companies tested each individual on his or her strength to plan and make decisions. Her conclusion was that most Black people she knew—schoolteachers like her and people who lived in the gentrified area of the inner city—fell prey to credit problems because they were not honest with themselves, they did not have a spending plan, and they did not set attainable goals. The schoolteacher, a middle-class woman who had traveled abroad, dressed in West African clothes bought in the boutiques of Leimert Park, and who was conscious of the social distance that separated her from the gang members who were participating in the class, was trying to make the point that she—as most better-off Blacks—also had problems with self-esteem. In this, therefore, middle-class Blacks were no different than the gangbangers. She overcame her debt problems, first with an assessment of her responsibility, and second by setting goals that could be met over a stipulated amount of time. Her experience, as well as those of ex-gangbangers, thus confirmed the validity of the program's emphases. Although she was not conscious of the steps she had taken to overcome her financial problems, she said it made her even more confident to see that those personal resolutions were part of a program aimed at primarily underprivileged people. She decided to fight for the implementation of the program in her school.

What is the substance of Amer-I-Can's notion of success? Introspection and rational setting of attainable goals can lead to overcoming drugs, crime, and debts. Self-sacrifice and hardships are certainly difficult but are character-forming: success cannot be dissociated from sufferings. More important, however, the essence of success is realized through work. It is only by being productive and accomplished in the job market that one can be truly successful. Obtaining a job is thus fundamental. The course devotes two chapters specifically to "how to get a job" and the necessary communications skills involved in interviews.[58] As important, one should strictly abide by the rules—rules of conduct and expectations similar to the ones at McDonald's. During the course, we were constantly warned about the fierce competition involved in finding and keeping jobs.[59] If the steps of the program are followed, material recompenses should ensue. Success, therefore, is mostly a matter of individual financial stability—the end to which the program is ultimately conceived.

The Amer-I-Can program clearly aims to overcome patterns of self-hatred and low self-esteem. Through a concise method, Jim Brown's course has the merit of facilitating introspection, confidence and, most important in the context of the gang truce, communication between the participants. First-hand experience and accounts from course instructors have also demonstrated that the program is instrumental in enhancing relations between persons of different social backgrounds, ages, races, sexualities, and genders. Furthermore, as it emphasizes the need to "return to old values at home," the program associates a successful professional life with family harmony and happiness (42). To those who consider the inculcation of bourgeois patriarchal values a solution for inner-city problems, the program is praiseworthy.

On the other hand, however, the Amer-I-Can program is conspicuously devoid of claims for social justice. Indeed, in Jim Brown's course there is not the slightest suggestion that self-hatred, low self-esteem, lack of initiative, difficulties in finding work, gender tensions, and propensity for drug use have some of their roots in historical and social conditions. No references are made to the role of the government in perpetuating poverty. A few allusions to the "community" prevent the program from operating in a total social vacuum, but the "community," as it appears in the course's descriptions, is a context of hardships (poverty, discrimination) and temptations (drugs, illicit sex, easy money) against which there is only one antidote: individual strength and perseverance. Individuals pursuing financial success, moreover, are to be docile and comply meekly with the preestablished rules. Unlike CSGT's programs for economic development, there are no communitarian preoccupations, nor is there the slightest hint that trade unions may be beneficial for the individual and his or her colleagues.

As we try to capture the program's hidden premises, we may ask: what about those who do not succeed? What if, after attending the classes, adopting the suggested strategies, and seeking a career "at least forty hours a week" (59), an individual is not able to find and maintain a job? The saddest irony of the program's emphasis on individual characteristics is that it feeds from, and confirms, the racialized matrix of thought that has become so hegemonic at least since the 1980s. In this matrix, as well as in Amer-I-Can's teachings, individuals who are not successful are seen as victims of their own deficiencies. Successful Blacks demonstrate the stamina needed to overcome their disadvantaged initial situations. The effects of these combined propositions are well known. Historical structures of racial discrimination and social injustices become occluded. The positing of an innate, qualitative difference between Blacks who succeed and those who do not, reifies differences of social class, generation, education, and justifies the long-term chasms between Blacks of different backgrounds.

ₒₒ

In April 1996, a series of celebrations marked the fourth anniversary of the gang truce. These celebrations realized one of CAPA's aspirations of bringing together people of different backgrounds. They also underscored, however, the persistent gulf between Blacks of different political aspirations and social classes. CSGT's message and the strategies it utilized to promote the public event were not appealing to most residents of the inner city. Attendance was sparse, well below the expected 10,000 participants.

Preparations for the event, set to take place at Will Rogers Park in the heart of Watts on Saturday, April 27, 1996, began at least three months before. The office that houses CAPA and CSGT served as the main headquarters. Meetings related to the march and rally took place there almost daily. Youngsters who supported the truce from Watts, Athens, Florence, Inglewood, Crenshaw, downtown, East L.A., Pasadena, Venice, and the San Fernando Valley—in other words, representatives from most of the major gangs in the Los Angeles region—discussed the event. Blacks, Latina/os, men and women, Catholics, Protestants, and Muslims all contributed to debates about the desired form and content of the gang truce celebration. CAPA's old-timers also participated in some of the meetings, but only spoke when requested or when they thought that their input was vital. Zinzun, for example, told me he made an effort not to intervene, arguing that it was "the young people's thing" and that, as always, he would work *with* them, and not *for* them. In spite of his self-imposed restraint, however, Zinzun made important contributions by setting up different committees (press relations, community outreach), intervening when meetings became too disorganized, and coordinating the celebration's general timetable. Obviously based on CAPA's manual of community mobilization,

Zinzun was attempting to transform the march and rally into a significant political event that would reverberate in the press and among inner-city residents.

Younger members of CSGT and other similar organizations supportive of the ceasefire determined the tenor of the meetings and made the major decisions about the celebration. In contrast to what usually happened in assemblies organized by CAPA personnel, the gatherings invariably started with an ecumenical prayer. All of us held hands and listened to the designated speaker, often someone connected with one of the numerous Protestant churches or mosques of South Central. Appeals were made for the maintenance and expansion of the peace, as well as a successful celebration.

A large proportion of the meeting participants were Latina/os. Although younger Latina/os and Blacks were taciturn in each other's presence, the more experienced members of CAPA, CSGT, and other mostly Black organizations displayed marked camaraderie toward representatives of Latina/o groups. The genuine friendliness was reciprocal. "Brother" and "sister" were used by both groups to address each other, and occasionally, Blacks would venture into using Spanish terms such as *compañero, compañera, hermano,* and *hermana,* and, of course, the easier *amigo* and *amiga.* Latina/o and Black activists have, in fact, become personal friends and lovers. The political meaning of these alliances is obvious. There exists a clear consciousness that the causes embraced by CAPA and CSGT including the gang truce are as much about African Americans as they are about (descendants of) peoples from Mexico, El Salvador, Guatemala, Puerto Rico, Dominican Republic, Cuba, and Nicaragua. Because of CAPA's long history and its experience in social movements, however, it is Latina/os who tend to join the Coalition and CSGT rather than the other way around. Yet, as similar organizations develop in East L.A., it is likely that Black activists will work for causes that are first raised and specific to the City of Angels' barrios. The seeds for this scenario have been planted. The politicization of the gang truce, in this sense, is realizing one of Black Power's goals, namely, the emergence of interracial alliances. One manifestation of this kind of alliance took place during a meeting attended by approximately fifty persons, most of whom were Latina/os. The group decided that the fliers announcing the anniversary were to be bilingual. (I was designated to write the text in the computer; Zinzun volunteered to have 5,000 copies made.) Following a suggestion from a CAPA old-timer, it was agreed that reminders about the event were to be placed in Spanish-language newspapers and radios. The same, of course, would be done in newspapers and radio stations that served mostly Black communities.

Organizations from out of town also participated in the gang-truce celebration. Among the most notorious was a small delegation of Black Stone Rangers, one of the larger and older gangs in Chicago. As well as expressing the national network of which CAPA and CSGT are part, the Rangers' presence also highlighted—if only through the awkwardness they generated among people at the office—the progress that had already taken place in the peace movement in Los Angeles. Heavily armed—indeed, most of those in the delegation were bodyguards to the two Rangers O.G.s— the men from Chicago seemed extremely cautious about establishing dialogues with unknown persons, and especially so with the Latina/os who were participating in the preparations of the event. Converted Muslims, the taciturn Rangers daunted most of those to whom they were introduced by Zinzun. (Zinzun, in fact, was their contact in Los Angeles. This particular alliance dates back to the 1960s and early 1970s, when the Black Stone organization acted closely with the Panthers.) The bodyguards reached for their guns every time a person with whom they had not been acquainted walked into the meeting room. Numerous bloody stories about the shootouts in which those particular Rangers had been involved only made their aura more intimidating. Unlike some of the Los Angeles gangsters—especially the Blacks and Browns who supported the ceasefire—the Chicago gangsters did not display any interest in establishing dialogues with local supporters of the truce. They made it clear that they were there chiefly to speak and be heard.

Escorted by LAPD officers, the march that preceded the rally at Will Rogers Park occurred calmly. Indeed, too calmly. Featuring loudspeakers mounted on a truck, the fewer-than-one-hundred-person procession passed some of the main streets and housing projects in Watts, but generated only lukewarm responses. Few locals joined in. At around 11 A.M., as the group arrived at the park where the rally was programmed to take place, only vendors, who had finished assembling their tents a few minutes earlier, and a few bystanders waited. The event drew more people when rappers and other artists performed on a large stage set in the middle of the park. Black and Latina/o artists were applauded and cheered as the rally reached its peak at around 1 P.M. At that point, approximately three hundred people had been attracted to the event. The crowd was a mixture of Latina/os and Blacks, mostly in their late teens and early twenties. At least sixteen young men in wheelchairs, victims of shootings, were there. In spite of—or perhaps because of—Nation of Islam's security personnel, the Fruit of Islam, the atmosphere was relaxed and calm. Zinzun had warned everyone working in the organization of the event to look for and discourage gun showing. Alcoholic beverages were also prohibited and, although some youths managed to sneak in bottles of beer in paper bags, no incidents took place.

Except for the middle-aged persons who were working as vendors, and who mostly belonged to South Central's Black middle class (there were few Latina/o merchants at the event), better-off African Americans were not seen at the park during the rally. Few residents of the immediate area—one of the poorest of the inner city—were in the crowd. So when the gathering reached its most important point—the various speeches by community activists, Blacks and Latina/os, who emphasized the importance of the truce and the need to collectively mobilize to redress the inner cities' social problems—the audience was composed primarily of local youngsters who, attracted by the earlier artistic performances, decided to listen to the speakers. Although most of those persons stayed until the end, the enthusiasm demonstrated for the activists' words was far less energetic than the responses generated by the artists.

Not surprisingly, no public celebrations marked the gang-truce anniversary in 1997. Although there are no signs that the peace among the major Black gangs of Watts—and between some of the Latina/o gangs in Venice and in the Orion Avenue area—is about to end, the peace movement does not seem to be expanding either. CSGT's ideological syncretism, in particular the adoption of the Amer-I-Can program, has made possible the formation of the very communicative basis from which the gang truce was drawn. Yet the ambiguous perspectives and organized actions, while still able to draw sympathy and support from progressive social movements, are nevertheless unable to gain widespread acceptance among the various social sectors of inner-city residents. A considerable number of Blacks, especially the relatively well-off, openly nurture a strong aversion to all that is related to gangs—and they remain aloof to both the market-oriented, individualistic wishes of success, and the claims for social justice that are part of

CSGT's programs. Without recognition and support, the gang truce and the significant results it has achieved are at risk. The peace movement runs against the grain of both contemporary politics, determined in great measure by the public-sanctioned necessity of ever-expanding law-enforcement apparatuses, and widespread perceptions about the social and racial components of poverty and social deviance. In this worldview, gangbangers will always be gangbangers, irrespective of their allegiance to the values and practices of the wider society: gangbangers are prisoners of their immanent social and racial essence.

℀

The gang truce's internal dilemmas are considerable. Aside from the obvious difficulties in keeping the peace among ever-younger and unaware members of warring sets, finding a balance between self-help ideologies and the more radical, community-oriented programs inspired by Black Power is a difficult and obviously ongoing challenge. While self-help programs such as Amer-I-Can command indisputable appeal among young and disillusioned men and women, they are not sufficient to formulate a powerful social and historical critique based on which a vital collective movement would bloom. Still, programs such as Amer-I-Can provide precious and necessary discipline guidelines based on a sense of self-worth and agency—vital elements that, when channeled into political organizing, can become powerful tools in the struggle for social justice.

Gender relations and the accompanying ideologies are another area of debate and timid change, and still in need of transformation. Young men and women at CSGT interact, think about responsibilities, and project an idealized future based on rigid notions of manhood and womanhood. Such rigid notions are closely connected to the misogynist gang worldviews, but they are also a product of this society's hegemonic, culturally shared patriarchal understandings. Although CSGT is a space where women are welcome and respected, the terms of their participation are not set by themselves, nor are they the product of an ongoing dialogue about the need to locate, deconstruct, and replace patriarchy with an equalitarian, revolutionary model of gender relations. There is much work to be done, but guaranteeing the preconditions for effective, decolonizing change seems to be crucial. Because CSGT and CAPA work closely together, and because CAPA, as we saw previously, is committed to a constant process of self-critique and reformulation, I see such commitment also impregnating the discussions and decisions lying ahead for CSGT activists.

How effective CSGT becomes in responding to the larger Black community's resistance against its constituency and programs, while continuing to hold on to a vision of change based on social justice, will in great measure depend on how the organization approaches its internal dilemmas.

CSGT idea   Pg 177

What gangs stand for Pg 182

downfall   Pg 189

CSGT demands Pg 191

misogeny pg. 198

aner-I-can 199, 201

...11 only individual Pg 207

BLACKNESS AS BLUEPRINT
FOR SOCIAL TRANSFORMATION

Blackness is a copmy mechanism [handwritten annotation]

What are the political implications of the distinct forms of blackness presented in this study? Blackness as solidarity and sorrow, blackness as mobilization and movement, blackness as artistry and achievement, and blackness as self-help and social critique are powerful tools for collective and individual survival, and for social transformation. The various forms of blackness emerging from the experience of racial discrimination are blueprints for strategies against imposed marginalization as well as for establishing a social world that is yet to be known.[1] An appreciation of how blackness is experienced can therefore provide important political guidelines not only for understanding and surviving contexts of extreme oppression, but also for devising just and egalitarian social relations and the strategies most adequate to achieve them.

Yet such manifestations of blackness are suffused in contradictions. The contradictions happen both *within* certain types of blackness, and *between* varied modalities of blackness. All the forms of blackness analyzed in this study demonstrate how Black people must draw on a constantly updated reservoir of wisdoms, knowledge, and strategies deriving from the awareness of specific, shared, racialized experiences. Nevertheless, blackness can often be divisive. As Blacks of varied genders, classes, sexualities, places of residence, and ages claim to be the bearers of authentic blackness, they exclude from their community all those who do not conform to their specific parameters of blackness—Blacks and non-Blacks alike. Furthermore, even within specific modalities of blackness that are defined by porous and changing boundaries, there can be moments in which exclusion of difference pervades the performance and definition of blackness. Ironically, therefore, as much as blackness is a crucial tool for locating, understanding, deconstructing, and surviving the historical and everyday assaults against Black people's humanity, it is also one that frequently discriminates against those not deemed worthy of the community of struggle built around specific definitions and performances of blackness.

Rather than asking how the contradictory aspects of blackness can be resolved, I argue that the very contradictory natures of blackness show that, if an ethical commitment to liberatory politics is the energizer of self-making, blackness is absolutely *necessary* as a source of knowledge of the social world, survival, resistance, and community maintenance. Whether blackness is also *sufficient* for liberatory, decolonizing transformation depends on how its manifestations lend themselves to establishing broad political alliances. Broad political alliances set the conditions of possibility for social change.[2]

The contradictions in and between modes of blackness express the gains and limits of identity politics as well as offer models for vital social movements. Identity politics based on blackness, however, are not necessarily opposed to broad alliance building. Inasmuch as flexible notions of blackness confront their own limits, they open up new possibilities for personal and political identification. Such is the case when Blacks at CAPA and CSGT, as well as those involved in artistic creation in Leimert Park, attempt to forge parameters of social and political belonging that do not depend exclusively on being Black, or that do not contradict being Black. That is, the experience of blackness at times points to the necessity of inventing identities that are based on politics, rather than inventing politics that are exclusively based on identities.[3] Even more restrictive notions of blackness that appear in the grassroots organizations and also in the apartment building have the potential for extrapolating their boundaries. In the specific case of the Black women living in poverty, the ethics of caring that they consistently lived by constitutes a powerful, crucial element for the establishment of alliances across lines of race, gender, sexuality, social class, place of residence, and nationality. In this way, certain modalities of blackness provide blueprints for truly innovative, liberatory, and broad-based political cultures and praxes. Blackness, therefore, can encapsulate both the emphasis on Black identity *and* the exploration of how new identities may be formed on the basis of a progressive and inclusive political program. Blackness's contradictory natures and its multiple manifestations are the very engine of its creative and revolutionary potential.

❝

Blackness often excludes when it draws on specific racialized experiences that intersect with gender, urban geography, and politics. The women in the tenement I lived in conceptualized their blackness in terms of race, gender, social class, and place of residence. These persons built their solidarity around singular and mutually reinforcing experiences deriving from the fact that they were poor Black women living in one of the most deteriorated areas of South Central. Their notion of blackness not only provided the cement for their social networks and their tense mutual understanding and support, but also served to delimit their own boundaries of blackness.[4] "Golden Hills snobs"—wealthier African Americans who lived in the more expensive parts of the inner city—were seen as Blacks who did not understand or never had to depend on the type of solidarity disadvantaged Black women relied on. The same was said of Black men and women who worked in hospitals and welfare agencies. Although the women in the tenement recognized them as Black people, they also made vivid distinctions between their experiences. Blacks who were able to pass judgment about, or were in positions of power regarding Black women living in poverty, were considered Blacks of a different kind: their apparent racial identity did not diminish the fact that they belonged to distinct social environments, and such contrast was enough to place them outside of underprivileged Black women's definition of blackness.

Black men who were also poor occupied a more ambiguous position, but they were still mostly marginal to the shared everyday experiences of the women in the apartment building I lived in. While lovers and partners were at times included in their networks of solidarity, Black men's transient condition impeded their consistent participation in women's lives. They also knew that, as Black women and poor, they were at times seen by persons outside their community with even greater suspicion than their male partners. The incident with the police officers who did not hesitate in taking Al's word instead of Vivian's, in spite of the overwhelming evidence of Al's physical abuse of Vivian, only underscored their perception.

Moreover, Black women were well aware of the derision with which they were talked about by many Black men. Even the respectful and loving partners who had been part of their lives ended up leaving and, in the process, removing themselves from the Black women's spheres of sociability.

The Black women in the tenement considered Whites the most distant from their networks of solidarity, and therefore in diametric opposition to how they conceptualized their own blackness. Whites had the power (landlords, police officers, welfare agents) and Whites posed immediate threats to their well-being. Yet "Whites" could also be those who, irrespective of their appearance, acted in such ways that made explicit Black women's imposed marginality and fragility. Whiteness, therefore, constituted the most obvious parameter against which Black women maintained their sense of belonging and dignity. It is in this light that the Latina/os who showed up at our building were seen as "White": not only were they believed to be taking Black people's jobs away, but also they were posing a threat to the communities of struggle so arduously maintained and so vital to the women who were already there.

The exclusive nature of such notions of blackness expresses the urgency with which they were experienced. For women struggling with intersecting forms of marginalization, it was *necessary* to maintain those boundaries and to reinforce them; it was *necessary* to constantly reassure themselves that they would be able to survive on their own, irrespective of the many obstacles they encountered. There is perhaps no better image of these notions of blackness's power than the many orange extension cords bringing electricity from one apartment to the other that marked our common courtyard—the expression "power to the people" acquired a surprising but no less compelling meaning. The power generated by the women's notion of blackness also materialized itself in the knowledge and wisdoms so necessary to make it to the next day. For example: their alternative understanding of drug dependence which, unlike the institutionalized knowledge they were subjected to, made drug use a condition and a process, not an essentialized tendency; the emphasis on mutuality over individualism; the confidence in Black women's opinions and strategies as sound and autonomous; and the willingness to endure.

For all the vital power they generate, these specific notions of blackness do not lend themselves immediately for broad political alliances. As Patricia Hill Collins noted when she analyzed the strategies Black women have employed in their struggles for autonomy and dignity, the forms of group solidarity (in this case derived from strict notions of blackness) are suited for everyday survival and temporary resistance, but ultimately they do not challenge institutions and norms.[5] While their wisdoms provide *necessary* foundations for political strategies that take Black women's experiences into account, their notions of blackness seem not to be *sufficient* for the elaboration of broad political alliances—the only route out of their oppressive conditions.[6] While this mode of blackness synthesized strong communitarian bonds based on caring and a sense of vital interdependence, it vigorously excluded from its realm both Blacks of different social classes, Black men, and nonblacks.

Rather than dismiss this mode of blackness as irremeably short-term focused and powerless to change institutions, I propose that it is precisely the acute gendered critique of how race operates in the United States, coupled with and expressed by the ethics of caring, which make it a necessary component of any project of social transformation in South Central. While the limits imposed by such mode of blackness are indeed problematic for alliance building—the incidents with Latina/os are a case in point—they nevertheless bring in them blueprints according to which these difficulties can be overcome. The historical juncture the marginalized Black women found themselves in was certainly not propitious for broader alliances; their strategies of survival can be seen as preparation for political protest.[7] Their experiences should nevertheless inform more organized efforts that often reproduce a normalized male-centric gaze.

C

Analogous potentials and limitations existed in the notions of blackness informing activists working for CAPA and CSGT. Race, as it intersected with and became inflected by gender, sexuality, place of residence, and age, produced distinct modalities of blackness according to which the social world was made comprehensible and performed. The particular notions of blackness CAPA activists embrace are part of a progressive historical and social consciousness that is systematically cultivated in everyday interactions, seminars, and social interventions. While blackness among old-timers stems directly from the Black Panther years and therefore, in theory, is open to the incorporation of non-Blacks into political alliances and networks of solidarity, reality is more complex.[8] There were, indeed, many non-U.S. Blacks working at the Coalition or collaborating with its members: Latina/os, Korean Americans, and Whites. There were also a number of women of varied races and sexual orientations working on different projects.

These examples show how a particular—perhaps dominant—notion of blackness informing the work of the Coalition, while based on historical awareness, pride, and on the celebration of the knowledge, intelligence and struggles of Blacks in the African diaspora, past and present, was able to attract and negotiate different racial, gender, and sexual identities. Due also in part to CAPA's involvement with organizations outside the United States, where notions of blackness are markedly distinct from those enacted in South Central, the fact is that former Panthers and their comrades often based their identities—their blackness—more on a set of political ideals than on a set of irreducible characteristics formed by the intersection of race, class, gender, and sexuality. By emphasizing a political program from which blackness radiated, Coalition members, in theory and often in practice, collaborated and formed lasting coalitions, solidarity, and friendships with non-Blacks, women, gays, and lesbians in the United States and various parts of the world.

This is not to discount more rigid notions of blackness that emerged at CAPA and CSGT. The ongoing tensions with middle- and upper-class Blacks not only prevent the formation of coalitions *within* the larger Black community, but they also reveal some of the boundaries of blackness enacted by Blacks of different social classes. Much in the same way that Black women who are poor and live in devalued areas of South Central considered more affluent African Americans to be lacking in Black authenticity, Black men and women involved in grassroots-organized struggles often excluded from their universe of honorable blackness Blacks who were not working class or poor. The derision and suspicion with which relatively affluent Blacks—those living in the unmistakable wealthier areas of South Central—were treated by activists only underscores this specific blackness's inflexible limits. Analogous limits, of course, define the notions and performance of excluding blackness held by wealthier Blacks against African Americans deemed poor, unsophisticated, and politically radical. Blackness in those moments reveals a set of political principles derived from a well-defined and unyielding racial identity built on the intersections of race, class, politics, and place of residence.

Rigid notions of blackness were also present among the younger members of the political organizations I described earlier. Tensions that still exist between Latina/o and Black gangs are carried into organizations supporting the gang truce. The profound political differences between old-timers and young gang members regarding one's insertion in the consumer market is another axis from which blackness is derived. For young people raised under the influence of the Reagan/Bush era, dreams of conspicuous consumption are often interwoven into their self-representation and performance as they relate to their singular idealizations of blackness. Amer-I-Can captures these dreams and, through disciplined activities and introspection, reconfigures them into programs for individual success. While the program's appeal is unmistakable among the younger supporters of the truce, CAPA old-timers see it with marked suspicion. Old-timers conceptualize their blackness as an eminently political attribute. As such, blackness is deeply associated with *collective* struggles and responsibilities, according to which, in theory at least, individual desires have little bearing. Still, what old-timers realize is that disciplined activities do matter and are important in creating social movements and new political identities; hence their emphasis on various supervised courses that aim precisely at providing youths with marketable skills (as in Amer-I-Can) *and* progressive political and social awareness.

The concerted efforts by old-timers as well as former gang members to contextualize the gang wars—and their racial dimensions—in the current and past political economy have been relatively successful in diffusing the most overt forms of prejudice and hatred between Blacks and Browns. Personal and political relationships built between young men and women from Black and Latina/o backgrounds are quite significant considering their previous deadly feuds and generalized disrespect. Such relationships render evident how a progressive, responsible, and sensitive political program can incorporate various modes of identity based on race, gender, age, and place of residence. Indeed, modes of blackness in these instances when new identities are forged become derivations, and not determinants, of political intervention and theory. The inclusive dimensions of blackness inform multiracial and intergenerational alliances between previously conflicting gangs whose identities depend much on their urban territories. These new identities, while not repressing awareness and celebration of racialized, gendered, urban space- and class-based experiences, nevertheless emerge from the shared understanding of broader historical forms of marginalization and a learned appreciation of collective action. Only broad, multiracial political fronts can challenge the various modes of imposed marginalization on communities of color. When blackness emanates from political programs and calls for new identities, its emancipatory power is revealed. Modes of blackness become powerful blueprints for coalitions that both value the historical forms of Black knowledge and resistance, and the incorporation of social groups defined by different axes of belonging into the political bloc.

Blackness as blueprint for social transformation is well expressed in Leimert Park's sociability networks. Poetry and music, as performed by Kamau Daaood, Juno Se Mama, Billy Higgins, Horace Tapscott, and so many other artists who develop their craft in South Central's jazz venues, openly stretch definitions of blackness. While shared imposed historical marginalization and collective struggle, as well as the pleasures drawn from vocabulary, foods, music, and sensuality constitute some of the axes around which blackness is performed and conceptualized, agency as it is translated in self-making also features prominently. By self-making I mean the capacity—indeed the responsibility—that Blacks in the Village invest themselves with as they utilize Black expressive modalities to not only celebrate their existence, but also to make sense of and transform the social world around them. Blackness as a transformative tool resides in the awareness of the traps inherent in closed, finished identities. It is expressed in the attempts to render poetry, for example, a conduit for dialogue between Blacks of different social classes, ages, genders, sexualities, places of residence, and political affiliations. Daaood's verses relentlessly stress the necessity of remaking ourselves as we engage with those who scare us, who challenge us, and who may transform us. His embrace of hip-hop culture and its young practitioners is an open invitation for bridging class, age, and political chasms that long have characterized South Central. It is also an attempt to present Black art—and blackness—as a blueprint for transformation. Blackness expressed in his poetry, as indeed it is expressed in jazz and other artistic manifestations devised, adopted, and perfected by Black folk, becomes itself a model for openness, for the invention of new identities that recognize the necessity of moving beyond the normalized boundaries of blackness.

Blackness as a model for the invention of new identities (that can in turn become catalysts for political movements) becomes the more pressing when competing modes of blackness happen in Leimert in ways that frontally exclude groups of persons from their boundaries. Leimert's regulars, similar to how the greater public justifies repressive law-and-order approaches, often dehumanize young gang members.[9] Many who socialize in the Village see derisively other Blacks who are poor, women, unemployed, young, or going through problems with drugs or the police. Moreover, common sense about non-Blacks' (especially Whites') purported inability to play jazz satisfactorily, as well as the continuing sexism against women of all races, added to the extensive homophobia in music performance venues: these facts reveal how notions and performances of certain modalities of blackness further divisions across race, gender, sexualities, urban geography, ages, and social class.

For all their transformative potential, the ethical and political perspectives informing the lives of those at CAPA, CSGT, and Leimert Park are still immersed in male-centric concepts that need to be deconstructed and replaced. Inasmuch as such perspectives are indeed deeply engaged with transformation, they must locate and question their patriarchal/principles. As bell hooks reminds us,

> it has been easier to challenge and change racism in the society than it has been to alter the rigid patriarchal thinking about gender that abounds in black life and is often reinforced by religion. Most black people are anti-racist (even those who have internalized self-hatred) and will not argue that whites are better, superior, and should rule over us. Yet most black people are not anti-sexist (even those whose life circumstances may make it impossible for them to rigidly conform to sexist roles) and will argue the natural superiority of men, supporting their right to dominance in the family and the world outside the home.[10]

The knowledge utilized in Black women's community of struggle described earlier in this work—as indeed the work by Black and U.S. second/third world feminists of color activists and academics—furnishes guidelines according to which the open-ended, transformative, and indeed revolutionary directions blackness indicate can be engaged with. It is not only attention to gender that is gained from this knowledge (although a gendered gaze is crucial if we are going to reorient our struggles for decolonization in a radical, nonhierarchical manner); it is above all the uncompromising need for dialogue, self-critique, difference, and open-endedness. There is no real change without the acceptance of our necessarily limited, partial, and therefore fragile standpoints.

If blackness, therefore, on the one hand can generate intolerance, on the other it can provide the basis for the construction of identities that depend not so much on imposed conditions or strict notions of belonging, but on the recognition that our only hope for overcoming our present state of oppression and fragmentation is to share political—collective and public—inclusive, progressive agendas. When blackness is defined by strict axes of belonging, it is often a necessary and vital instrument for social understanding and physical and psychological well-being, but it is definitely not sufficient for overcoming our unavoidably fascist subjectivities,[11] or the genocidal histories and policies that continue to relegate Blacks to segregation, institutional abuse, and early death. In this sense, SNCC activist Courtland Cox's opinion that "blackness is necessary. But it is not sufficient," quoted in Kwame Ture's autobiography, is certainly applicable.[12] Yet, when blackness is predicated on a set of progressive political propositions that enable the formation of new identities—among which new *Black identities that value and understand the vast, ever changing, radical legacy impregnating modalities of blackness*—it serves as enabling guidelines according to which differential and oppositional consciousness,[13] liberation, nonhierarchical subjectivities, and social justice can be fought for. Blackness can thus offer formidable blueprints for imagining and constructing James Baldwin's another country.

ACKNOWLEDGMENTS

This book has been in the making for at least a decade, hence these seemingly endless pages of acknowledgment. It will be impossible to provide a dimension of how fortunate I have been to be able to draw on the wisdom of so many extraordinary people, and how, in our long history of struggles, very little of this book's substance is my own—not much beyond mistakes and misunderstandings, for which I take full responsibility.

I do not have enough or good enough words to express my deep gratitude for all the persons and collectives that made this work possible. In South Central, with their lives on the line, my neighbors always found time to check if I wasn't skipping any meals (even though most of them were), and if I wasn't forgetting to lock all my doors and windows at night. They warned about drive-bys and police sweeps, and made sure that I fulfilled my obligations toward the well being of our expanded family. While taking care of the kids, making runs to the grocery store or to the hospital, lending money, sharing food, or just listening and talking, I borrowed some of their courage as we did our best to simply hang in there. In the midst of routinized chaos, we fought the good and necessary fights against the oppressive arms of powerful individuals and the state—both of which were often murderous. If only a tiny fraction of their courage and dignity could be socialized, we would be living in a much better world.

The comradeship of Michael Zinzun, Florence Zinzun, Bilal Mafundi, Jasone Watkins, Maybe Settlage, Twilight Bey, Red, Lisa, Gerardo, and many others made my daily work at the Coalition Against Police Abuse and at the Community in Support of the Gang Truce a genuinely warm, serious, and ongoing vital experience. Along the years, I have learned to appreciate Michael's true revolutionary spirit, one that depends less on clear programs than on the unrelenting self-critique and experimentation, always framed by a profound sense of justice. Michael's integrity, perseverance, cultivated vulnerability, and plain survival incarnate the crucial importance of CAPA and CSGT: they are reinventing a Black radical tradition of resistance, and in the process deflecting some of the most pernicious aspects of antiblack racism. They have kept me red and Black and real and open to our many truths.

In Leimert Park, Don Muhammad at the World Stage, Richard Fulton at Fifth Street Dick's, and many wonderful musicians contributed to my sanity and are still teaching me about the laborious beauty of freedom— lessons that I could have never learned elsewhere. Jamming, practicing, gigging, and learning in the company of Bill Madison, Phil Farris, Bob, Tracy, Buddy, Jonathan, Curtis, and many others, was an interstellar privilege. Juno Lewis's wisdom, support, and encouragements, as well as Billy Higgins's warmth and generosity were great sources of inspiration. Higgins also introduced me to Rizza Khalilullah, imam of a local mosque where, for a period of time, I regularly attended its Juma prayers. Khalilullah opened my eyes and soul to key elements of Islam. I can't say how much our conversations in Portuguese, while hell was breaking loose around us, were important in their simple, comforting, and yet surreal depths. Fulton, Higgins, and Lewis have passed on: their beautiful spirits energize the music and utopian musings I'll always carry with me.

The first four years of graduate school and research in the United States was funded by Brazilian taxpayers via the Conselho Nacional de Desenvolvimento Científico e Technológico (CNPq), for which I am not only grateful but also committed to paying forward. I know my community work in Rio de Janeiro and the vibrant group of Afro-Brazilian students I am helping to consolidate in the African Diaspora Graduate Program in Anthropology at the University of Texas, Austin, is just the beginning.

At U C–San Diego, the staff of the Department of Anthropology was kind and efficient. Many thanks to J. C. Krause, David Marlowe, Liz Roth, Marian Payne, and Kay Knight. I also thank the department for conceding much needed research and writing up grants.

While jumping through the hoops of graduate school, I was very fortunate to benefit from the kindness and support of a number of professors, committee members, and commentators. They have helped shape and complete this work, in content and form. With great generosity and skill, psychologist Lee Jaffe analyzed with me many hidden aspects of my experience as a racialized person no matter where I found myself, breaking down and finding strategies to deal with the ensuing traumas. I am convinced psychological therapy must be part of the reparations program.

My committee chair, James Holston, was a source of serious debate and encouragement from day one, always finding last-minute solutions when all seemed doomed. Besides being acute interlocutors, Teresa Caldeira and he were good friends during some of the roughest times, for which I am very grateful. How important were the many dinners they cooked while we were trying to make the best of our Southern California experience. Michael Meeker keenly accompanied all the stages of this work, offering many key insights along the way. Gesine Meeker and he provided much needed lightening up on many occasions. F. G. Bailey patiently corrected my faulty English and made sure my prose made sense. Michael Bernstein's earnest teachings, commentaries, and his embarrassing praises were appreciated. Leland Saito and Charles Briggs offered their much appreciated support and knowledge.

James Cheatham and George Lewis, dedicated professors and performers of jazz, made it possible for me to better understand and embrace the necessary discipline, humility, and vulnerability and strength of improvisation, this key aspect of the diasporic Black radical tradition. I cannot imagine how I would be looking at and approaching the world around me had I not participated in their ensembles/classes and witnessed their brilliance. Thank you.

George Lipsitz's contributions to this work go beyond his unrelenting support from a day in 1995 when I cornered him in the campus library and asked if he could read a rough, overtly ambitious, and ridiculously long master's report. What was my surprise when, a few weeks later, I received a letter from him in my South Central apartment mailbox with detailed comments and bibliographic suggestions. For over a decade, I have benefited immensely from his encyclopedic knowledge and the vision of liberation he encourages and shares with me. His generosity, therefore, cannot be recounted only by the many times he dug into his resources: when he made sure I went to several out-of-town academic events, as well as to my first American Anthropological Association meeting when I was looking for a job (after the plans of returning to my motherland fell through); or when he gave up teaching classes so that I could take them over and make a living. George's imprint is in every line of this work—I lost count of how many times he meticulously read and corrected and suggested reformulations, all while managing his own hectic schedule as a writer, activist, and public intellectual. He went through everything from chapter titles, to sentences, to footnotes, references and theoretical orientations. I would not be writing these acknowledgments if it were not for his critical interventions—as a mentor, friend, and colleague—in key moments of my life. It is only a testament to his revolutionary and deeply ethical spirit that, until I read *The Possessive Investment in Whiteness,* I interacted with him as if he was a stately Black person. The only difference is that now I know he is one of our overcover agents.

My long-time friends in Brazil and in the United States have been fundamental bases of support: Guilherme, Dani; Paulo and Taís; Marcos Antônio; Heitor, Bia, Marina e Tiago; Lindy, Kyle and Glenn; Paul; Bess; Gabriela, Cátia; and Andrew and Vasantha. Lindy, Tamera, Linda and Roger, and John and Gail—each in their affectionate way, made me feel part of their families while I was writing the first version of this book, for which I am fondly thankful. My cumpadres, Marcia and Hermes, have made life in Uncle Sam's land all the more bearable; Julia, my afilhada has been a source of great happiness

Moon-Kie Jung has been a dear friend since we met in the corridor of the Ethnic Studies Department at UC–San Diego, in what seems like an eternity and yet a few days ago. Generous to a fault, he has had to hear about and participate in more than the share of drama, emotional imposition, and uncooked ideas he has ever hoped for. (I won't even mention that, over the years, he has made several extravagant contributions to CAPA.) To say that I am deeply grateful for his presence, loyalty, and understanding does not even begin to acknowledge how important he is as a sweet brother in both my various personal battles and the broader struggle. I look forward to the many more exchanges we'll have over Korean food, no matter where.

Since 2000 I have made Austin my newest refuge. Pam Becker, Stephanie Osbakken, Susan Lane, Jenni Jones, and Andi Shively much contribute to making the everyday grind at the University of Texas one that is efficient and never devoid of humor. The Department of Anthropology is unparalleled in its friendliness, support, and cutting-edge perspectives. James Brow and Samuel Wilson, in particular, embody the vision, understanding, and camaraderie so necessary for young scholars of color who, like me, are reminded on an everyday basis that institutions such as this are not meant for us. I greatly value James's love of jazz and support in key moments. I am also grateful to Dean Larivierre's support throughout the years.

The number and quality of graduate students of color and progressives at UT—colleagues whose future employers will be fortunate indeed to hire them—is of epic proportions. Pablo Gonzalez, Juli Grigsby, Celeste Henery, Mariana Mora, Courtney Morrison, Athayde Motta, Raquel de Souza, Damien Schnyder, Keisha-Khan Perry, Jacqueline Pólvora, Sônia Santos, Lynn Selby, Teresa Velasquez, Amanda Walker, and many others who have taken my classes have actively contributed to my own development. They must be tired of listening to my endless utopian meanderings. Mohan Ambikaipaker and Briana Mohan are trusting friends of whose contagious caring I am extremely lucky to be a recipient.

In New York City, while holding an Andrew W. Mellon postdoctoral fellowship on Race, Crime, and Justice, at the Vera Institute of Justice, I had the unmatched opportunity of having two years to improve the all-too-convoluted manuscript. Tim Ross, Suzane Mueller, Hesther Lyons, Chris Stone, Joel Miller, Jim Parsons, Nichole Henderson, Cybelle Merrick, Geoff Ward, Zaire Flores, Zainab Latif, Ali Knight, Jeff Lin, and Delma McDonald made that experience fruitful and worthwhile. Jon Wool has become a thoughtful and sensitive friend. Khalil Muhammad, brother in arms, and his lovely family have provided the intellectual and affective support in yet another strange land—Khalil was the lightening in blue skies in my second year at Vera, and I look forward to implementing our plans of rebellion. While living in Brooklyn, I had the good fortune of performing in various venues with Shaun and Gershwyn Broadbelt—thank you for the musical experiences.

My second year in New York was greatly enriched while at the Du Bois retreat house for scholars, of the CEJJES Institute, in Pomona. Amid the Rockland County woods, what a privilege and pleasure it was to have Drs Edmund W. and Susan Gordon as neighbors and friends. Their unwavering commitment to social justice left a deep, life-affirming mark. I will always affectionately remember our long conversations over the delicious meals. Thank you also to all who work daily at the institute, especially Heather and Joe.

Many thanks to the anonymous reviewers who had to go through mountains of pages. Barbara Ransby made key and generous interventions as she suggested improvements, all of which I took to task. Richard Ralston doesn't know it, but he continues to inspire. Robin Kelley was generous with his time, comments, and preface, for which I am grateful. I want to thank David Pieribone, who took the front cover's photograph out of sheer kindness for a stranger he does not know. Thank you also to Richard Morrison and the staff at the University of Minnesota Press for supporting the project and helping to package it. I thank Therese Boyd for her patient and careful editing. Thank you to the University Cooperative Society Subvention Grant awarded by the University of Texas at Austin.

More recent as well as reemerging friends need to be acknowledged. Tayari Jones keeps all in perspective while selflessly sharing her wit. Asale Angel-Ajani always brings it back to what really matters, humorously. Joy James has generously engaged with my projects and ideas in ways that encourage me to keep searching for an emancipatory grammar and impossible utopia, for which I am grateful. Kevin Witt, David Chao, Jeremy Bell, and Paul Matthews have embarked with me on musical experiments that accept discomfort as a creative tool, sometimes transforming our gigs around town as true acts of insurgency. Ney and Lelia Oliveira have been affectionate and welcoming friends in New York and Rio.

Compatriots at the Center for African and African-American Studies, working hard in the construction of a black community in what still is a typical U.S. academic plantation, have provided a supportive and caring environment. I am grateful to all the true Center's affiliates, as well as the good work of Pam Haith, Stephanie Lang, Jin Kyung Lee, and Jennifer Lawton. Joni Jones/Iya Omi Osun Olomo, Center codirector, and Sharon Bridgforth, both performers extraordinaire, share with grace and beauty their dreams and knowledge of community and freedom; they understand all our internal and collective struggles—thank you.

An impressive group of scholars of color and allies make UT the ultimate people's republic of activist research, smack in the middle of the beast's belly. For a while, we had what must have been the greatest concentration of Afro-Brazilian scholars-activists in a campus, anywhere: besides our imported locals, Joel Zito Araújo, Diva Moreira, and Rumba Gabriel, from whom I continue to learn. Thanks to Sharmila Rudrappa for her friendship and good sense. Michael Ray Charles inspires me to keep searching for a language of social change outside our various cages.

Charlie Hale is the rare race traitor whom we Black folks love to love. He and Melissa Smith, Amalia, and Sofia are not only revolutionary people but also friends for all weathers.

Colleagues and friends at the Center, of the Austin School, and the Black Diaspora Consortium have challenged and motivated me to better express my views. Special thanks to Jemima Pierre, Faye Harrison, Kia Caldwell, Ben Carrington, Kevin Foster, Marc Sawyer, Bettina Ng'weno, Kaushik Ghosh, Shannon Speed, Frank Guridy, Jennifer Wilks, Juliet Hooker, Michael Hanchard, and Angela Gilliam.

Jafari Allen and Phillip Alexander, brother comrades, and all-around artists, constantly remind me of the necessity and processual nature of serenity, as well as the analytical, in-your-face, productive, caring, and honest dialogue. Jafari has much contributed to my endless process of decolonization, gently suggesting and recognizing new directions of personal and political transformation.

Edmund T. Gordon, pragmatic and loving, ruthless and placid, the relentless visionary, is the self-effacing mastermind liberation strategist behind this unprecedented experiment of building a community of Black progressive scholar-activists in Tejas. I, like most, if not all, Black folks in the College of Liberal Arts—graduate students and faculty—owe my presence at UT to his vision, for which he refuses to take credit. From revolutionary Nicaragua to the Austin School, guided by the sounds of Coltrane, Jimi Hendrix, Bob Marley, and Nina Simone (and Bob Dylan), from the Black Diaspora Consortium to whatever collective project must come next, Ted is the ultimate guerrero del amor—utopian in spite of his second-nature Hall/Foucault/Gramsci syncretism. His loyal, enabling, and caring comradeship has not only opened up revolutionary possibilities, but also saved my life a few times. I have enjoyed and abused Ted and Daisy Garth's friendship, Creole hospitality, innumerable banquets, endless patience, and infinite kindness; together with Wyatt and Ishan, they have a huge hand in helping me transform Austin into a refuge that almost feels like home, which is probably as good as it gets.

Toussaint Pierre-Vargas, born on the two-hundredth year of the Haitian revolution, inspires me to adoringly resist our oppressions and fight for liberation. The Pierres have been wonderful grandparents, aunts, and uncles, for which I am thankful. A profound thank you, Jemima, for the loving coparenting, and sharing the vision and so much more. I am grateful to my sisters, Mônica and Zaíra, and their families—especially my wonderful Anna Clara, Pedro Paulo, and Uma—as well as to Anna and Helion, my parents, who have always been supportive, accepting while trying to understand my choices.

COALITION AGAINST POLICE ABUSE COMMUNITY ORGANIZING MANUAL

Abridged Version

Statement of Purpose

What We Want

What We Believe

Program for United Action

Police Review Board: Summary

CAPA Community Organizing Manual

Introduction. Police Abuse: The Reign of Terror

I. Document the Case

II. Reach the People

III. Mobilize the People

IV. Legal Tips

V. Ongoing Committee Work and Block Organizing

STATEMENT OF PURPOSE

WHEREAS, for as long as we can remember, poor people, especially in the black and brown communities, have been victims of abusive and criminal acts committed by racist police officers;

WHEREAS, the present pattern of police terror is well established, taking the form of senseless beatings, brutal murders, illegal and unconstitutional stops, searches and arrests;

WHEREAS, lurking behind these cases of murder and oppression lies a worsening economic and political crisis in which the government, guided by a false notion of law and order, has begun to legislate and order through the courts more repressive acts by the police;

WHEREAS, by legislating away the few human rights we have won through constitutional amendments, the government has put more and more power into the hands of the police;

BE IT RESOLVED that THE COALITION AGAINST POLICE ABUSE has been formed by community people who feel that the reign of terror by the police has remained unchecked for too long, that it is time to let the authorities know that we will no longer tolerate the senseless harassment, injury and murder of community people by the police, and that we have resolved as our main purpose to organize and mobilize the masses in the black and brown communities as well as other poor communities, through block clubs, church groups, labor committees, youth groups, women's groups, gay organizations, senior citizen clubs and concerned individuals and families, to organize against police terrorism in our communities.

What We Want

1. Suspend without pay from the police department, indict and jail all officers involved in or accused of cases of police harassment, beatings and murders of community people.

2. Elimination of the Internal Affairs Division, the current investigative arm of the police department, and the establishment of a community selected and controlled agency to investigate charges of police abuse

and criminal misconduct. This new agency can set up a bureau in each of the 16 divisions patrolled by the LAPD. It should be city funded and staffed by community people—not funded by police agencies such as LEAA or staffed by police personnel.

3. Establishment of a special prosecutor for all cases of police abuse crimes. This special prosecutor should be appointed by concerned community organizations. This is necessary because most officials responsible for appointing prosecutors are far removed, both economically and socially, from most of our people who suffer from police abuse crimes. This special prosecutor should be financed by the City of Los Angeles.

4. Stop deportations and harassment by racist police and immigration officials. The repeated deportations, harassment, beatings and murders by these agencies of undocumented workers is a conscious move by the city, state and federal governments to politically and economically enslave these workers who were forced from their homes by U.S. capitalist corporations, forced to accept ridiculously low wages and humiliating living conditions in America.

5. Elimination of special tactics squads, such as SWAT, CCS, SSI and undercover agencies and agents because of the general threat they pose to the safety and welfare of civil and human rights of black and brown communities. We have evidence that these special tactics squads and undercover agencies' main objectives have been to spy on us and collect information to be used to destroy us and other legitimate community organizations and their organizing efforts, and to show massive military force when entering our community. The SLA shootout in 1974 is a good example.

6. An independent investigation of the Los Angeles County District Attorney's office for its lack of indictments of police who have abused and terrorized community people. From 1975 to 1978 almost 150 people have been killed and hundreds of others shot. There have been no indictments.

7. Stop, indict and jail all officers involved in sexist and racist harassment, beatings, murders and rapes of women, particularly black and brown women.

8. Remove all city officials who sit back and condone or refuse to fire and jail police who have records of police abuse, or have been shown clearly to have committed crimes of murder in our communities.

What We Believe

We believe that the police in our communities were not placed there to "protect and serve" the people. In fact, by their past actions they have proven to us that police:

Are not in reality members of the communities in which they patrol and do not relate to our communities on any other level than as "armed enforcers" of racism, sexism and other forms of oppression;

Are not sincerely working to help our communities' progress, but are actually in our communities for the purpose of intimidation, confinement and control;

Treat the people in our communities with attitudes of suspicion, racism and general disrespect;

Place little value on the lives and safety of the people in our communities and do not hesitate to use excessive force and violence.

Program for United Action

In the direct interest of the numerous defense and justice committees who are struggling with particular instances of senseless killings and abuse, CAPA has chosen the following actions to achieve our immediate and long range goals:

To actively call public attention to these particular instances of police abuse and crime, and to bring public pressure to bear in obtaining justice;

To politically educate people as to the origins of increasing police terror, and in particular the growing menace of an all-out police state;

To educate people about both our human and constitutional rights and to organize a mass base in the communities, train new leadership in order that people may unite to defend themselves and their democratic rights from further attack in our communities, jails and prisons;

To mobilize, rely on, and give concrete direction to the people of our communities to stand up for their rights against police harassment, beatings, racist insults, murders;

To unite as many organizations and individuals of all nationalities as possible so that in our numbers we will have the unity and strength to defend our homes, families and democratic rights from attack.

Police Review Board: Summary

The following represents the basic points to be included in a petition to change the Los Angeles City Charter. The charter amendment will establish a Civilian Police Review Board to be elected by the voters.

1. The Civilian Police Review Board will be made up of 15 members, one elected from each City Council District. They will be salaried and work full-time.

2. The Review Board will judge complaints of unnecessary force, false arrest, harassment, tampering with evidence, abuse of authority, violation of civil rights, illegal surveillance, abusive language, gay bashing, racial or ethnic slurs.

3. The Board will have the power to review and alter police procedures and policies concerning the above areas.

4. The Board will have the power to discipline (ranging from censure to suspension without pay for up to six months) and the power to fire officers. It will also have the power to recommend criminal prosecutions and power to award civil damages up to $50,000,000.

5. The Board will also have an independent staff of investigators with full subpoena power, plus immediate and unrestricted access to shooting areas.

6. A Special Prosecutor will be elected, whose job will be to handle cases of misdemeanor criminal charges against police officers.

7. All Review Board members will be required to hold community meetings at least once per month in their districts, where they will present reports to the people and listen to the peoples' views and suggestions.

8. The Review Board will give quarterly reports on all incidents involving complaints against police officers.

9. Complaints may be filed by mail, telephone, or at any of the 15 City Council district offices.

10. Any accused officers will have the full right to defend themselves during all Review Board proceedings.

11. Any Police Officer who threatens, harasses or discriminates against another officer of the LAPD who witnesses an act of police abuse and reports it to the Civilian Police Review Board is subject to the penalties as outlined in the Review Board Initiative.

COALITION AGAINST POLICE ABUSE

COMMUNITY ORGANIZING MANUAL

Introduction

Police Abuse—The Reign of Terror

There is a reign of police terror in cities throughout the United States that has gone unchecked for many years. Recently it has grown much worse.

In Los Angeles, police officers shot over 270 citizens from January, 1975 to January, 1979. Over 127 persons have been killed or choked to death.

In Detroit, Chicago, Philadelphia and Houston, murderous rampages by police far exceed those in Los Angeles.

In cities everywhere police harassment, brutality, and abuse are rampant.

The situations continue to worsen because police act as armed storm troopers against any person who opposes the wretched and oppressive conditions of this society.

The police are in our communities to intimidate, confine and control. They treat people in our communities with racism, suspicion and disrespect. They place little or no value on our lives and safety. They do not hesitate to use excessive force and violence to protect the interests of the ruling class of this country.

The Coalition Against Police Abuse believes it is time to declare an absolute end to this kind of senseless harassment and murder. In the firm belief that the key to achieving this goal is an organized, unified community, CAPA has resolved to mobilize masses of community people—community groups, youth organizations, women's groups, individuals and families—to organize against the scourge of police terror in our community. To this end CAPA has developed what it believes to be a highly effective organizing technique applicable to the communities.

This technique is based on organizing in the wake of specific cases of police abuse. It can be done most effectively in three steps:

1. Document the case,

2. Reach the people, and

3. Mobilize the people.

Drawing from a wide variety of actual experiences of police abuse in the Los Angeles area, CAPA is pleased to present this practical, step-by-step guide to effective community organizing.

I. Document the Case

Effective community organizations cannot thrive around abstract ideas. To succeed, they need concrete issues—specific instances of police abuse. Specific cases need hard facts to back them up. Gathering these facts is a vital first step in building and maintaining community organizations.

Find and Interview Witnesses

The victims of abuse may be able to supply a list. If not, visit the scene and seek out witnesses by talking to people who live and work in the area.

A few pointers: Interview witnesses only in person, not by telephone. Find interviewers who can talk comfortably to witnesses and make them feel relaxed. Perhaps someone who knows the witness personally can go along. Witnesses should be allowed to tell the story in their own words, while being gently encouraged to keep things in the order they occurred and to stick to the facts. Take notes of everything the witness says. Find out if the witness is willing to talk to a lawyer and to tape the interview. Find out whether the witness will testify in court.

Interview Public Officials

Many officials, such as the mayor, city council members, police community affairs officers, representatives of the district attorney and others, are in positions to know or find out crucial information about the incident. They can be surprisingly helpful, if only when they accidentally contradict official public statements about the case. Take notes and make tape recordings whenever possible.

Keep a Record of All Written Public Statements about the Case

This means newspaper and magazine articles, as well as other sources of statements by police or public officials. Compare these to statements taken in your own interviews and check for contradictions.

With the facts in hand, you should consult the victims and/or their friends or family to decide on the next step. The victim may wish to consult a lawyer before continuing. If the victim agrees to begin a community action, your actual organizing now begins.

II. Reach the People

Well organized communities must be well informed, not only in the initial stages of a case, but later on as it continues and still later as your organization responds to future incidents and expands its scope.

Basically, there are six ways of keeping people informed:

1. Flyers or fact sheets

2. Leaflet and newsletters

3. Educational meetings

4. Face-to-face contacts

5. Fax and E-mail

6. Media exposure

Fact Sheets and Flyers

Distributing these throughout the community are good ways of initially alerting people about the facts of a case. They can also spread the word about community meetings, and help keep communities informed about new developments. Fact sheets should be kept brief and to the point; they should be hand-delivered to homes and placed in strategic public locations such as stores, markets, community centers, recreation centers and meeting halls.

Leaflets and Newsletters

Supplement or replace the fact sheets as your group expands its ongoing cases, sets its goals and begins work on broader issues of police repression. Background leaflets or brochures should briefly and persuasively summarize your group's purposes and goals, while newsletters should provide clear and interesting updates of your latest activities. For printing and other technical tips, see the Manual's Resource Appendix [*author's note:* not included in this volume].

Educational Meetings

Feature discussions, films, speakers, guerrilla theaters, or debates can be extremely effective in reaching people and building community awareness of the problem. Be sure to pass our sign-up sheets at all meetings, asking names, address and phone numbers of those attending.

Face to Face Contacts

On a one-to-one basis is probably the most effective way of reaching people. Besides meetings, door-to-door canvassing in early organizational stages and block organizing later on can provide excellent opportunities for face to face communication.

Fax or E-mail

Develop a fax phone list of organizations or individuals who can "pass the word along"—including denominational offices of churches, local press, religious news media, colleges (sympathetic faculty, for example), civic organizations such as NOW or gay rights groups; the League of Women Voters, or other groups concerned with public policy; and groups in solidarity with your cause such as Clergy and Laity Concerned, N-COPA (National Coalition on Police Accountability); peace and justice groups such as the American Friends Service Committee and trade union groups. Set your fax for automatic faxing to a predetermined list of these fax numbers to save time. E-mail within corporations can be accessed through one employee with the right access codes.

Media

Media coverage is an effective way of seeking wider public support outside your immediate community, while displaying your group's effectiveness and "muscle." At the same time, public officials are less likely to cause trouble for you if they know the media is interested in your case. You should seek coverage from daily television and radio newscasts, and newspapers, public service announcements from TV and radio station announcers, and plugs from radio personalities such as disc jockeys. For tips on how to go about getting this coverage, see the Manual's "Media Appendix" [*author's note:* not included in this volume].

III. Mobilize the People

Well-organized communities should be able to respond effectively to specific cases of police abuse on a continuing basis and to seek remedies for wider problems of police terror and repression. To do so, they must be able to mobilize people—to call on people to perform specific tasks, and to turn out large numbers for specific events such as rallies, pickets and marches.

Community organizing is always most effective when begun in reaction to a specific episode of police abuse, rather than around an abstract idea. Essentially, the same techniques used in early stages of organizing can be used again as the group increases its scope. For instance, your early meetings should be narrowly confined to a single incident. Later on, the meetings can use films, speakers and other tools to address broader issues of police abuse. Also, a rally or picket line might be used at an early stage to show some "muscle" and boost community interest in your group and your issue. These same actions can be used again to continue addressing specific incidents, as well as broader issues. Door-to-door canvassing may be used at first to help build interest in your group. Later it is best to build a block-by-block organization (more on this later).

Remember, organizations thrive on specific actions and concrete issues. They die on inaction and abstract themes. Positive action, in particular, can help achieve goals and increase community awareness. Organizers should focus on realistic, attainable goals, while keeping in mind that any specific case is part of the larger issue of police repression. Again, this whole system of organizing is based on responding to specific episodes of police abuse. Take a step-by-step approach, plan short-range goals with a high probability of success and seek "small" victories as a way to build confidence among your members. The following presents a general approach on organizing after a specific incident of police abuse.

Call a Community Meeting

An especially loathsome episode of police abuse has aroused the anger of the community. Compile the facts, tell people what really happened—by face-to-face contact and fact sheets—and call a community meeting.

Some pointers about the meeting: Pick a chairperson acceptable to the people whom you expect to attend. Don't let the meeting drag on or be distracted from the main issue at hand. If necessary, set time limits on speakers and use Robert's Rules of Order—available in paperback—to keep the meeting moving along. Be sure to pass out a sign-up sheet asking for names, addresses and telephone numbers. Stick to two essential themes: (1) Tell people about the case with fact sheets and discussion, and (2) decide on a definite action to expose and protest the incident. Do not let this meeting adjourn without deciding on some action.

Forming a Justice Committee

The likely action or result of this community meeting will be the formation of a defense or justice committee. This may seem like a modest beginning, but it is crucial to get this far. Those who join the committee should immediately set a date for their first meeting and, as soon as possible, decide:

1. How much time each person can work for the group.

2. A regular meeting time, scheduled at least once a week.

3. An organizational structure, such as committee or officers, and

4. Goals and how to reach them (see below).

Organizing the Committee—Goals and Demands

Your justice committee has gotten the basics out of the way (the first three points just above). Your committee should formulate a brief statement of its goals, purposes and intentions. Its first goal most likely should be to draw up and present a set of demands. Here are some pointers:

1. Be sure of your demands. Research them thoroughly and try to come up with the best possible statement of what you want.

2. Avoid negotiating with any individual or group which does not have the power to agree and implement your demands.

3. Research the people with whom you will be negotiating. That is, has he or she been vocal against police abuse in the past? Is it an issue in his/her district?

4. Take as many people as you can to the negotiations.

5. Be skeptical. Do not be fooled by people who try to pretend to be nice, polite and concerned. Don't deal in personalities. Keep the issues and concrete demands in mind.

6. Stick to your demands. Don't deal with other subjects unless they relate directly to your demands.

7. Watch out for attempts to divide your forces.

8. Avoid negotiations which lead to time-consuming committees or commissions to "study" the matter. Good demands keep the momentum of a committee moving.

IV. Legal Tips

At the same time you are drawing up your demands, you should be considering filing a formal complaint with the police or filing civil suit. For either of these, you should contact a lawyer. You may contact the American Civil Liberties Union, the National Lawyers Guild, Peoples College of Law or a community legal assistance group such as the Los Angeles Greater Watts Justice Center. Remember the legal system is slanted heavily against you. Your only chance is to have someone working for you who knows it and knows how to use it to benefit people. Although the legal solution will rarely be satisfactory, you should exhaust it fully—if only to understand the need for taking more militant action. Moreover, it is one more method of dealing with police abuse. Finally, as citizens of the United States we are supposed to be able to address different government institutions with any complaint we have. We should utilize this right!

Also remember that the legal action should not be separated from the issue of police abuse itself. First, the announcement of legal action, or the presentation of demands are suitable for a press conference. See Media Appendix [*author's note:* not included in this volume]. Second, you should at the same time be planning a major demonstration designed to show community sentiment about the issue. The demonstration is also suitable for media coverage.

As to the legal action itself, it is generally advisable to consult with community legal groups before proceeding. Below are some general tips and specific information on how to complain against police misconduct in the Los Angeles area.

(A) Recruit professional help

Include lawyers, paralegals, law students and legal workers in your Committee. It is important that the general membership and/or special committees include some persons who are familiar with working on legal problems. Legal workers should not be permitted to dominate or change the radical nature of the organization, but they should be politicized and consulted regarding on-going projects and activities so that major cases can be nurtured from the earliest possible opportunity.

(B) Choose concrete, specific issues to attack

Most victims of police abuse have a large number of legitimate complaints to make about their treatment at the hands of the police. Many sound like this: "He told me to move on even though I was just standing around watching. He put a choke hold on me, didn't give me my rights, called me a 'nigger,' didn't give me medical treatment in jail, held me for 3 days, charged me with a high bail, and later caused me to serve 90 days for interfering with and obstructing a police officer."

In trying to launch a major civil suit, try to isolate one or two key issues that you can organize around and which provide an attorney with a basis for going to court. This is where legal people close to the organization can aid in selecting the issues. Perhaps you want to isolate the specific, concrete issue of a person's right to witness. By this we mean that a person should have the right to peaceably observe police action without being forced by the police to "move on." The basic argument would be that the First Amendment protects this right. This is also an issue which the liberal press and the general public can identify with. Perhaps this is not the case to try and raise Miranda rights issues or even bail issues, but it may be great for the right to witness issues.

(C) Choose the proper clients

Recognizing that all persons deserve a vigorous defense to criminal cases, nevertheless, all cases and clients don't make good lawsuits. Therefore, choose a situation that contains the issue you're seeking to redress, but that also contains favorable facts. For example, a client without a felony record will usually be preferable for most issues. Choose situations where independent witnesses are most easily available, where public sympathy can easily be aroused, and where your client is most disciplined and poised to endure long and painstaking legal procedures and cross-examinations.

(D) Organize legal helpers

Once a case and strategy are chosen, have people around who are willing to interview many witnesses, go through court records, serve subpoenas, run errands, or find documents.

(E) Mobilize mass support

As stated before, legal remedies are not the solution for police misconduct. Any real impact will be the result of our ability to organize and education the community around the issue.

(F) Use of the mass media

Also discussed earlier was the need to utilize the media fully before filing a lawsuit. Try to get on talk shows and explain the issues. Finally, have a news conference upon filing the lawsuit.

V. On-Going Committee Work and Block Organizing

You've done an enormous amount of work, successfully staged some meetings, actions and events and drawn considerable attention to your issue. There are still great numbers of tasks to perform in eliminating widespread police abuse and repression. With the amount of work you've already done, your wisest course is naturally to develop and maintain the organization you have begun. As already stated, you can continue to use a combination of actions, community meetings, and educational tools. In addition, a key way to build and develop lasting and responsible organization is block organizing. It is an excellent way to maintain a firm, grassroots base in the community. And it's a perfect pipeline; you can spread information and you can learn what the community is concerned about and what it thinks of the work you have been doing. Here are some pointers on how to organize a block:

1. Draw a map of blocks in the immediate area of the incident.

2. Assign members of your committee to each block.

3. These members—block contacts—should go door-to-door and let people know what the committee is doing. They should enlist

support by getting people to talk to their families, friends, relatives and neighbors about your issue and about being part of the block organization.

4. The block contact should note which people on the block seem most receptive. These people should be asked to host a block meeting at their home.

NOTES

1. I capitalize the term *Black* as it describes and locates the social dynamics of racialized communities with specific experiences, histories, and politics in both the United States and in other nation-states of the African diaspora. *Black,* capitalized, connotes simultaneous processes: it is a self-defined racial identity; it is a result of state classification (as in the 2000 U.S. census); and it emerges from political struggles within and between racialized communities and the state. *Black,* capitalized, is synonymous with African American, Black American, and people of African descent, among others. As a noun, adjective, and ideology, Black refers to both the specificity of racialized experiences and their imminently socially constructed character. The capitalization of White follows the same logic. For a useful related discussion, which I closely follow here, see Patricia Hill Collins, *Black Sexual Politics: African Americans, Gender, and the New Racism* (London: Routledge, 2004), 17, 310.

2. I am aware that such figures may be inflated. A study suggests that in the late 1980s the average crack dealer made about $700 a month. Peter Reuter, Robert MacCoun, and Patrick Murphy, *Money for Crime: A Study in the Economics of Drug Dealing in Washington, D.C.* (Santa Monica, Calif.: Rand Drug Policy Research Center, 1990). Still, Kody's reputation in the drug market may explain his higher gains.

3. It must be stressed that babies born under conditions of poverty and hopelessness are likely to be unhealthy regardless of their mothers' use of crack. For a more detailed explanation, see Dorothy Roberts, *Killing the Black Body: Race, Reproduction, and the Meaning of Liberty* (New York: Vintage, 1997), esp. chap. 4.

4. Throughout this work, South Central Los Angeles will be understood in accordance to *An Atlas of South Central Los Angeles,* published by the Rose Institute of Local and State Government at Claremont McKenna College. South Central is defined there as "bounded by West Hollywood and Beverly Hills on the Northwest; Culver City, Ladera Heights, Inglewood, Lennox, and Hawthorne on the West; Lawndale,

Gardena, and Compton on the South; and Lynwood, South Gate, Huntington Park, and Vernon on the East." It should be understood that not all census tracts included in this area pertain to the City of Los Angeles: of the 526 census tracts that correspond to South Central, only 346 are in the city's perimeter. Cited in Armando Navarro, "The South Central Los Angeles Eruption: A Latino Perspective," in *Los Angeles— Struggles Toward Multiethnic Community: Asian American, African American, and Latino Perspectives,* ed. Edward T. Chang and Russell C. Leong (Seattle: University of Washington Press, 1994), 83. See map 2.1 for South Central's neighborhoods.

5. See, e.g., Jerome G. Miller, *Search and Destroy: African-American Males in the Criminal Justice System* (New York: Cambridge University Press, 1996). "The figures suggested that the absolute majority of young black males in Los Angeles could expect to be dragged into one or another of the county's jails, detention centers, camps, or prisons as they traversed the years between adolescence and age 30. Similar patterns were showing up in other large cities" (5).

6. Robert M. Fogelson, *The Fragmented Metropolis: Los Angeles, 1830–1930* (Cambridge: Harvard University Press, 1967); James N. Gregory, *American Exodus: The Dust Bowl Migration and Okie Culture in California* (New York: Oxford University Press, 1989); John H. M. Laslett, "Historical Perspectives: Immigration and the Rise of a Distinctive Urban Region, 1900–1970," in *Ethnic Los Angeles,* ed. Roger Waldinger and Mehdi Bozorgmehr (New York: Russell Sage Foundation, 1996); David O. Sears and John McConahay, *The Politics of Violence: The New Urban Blacks and the Watts Riot* (Boston: Houghton Mifflin, 1973); Kenneth Jackson, *Crabgrass Frontier: The Suburbanization of the United States* (New York: Oxford University Press, 1985); Keith Collins, *Black Los Angeles: The Maturing of the Ghetto, 1940–1950* (Saratoga, Calif.: Century Twenty One Publishing, 1980); J. Max Bond, *The Negro in Los Angeles* (1936; San Francisco: R and E Research Associates, 1972); Charles Mingus, *Beneath the Underdog* (1971; New York: Vintage, 1991); Lynell George, *No Crystal Stair: African-Americans in the City of Angels* (London: Verso, 1992).

7. It can be argued that civil rights–era gains in education and employment disproportionately benefited middle-class Blacks in comparison to poorer Blacks. Studies on several comparable cities in the United States have shown how the process of class formation among Blacks was also shaped by the state's influence on the political possibilities at the neighborhood level. Steven Gregory, in his study of Corona and East Elmhurst, Queens, New York, argued that the state "incited the production and exercise of particular forms of black 'middle class' identity and disproportionately empowered middle-income, largely home owning residents of East Elmhurst." The Black poor, meanwhile, were categorized and isolated as "clients in bureaucratic agencies." In sum, "this bureaucratization of the community's service infrastructure increased the social, political, and ideological distance between low and middle-income residents by differentiating the institutional settings in which the needs and interests of the two groups were defined and addressed." *Black Corona: Race and the Politics of Place in an Urban Community* (Princeton, N.J.: Princeton University Press, 1998), 144–46. See also Thomas Sugrue, *The Origins of the Urban Crisis: Race and Inequality*

in Postwar Detroit (Princeton, N.J.: Princeton University Press, 1996). Similar processes took place in Los Angeles' Black neighborhoods. The fact that the Black poor became, especially in the wake of the 1960s activism, preferential *clients* of the state-sponsored social welfare programs, while the well-to-do Blacks became *participants* in the bureaucratic agencies set to (theoretically, at least) challenge neighborhood problems provides yet another explanation for the contemporary chasms between Blacks of different social backgrounds.

8. Melvin Oliver and Thomas Shapiro, *Black Wealth/White Wealth: A New Perspective on Racial Inequality* (London: Routledge, 1997).

9. Stuart Hall, "Encoding/Decoding," in *Culture, Media, Language,* ed. Stuart Hall, Dorothy Hobson, Andrew Lowe, and Paul Willis (London: Routledge, 2002), 128–38.

10. In order to make sense of the various class denominations that appear in this text, a set of references is necessary. To do so, let me heuristically define a few parameters according to which we can envisage a Black class structure, keeping in mind that such parameters are always dependent on the context, they are contrastive (i.e., working class versus middle class), and above all else, serve as a conduit through which to detect and interpret tensions among Blacks. By attempting to initially define the Black middle class, I thus also draw a provisory line between the middle class and the working class. A person or a family, unless otherwise noted, will be part of the Black middle class if at least one of the following applies:

    a. earning income at least twice the poverty level income, which for a family of four in 1995 stood at $15,569;

    b. having a college degree; or

    c. holding white- or specialized blue-collar employment.

These incomplete and necessarily partial criteria take on historical specificity and sociological depth in this study. My principal concern when utilizing, engaging with, and interpreting notions of class is to develop a historical comprehension of the various conflicts—as well as their solutions—within South Central. For studies on contemporary manifestations of Black social class, see Thomas M. Shapiro, *The Hidden Cost of Being African American: How Wealth Perpetuates Inequality* (Oxford: Oxford University Press, 2004), esp. 87–88; Mary Patillo-McCoy, *Black Picket Fences: Privilege and Peril among the Black Middle Class* (Chicago: University of Chicago Press, 1999); on the mutual determinations of class and race in Harlem, see the ethnography by John L. Jackson, *Harlemworld: Doing Race and Class in Contemporary Black America* (Chicago: University of Chicago Press, 2001).

11. My view on anti-Black genocide taking place in the United States, as well as in other countries of the African diaspora, builds on the 1951 formal accusation made by the Civil Rights Congress against the United States at the United Nations. Presented by a delegation supported by W. E. B. Du Bois and Paul Robeson, among others, the accusation described the United States' practice of genocide against African Americans. See William Patterson et al., *We Charge Genocide: The Historic Petition to the United Nations for Relief from a Crime of the United States Government*

Against the Negro People (New York: Civil Rights Congress, 1951). An analysis of the document reveals a complex understanding of genocide as both multidimensional (including not only lynchings, but also residential segregation and discrimination in the labor market, for example) and part of a continuum (in which a cultural climate supported the symbolic and actual violence against Blacks and the social and economic entitlements to which Whites felt entitled). See João H. Costa Vargas, "Hyperconsciousness of Race and Its Negation: The Dialectic of White Supremacy in Brazil," *Identities* 11 (2004): 443–70, and also "Black Genocide: Brazil, United States, and the Need for a Holistic Approach, *Cultural Dynamics* (2005, forthcoming). For analyses of Black genocide in the contemporary United States, see, e.g., Manning Marable, *How Capitalism Underdeveloped Black America* (1983; Cambridge, Mass.: South End Press, 2000), and also Joy James, *Resisting State Violence: Radicalism, Gender, and Race in U.S. Culture* (Minnesota: University of Minnesota Press, 1996).

12. For a critique of self-help ideology, see Kelley, *Yo' Mama's Disfunktional!: Fighting the Culture Wars in Urban America* (Boston: Beacon Press, 1997), esp. chap. 3.

13. Among these varied experiences and outlooks, consider the fact that many impoverished Blacks, unlike their middle-class, home-owning counterparts, are unable to maintain the same address for any extended period of time, as chapter 3 shows. This fact alone creates not only immense hardships for those constantly moving from residence to residence to keep in touch with community-based organizations, but also reinforces a perception of the inner city that is very different from that held by well-to-do Blacks. This brief, introductory example points to some of the difficulties, on the one hand, of getting persons actively and consistently involved in social movements and, on the other, of reconciling different views of the ghetto within the same organization (supposing, of course, a class-inclusive program).

By "ghetto" I understand "a set of neighborhoods exclusively inhabited by members of one group, within which virtually all members of that group live. By this definition, no ethnic or racial group in the history of the United States, except one, has ever experienced ghettoization, even briefly. For urban Blacks, the ghetto has been the paradigmatic residential configuration for at least eighty years." Douglas Massey and Nancy Denton, *American Apartheid: Segregation and the Making of the Underclass* (Cambridge: Harvard University Press, 1993), 19. While I am aware of the uneasiness that the "ghetto" can generate, especially among Blacks and when employed as an adjective, I chose to use it as a noun to underscore its deeply historical and systematic dimensions.

14. Various authors have made similar claims regarding the Black radical tradition. See, e.g., Cedric Robinson, *Black Marxism: The Making of the Black Radical Tradition* (1983; Chapel Hill: University of North Carolina Press, 2000); Patricia Hill Collins, *Black Feminist Thought: Knowledge, Consciousness, and the Politics of Empowerment* (London: HarperCollins Academic, 1991); Robin D. G. Kelley, *Freedom Dreams* (Boston: Beacon Press, 2002).

15. Chaim Perelman, *Le Champ de l'Argumentation* (Bruxelles: Presses Universitaires de Bruxelles, 1970).

16. See, e.g., Elijah Anderson, *Streetwise: Race, Class, and Change in an Urban Community* (Chicago: University of Chicago Press, 1990); Mitchell Duneier, *Slim's Table: Race, Respectability, and Masculinity* (Chicago: University of Chicago Press, 1992); Philippe Bourgois, *In Search of Respect: Selling Crack in El Barrio* (New York: Cambridge University Press, 1995).

17. Bourgois, *In Search of Respect,* 11.

18. Duneier, *Slim's Table,* 126.

19. Among relatively recent ethnographies, Jay McLeod's *Ain't No Makin' It: Leveled Aspirations in a Low-Income Neighborhood* (Boulder, Colo.: Westview Press, 1987) is an exception. It addresses and provides a compelling explanation for the reproduction of social inequalities among poor youths through local sociabilities, school, and work. In this sense, it is attuned to broader structures of oppression, although it does not address the historical developments of such structures. Likewise, Gregory's *Black Corona* reconstitutes the histories of a Black community from the memories of those who participated in its making. Anderson's *Streetwise* includes a chapter about "Police and the Black Male." Here again, however, the analysis is restricted to local representations of the police, without attention to its organization and programs.

20. On the knowledge produced by Black women, see Collins, *Black Feminist Thought,* and *Fighting Words: Black Women and the Search for Justice* (Minneapolis: University of Minnesota Press, 1998). For a perspective on the Black radical tradition, see Robinson, *Black Marxism.* I am obviously making the argument that what Collins locates, describes, and analyzes as Black feminist thought is precisely an expression of the Black radical tradition as foregrounded by Robinson in his classic study. Inflected/corrected by Black feminist thought, the Black radical tradition becomes one that asserts the intersectionality of race, class, gender, sexuality, and nationality, among others, while centering on the experiences of Black working-class women's theorizations and everyday politics of resistance. In a world defined by imperialist White supremacist capitalist patriarchy, as bell hooks often reminds us, progressive Black feminist perspectives, when grounded in actual lived experiences, provide crucial elements for critique and liberation. See, e.g., bell hooks, *We Real Cool: Black Men and Masculinity* (London: Routledge, 2004). Because it emerges from and opposes the intersectional oppressions of race, gender, social class, and sexuality, Black feminist thought presents universalistic claims insofar as its commitment to social justice necessarily implies justice to all social groups objectified by any of such axes of oppression. A consequence of this perspective that affirms both the knowledge and the limitation of various standpoints is the need for coalitional politics. The U.S.-specific dimensions and limitations of Black feminist thought, however, also need to be acknowledged. See Barbara Smith, *The Truth That Never Hurts: Writings on Race, Gender, and Freedom* (New Brunswick, N.J.: Rutgers University Press, 2000), and Chandra Talpade Mohanty, *Feminism Without Borders: Decolonizing Theory, Practicing Solidarity* (Durham, N.C.: Duke University Press, 2003).

21. On the oppressor within, see Audre Lorde, *Sister Outsider* (Freedom, Calif.: Crossing Press, 1996). For an account of coalitional politics in the context of England,

see Julia Sudbury, *"Other Kinds of Dreams": Black Women's Organisations and the Politics of Transformation* (London: Routledge, 1998). Gloria Anzaldúa and Elizabeth Keating, eds., *This Bridge We Call Home: Radical Visions for Transformation* (London: Routledge, 2002), focuses on both the personal and the political processes of decolonization and radical social transformation. On the possibilities and dangers of alliances between profeminist males and feminists of color, see, e.g., Joy James, *Shadowboxing: Representations of Black Feminist Politics* (1999; New York: Palgrave, 2002). Based on a critical analysis of the academic work of important self-professed male profeminists, Joy remarks: "At best, the feminization of male discourse confronts gender hierarchy, inextricably linked to heterosexism, racism, and classism, *and* the institutional privilege of the feminized male voice. At its worst, in the absence of a radical practice and theory, profeminism will foster a coalition politics that stops before full justice is achieved. Consequently, its politics will downplay disputes between professed feminists, adding to the restive uneasiness among profeminism's natural allies" (170).

22. On controlling images, see Collins, *Black Feminist Thought,* chap. 4. See also Roberts, *Killing the Black Body,* and Angela Davis, *Blues Legacy and Black Feminism* (New York: Vintage, 1999). For an examination of how "controlling images" influence the criminalization of young Black men, see Kathryn Russell, *The Color of Crime: Racial Hoaxes, White Fear, Black Protectionism, Police Harassment, and Other Macroaggressions* (New York: New York University Press, 1998). While I am aware of the connection between the notion of controlling images and Black feminist thought, I suggest that, with the necessary caveats about the specificities of Black women's gendered racialization, the notion can be applied to how Black males are construed as either super- or infra-human and thus dehumanized.

23. See, e.g., hooks, *We Real Cool,* 57.

24. On the boundaries of blackness and how they are imagined, enforced, and negotiated among African Americans, see Cathy J. Cohen, *The Boundaries of Blackness: AIDS and the Breakdown of Black Politics* (Chicago: University of Chicago Press, 1999).

25. Anderson, *Streetwise,* 101.

26. See, e.g., Eliot Liebow, *Tally's Corner: A Study of Ghetto Streetcorner Men* (Boston: Little, Brown, 1967); Ulf Hannerz, *Soulside: Inquiries into Ghetto Culture and Community* (New York: Columbia University Press, 1969); David Schulz, *Coming Up Black: Patterns of Ghetto Socialization* (Englewood Cliffs, N.J.: Prentice-Hall, 1969); Carol Stack, *All Our Kin: Strategies for Survival in a Black Community* (New York: Harper and Row, 1974).

27. Anderson, *Streetwise,* 103, 104–5.

28. William J. Wilson, *When Work Disappears: The World of the New Urban Poor* (New York: Knopf, 1996), 73.

29. Wilson does not make the claim that new urban poor act irrationally by opting for welfare in the face of the economic constraints of badly paid work. But he affirms that the rationality involved in this calculation is sanctioned by the environment in which such decisions are common and tolerated (ibid., 84).

30. Ibid., 75.

31. For descriptions and analyses of the 1965 Watts uprising, as well as pertinent literature on the political, social, and psychological contexts of the 1950s–1960s, see Lonnie G. Bunch, "A Past Not Necessarily Prologue: The Afro-Americans in Los Angeles," in *20th Century Los Angeles: Power, Promotion, and Social Conflict,* ed. Norman Klein and Martin Schiesl (Claremont Calif.: Regina Books, 1990), 119, 120; Spencer Crump, *Black Riot in Los Angeles: The Story of the Watts Tragedy* (Los Angeles: Trans-Anglo Books, 1966); George, *No Crystal Stair;* Robert Conot, *Rivers of Blood, Years of Darkness* (New York: Bantam, 1967); Erin J. Aubry, "The Legacy of the Eastside Boys," *Los Angeles Times Magazine,* July 20, 1997, 12–16, 30; Brian Cross, *It's Not about a Salary: Rap, Race and Resistance in Los Angeles* (London: Verso, 1993); Raphael Sonensheim, *Politics in Black and White: Race and Power in Los Angeles* (Princeton, N.J.: Princeton University Press, 1993); Kenneth B. Clark, *Dark Ghetto: Dilemmas of Social Power* (New York: Harper and Row, 1965); Johnathan Kozol, *Death at an Early Age: The Destruction of the Hearts and Minds of Negro Children in the Boston Public Schools* (Boston: Houghton Mifflin, 1967); Frances F. Piven and Richard A. Cloward, *The Politics of Turmoil: Essays on Poverty, Race, and the Urban Crisis* (New York: Pantheon Books, 1965); Elaine Tyler May, *Homeward Bound: American Families in the Cold War Era* (New York: Basic Books, 1988); Staff of the Los Angeles Times, *Understanding the Riots: Los Angeles Before and After the Rodney King Case* (Los Angeles: Los Angeles Times, 1992); Sears and McConahay, *The Politics of Violence.* Based on this literature, as well as on archival research, I provide a more detailed interpretation of the uprising in João H. Costa Vargas, "Blacks in the City of Angels' Dust," Ph.D. diss., University of California, San Diego, 1999.

32. For a seemingly dissonant view coming from mass media, see the front cover article by Ellis Cose, "The Good News about Black America," *Newsweek,* June 7, 1999, 28–40. Although Cose for the most part argues that "[i]t's the best time ever to be black in America," the article also presents information about those considered "beneath the surface of socioeconomic viability" (quoting Elijah Anderson) and affirms that they "are worse off than ever." Chapter 1 will discuss these disparities and show how and why, in spite of the few Blacks who are able to succeed economically in American society, most are experiencing intense impoverishment, further repression, and death.

33. CAPA's logo is a black panther encircled by "All Power to the People," the emblematic Black Panther phrase that condensed much of the party's goals. Kwame Ture (then Stokely Carmichael) chose the black panther to represent the Lowndes County Freedom Organization, an independent party he cofounded in Alabama in the mid-1960s. He later gave permission to Huey Newton and Bobby Seale to use it for the Black Panther Party for Self-Defense. Lee Sustar, "The Life of Kwame Ture: Freedom Rider to Revolutionary," *Socialist Worker,* Dec. 4, 1998, 6.

34. See, e.g., Frantz Fanon, *Black Skin, White Masks* (New York: Grove Press, 1967), and *The Wretched of the Earth* (New York: Grove Press, 1963).

35. Vargas, "Hyperconsciousness of Race and Its Negation," 443–70.

1. BLACKNESS AS EXCLUSION AND ISOLATION

1. D. Grant and J. Johnson Jr., "Conservative Policy-Making and Growing Urban Inequality in the 80s," in R. Ratcliff et al., *The Politics of Wealth and Inequality,* special issue of *Research in Politics and Society* 5 (1995): 135.

2. D. Braun, "Negative Consequences to the Rise of Income Inequality," in Ratcliff et al., *Politics of Wealth and Inequality,* 13. Furthermore, the loss of international competitiveness and the transition to a service and more flexible economy meant that many well-paying jobs in the more traditional industrial sector were lost. During the 1970s, "there were fewer well-paying jobs than at any time since 1930." Michael Bernstein, "Understanding American Economic Decline: The Contours of the Late-Twentieth-Century Experience," in *Understanding American Economic Decline,* ed. M. Bernstein and D. Adler (Cambridge: Cambridge University Press, 1994), 20. See also Juliet Schor, *The Overworked American: The Unexpected Decline of Leisure* (New York: Basic Books, 1992).

3. D. Braun, "Negative Consequences to the Rise of Income Inequality," 8-13. See also Cedric Robinson, "Race, Capitalism, and Antidemocracy," in *Reading Rodney King/Reading Urban Uprising,* ed. Robert Gooding Williams (New York: Routledge, 1993). Between 1977 and 1989, according to the Congressional Budget Office, the poorest 20 percent of the "superpoor" saw their income diminish 9 percent. In the same time span, "chief executive salaries rose from 35 to 120 times the average worker's pay, and the number of (primarily corporate) lawyers doubled to 174,000" (ibid., 75).

4. This is the point repeatedly made by E. Wolff, "The Rich Get Increasingly Richer: Latest Data on Household Wealth during the 80s," in Ratcliff et al., *Politics of Wealth and Inequality.* In Wolff's study, "the terms wealth and net worth represent the current value of all marketable or fungible assets (such as bank accounts, bonds, stocks, and unincorporated businesses) less the current value of debts. Debts is thus the difference in value between total assets and total liabilities or debt" (59). Because this definition emphasizes "wealth as a store of value, and therefore a source of potential consumption," it "excludes two kinds of assets that are sometimes included in broader concepts of wealth: consumer durables and retirement wealth" (60).

5. Ibid., 35, 43.

6. Braun, "Negative Consequences," 15.

7. Unemployment's highest point was registered in the period between September 1982 and the summer of 1983, when more than 10 percent of the labor force was out of work. This figure was, depending on the data considered, two or three times the rates of unemployment during the post–World War II years. Reynolds Farley, *The New American Reality: Who We Are, How We Got Here, Where We Are Going* (New York: Russell Sage Foundation, 1996), 84, 85, 88.

8. Thomas Byrne Edsall with Mary D. Edsall, *Chain Reaction: The Impact of Race, Rights, and Taxes on American Politics* (New York: Norton, 1992), 191, 192. For the effects of these polices on children, see B. Katz, *The Undeserving Poor: From the War on Poverty to the War on Welfare* (New York: Pantheon Books, 1989), 126, 127. Furthermore,

"estimates are that one in every eight American children under the age of 12 suffers from hunger, totaling 5.5 million children. Ten thousand children die from poverty in the United States each year." Braun, "Negative Consequences," 15.

9. Grant and Johnson, "Conservative Policy-Making," 134. To facilitate U.S. industries' domestic recovery and international competitiveness, the Reagan administration's supply-side economics cut taxes and loosened or simply eliminated regulations. In the summer of 1981, as Congress enacted the Economic Recovery Act, federal income taxes were cut by almost one-third.

10. Grant and Johnson, "Conservative Policy-Making," 135.

11. Edsall and Edsall, *Chain Reaction,* 152.

12. White Republicans and White Carter voters, by contrast, were not as assertive about this view: they supported it by a margin of 57–38 and 55–41, respectively. Ibid., 164. Debates on the role of the state with relation to poverty are, of course, still heated and undefined. Clinton's workfare program—which conditions welfare assistance to the recipients' incorporation into the job market—has polarized opinions in ways that betray historical continuities with the 1980s debate. "With the dawn of the new welfare age, America ordered 11 million aid recipients to get a job. Now, should 3 million residents of public housing be told to secure places of their own? What about the 7 million more whose rent is partially paid by government vouchers?" asked the *Los Angeles Times* of July, 17, 1997, A5, in an article entitled "Should Door to Public Housing Ever Be Closed?"

13. On the centrality of race in organizing this society, see Michael Omi and Howard Winant, *Racial Formation in the United States: From the 1960s to the 1990s* (New York: Routledge, 1994). Toni Morrison, among others, in *Playing in the Dark: Whiteness and the Literary Imagination* (Cambridge: Harvard University Press, 1992), had in fact made the point emphasizing the role Blacks play in the American imagination, laws, attitudes, and expectations.

14. R. Williams, "Accumulation as Evisceration: Urban Rebellion and the New Growth Dynamics," in *Reading Rodney King,* ed. Williams, 84-85. Low earning is relative to men employed with remunerations below $12,000 in 1987 dollars.

15. Ibid., 87.

16. Wolff, "The Rich Get Increasingly Richer," 48.

17. The Social Security Act of 1935 is a case in point. It "effectively denied two-thirds of the Black population access to the largest monetary transfer program in U.S. history; the government has actively assisted and contributed to racial inequality in the wealth generating arena. Contemporary welfare policies that mandate a spend down of all assets for eligibility inhibit the ability of poor people to secure assets. This 'racialization of the state' has produced a politics in which administrative policy at the local and national level has produced differential opportunities for the accumulation of wealth for blacks and whites." M. Oliver, T. Shapiro, and J. Press, "Them That's Got Shall Get," in R. Ratcliff et al., *The Politics of Wealth and Inequality,* 75.

18. Ibid., 84.

19. Ibid., 84. Data were extracted from the 1987 Survey on Income and Program

Participation (SIPP), which is statistically representative of the U.S. adult population. 11,257 households were considered. For more information on the survey's details, see ibid., 76, 77.

20. Ibid., 87.

21. Massey and Denton, *American Apartheid*, 83. For a thorough historiography of racial segregation in Detroit, see Sugrue, *Origins of the Urban Crisis*.

22. Mike Davis, "Who Killed L.A.?," *Crossroads* (June 1993): 11.

23. Surveys indicate persistent discrimination in the real estate market. Almost 70 percent of Black respondents to a 1988 Lou Harris poll indicated their awareness of being disadvantaged in terms of housing when compared to other ethnic and racial groups with similar income and status. Massey and Denton, *American Apartheid*, 105.

24. A comparison with the politics developed by other racial and ethnic minorities may be instructive. "Underneath the umbrella of rainbow rhetoric, contemporary black politicians are practicing ethnic particularism a la the Irish power brokers. . . . There is little reason to believe that black politicians can succeed at cross-ethnic rainbow politics where the legendary Irish bosses failed." Furthermore, "black politicians lack integrating mechanisms like the machine that can fuse the disparate elements of today's urban politics—national versus local, bureaucratic versus electoral. As a result, big-city and politics of color reflect their unreconciled imperatives. The continued flow of welfare-state jobs, transfer payments, and social services, which sustain the black middle class and underclass, depends on group influence and alliance building at the national and the state levels where social policy is made and funded. *Blacks, however, are not as well organized to press their claims outside the local political arena*" (emphasis added). Steven Erie, *Rainbow's End: Irish-Americans and the Dilemmas of Urban Machine Politics, 1840–1985* (Berkeley: University of California Press, 1988), 190 and 265, respectively.

25. Collins, *Black Los Angeles*.

26. Sonensheim, *Politics in Black and White*, 148, 150, 152.

27. "While supervising the immiseration of the city's working class, the Bradley administration forged a truly multinational, multiracial coalition *at the top*. In his dealings with Japanese-American businesspeople, Korean-American merchants, Hollywood studio heads, members of the Jewish establishment, Latino political and economic leaders, labor-union bureaucrats, international investors from Japan, Hong Kong, and elsewhere, and members of the African American capitalist/managerial class, Bradley created a model for the inclusion of the broadest spectrum of elites into the political life of the city." Labor/Community Strategy Center, "Reconstructing Los Angeles—and U.S. Cities—From the Bottom Up: A Long-Term Strategy for Workers, Low-Income People, and People of Color to Create an Alternative Vision of Urban Development," Los Angeles, 1992, 4.

28. Sonensheim, *Politics in Black and White*, 174.

29. Susan Anderson, "A City Called Heaven: Black Enchantment and Despair in Los Angeles" in *The City*, ed. Allen Scott and Edward Soja (Berkeley: University of California Press, 1996), 350.

30. Labor/Community Strategy Center, "Reconstructing Los Angeles," 5.

31. Wilson, *When Work Disappears,* 25.

32. Ibid., 33.

33. Quoted in ibid., 69.

34. Davis, "Who Killed L.A.?," 9, 10.

35. Joel Kotin, "Back to Basics," *Los Angeles Times,* Feb. 16, 1997, M1, M6.

36. Data are from a study conducted by James P. Allen and Eugene Turner, "The Ethnic Quilt: Population Diversity in Southern California." See Efrain Hernandez Jr., "Growing Gap Seen Between Minority and White Income," *Los Angeles Times,* May 11, 1997, A3, A25.

37. Richard P. Applebaum, "Using Religion's Suasion in Garment Industry," *Los Angeles Times,* Feb. 16, 1997, M1, M6.

38. Davis, "Who Killed L.A.?," 10.

39. U.S. Bureau of the Census, 1990 CPH-L-4, Table 1.

40. William H. Webster and Hubert Williams, *The City in Crisis: A Report by the Special Advisor to the Board of Police Commissioners on the Civil Disorder in Los Angeles* (Los Angeles: Board of Police Commissioners, 1992), 35, 36.

41. An examination of its neighborhoods' composition illustrates the point. In Brentwood, Anglos comprise 90 percent of its inhabitants; Hispanics are 5 percent, Asians are 5 percent, and African Americans 1 percent. Palms, where the predominance of non-Hispanic Whites is *less* prevalent, has 54 percent Anglos, 26 percent Hispanics, 14 percent Asians, and 6 percent African Americans.

42. The area defined by West Adams, Baldwin Hills, and Leimert is 48 percent African American, 45 percent Hispanic, 5 percent Anglo, and 3 percent Asian. The Southeast is mainly Hispanic, but has a large minority of Blacks. Its composition is as follows: 59 percent Hispanic, 39 percent African American, 1 percent Anglo, and 1 percent Asian.

43. A few examples illustrate the point. Brentwood, while presenting the highest percentage of Whites, has the lowest proportion of unemployed inhabitants and the lowest percentage of people below the poverty line *amid all areas in the city.* As of 1990, the mean household income in Brentwood was $123,000, well above the $46,000 for the city. Blacks and Hispanics live in this area in fewer numbers than in any other neighborhood. In the other extreme, represented by the district of Southeast, where Whites are fewer than anywhere in L.A., those below poverty level and unemployed exist in more numbers than in any other area. There, compared to the rest of the municipality, the neighborhoods present the highest unemployment rates (17.4%) and poverty (40%).

44. John Horton, *The Politics of Difference: Immigration, Resistance, and Change in Monterrey Park, California* (Philadelphia: Temple University Press, 1995); Leland Saito, *Race and Politics: Asian Americans, Latinos, and Whites in a Los Angeles Suburb* (Urbana: University of Illinois Press, 1998); Nancy Abelmann and John Lie, *Blue Dreams: Korean Americans and the Los Angeles Riots* (Cambridge: Harvard University Press, 1995).

45. The information in this paragraph comes from William A. V. Clark, "Residential Patterns: Avoidance, Assimilation, and Succession," in *Ethnic Los Angeles,* ed. Waldinger and Bozorgmehr, 125.

46. I thank George Lipsitz for emphasizing this point.

47. Clark, "Residential Patterns," 133.

48. Ibid., 135.

49. Ibid., 136.

50. The argument I am presenting here does not focus adequately on Asian immigration in Los Angeles and its impact on South Central's political economy. Because my analysis is closely connected to everyday experiences in Black segregated neighborhoods, I chose to focus instead on the most urgent and immediate structural processes affecting African Americans. As the next two chapters will suggest, Latina/os were a constant presence in formerly all-Black areas in South Central, and from the perspective of a considerable number of Blacks living in poverty, a source of anxiety, fear, and even hatred. However, Asian immigration patterns do impact and indeed add to the tensions between Blacks and Latina/os as Los Angeles' economy pits racialized groups against each other, in the process maintaining its historic hierarchies based on race, gender, urban space, and nationality. For analyses of Asian immigration in Los Angeles, see Paul Ong, Edna Bonacich, and Lucie Cheng, eds., *The New Asian Immigration in Los Angeles and Global Restructuring* (Philadelphia: Temple University Press, 1994). On Korean-Black tensions, see, for example, Paul Ong, Kye Young Park, and Yasmin Tong, "The Korean-Black Conflict and the State," in *The New Asian Immigration in Los Angeles,* ed. Ong, Park, and Tong. For detailed studies on the impact of race, gender, urban space, and immigration on Los Angeles political economy, see Lawrence D. Bobo, Melvin Oliver, James Johnson, Jr., and Abel Valenzuela Jr., eds., *Prismatic Metropolis: Inequality in Los Angeles* (New York: Russell Sage Foundation, 2000).

51. Paul Ong and Abel Valenzuela Jr., "The Labor Market: Immigrant Effects and Racial Disparities," in *Ethnic Los Angeles,* ed. Waldinger and Bozorgmehr, 172.

52. For an analysis of the restaurant and hotel sectors, see Roger Waldinger, "Who Makes the Beds, Who Washes the Dishes? Black/Immigrant Competition Reassessed," in *Immigrants and Immigration Policy: Individual Skills, Family Ties, and Group Identities,* ed. Harriet Dunlup and Phanindra Wannara (Greenwich, Conn.: Jai Press, 1996).

53. Cf. Ong and Valenzuela, "The Labor Market," 179, 191.

54. For an interpretation of this survey, see Melvin L. Oliver and James H. Johnson, "Inter-Ethnic Conflict in an Urban Ghetto: The Case of Blacks and Latinos in Los Angeles," in *Research in Social Movements, Conflicts, and Change,* ed. Richard Ratcliff and Louis Kriesberg, vol. 6 (Greenwich, Conn.: Jai Press, 1984), esp. 76–85. According to the same survey, Latina/os were more antagonistic toward Blacks than Blacks were toward them. They tended to hold prejudiced ideas about African Americans similar to those found among Whites, and thus questioned their work ethic, their cleanliness, and sexual conduct. Latina/os who felt trapped in the poorer and more violent neighborhoods, and who competed with Blacks for jobs and residence more directly, were the most prejudiced. Adding to this animosity, Latina/os also felt

that Blacks controlled much of the public bureaucracy in Los Angeles and, in general, considered them to be better off politically.

55. Compare the lower rates of racial segregation registered in Los Angeles relative to other metropolitan regions of the United States in Massey and Denton, *American Apartheid.*

56. David M. Grant, Melvin L. Oliver, and Angela D. James, "African Americans: Social and Economic Bifurcation," in *Ethnic Los Angeles,* ed. Waldinger and Bozorgmehr, 384, 385.

57. Edward W. Soja, "Los Angeles, 1965–1992: From Crisis-Generated Restructuring to Restructuring-Generated Crisis," in *The City,* ed. Scott and Soja, 446.

58. Grant, Oliver, and James, "African Americans," 394.

59. Ibid., 396. There are some factors, however, that make us approach this conclusion with caution. While growing levels of education among women may have indeed increased, there is no conclusive data on the better educational performance of Black women vis-à-vis Black men. Furthermore, what is known about the city's school system is rather dismal: the Los Angeles Unified School District is ranked among the lowest in academic achievement in the country, and its worst schools are precisely the ones located in the inner city, where practically no White students are enrolled. *Los Angeles Times,* Dec. 15, 1996, B3, and Aug. 1, 1997, B1, B6. In this latter article, we are told that 75 percent of the LAUSD's South Region are among the 100 poorest-performing schools. Jordan High (fourth worse among L.A.'s schools), Jefferson (fifteenth worse), and Locke (twelfth worse) are all in South Central. Moreover, the rate of students not completing high school in Los Angeles County is 28 percent, more than twice the national rate measured in 1995 of 12 percent. Indeed, in California, 33 percent of Black students do not complete high school, against 28 percent of Latinos, 12 of Whites, and 10 of Asians. *Los Angeles Times,* Aug. 1, 1997, A16. This information suggests that, if better educational performance among Black women exists when compared to previous periods and when compared to Black men, it must be marginal and acquired through great pains, for the structural conditions affecting the education of those in Los Angeles' public school system are the same for Black women and men.

60. Wilson, *When Work Disappears.*

61. Grant, Oliver, and James, "African Americans," 395.

62. In the guise of temporal perspective, consider the following: in 1970, 75 percent of all Black high-school dropouts worked; in 1990, only 33 percent did. Even Black males with a high school diploma experience today greater difficulties: in the 1970s, their employment rate was almost 90 percent; in the beginning of the 1990s, their participation in the formal job market was down to 60 percent. Ibid., 38. Consider specific occupational sectors. Between 1970 and 1990, the durable manufacturing and construction industries registered a diminution of almost 50 percent of Black men employed in each of their ranks; in the same period, the proportion of Black men in laborer occupations fell almost 75 percent. For all men, independent of race, the respective rates were the following: a similar diminution of 50 percent in durable

manufacturing; an increase of more than 60 percent in the construction sector; and a negligible increase in laborer occupations. Ibid., graph in 393.

63. Ibid., 388, 391.

64. Ibid., 393, 398. See also Sonensheim, *Politics in Black and White.*

65. Bunch, "A Past Not Necessarily Prologue," 119, 120. As a result of this process, Watts and the central parts of South Central witnessed a considerable economic decline. By 1965, an estimated four in ten families in Watts lived below poverty level. Unemployment stood between 25,000 and 50,000. See Crump, *Black Riot in Los Angeles,* 21; Conot, *Rivers of Blood, Years of Darkness;* George, *No Crystal Stair;* Aubry, "Legacy of the Eastside Boys"; Cross, *It's Not About a Salary.*

66. Denise Hamilton, "Land of Opportunity," *Los Angeles Times,* Dec. 22, 1996, D13.

67. Grant, Oliver, and James, "African Americans," 405. A recent newspaper article reported on the fate of a middle-class Black family that decided to stay in South Central Los Angeles. Sean Murray, 20, the son of Rodney and Vivian Murray, was killed in a drive-by shooting. The tragic event was portrayed as one of the main reasons why middle- and working-class families were leaving South Central in great numbers. Jill Levoy, "Tenacity Turns to Tragedy in South L.A," *Los Angeles Times,* May 6, 2004, http://www.latimes.com/news/local/la-me-defiant6may06,1,781493.story?coll =la-home-headlines.

68. Hamilton, "Land of Opportunity," D13.

69. U.S. Bureau of the Census, 1992, cited in ibid.

70. Grant, Oliver, and James, "African Americans," 402.

71. Miller, *Search and Destroy,* 7. For further analysis and numbers on the ongoing genocide of Blacks, see Steven A. Donziger, ed., *The Real War on Crime: The Report of the National Criminal Justice Commission* (New York: HarperPerennial, 1996).

72. *Los Angeles Times,* Dec. 3, 1996, B1, B8. In the incident reported, forty-three illegal immigrants, forty of whom were young men in their twenties and thirties, had just arrived from eastern San Diego County and were waiting to be conducted to their final destination in Los Angeles. "Coyotes" are the smugglers who bring the illegal immigrants.

73. Mike Davis, "Chinatown Revisited? The 'Internationalization of Downtown Los Angeles,'" in *Sex, Death, and God in Los Angeles,* ed. David Reid (New York: Pantheon, 1992), 44. Remember also that, since 1992, suburban voters and their representatives have become the political majority in the country. Los Angeles is no exception, and this political power has created, maintained, and is augmenting, the autonomy suburban areas have with relation to core cities.

74. I thank George Lipsitz for the latter point and also for suggesting that one of the main goals of the two major political parties at this moment is people of color's vote dilution and low voter turnout.

75. Ibid., 32.

76. *Los Angeles Times,* Dec. 20, 1996, A1, A46.

77. Jennifer Wolch, "From Global to Local: The Rise in Homelessness in Los Angeles During the 1980s," in *The City,* ed. Scott and Soja, 405.

78. *Los Angeles Times,* Dec. 20, 1996, B6.

79. Wolch, "From Global to Local," 405.

2. BLACKNESS AS SORROW AND SOLIDARITY

1. Earl Lewis, *In Their Own Interests: Race, Class and Power in Twentieth Century Norfolk Virginia* (Berkeley: University of California Press, 1991), 90–91.

2. On the systematic exclusion and blatant discrimination Black women experience vis-à-vis law enforcement and the criminal justice system, and how this compounds domestic abuse by male partners, see Beth Richie, "The Social Impact of Mass Incarceration on Women," in *Invisible Punishment: The Collateral Consequences of Mass Imprisonment,* ed. Marc Mauer and Meda Chesney-Lind (New York: Free Press, 2002). Richie states: "In effect, perpetrators of violence against women in low-income communities who may have a substance abuse history, who may be involved in the illegal sex industry or who may be homeless are typically not held accountable" (145); see also hooks, *We Real Cool.*

3. The phrase "circles and circles of sorrow" comes from the following passage: "'Suddenly Nel stopped. Her eye twitched and burned a little. 'Sula?' she whispered, gazing at the tops of the trees. 'Sula?' Leaves stirred; mud shifted; there was the smell of overripe green things. A soft ball of fur broke and scattered like dandelion spores in the breeze. 'All that time, all that time, I thought I was missing Jude.' And the loss pressed down on her chest and came up into her throat. 'We was girls together,' she said as though explaining something. 'O Lord, Sula,' she cried, 'girl, girl, girlgirlgirl.' It was a fine cry—loud and long—but it had no bottom and it had no top, just circles and circles of sorrow." Toni Morrison, *Sula* (New York: Plume, 1982), 174.

4. Some of the historical antecedents to this context can be grasped in the following. In 1972 Johnnie Tillmon, then director of the National Welfare Rights Organization, wrote to *Ms.* describing the situation of Black women under welfare. She wrote from personal experience as well as from the knowledge she acquired as a militant in the welfare rights movement. Her history was a familiar one: "I am forty-five years old. I have raised six children. I grew up in Arkansas, and I worked there for 15 years in a laundry, making $40 to $30 a week, picking cotton on the side for carfare. I moved to California in 1959 and worked in a laundry there for nearly four years. In 1963, I got too sick to work. My husband and I split up. Friends helped me to go on welfare. They call it AFDC—Aid to Families with Dependent Children. Each month I get $363 for my kids and me. I pay $128 a month rent; $30 for utilities; $120 for food and nonedible household essentials; $50 for school lunches for the three children, who are not eligible for reduced-cost meal programs.

"This leaves about $5 per person per month for everything else—clothing, shoes, recreation, incidental personal expenses, and transportation. This check allows $1 a month for transportation for me but none for my children. That's how we live." "Welfare," *Ms.* (1972), reprinted July/Aug. 1995, 50–55. Diabetes disabled her in 1990 and she died five year later, after having a foot and five fingers amputated.

After noting that the majority—two-thirds of all poor families and potential welfare recipients—is White, Tillmon elaborated on the nature of welfare as an institution: "Welfare is the most prejudiced institution in this country, even more than marriage, which it tries to imitate. Let me explain that a little.

"Women head forty-four percent of all poor families. That's bad enough. But 99 percent of the families on AFDC are headed by women. There is no man around. In half the states there can't be men around because AFDC says if there is an 'able-bodied' man in the house, you can't be on welfare. If the kids are going to eat, and the man can't get a job, then he's got to go. So his kids can eat. AFDC is like a supersexist marriage. You trade in *a* man for *the* man. But you can't divorce him if he treats you bad. He can divorce *you*, cut you off anytime he wants. But in that case, *he* keeps the kids. *The* man runs everything. In marriage, sex is supposed to be for your husband. On AFDC, you're not supposed to have sex at all. You give up control of your body. You may even have to get your tubes tied so you don't have more children just to avoid being cut off welfare. *The* man, the welfare system, controls your money. He tells you what to buy, where to buy it, and how much things cost. If something—rent, for instance—costs more than he says it does, it's just too bad for you. He's always right. Everything is budgeted down to the last penny, and you've got to make your money stretch. *The* man can break into your house anytime he wants and poke into your things. You've got no right to protest. You've got no rights to privacy when you go on welfare.

"Like I said, welfare's a supersexist marriage" (50, 51).

Tillmon also addressed AFDC's historical roots. "Welfare's ideology has always been linked to what the broader society considered the 'proper' domestic arrangement and the gender roles within this arrangement. In fact, welfare was invented mostly for women. It grew out of something called the Mother's Pension Laws. To be eligible, you had to be female, you had to be a mother, you had to be 'worthy.' That meant your kids had to be 'legitimate,' your home 'suitable,' and you had to be 'proper.' In 1935, the Mother's Pension Laws became part of the Social Security system, and they changed the name of the program to Aid to Families with Dependent Children. Now there are other welfare programs, other kinds of people on welfare—the blind, the disabled, the aged. (Many of them are women, too, especially the aged.) Those others make up just over a third of all the welfare cases. We AFDCs are two thirds. But when the politicians talk about the 'welfare cancer eating our vitals,' they're not talking about the aged, blind or disabled. They're the 'deserving poor.' Politicians are talking about us—the women who head up 99 percent of the AFDC families—and our kids. We're the 'cancer,' the 'undeserving poor.' Mothers and children" (51).

Underlying AFDC's organization and the critiques its recipients received from (at the time) conservative politicians was the American notion of the "work ethic." Tillmon points to the force and contradictions within this notion and its effects on underprivileged women. "In this country, we believe in something called 'work ethic.' That means that your work is what gives you human worth. But the work ethic is a double standard. It applies to men, and to women on welfare. It doesn't apply to all women. If you're a society lady from Scarsdale and you spend all your time sitting on your prosperity paring your nails, that's O.K. Women aren't supposed to work. They're supposed to be married. But if you don't have a man to pay for your things, particularly if you have kids, then everything changes. You've 'failed' as a woman, because you've failed to attract and keep a man. It can't possibly be the man's fault, his lack of responsibility. It must be yours. That's why Governor Reagan can get away with calling AFDC recipients 'lazy parasites' and 'pigs at the trough.' We've been trained to believe that the only reason people are on welfare is because there's something wrong with their character. If people only *want* to work, they can, and they will be able to support themselves and their kids in decency" (54).

5. I am aware of the long history of imposed birth control in Black communities. Such history is important to consider in the suspicion against women's health facilities in South Central. See, e.g., Robert G. Weisbord, *Genocide? : Birth Control and the Black American* (Westport, Conn.: Greenwood Press, 1975); and Roberts, *Killing the Black Body.*

3. BLACKNESS AS LIABILITY AND POWERLESSNESS

1. The debate on welfare that transpired in news broadcasts, early evening programs, and that certainly found some of its perverse effects in the threats delivered by welfare agents was greatly influenced by Clinton's signing of the Personal Responsibility and Work Opportunity Reconciliation Act of 1996, which became known as the "welfare reform bill." As well as giving the states new independence to design their own welfare systems, the bill eliminated Aid to Families with Dependent Children, a federal, state, and locally funded program. AFDC was substituted with block grants (Temporary Assistance for Needy Families), which were to be molded according to each state's particularities. Still, the greater impacts of the federal reforms were on the time allowed for benefits. Under the new law, adults will be required to get a job within two years, and the lifetime limit on benefits for any recipient will be five years. In California, the debate on welfare reflected the even more conservative climate well maintained by Governor Pete Wilson's administration. It culminated with Wilson's welfare reform proposals publicized in early 1997. More drastic than the federal law, it proposed to cut aid to new recipients after one year if they did not find jobs (the federal bill allowed two years in such cases). In addition to the harsher time limits, the governor's proposal subjected prospective and current welfare recipients to even more intrusive requirements to qualify for relief. For example, a new screening process at welfare offices would determine ability to work and categorize applicants according to need for training or other services; cash grants would be ended for any woman who did not establish paternity for all of the children in her care; and a new Minor Parent Program would establish government home visitations of families in which the mother is under 18—the home visitations would also assess the problems of the household, such as delinquency and substance abuse. See *Los Angeles Times,* Jan. 8, 1997, A1, A13; Jan. 12, 1996, A1, A25; Jan. 10, 1997, A1, A18; Nov. 25, 1996, A1, A18. For a critique of the history of welfare in this country, and the exposure of its control mechanisms of

the poor, see Frances F. Piven and Richard A. Cloward, *Regulating the Poor: The Functions of Public Welfare*, updated ed. (New York: Vintage, 1993.) A thorough critical review of welfare-reform literature, from a feminist standpoint, can be found in Karen Christopher, "Welfare as We [Don't] Know It: A Review and Feminist Critique of Welfare Reform Research in the United States," *Feminist Economics* 10, no. 2 (2004): 143–71. Many of the everyday struggles the women experienced in the apartment building in South Central Los Angeles—especially those related to food, housing, healthcare, childcare, and domestic violence—are indeed common to those who left welfare following Clinton's 1996 welfare reforms (150–52). It is evident that Christopher's view on welfare as paternalistic and racist, as it allegedly attempts to strengthen marriage and decrease nonmarital fertility among women of color, corroborates the analysis and description presented in the last two chapters. For an expanded critique of welfare racism, see Kenneth J. Neubeck and Noel A. Cazenave, *Welfare Racism: Playing the Race Card against America's Poor* (New York: Routledge, 2001).

2. Kwanzaa is an African American holiday that starts on the day after Christmas. It is based on several African harvest celebrations, and it is not meant to replace Christmas or any other holiday. Created by Maulana Karenga during the 1960s, it was part of the cultural and political ferment inspired by the Black power movement.

3. The effects of this type of environment on children have been documented. "To protect themselves, said the doctors, these children are always at the ready, hyperaware of loud sounds and easily startled." This readiness, however, interferes with children's ability, among others, to sleep and concentrate in school. The same article notes that some children in violent areas develop just the opposite problem, that is, tuning out noises. See Joanne Wasserman, "Some Children Living in Violent Neighborhoods Are Developing Heightened Senses," *New York Daily News,* Jan. 9, 1995.

4. I was unable to find out how much the women owed for crack. Still, a hit was going for ten or fifteen dollars at that time, depending on the quality of the drug, and Vivian hardly missed a day without having at least one hit. As for Shannon, although less regular in her use of crack cocaine, she nevertheless went at least twice a day during the height of her crisis. These figures, however, only represent what I observed and heard from my apartment, which was at the ground floor of our building, parallel to, and less than ten feet away from the crack house. From my kitchen window I could see who was walking in and out of the crack house through the gap in the fence; from my bedroom I had a clear view of the crack house's front and lateral door. But I was not home all day, and after my initial months of adaptation, I managed to sleep fairly well through most of the busy nights.

5. See, for example, hooks, *We Real Cool.*

6. The gendered skills Elen and Nadine employed to both maintain the community united and push for common approaches to collective problems clearly connect them to the centerwomen or bridge leaders analyzed by Belinda Robnet, *How Long? How Long?: African-American Women in the Struggle for Civil Rights* (New York: Oxford University Press, 1997), esp. 17–22. I thank Barbara Ransby for this insight. Her definitive *Ella Baker and the Black Freedom Movement: A Radical Democratic Vision*

(Chapel Hill: University of North Carolina Press, 2003), narrates how Baker exemplarily embodied the qualities of bridge leaders in spite of the gendered hierarchies shaping the structures and many of the outlooks of the civil rights movement.

7. For an analysis of the "transformative power of mutuality," group survival, and how these are crucial aspects of Black feminist thought, see Collins, *Black Feminist Thought,* chaps. 6 and 7. See Davis, *Blues Legacy and Black Feminism* for a perspective on how art produced by blues women constituted groundwork for protest and politicization. I propose an analogous argument regarding the strategies utilized in the apartment building: if on the one hand they were temporarily quelled, on the other they build on shared knowledge that carries unmistakable transformative potential that can/needs to be mobilized in/by liberatory organized movements. On the primacy of the "ontological totality" over the individual, found to organize the enslaved revolts in the Americas starting in the sixteenth century, see Robinson, *Black Marxism.*

4. BLACKNESS AS MOBILIZATION AND MOVEMENT

1. As was reported in *The Pelican Bay Prison Express,* April 1996, 25. CAPA has been successful in expanding its geographical horizons, maintaining contacts and frequent interchange visits with organizations of various cities in the United States and abroad. In recent years, Coalition members have visited England, France, Namibia, and Brazil. Persons from these countries and American cities are constantly coming to Los Angeles and spending time at the Coalition, exchanging information and techniques of community organization. Zinzun's national and international visibility—and that of other Coalition and CSGT members—has projected their cause well beyond the City of Angels' core neighborhoods. For an account of the political alliances between CAPA, CSGT, and Black activists in Rio de Janeiro, see João H. Costa Vargas, "The Inner City and the Favela: Transnational Black Politics," *Race and Class* 44, no. 4 (2003): 19–40.

2. Due to all the more immediate chores at the office that kept preventing me from finishing the task, the word-processed manual had to wait until mid-1997 to be completed. Zinzun told me a USC student did the work.

3. Coalition Against Police Abuse, *Organizing Manual* (Los Angeles, n.d), 4.

4. Ibid., 5.

5. The photograph of the young Black hanged also resonated with a wave of similar events that were taking place in South Central at that same time. Gang members were being killed and hanged by enemy gangsters. The bodies were left for public display until authorities removed them. Whether the lynching in the south inspired those attitudes remains to be investigated. The photograph in the office, however, had the additional importance of showing to gang members that such lynching and hangings are part of a broader historical context of everyday and institutional forms of oppression.

6. CAPA, *Organizing Manual,* 5. Subsequent page numbers appear in the text.

7. "Establishmentarian" comes from the following quote and reference. "Since the doctrine of objectivity [prevalent in American news media] called for the meticulous

certification of almost every phenomenon by an authority with a title, the news came increasingly to be presented by the authorities. In fact, American news, under that doctrine, has become increasingly conservative, but not truly neutral, and too often devoid of meaning. The doctrine led journalists in the standard media to 'safe,' politically neutral subjects like crime and natural disasters, and it delayed for decades intelligent examination into the causes of events. Doctrine of objectivity . . . has led to episodes like that of Senator Joseph McCarthy, whose fantasies were accepted because he was a certifying authority under the rules of objectivity. It has given American standard news a profoundly establishmentarian cast under the guise of a press independent of established authority." Ben Bagdikian, *Media Monopoly* (Boston: Beacon Press, 1987), 130. Note how the techniques exposed in CAPA's manual are pitched according to the "doctrine of objectivity." What makes the Coalition's strategy interesting is that, in emulating the standards of objectivity, it aims to subvert the establishmentarian inclinations of mainstream media.

8. I use "old-timer" to refer to those who participated in the BPP in the late 1960s and early 1970s. Those persons are usually in their late forties and early fifties. Old-timers, in this case, are not elderly persons, even though youngsters often call them "Grandpa." Still, "Grandpa" works more as an affectionate calling than as an expression of old age. Michael Zinzun, for example, in spite of being in his late forties, is called "Grandpa" by most of the out-of-town youngsters who came to L.A. during our 1996 summer computer classes.

9. The following quote, albeit relative to TV news, can be expanded to news media in general. It echoes concepts commonly discussed at the Coalition. "Television is clearly in some sense an actor on the political stage as well. It doesn't merely transmit to the public information about what is going on. One of the things that is most distinctive about TV news is the extent to which it is an ideological medium, providing not just information or entertainment, but 'packages of consciousness'— frameworks for interpreting and cues for reacting to social and political reality." Daniel Hallin, *We Keep America on Top of the World: Television Journalism and the Public Sphere* (New York: Routledge, 1994), 90.

10. CAPA, *Organizing Manual,* 3, 4. Subsequent page numbers appear in the text.

11. The incapacity to be "rational"—rather, the internalized impression that Blacks are incapable of objective judgment and behavior—is obviously akin to the various forms of internalized racism as they are analyzed in Kenneth Clark's *Dark Ghetto,* and Stokely Carmichael and Charles Hamilton's *Black Power: The Politics of Liberation in America* (New York: Random House, 1967). These works, among others, described the ghetto as a result of colonial powers that were maintained through intense economic exploitation, police repression, and, no less, by an intense (if only muted) psychological warfare that bombarded Blacks with self-deprecating—and self-fulfilling—thoughts and behaviors. The idea of emotionalism should not be confused with the expressions of Black emotions. Emotions that appear formalized in art forms, such as music, poetry, and painting, are generally much appreciated. I will discuss this at greater length in a forthcoming chapter. For now, I stress the consciousness that some political and

religious groups share about the need to overcome the *myth* of Black emotionalism, ratified by hegemonic discourses about Blacks. A Los Angeles Black Muslim leader once wrote, "There is a saying in the Holy Quran which reads, 'Do not take your emotions as god.' This is saying to us, 'do not allow our feelings to be our guide in life.'" Rizza M. Kalilullah, *The Whiteman Made Me Do It* (Los Angeles: Harrell Press, 1994), 116.

12. These facts are also narrated in Edward J. Escobar, "The Dialectics of Repression: The Los Angeles Police Department and the Chicano Movement, 1968–1971," *Journal of American History* (March 1993): 1483–1514.

13. Such programs were extensively analyzed by Ward Churchill and Jim Vander Wall, *Agents of Repression: The FBI's Secret Wars Against the Black Panther Party and the American Indian Movement* (Boston: South End Press, 1990).

14. In 1992, for example, following the uprisings, a more radical "robbery" was conducted. Videocassette players, televisions, tapes and other valuables were taken. Yet even though several offices were housed in the same building, only CAPA drawers were searched—a clear sign that the "robbers" knew exactly where to look and what to look for.

15. See chapter 1.

16. Mace is a liquid propelled by spray can and causes severe eye pain (sometimes temporary and even permanent blindness), as well as difficulty in breathing. Mace cans contain tear gas, kerosene, and a propellant, usually freon, which is inert.

17. *Los Angeles Times,* April 4, 1991, B1, B12, and May 11, 1991, B1.

18. Two weeks prior to the verdict on Zinzun's case, another Superior Court jury awarded a record $8.75 million to a former Coliseum groundskeeper who was wounded and left paraplegic by an off-duty LAPD officer in 1987. "The two combined verdicts of $12.58 million exceed the record $11.3 million the city paid out to settle all police-related lawsuits last year." *Los Angeles Times,* May 11, 1991, B3.

19. Ibid., B1.

20. Ibid., May 15, 1991, B8.

21. Ibid.

22. Ibid., May 11, 1991, B3.

23. Ibid.

24. *Los Angeles Sentinel,* April 17, 1991, A1.

25. On April 24, 1991, the *Sentinel* displayed on its first page photographs of a Carson resident victimized by L.A. County Police. His injuries were similar to those of Rodney King and had taken place a month prior to the infamous incident. On the same page, actor Wesley Snipes was reported to have been abused by LAPD. On May 8, 1991, it showed first-page photos of people who claimed to have been brutalized by the police. They are all Black and have severe bruises on their faces. The photographs were part of State Sen. Diane Watson's campaign to oust Gates. She claimed that the photos prove that "the beating of Rodney King was not 'aberration' as Chief Gates has characterized it." These examples show the pattern of the *Sentinel*'s first page during the months following the King beating.

26. *Los Angeles Times,* July 28, 1994, B1, B8.

27. Based on data collected by CAPA, Zinzun stated: "The police assault on Rodney King was not an aberration. In 1990 alone, 72 people were shot by the LAPD. Thousands of complaints for other abuses were filed, but none of the officers involved were indicted." "Civilian Police Review Board Campaign Launched in L.A.," *Random Lengths,* Aug./Sept. 1991, 2.

28. CAPA, "Statement to the Media: On a Civilian Police Review Board in Los Angeles," Aug. 9, 1991, 2, 3.

29. Ibid.

30. "Civilian Police Board Campaign," 2.

31. One of these bits of advice—and this example illustrates the committee's meticulous legal concerns—regarded free speech rights at shopping centers and supermarkets. The ACLU responded, in a letter sent to Zinzun dated December 3, 1991, with a general overview of the "constitutional right to gather signatures on a petition, leaflet, and generally engage in speech activities at these places." The letter was two pages long, and its information served to assert the activists' legal rights to gather signatures in various public spaces. It also provided advice as to how to deal with owners and managers of commercial establishments who restricted the circulation of petitions for signatures.

32. The *New York Times* has a distinct view on Berry, whose political stance it summarized as follows: "Ms. Berry, 66, made a reputation in her 25 years on the commission for haranguing presidents for not doing enough to recognize what she considered the persistent vestiges of discrimination." Ms. Berry was replaced by Gerald Reynolds, an African American lawyer, who is openly conservative on matters of race and discrimination. See Randal C. Archibold, "Shift Toward Skepticism for Civil Rights Panel," *New York Times,* Dec. 10, 2004, http://www.nytimes.com/2004/12/10/national/10reynolds.html.

33. *CAPA Report: 1989 through 1993,* n.d., n.p.

34. Ward Churchill, "'To Disrupt, Discredit and Destroy': The FBI's Secret War Against the Black Panther Party, " in *Liberation, Imagination, and the Black Panther Party,* ed. Kathleen Cleaver and George Katsiaficas (New York: Routledge, 2001); "Panther Special International Edition—A True History of the Black Panther Party (BPP)" (Summer 1995); Manning Marable, *Race, Reform, and Rebellion: The Second Reconstruction in Black America* (Jackson: University Press of Mississippi Press, 1991); Edward M. Keating, *Free Huey! The True Story of the Trial of Huey Newton* (San Francisco: Ramparts, 1971); Huey Newton, *Revolutionary Suicide* (New York: Harcourt, 1973).

35. Churchill and Vander Wall, *Agents of Repression.*

36. Pratt's case provides a window into the types of assaults by local police and FBI personnel Panthers were subjected to. For an account of the form and content of the racist training that the Los Angeles Police Department provides, see Mike Rothmiller and Ivan Goldman, *L.A. Secret Police: Inside the LAPD Elite Spy Network* (New York: Pocket Books, 1992). For anthropological analyses of the LAPD, see Steve Herbert,

Policing Space: Territoriality and the Los Angeles Police Department (Minneapolis: University of Minnesota Press, 1997); and Joan C. Barker, *Danger, Duty, and Disillusion: The Worldview of Los Angeles Police Officers* (Prospect Heights, Ill.: Waveland Press, 1999). San Francisco attorney Stuart Hanlon accompanied Pratt's case since he was a third-year law student and was volunteering legal assistance at San Quentin Prison in 1974, until Pratt's release in 1997. See by Edward J. Boyer, "Lawyer Presses 23-Year Battle on Behalf of 'Geronimo' Pratt," *Los Angeles Times,* March 13, 1997, B1, B6; "Hearing Set on 'Geronimo' Pratt's Request for New Trial," *Los Angeles Times,* Nov. 23, 1996, B1; and "Pratt Strides Into Freedom," *Los Angeles Times,* June 11, 1997, A1, A17.

37. Assata Shakur, *Assata: An Autobiography* (Westport, Conn.: L. Hill, 1987); Elaine Brown, *A Taste of Power: A Black Woman's Story* (New York: Pantheon Books, 1992).

38. "Panther Special International Edition," 3.

39. Replacing Huey Newton as the party's chairman, Elaine Brown, it seems, provided evidence against the Panther's patriarchy. Yet her account can be read as evidence of how Brown consciously deployed patriarchal, hierarchal, centralized, and often despotic measures as a party leader, thus revealing how the Panther dominant political culture hardly depended on the gender of its leader.

40. Newton, *Revolutionary Suicide,* cited in "Panther Special International Edition," 3.

41. Newton and Seale were the objects of numerous documentaries and television programs. It is clear from the footage available today that the founders of the Panthers, as well as other prominent leaders, thought the party's fate a matter to be resolved by its higher officials. Even independent films fall prey of the perspective according to which the Panthers were, after all, its leaders. Consider Lee Lew Lee's *All Power to the People* (1997). This former Panther's film attempts to reconstruct the rise and fall of the party. The film's main narrative and tone are given by Bobby Seale's series of testimonies, uncritically corroborated by other well-known ex-militants. The party's rank-and-file are either silent or invisible. In the rare moments that they speak, their testimonies support the main narrative.

42. "Panther Special International Edition," 3.

43. Earl Ofari Hutchison, "Black Conservatives Have a Place at the Table," *Los Angeles Times,* Dec. 8, 1997, B5.

44. The stories about middle-class Blacks by middle-class Black volunteers at CAPA tended to expand with each telling. Every time one of these narratives surfaced, they involved an increased amount of (often contradictory) detail and scorn compared to the previous time they had been uttered. One narrative related how the storyteller noticed many large boxes standing by his neighbor's trash can at the end of Christmas day. The packages had colorful wrappings, easy to spot. The narrator later discovered, while his children were playing with the neighbor's children, that the boxes had been made for the sole purpose of being exposed to the public. No actual presents corresponded to the boxes. The family next door experienced financial difficulties when the father recently lost his job, and the wrappings were all for show, to give the

appearance of prosperity to others. Each time the story was told, however, it gained in detail and drama. I eventually heard a version, produced by the same narrator, in which the neighbors had bought several pounds of chicken innards and left them in the trash can, next to the empty boxes, many days before the trash collection was due. According to the storyteller, the family with the stinking and overflowing garbage tried to convey to the neighbors that it had a plentiful Christmas, with no shortage of food or presents. Each time the story was told, more neighbors were described doing the same thing in more intense and imaginative ways.

45. The fact that most of the Black Power theses' defendants were from upwardly mobile working-class or middle-class backgrounds only adds to the tensions within the organizations they represented. Carmichael was a graduate of Howard University; Newton and Seale were students at Oakland's Merritt College, and Newton would later pursue his doctoral degree. "Only a small fraction of the major proponents of Black Power had the gritty background of Malcolm X, whose actual ordeal as part of the ghetto underworld served as a crucible for his ultimate political trajectory." Marable, *Race, Reform, and Rebellion*, 110, 111.

46. "Why Pratt Case Didn't Grab More Attention," *Los Angeles Times,* June 5, 1997, B1, B6. See also George Lipsitz, *The Possessive Investment in Whiteness: How White People Profit from Identity Politics* (Philadelphia: Temple University Press, 1998), where he discusses why Geronimo's case did not get as much attention as O. J. Simpson's.

47. These concepts are discussed at length in Carmichael and Hamilton, *Black Power.*

5. BLACKNESS AS ARTISTRY AND AFFIRMATION

1. This characterization is not exclusive to Blacks who live in the area. The *Los Angeles Times* has described Leimert Park as "a center for African American culture in Los Angeles" that "has blossomed in recent years." Peter Y. Hong, "Merchants Rally Against Parking Meters," *Los Angeles Times,* April 5, 1997, B3. See also Frank Williams, "The Poet of Leimert Park," which presents the area in similar terms (*Los Angeles Times,* Sept. 23, 1997, B2). The dominant class, ideological, and generational character of this "renaissance" will become clear as this chapter unfolds.

2. Throughout most of this chapter, especially when describing performance-related events, I will be employing the ethnographic present tense. This is not to diminish the time-specific quality of the research I conducted between 1996 and 1998. Rather, my intention is to preserve that very specificity and give the reader a sense of the social processes that were taking place in Leimert Park during that period. Many significant changes have materialized since. Billy Higgins and Juno Se Mama Lewis, among others, have died. Fifth Street Dick's closed shortly after Fulton's death. For an analysis on ethnography and how it represents reality and time, see for example Johannes Fabian, *Time and the Other: How Anthropology Makes Its Object* (1983; New York: Columbia University Press, 2002).

3. Males dominate the jam sessions at the World Stage. A few women participate, usually as singers. The antipathy that instrumentalists often express toward singers,

however, has less to do with the fact that the singers are women than with the fact that singers usually request odd keys which they want to perform.

4. I utilize "amateur" to differentiate from "professional." The amateurs at the World Stage are not able to make a living off music. But this distinction does not necessarily describe amateurs' musical abilities or their performance experience. While most of the amateurs who play at the World Stage are conscious of their technical deficiencies, especially when compared to established musicians, they have an extensive experience playing, not only at the Stage, but also in various restaurants, cafés, clubs, and hotels in Los Angeles, in other cities of the United States, and occasionally abroad.

5. This, of course, does not diminish some of the advantages of Dick's arrangements relative to the Stage: better organized sessions, in which players sign a list and are called by order of arrival; and the guarantee that there will always be musicians to accompany those who want to play.

6. "The Coltrane Quartet . . . was the most influential band of the post-war period. It was the one group that amalgamated all the threads that had gone into creation of Black music up to that point and did so in a musicianly way, based on the traditions of the great jazz heritage. . . . The unique tone and the hypnotic mood that John Coltrane established the minute he started to play have become the norm." Valerie Wilmer, *As Serious as Your Life: The Story of the New Jazz* (1977; Westport, Conn.: Lawrence Hill, 1980), 31, 32. It is significant that the June 1998 issue of *Down Beat,* one of the most read jazz and blues magazines, featured a cover article on Coltrane's enduring legacy. "The sound and spirit of John Coltrane fills the air. Though the man himself died of liver cancer 32 years ago this July 17, two months short of age 41, his music and his personal example still exercise their profound effect, having an impact on the music we call jazz greater than any single figure since Charlie Parker. . . . It's not just the release of *The Complete 1961 Village Vanguard Sessions* that brings Trane's deep, fleet, probing sensibility to the fore. There are also a flood of homages that refresh our memories and perspectives on his work, streaming from artists as diverse as [White virtuoso tenor saxophonist] Michael Brecker (playing "Impressions") and [singer] Kevin Mahogany in a February concert of Coltrane's music with the Carnegie Hall Jazz Orchestra, [ex-Miles Davis alto saxophonist] Kenny Garrett (on *Pursuance,* featuring Pat Metheny), [British guitarist] John McLaughlin (*After the Rain,* with Elvin Jones and Joey DeFrancesco), the ROVA Saxophone Quartet and guests (*John Coltrane's Ascension*), Prima Materia with Rashied Ali, Dave Liebman, Benny Colson and other Arkadia Records artists (anthologized on *Thank You, John!,* released early this year)." Howard Mandel, "Louder Than Words: The Enduring Legacy of John Coltrane," *Down Beat,* June 1998, 20. Garrett's *Pursuance: The Music of John Coltrane* was voted, by the magazine's readers, the best album of 1997.

7. Coltrane's spirituality, as amateurs describe it at the Stage, has been widely documented by fellow musicians and students of his life and work. "In addition to his musical importance, Coltrane exerted a profound spiritual influence on the musicians who followed in his footsteps. He was, according to all accounts, a modest man

involved in a continual search for new areas of self-expression, and he projected a personal quality that the younger musicians have drawn and used as a model for their own behavior. He was not the first musician to speak of spiritual matters, but his example was one of the most compelling and persuasive. As Frank Lowe put it: 'In the beginning, I wanted to be a "hip jazz musician." But Coltrane changed all that. Of course, the musicians have always been a part of the community, from Buddy Bolden on down. But Coltrane re-emphasized this. He took it out of being a "hip" musician and into being a musician of value or worth to the community. A musician to inform, a musician to relate to, a musician to raise kids by.'" Mandel, "Louder Than Words," 34. Albert Ayler perhaps best expressed what still is the most common impression on the saxophonist: "John was like a visitor to this planet. He came in peace and he left in peace; but during his time here, he kept trying to reach new levels of awareness, of peace, of spirituality. That's why I regard the music he played as spiritual music—John's way of getting close and closer to the Creator." Quoted in Nat Hentoff's notes to *Albert Ayler Live in Greenwich Village* (Impulse A-9155), cited in Wilmer, *As Serious as Your Life*, 45. Along this same line of thought, an ex–Miles Davis sideman, Dave Liebman, recently gave the following testimony. "As in the case of any great artist, his legacy is a sum greater than its parts—in this case a coherent feeling, a vibe, an effect on the spiritual level. *You can absorb his specific musical accomplishments or not—but what really matters is the spiritual aspect.* It's as though he had a link to a greater force, and the later music is a trail of that. . . . His legacy is that feeling he put out, absolute sincerity and conviction of the music, and something passionate that I've never heard from anyone else—well, maybe Beethoven, a man who really meant business—without any pretension. . . . There is no one comparable, if you think about it. Miles's music is great and artistic and clever and beautiful and powerful—maybe he comes closest because of the duration and scope of his career, but he's not so spiritual, not so deeply moving. Coltrane's maybe not as clever as Miles, not as stylish, but has everything else in it, speaking louder than styles, louder than words. You know, Coltrane seldom spoke in public; he was shy, quiet, understated, gentle—a nice guy, not ominous, always with the horn in his mouth. He *was* like a train, on a path, not to be swerved, with a light in front of him that he went towards till the day he died." Quoted in Mandel, "Louder than Words," 24, 25, my emphasis. For a thorough analysis of the relation between Coltrane's spirituality and the structure of his compositions and use of musical techniques, see Lewis Porter, *John Coltrane: His Life and Music* (Ann Arbor: University of Michigan Press, 1998). Among other convincing and creative examples of the spiritual-technical connections in Coltrane's work, Porter juxtaposes the words in Coltrane's poem "A Love Supreme," which appears in the homologous disc's liner notes, with Coltrane's solo in "Psalm," the last song of the disc. "A comparison of the poem with Coltrane's improvisation reveals that his saxophone solo is a wordless 'recitation,' if you will, of the words of the poem, beginning with the title 'A Love Supreme'" (244). By the time Coltrane recorded *A Love Supreme*, "he was leaning more and more toward a kind of universal religion." As Coltrane said in 1966, "My goal is to live the truly religious life and express it in music. If you live it, when you play there's no problem because the music is just part of the whole thing. To be a musician is really something. It goes very, very deep. My music is the spiritual expression of what I am—my faith, my knowledge, my being. . . .When you begin to see the possibilities of music, you desire to do something really good for people, to help humanity free itself from its hangups. I think music can make the world better and, if I'm qualified, I want to do it. I'd like to point out to people the divine in a musical language that transcends words. I want to speak to their souls." From Paul D. Zimmerman, "The New Jazz," *Newsweek,* Dec. 12, 1966, 108, and Paul D. Zimmerman, "Death of a Jazzman," *Newsweek,* July 31, 1967, 78, 79; quoted in Porter, *John Coltrane,* 232. Attesting to the spiritual power of *A Love Supreme,* Porter reminds us that, to this day, "a church in San Francisco even builds its services around this album and reveres Coltrane as a saint. Although this is surely not what Coltrane had in mind, he obviously meant the album to be an important statement" (232).

8. Such argument can be extrapolated from Frank London Brown, "McDougal," *Phoenix Magazine* (Fall 1961), reprinted in *Black Voices: An Anthology of Afro-American Literature,* ed. Abraham Chapman (New York: The New American Library, 1968). For a historical analysis of Black masculinity focusing on Charles Mingus, see Nichole T. Rustin, "Mingus Fingers: Charles Mingus, Black Masculinity, and Postwar Jazz Culture," Ph.D. diss., New York University, August 1999.

9. Whether this contrast between White and Black jazz settings is valid outside my ethnographic universe remains to be investigated. I refrain from generalizations of that magnitude since my analysis is concerned with very specific social situations. J. C. Thomas, however, one of John Coltrane's biographers, compares Coltrane's musical expressions with that of another great jazz tenor player, Stan Getz, who was White. While Getz's sadness was, "as he said it, his own, accruing to no one else except himself . . . John's melancholy was more of a universal nature, not so much from his own experiences as from the suffering and sadness of others, the wasted lives and worried people he'd observed during his years of traveling. He was, in the continuing quest for perfection in his music and compassion for others, acquiring a preacher's consciousness; not pejoratively, not in telling others not to do this or that, but in trying to make other people's lives more meaningful through music. And those who listened close to Coltrane could tell, could certainly *feel* the persuasive intensity and personal message to his music; he was 'talking' with his saxophone voice, and his sound so perfectly expressed what musicians called the 'cry' of the preacher, a mystic, or a prophet." J. C. Thomas, *Chasin' the Trane: The Music and Mystique of John Coltrane* (New York: Doubleday, 1975), 136.

10. Black music instructors with whom I have studied often mentioned the "ghetto" component of note articulations. "Think of the streetcorners of L.A., think of the fights you've seen, the women." Such comments were produced when I was playing written music too literally, without the necessary interpretation that rendered it expressive from their standpoint. Here again, Black social life was the eminent reference, the repository of knowledge that made possible the translation of notated music into the production of meaningful statements. This exemplifies the difficulties

some of my Black instructors encountered when attempting to teach jazz idioms to persons not familiar with Black social life.

11. Indeed, this maxim is often repeated in workshops conducted by experienced musicians at the World Stage. On a hot Saturday afternoon, in July of 1997, for example, Barry Harris, Black pianist-educator and veteran sideman for, among others, Coleman Hawkins, Sonny Stitt, Cannonball Adderley, and Dexter Gordon, coordinated one of those workshops for jazz vocalists and instrumentalists. Attended by several musicians of different levels of skill, young and older, Black, White, Latina/o, and Asian, the workshop encompassed not only harmony and improvisation theory and application, but also several pieces of advice that touched on the spirit of music. As it was reported by a newspaper, "Jazz is about feeling," said Harris. "It's about beauty. It's about expression. Jazz is a beautiful way *of expressing yourself*" (emphasis added); Don Heckman, "A Low-Key Cultivation for Jazz," *Los Angeles Times,* July 8, 1997, F1. The workshop was also attended by Billy Higgins who, by way of his presence and enthusiastic impromptu singing, obviously provided further legitimization for Harris's teachings. "Higgins scats with swing, intensity and originality, his lines unfolding with the drive and imagination of a world-class horn player. The audience is captivated, and the room is filled with a mass feeling of communal swing—exactly the kind of feeling Harris has been trying to communicate in his teaching." Ibid., F6.

12. In addition to the influence of Elvin Jones, most drummers also have a special admiration for Billy Higgins. But this admiration entails, curiously, a reduced number of persons who openly pursue a style that is mirrored in his technique. Except for one drummer who occasionally plays in the jam sessions, but who is closer to being a professional than an advanced amateur since he has constant gigs and draws a considerable part of his income from them, there are no regulars who talk and act as if they would like to play somewhat like Higgins as there are those who readily acknowledge their desire to sound similar to Jones. This is perhaps due to the precision and difficulty of Higgins's technique, added to the fact that Higgins is a beloved local figure, who can be seen almost every day in Leimert—which makes him too close to be idolized in the same way Jones is. Another factor that might explain this situation is that amateurs may feel that their rendition of Higgins's style may be too awkward and off the mark and thus cause embarrassment for them and imply disrespect toward Higgins. Moreover, it should be noted that Higgins was Coltrane's last drummer before the formation of his famous quartet. Jones was serving time in jail and, as soon as he was released, he replaced Higgins. According to some of the Stage's regulars, one of the reasons for Higgins's substitution was that he played invariably on top of the beat, while Coltrane was looking for somebody who, by playing around and mostly ahead of the beat, would, as it were, push the music forward—create an accompaniment that would help define more dynamic and energetic executions. A similar point is made in Thomas, *Chasin' the Trane.*

13. Billy Higgins had recently undergone a liver transplant. Although still recovering (as I witnessed at the Juma prayer the previous Friday at the Crenshaw Blvd. mosque), his playing was as fresh and inspired as ever.

14. For other fundamental differences, see Mustafa El-Amin, "The Religion of Islam and the Nation of Islam: What Is the Difference?" A Muslim friend who practiced Al-Islam gave me this undated paper. According to him, this paper is widely read in prison—where, like this friend I just mentioned, a considerable part of Blacks become Muslims—and in Muslim study groups in Los Angeles' inner city.

15. Malcolm's dissent with relation to the teachings of the Nation of Islam—and some of the motives that led to his leaving the Nation—can be seen in various passages of his autobiography. "I was to learn later that Elijah Muhammad's tales, like this one on 'Yacub' [a Black man who, "about sixty-six hundred years ago," by genetic manipulation, created whites and taught them wickedness and how to rule Blacks], infuriated Muslims of the East. While at Mecca, I reminded them that it was their fault, since they themselves hadn't done enough to make real Islam known in the West. Their silence left a vacuum in which any religious faker could step in and mislead our people." Malcolm X, with Alex Haley, *The Autobiography of Malcolm X* (1964; New York: Ballantine, 1993), 171. Minister Louis Farrakhan, head of the Nation of Islam, incidentally, is still telling Yacub's story.

16. These general guidelines can be extracted from the Friday sermons (*khutbah*) I heard from Rizza Khalilullah, iman of a local mosque, the tape recordings of these sermons that can be purchased at the mosque, and the literature that was suggested to me by (non–Nation of Islam) Muslims in South Central. Among this literature are the weekly *Muslim Journal,* the monthly *al-talib,* a Muslim newsmagazine at UCLA, and the following books, found in local Muslim bookstores and known by a majority of local Muslims: Hammudah Abdalati, *Islam in Focus* (Indianapolis: American Trust Publication, 1975); Maryam Jameelah, *Islam and Western Society* (Delhi: Adam Publishers, 1988); Khalilullah, *The Whiteman Made Me Do It;* H. M. Baagil, *Christian-Muslim Dialogue* (Los Angeles: n.p., 1984); and, of course, the Qur'an. Such orientation is obviously less sectarian toward non-Blacks and American society than other Muslim currents such as the Nation of Islam and those represented by authors such as Ameer Abdul-Hakeem Muhammad, who wrote *Maintaining Slaves in America* (Rialto, Calif.: Hakeem's Productions, 1995).

17. LeRoi Jones (Amiri Baraka) makes this point in his *Blues People: Negro Music in White America* (New York: William Morrow, 1963). "If Negro music can be seen to be the result of certain attitudes, certain specific ways of thinking about the world (and only ultimately about the *ways* in which music can be made), then the basic hypothesis of this book is understood" (153). According to Jones—and here the parallels with what some of Leimert's jazz players usually affirm is evident—"the jazz player could come from any part of that [Afro-American] social-cultural spectrum, but if he were to play a really moving kind of jazz, he had to reflect almost all the musical spectrum, or at least combine sufficiently to older autonomous blues tradition with the musical traditions of the Creoles or the ragtime orchestras of the North" (139). For further insights into the relation between Afro-American culture and blues, see Houston A. Baker Jr., *Blues, Ideology, and Afro-American Literature: A Vernacular Theory* (Chicago: University of Chicago Press, 1984). According to Baker, "Afro-American

culture is a complex, reflexive enterprise which finds its proper figuration in blues conceived as a matrix. A matrix is a womb, a network, a fossil-bearing rock, a rocky trace of a gemstone's removal, a principal metal in an alloy, a mat or plate for reproducing prints of phonographic records" (3). The blues, moreover, are "the multiplex, enabling *script* in which Afro-American cultural discourse in inscribed" (4). Baker makes the suggestive point that the blues "constitute an amalgam that seems always to have been in motion in America—always becoming, shaping, transforming, displacing the peculiar experiences of Africans in the New World" (5). This quality of restlessness will appear again in this chapter, when I discuss part of Leimert's public ethic. In *We Real Cool,* bell hooks sees the blues as one of the few outlets for non-patriarchal forms of Black male expression of emotions, in which vulnerability and sensitivity are seen as valued aspects of artistic performance.

18. For a characterization of the various currents of blues that is still applicable, see Charles Keil, *Urban Blues* (1966; Chicago: University of Chicago Press, 1991). Keil's words about the relation between the Black Muslims of the 1960s and what they perceived as objectionable, embarrassing mores of disadvantaged Blacks, can perhaps serve as a point of reference for what happens in contemporary Leimert Park. "Cloaked in an Islamic and Zionist ideology, the Muslim program is based on a complete, harsh, and puritanical negation of the Negro lower-class stereotype. It is this stereotype of course that the proponents of soul hope to refurbish, reshape, and revive. For the Muslims, 'the collard green is a weed,' 'the pig is a poison animal,' and both are strict taboo; for the soul brother, 'hocks and greens sustained us during slavery times, and they're the source of our strength today.' . . . The soul strategists try to turn old liabilities into new assets; the Muslim ideologists continue to mint a new currency altogether, although the coins are clearly stamped with the Protestant ethic" (186). In Leimert Park, the diffused Muslim ideology cannot be held solely responsible for the negative views on blues. Many of the local celebrities—musicians, poets, artisans, writers, the group of people who seem to express with greater impact the Village's public codes—have shaped their views in the same period studied by Keil. Today, however, these artists attempt to integrate elements of a Muslim ethic with traits of local and international Black cultural manifestations.

19. Tapscott was also a key member of UGMAA, the Union of God's Musicians and Artists Ascension, which encompassed the Arkestra and organized activities that focused on the inner city. Horace Tapscott and Steven Louis Isoardi, *Songs of the Unsung: The Musical and Social Journey of Horace Tapscott* (Durham, N.C.: Duke University Press, 2001); Central Avenue Sounds Editorial Committee, Clora Bryant et al., *Central Avenue Sounds: Jazz in Los Angeles* (Berkeley: University of California Press, 1998). Explaining the reasons why in 1959/60 he left Lionel Hampton's big band, Tapscott said that he "got off the road to start my orchestra, to preserve black music. I wanted to preserve and teach and show and perform the music of black Americans and Pan-African music. To preserve it by playing it and writing it and taking it to the community. And that to me was what it was about, being part of the community" (301). As the introductory note on Tapscott's biography tells us, "From leading a

marching band to the annual Kwanzaa parade and teaching kids in the neighborhood, to late night jams in Leimert Park and standing in his front lawn near Crenshaw High School chatting with neighbors, Horace remains an influential presence in his community" (282).

20. For a comprehensive study on this current of improvised music that emerged around the mid-1960s in several American Black communities, especially in Chicago and New York, see Wilmer, *As Serious as Your Life*. See also George Lewis, "Improvised Music After 1950—Afrological and Eurological Perspectives," *Black Music Research Journal* 16, no. 1 (Spring 1996): 91–122.

21. See Cross, *It's Not about a Salary*, 10-12.

22. Quoted in Williams, "The Poet of Leimert Park," B2.

23. As have most jazz veterans who have performed and developed their art with social awareness (and sometimes social activism), Max Roach has made the following statement about hip-hop: "[T]he thing that frightened people about hip-hop was that they hear people enjoying rhythm for rhythm's sake. Hip-hop lives in the world—not the world of music—that's why it's so revolutionary." Quoted by Greg Tate, *Flyboy in the Buttermilk: Essays on Contemporary America* (New York: Simon and Schuster, 1992), 129.

24. Quoted in Williams, "The Poet of Leimert Park," B2.

25. Quoted in ibid.

26. Quoted in ibid.

27. See, e.g., Malcolm X with Haley, *The Autobiography of Malcolm X*, 371. For a discussion of the Black Power theses, Vargas, "Blacks in the City of Angels' Dust."

28. Recorded in Los Angeles in 1965, *Kulu Se Mama* had an unusual personnel roster: aside from his regular rhythm section of pianist McCoy Tyner, bassist Jimmy Garrison, and drummer Elvin Jones, Coltrane added drummer Frank Butler, Pharoah Sanders on tenor saxophone, Donald Garrett on bass clarinet and bass, and the percussion and vocals of Juno Lewis—all playing simultaneously. A drawing of Juno, and a transcription of "Kulu Se Mama (Juno Se Mama)," his poem that gave the record its title, illustrate the inside cover of the original LP. The date, location and substance of the recording are no accident. The radical experimental character of *Kulu Se Mama*, with its iconoclast stances toward bebop's usual time, harmony and improvisations, can be readily associated with the post-uprising cultural climate that included, among others, the no-less-radical experiments undertaken in Watts by local poets and musicians. Coltrane's innovative approach to rhythm and his obvious search for greater freedom in tonality can be contextualized, and indeed acquire further meaning, within the effervescent political and artistic expressions of the mid-1960s. I thank George Lipsitz for pointing out that Frank Kofsky made a similar argument in his *Black Nationalism and the Revolution in Music* (New York: Pathfinder Press, 1970).

29. Higgins's achievements as a musician have been recognized and prized several times. One of the most recent homages to him is described in the following lines. "On Jan. 12 at Merkin Hall in New York City, the 61-year-old Higgins was presented the fourth annual Phineas Newborn Jr. Award, created by pianist [James] Williams to

honor the living legends of jazz. Past recipients of the award, named after piano genius Phineas Newborn Jr., have been Ron Carter, Milt Jackson and Jimmy Heath. That same night, Higgins was also presented with a Barry, an award created by pianist and educator Barry Harris for those who exemplify musical excellence in jazz." *Down Beat,* April 1998, 10. A large number of acclaimed jazz musicians either performed in different all-star combinations for Higgins or were there to pay tribute to him: Billy Hart, Tommy Flanagan, George Coleman, Victor Lewis, Carl Allen, Chris Anderson, Ron Carter, Dave Holland, Harold Mabern Jr., Buster Williams, Joe Lovano, Javon Jackson, Vanessa Rubin, and Bob Cranshaw, among others. This peer recognition, together with an enthusiastic sold-out audience, only reinforced the generalized knowledge that has existed for a long time among Leimert's regulars about Higgins's importance to music.

30. This, of course, is only *part* of the Nation of Islam's complex messages. For articles on the organization's outlooks, see Benjamin Playthell, "The Attitude Is the Message: Louis Farrakhan Pursues the Middle Class," *Village Voice,* Aug. 15, 1989, 23–31. See also Henry Louis Gates Jr., "The Charmer," *New Yorker,* April 29/May 6, 1996, 116–31. Both articles seem to agree that the Nation of Islam's main support—if not its moral principles—comes from middle-class Blacks. "Farrakhan's level of support among black Americans is vigorously debated. If you gauge his followers by the number who regularly attend mosques affiliated with the Nation of Islam and eschew lima beans and corn bread, they are not very numerous. Estimates range from twenty thousand to ten times that. On the other hand, if you go by the number of people who consider him a legitimate voice of black protest, then ranks are much higher. (In a recent poll, more than half the blacks surveyed reported a favorable impression of him.) The [Million Man] march was inspired by the Muslims but not populated by them. Farrakhan knows that the men who came to the march were not his religious followers. They tended to be middle class and college-educated and Christian. Farrakhan is convinced that those men came to a 'march called by a man who is considered radical, extremist, anti-Semitic, anti-white' because of a yearning 'to connect with the masses'" (128).

31. A similar point, albeit made in a more general manner, can be extracted from Paul Gilroy's *The Black Atlantic: Modernity and Double Consciousness* (Cambridge: Harvard University Press, 1993). For example: "It bears repetition that the premium which all these black diaspora styles place on the process of performance is emphasized by their radically unfinished forms—a characteristic which marks them indelibly as the products of slavery" (105).

32. For example, in April 1997, a group of approximately twenty-five small-business owners and neighborhood residents rallied against the city's intention to install additional parking meters in the area. "They liken the parking meters scheduled to crop up in two city-owned lots, to weeds that could destroy their cultural garden spot." Hong, "Merchants Rally Against Parking Meters," B3. The photograph that accompanied the article showed a mix of shop owners, artists, and residents carrying large signs expressing their demands. Some people were wearing African and Eastern clothes,

African drums were being played, and some people were wearing standard Western clothing.

33. Cohen, *Boundaries of Blackness,* esp. chap. 2.

34. For a historical analysis of how the 1920s' northern urban Black middle class engaged in policing practices as it focused on the migrating working class, and especially on young Black working-class women coming from the south, see Hazel Carby, "Policing the Black Woman's Body in an Urban Context," *Critical Inquiry* 18 (1992): 738–55.

35. Cohen, *Boundaries of Blackness,* 75.

36. Graham Lock, *Blutopia: Visions of the Future and Revisions of the Past in the Work of Sun Ra, Duke Ellington, and Anthony Braxton* (Durham, N.C.: Duke University Press, 1999), 184.

6. BLACKNESS AS SELF-HELP AND SOCIAL CRITIQUE

1. Garry Webb, *Dark Alliance: The CIA, the Contras, and the Crack Cocaine Explosion* (New York: Seven Stories Press, 1999); Michael Levine, *The Big White Lie: The CIA and the Cocaine/Crack Epidemic* (New York: Thunder Mouth, 1993); Alfred McCoy, *Politics of Heroin: CIA Complicity in the Global Drug Trade* (New York: Lawrence Hill Books, 1991); James William Gibson, *Warrior Dreams: Violence and Manhood in Post-Vietnam America* (New York: Hill and Wang, 1994).

2. Robin D. G. Kelley, *Race Rebels: Culture, Politics, and the Black Working Class* (New York: Free Press, 1994), 181.

3. Allen S. Gordon, "Resurrection of Principles," *The Source,* April 1996, 60.

4. Mike Davis, *City of Quartz: Excavating the Future in Los Angeles* (New York: Verso, 1990), 297.

5. Yusuf Jah and Sister Shah'Keyah, *Uprising: Crips and Bloods Tell the Story of America's Youth in the Crossfire* (New York: Scribner's, 1995).

6. Ibid., 329. Skeptically, Mike Davis, quoting Donald Bakeer's *CRIPS: The Story of the L.A. Street Gang from 1971–1985* (Los Angeles: Precocious, 1987), adds another suggestion to the list. CRIP, according to what Bakeer had heard from an O.G. ("Original Gangster), "originally stood for 'Continuous Revolution in Progress.'" Davis, *City of Quartz,* 299.

7. O.G.s—Original Gangsters—are individuals who claim or are known to be founders of gangs. The term can also be used to designate someone who participated, with distinction, in gangs during times far removed from the present. O.G.s, moreover, are gang members whose age—late twenties and up—distinguishes them from most younger gang members. O.G.s' experiences give them a historical perspective that youngsters obviously do not have.

8. As noted by Conot, *Rivers of Blood, Years of Darkness.* Cited in Davis, *City of Quartz,* 297.

9. Jah and Shah'Keyah, *Uprising,* 151, 152. Subsequent page numbers appear in the text.

10. In this text, *gangbanger* stands for the gang member who engages in violence, especially shootings of enemy gangsters. While those supportive of the truce may

remain gang members—part of the social network defined by gang affiliation—they do not participate in the violence.

11. According to Leibo, an ex-Watts Crip who is today a Muslim and who is now devoted to expanding the truce.

12. The drug business in the ghetto emerges from gangsters' accounts as a multitude of unrelated and competing small organizations usually commanded by O.G.s. who, in turn, are part of different distribution hierarchies. Perhaps due to the myriad of pulverized and complicated networks within which drug operations take place, Malcolm Klein, Cheryl L. Maxon, and Lea C. Cunningham, utilizing data from narcotics investigation files and homicide files of five LAPD and L.A. sheriffs' departments, affirm that crack distribution is *not* a primarily street gang phenomenon. Klein, Maxon, and Cunningham, "'Crack,' Street Gangs, and Violence," *Criminology* 29, no. 1 (Nov. 1991): 623–50. Ethnographic evidence, however, shows that most gangsters are involved with the drug trade. Davis, moreover, supports this argument, in *City of Quartz,* 313.

13. Klein, Maxon, and Cunningham, "'Crack,' Street Gangs, and Violence," 643, 644. The authors consider homicides with drug involvement those that occur accompanied by "paraphernalia, drug use or sales by victim or suspect, evidence of drugs at the scene, etc." (643).

14. Ted Rohrlich and Frederic Tulsky, "Gang Killings Exceed 40% of L.A. Slayings," *Los Angeles Times,* Dec. 5, 1996, A22.

15. Consider a study conducted by the National Center on Institutions and Alternatives which found that 42 percent of Black men in Washington, D.C., between the ages of 18 and 35 were in jail, on probation or parole, or awaiting trial or awaiting sentencing. It also reported that "as many as 70 percent of black men in the city have been arrested by the time they turn 35, and as high as 85 percent of black men in Washington, D.C., face arrest at some time in their lives." Quoted in Thomas Dumm, "The New Enclosures: Racism and the Normalized Community," in *Reading Rodney King,* ed. Gooding-Williams, 75. There is no reason to believe that these rates are any smaller for Los Angeles, considered the "gang capital" of the nation and notorious for its violent and biased police force.

16. Davis, *City of Quartz.*

17. *Los Angeles Sentinel,* Feb. 27, 1997, A7.

18. For an analysis of such operations in San Jose, see Christian Parenti, *Lockdown America: Police and Prison in the Age of Crisis* (London: Verso, 1999).

19. *Los Angeles Sentinel,* Feb. 27, 1997, A6. In the same vein, Davis has noted how even progressive middle-class Blacks share this revulsion against youth criminality. Novelist Ishmael Reed and former Minister of Propaganda for the BPP Harry Edwards (now a professor of sociology at UC–Berkeley) support the idea of a curfew for eighteen- to twenty-four-year-olds. Edwards, moreover, when asked about what should be done with a thirteen-year-old crack seller, emphatically replied, "Turn him in, lock him up. Get rid of him. Lock him up for a *long* time. As long as the law will allow, and try to make it as long as possible. I'm for locking 'em up, gettin' 'em off the

street, put 'em behind bars." Interview by Ken Kelly, *San Francisco Focus,* March 1988, 100; quoted in Davis, *City of Quartz,* 292.

20. Miller, *Search and Destroy,* 91. Such rates are per 100,000 homicides.

21. Ibid., 91, 92.

22. Anyone familiar with the Million Man March knows that the event was more than simply a celebration of the gang truce. Middle- and working-class Blacks, indeed, formed the core of the massive Washington audience, estimated to have been close to one million people. Not surprisingly, "personal responsibility" was one of the main *official* themes of the march which, obviously, exempts the government of any accountability regarding the situation of Blacks and other persons of color. The truce, however, enabled the participation of many Black youths who supported the peace agreements and who, if on the one hand identified with the March's spirit of unity based on self-help, on the other, as the case of Twilight well illustrates, defended a view of the future which included a powerful critique of the government and the need to organize collectively around strong social movements.

23. This according to Angelo in *Uprising,* 74. Subsequent page numbers appear in the text.

24. Ibid., 92. Indeed, one explanation for the gang truce's limited scope is its low receptivity among younger gang members. As Twilight put it, in the beginning of the ceasefire negotiations, in the early 1990s, "the treaty was discussed only amongst the older generation, and even though they may have agreed to certain terms, it never got down to the younger generation. In Watts, I can go anywhere, but my younger homeboys can't, because you have bad apples in every bunch. . . . One of my homeboys got shot recently, and the guy that was behind it is older than me, but he just doesn't want peace. He's manipulating the mind of the younger kids from his neighborhood and sending them on these missions" (306).

25. Anthony Perry, *Original Gang Truce* (Los Angeles: Ant Valley Book Productions, 1995), 14.

26. Playmate, echoing widespread complaints, said the following. "I graduated from Jordan High School in 1984, and I was totally illiterate. I could not read a lick, but I graduated from high school. How? How did I graduate from high school and couldn't read?" (Jah and Shah'Keyah, *Uprising,* 93).

27. Quoted in Perry, *Original Gang Truce,* 36.

28. *Los Angeles Times,* June 17, 1992, B1, B8.

29. See, e.g., Marsha Mitchell, "Gang Truce Brings Hope of Peace," *Los Angeles Sentinel,* May 14, 1992. Given the newspaper's tendency to discredit all that is associated with gangs, the tone of the article was unusually optimistic. "Although many in South Los Angeles do not believe the truce will last, these young people who were called 'notorious, archenemy federations' by the media recently, have vowed that their armistice will stay in effect. . . . In an effort to back their words with actions, organizers have begun planning positive programs around the community to keep the feeling of good vibes circulating" (A16).

30. The list of community organizations that emerged following the truce, or that

devote a substantial part of their energy to the truce's maintenance, is rather large. Among these organizations are Unity One, No Guns, Fokus, Exodus, Hope, Rise, Solomon Group, Coalition of Brothers and Sisters Unlimited, M.A.D.D. Dads, Mothers Reclaiming Our Children (Mothers ROC), New African Vanguard Movement, and Malcolm X Grass Roots Movement. They are composed largely of ex-gangbangers and operate on little or no budget.

31. Community in Support of the Gang Truce, "Fund for a New L.A.," proposal, December 1994, 1, on file in CSGT office.

32. Both institutions have a 501(c)3 nonprofit status.

33. CSGT has a board of directors, also called the steering committee, formed by ten persons who have either participated directly in the gang truce or that have been long-time members of CAPA. Besides Zinzun and Twilight Bey, four Latina/os (two men, two women), plus one Black woman, one White woman, and two other Black men form the steering committee.

34. The point has been made, among others, by Mike Davis. "But the Crips and Bloods—decked out in Gucci T-shirts and expensive Nike airshoes, ogling rock dealers driving by in BMWs—are also authentic creatures of the age of Reagan. Their world view, above all, is formed of an acute awareness of what is going down on the Westside, where gilded youth practice the insolent indifference and avarice that are also forms of street violence. Across the spectrum of runaway youth consumerism and the impossible fantasies of personal potency and immunity, youth of all classes and colors are grasping at undeferred gratification—even if it paves the way to assured self-destruction." *City of Quartz,* 315.

35. Community in Support of the Gang Truce, "Our Demands: What Our Community Needs," n.d., 8, on file in CGST office.

36. Ibid.

37. CAPA's influence is also evident in the legal advice CSGT provides for juveniles involved with the criminal justice system. Of great concern among Black youth is the "three-strikes law," which sentences persons with three felony convictions to a mandatory sentence of twenty-five years to life in prison. Juveniles sixteen years and older can face adjudications that can be counted as "strikes." These strikes become a permanent part of one's police record. "*Do not plead guilty* to any felony without first understanding that the *plea will result in an automatic strike* on your record," advises CSGT. "It is unethical for your attorney to not clearly explain the danger of life imprisonment with a guilty plea to felony charges in the '3 Strikes' environment. . . . Juveniles 16 years or older who face adjudications that can be counted as 'strikes' should demand *an adult trial with legal representation and all constitutional protection, including a jury trial.*" Ibid., 11.

38. Information in this and the previous paragraphs is extracted from ibid., 9–10.

39. Community in Support of the Gang Truce, "Statement of Economic Development," n.d., 3.

40. Ibid.

41. In spite of Ueberroth's convictions against government direct interventions in

the economy, the subsidies RLA offered for business willing to invest in South Central were to be sanctioned by public administration: tax incentives, deregulatory legislation, and enterprise zones.

42. Labor/Community Strategy Center, "Reconstructing Los Angeles," 1. With relation to the interests RLA represented, consider the following. "Although several dedicated community activists and advocates were recruited to RLA (some having serious misgivings about its legitimacy), the power on the board was firmly in the hands of representatives of Arco, IBM, Warner Brothers, Southern California Edison, U.S.C., Disney, and the Chamber of Commerce. At the staff level, power was held by Ueberroth and his cochairmen, Bernard Kinsey, a former Xerox vice-president; Barry Sanders, of the corporate law firm Latham and Watkins; and Tony Salazar, formerly with a St. Louis–based housing developer." Ibid., 2.

43. See, e.g., *Los Angeles Sentinel,* May 7, 1992, A3, B8, B7.

44. Labor/Community Strategy Center, "Reconstructing Los Angeles," 22.

45. The Black Business Association is a good example of organized business interests. Note its emphasis on procuring public support for private enterprises. Founded in 1970 by "a group of insightful Black entrepreneurs," this South Central organization vows to "maintain very effective working relationships with elected officials for support of the Black business development. We serve as a liaison between BBA members and the city, state, and federal government agencies, schools and public interest groups." Black Business Association brochure, n.d.

46. Labor/Community Strategy Center, "Reconstructing Los Angeles," 22.

47. See, e.g., Davis, *City of Quartz,* and Byran O. Jackson, quoted in *Los Angeles Times,* July 17, 1992, B8.

48. Community in Support of the Gang Truce, "Statement of Economic Development," 3.

49. Community in Support of the Gang Truce, "Economic Development Project," n.d., 4.

50. Ibid.

51. Labor/Community Strategy Center, "Reconstructing Los Angeles," 21, 23.

52. Asked what role Black women play in getting gang wars started, General Robert Lee said the following. "They play key roles. Most drive-bys and most trouble is usually behind a woman." In Jah and Shah'Keyah, *Uprising,* 139. T. Rogers, another O.G., added that disputes over females were one of the key factors that started the killings between gangs. "The same females that would go and sleep with someone else started a lot of killings" (209).

53. Ibid., 92, 93.

54. *The Amer-I-Can Program* (Los Angeles, 1991), 4. Subsequent page numbers appear in the text.

55. Don Gordon in Jah and Shah'Keyah, *Uprising,* 99, my emphasis.

56. The Amer-I-Can Program, 10, 12. Subsequent page numbers appear in the text.

57. Ibid., 52. Further proof of McDonald's success is the fact that its franchises "tell us that once youngsters (some still in high school) have absorbed themselves in the

McDonald's Corporation system, they exhibit tremendous growth and maturity. Franchises say that these high schoolers become more Focused and Determined to Succeed when they apply themselves and follow the rules laid out for them. This Success spills over their school life and family life as well." Ibid.

58. Careful explanations about several aspects involved in searching for, keeping and progressing in a career is given in chapters 13 and 14. A person looking for a job must be confident, communicative and possess the skills required. Information is also given on where to look for a job, the preparation of the resume, appearance, behavior and strategies during the interview. Finally, instructions are given for asking for a raise and considering other careers. Ibid., 55-62.

59. For example: "If we are not resolved and Committed, if our Attitude is not totally positive, and if we are not willing to do whatever is necessary to achieve this GOAL [i.e. financial security], we will be trampled by those members of society who are prepared and actively seeking financial security." Ibid., 47.

CONCLUSION

1. Charles Lawrence III asserts the need to dream and imagine a world not yet realized. This radical, transfigurative project accepts the dream but cannot settle. To settle would be to give up on the fundamental need of constant reinvention. See his "The Word and the River: Pedagogy as Scholarship as Struggle," in *Critical Race Theory: The Key Writings that Formed the Movement,* ed. K. Crenshaw et al. (New York: New Press, 1995).

2. Collins, *Fighting Words;* Smith, *The Truth That Never Hurts;* Kelley, *Freedom Dreams;* Lipsitz, *The Possessive Investment in Whiteness;* Anzaldúa and Keating, eds., *This Bridge We Call Home;* Mohanty, *Feminism Without Borders.*

3. Lipsitz, *The Possessive Investment in Whiteness.*

4. For a thorough study of divisions within Black communities and how those are related to conceptions of Aids/HIV, see Cohen, *Boundaries of Blackness.*

5. Collins, *Black Feminist Thought.*

6. Smith, *The Truth That Never Hurts.*

7. In a way similar to how blues songs performed by Black working-class women starting in the 1920s can be seen as historical preparation for organized political protest. See Davis, *Blues Legacy and Black Feminism,* esp. "Blame it on the Blues: Bessie Smith, Gertrude 'Ma' Rainey, and the Politics of Blues Protest."

8. As Huey Newton stated, "As far as our party is concerned, the BPP is an all black party, because we feel as Malcolm X felt that there can be no black-white unity until there is first black unity. We have a problem in the black colony that is particular to the colony, but we're willing to accept aid from the mother country as long as the mother country radicals realize that we have, as Eldridge Cleaver says in *Soul on Ice,* a mind of our own. We've regained our mind that was taken away from us and we will decide the political as well as the practical stand we'll take. We'll make the theory and we'll carry out the practice. It is the duty of the white revolutionary to aid with this. . . . Our alliance is one of the organized black groups with organized white

groups. As soon as the organized white groups do not do the things that would benefit us in our struggle for liberation, that will be our departure point. So we don't suffer in the hangup of a skin color. We don't hate white people, we hate the oppressor. And if the oppressor happens to be white then we hate him. And right now in America you have the slave-master being a white group. We are pushing him out of office through revolution in this country. I think the responsibility of the white revolutionary will be to aid us in this. And when we are attacked by the police or by the military then it will be up to the white mother country radicals to attack the murderers and to respond as we respond, to follow our program." *The Movement,* cited in *The Black Panthers Speak,* ed. Philip S. Foner (Philadelphia: J. B. Lippincott, 1970), 55, 57, 58.

9. Davis, in *City of Quartz,* describes how sectors of the Black middle class in Los Angeles adopt perspectives about the innate criminal nature of gang members that end up supporting the ongoing massive incarceration, surveillance of young people of color, and the corresponding legislation.

10. hooks, *We Real Cool,* 117.

11. Audre Lorde, *Sister Outsider.*

12. Kwame Ture, *Ready for Revolution* (New York: Scribner's, 2003). I thank George Lipsitz for suggesting this quote.

13. Chela Sandoval, *Methodology of the Oppressed* (Minneapolis: University of Minnesota Press, 2000).

INDEX

addiction. *See* drug dependence
AFDC (Aid to Families with Dependent
  Children), 8, 37, 263n.4, 265n.1
affirmative action, 37. *See also under*
  discrimination; work opportunities
African American Community Unity
  Center, 126
age. *See* generational issues; youth
agency, 171–72, 222
Aid to Families with Dependent
  Children (AFDC), 263n.4; war on
  welfare and, 37
Ain't No Makin' It (McLeod), 253n.19
All Power to the People (1997), 271n.41
American Civil Liberties Union, 119,
  129, 270n.31
American Friends Service Committee,
  128
Amer-I-Can program, 177, 204–5,
  206–8, 221, 285n.57
Americans for Democratic Action,
  128
Anderson, Elijah, 24–25, 26, 253n.19,
  255n.32
anti-Black genocide, 251n.11
Arkestra (Pan-Afrikan Peoples Arkestra),
  161, 278n.19

arts, the: transformative power of, 107,
  163–64, 222–23, 267n.7
Asians, 48, 259nn.42–44, 269n.50
Ayler, Albert, 273n.6

Bagdikian, Ben, 267n.7
Baker, Ella, 266n.6
Baker, Houston, 277n.17
Baldwin, James, 224
Baldwin Hills, 57, 141, 144, 259n.42
Baraka, Amiri (Leroi Jones), 277n.17
Barnes, Jimel, 180
Bates, Karen Grigsby, 138–39
Berg, Michael (Judge), 124
Bernstein, Michael, 256n.2
Berry, Mary Frances, 129, 270n.32
Bey, Twilight: educational achievement
  of, 283n.24; gang histories and, 179–
  80, 181; gang truce and, 185, 189,
  202–3, 205–6, 283n.24, 284n.33; as
  role model, 205–6; work with
  Amer-I-Can, 199, 200–202, 203
Black: definitions of, 31–33, 249n.1
Black Atlantic, The (Gilroy), 280n.31
Black Business Association, 285n.45
black consciousness, 32, 164–65, 167,
  168–69, 220, 251n.11, 280n.31

Black Corona (Gregory), 253n.19

Black feminist thought: Black radical traditions and, 22–23, 253n.20; controlling images and, 23–24, 254n.22; everyday experience and, 22; group survival and, 22, 223–24, 267n.7; social transformation and, 223–24, 267n.7; transformative power of mutuality, 107, 267n.7

Black Feminist Thought (Collins), 253n.20

Black/Jewish relationships, 43, 44, 170, 258n.27

Black Marxism (Robinson), 253n.20

blackness: autheticity and, 15–16, 150–51, 174, 220–21; boundaries of, 170, 174–76, 215–17, 217– 223, 254n.22; citizenship and, 16; class structures and, 15–17, 219–21; coalition building and, 217–19, 220; as conflict, 17, 174–75; consumption and, 221; contradictions and, 215–17; diasporic consciousness, 32, 164–65, 167, 168–69, 220, 251n.11, 280n.31; emotionalism and, 118–19, 268n.11; essentialism and, 29–30, 169–72, 175; exclusion and, 217–19; expressive culture and, 151–52, 153, 222; gender and, 145, 151–52, 169–71, 173–74, 217–20, 223–24; generational issues and, 219–22, 222–23; identity construction and, 219–24; individualism vs. collective responsibility, 221; inter-ethnic relations, 217; Latinas/os and, 217; masculinity and, 150–51; mutual recognition and, 17; political implications of, 215–17; self-making and, 222; social mobility and, 16–17, 221–22; social movements and, 216–17; social transformation and, 22, 176, 215–17, 221–24; as solidarity, 16–17, 66, 83, 215–17, 217–19; structural inequities and, 15–18; women and, 217–18, 221–22

Black-owned businesses, 58–59

Black Panther Party (BPP): black unity and, 286n.8; class diversity of, 133–34; Coalition Against Police Abuse and, 110, 111, 114, 118–19, 130–34; educational achievement and, 272n.45; gangs, 179; gender and, 132, 271n.39; generational issues, 219, 268n.8; leadership within, 271n.39, 271n.41; as membership organization, 133–34; middle class people and, 272n.45; use of panther imagery, 255n.323; women and, 271n.39; working class people and, 272n.45

Black Power, 131, 136–37, 139, 180, 189, 190, 193, 199, 212, 268n.11, 272n.45

Black radical traditions, 18–19, 138–39, 253n.20. *See also* Black feminist thought

Black Stone Rangers, 210

black unity, 286n.8

blues, the, 145, 160–61, 286n.7

Blues People (Jones), 277n.17

boundaries of blackness, 170, 174–75, 215–17, 217–23, 254n.22

Bourdieu, Pierre, 25

BPP. *See* Black Panther Party (BPP)

Bradley, Thomas (mayor), 43, 191, 258n.24

Bradley administration (1973–1993): coalition building and, 43–44, 258n.27; elitism and, 43–44, 258n.27; housing and, 43–44; Los Angeles Police Commission, 124, 188, 199; Rebuild Los Angeles (RLA), 191–93, 194, 284nn.41–42, 285n.42, 285n.45; work opportunities and, 43

Braxton, Anthony, 161

Brazil, 32–33, 109

Brecker, Michael, 273n.6

Brentwood, 259n.41, 259n.43

Breye, Bryan, 162

Brother Crook (Ron Wilkins), 179
Brown, Elaine, 271n.39
Brown, Jim, 29, 177, 200, 204, 207
business interests: Amer-I-Can program,
    177, 204–5, 206–8, 221, 285n.57;
    Black Business Association, 285n.45;
    Black-owned businesses, 58, 191–93;
    entrepreneurs, 15–16, 165, 175, 192,
    285n.45; McDonald's Corporation,
    204–5, 285n.57; NOI and, 170; post-
    1992 rebellions, 191; Rebuild Los
    Angeles, 191–92, 194, 285n.45;
    vocational training and, 195–97
Butler, Frank, 279n. 28

CAPA. See Coalition Against Police
    Abuse (CAPA)
Carmichael, Stokely (Kwame Ture),
    255n.33
Carter, Alprentice "Bunchy," 162, 179
Carter administration (1977–1981),
    257n.12
Central American immigration, 27–28,
    35, 51
CETA (Comprehensive Employment
    and Training Act), 37
Christopher, Karen, 265n.1
circles of sorrow, 65–66, 83, 263n.3
citizenship: blackness and, 16; gender
    and, 55; interethnic conflict and, 53,
    55; rights of the people, 118, 121, 127,
    194; work opportunities and, 55
City of Quartz (Davis), 282n.10,
    284n.34, 287n.9
Civilian Police Review Board, 126–29,
    190–91
Civil Rights Congress, 251n.11
class differences: the blues and, 160–61;
    coalition building and, 135, 258n.27;
    community-based organizations and,
    133–34, 136; expressive culture and,
    145; popular mobilization and,
    133–34, 135, 136

class structures: blackness and, 15–17,
    219–21; class mobility and, 39–41;
    definitions of, 251n.10; occupational
    status and, 39–41; respectability and,
    174–76; structural inequities and,
    15–18, 37, 44–45
Cleaver, Jim, 133, 183, 286n.8
Clinton administration (1993–2001),
    42–43, 88, 129, 257n.12, 265n.1
Coalition Against Police Abuse (CAPA):
    blackness and, 220–22, 223; Black
    radical traditions and, 139–40; BPP
    and, 109, 110, 111, 114, 118–19, 130–34,
    219–20; Civilian Police Review
    Board, 126–29, 190–91; coalition
    building and, 130, 219–20; commu-
    nity organizing and, 110, 111; CSGT
    and, 119, 130, 184, 189, 208–12,
    267n.1, 284n.37; doctrine of objectiv-
    ity and, 267n.7; gang members and,
    129–30; gender issues and, 30–31,
    131–33, 136–37, 223; generational
    issues, 219–22; history of, 28–29, 109,
    130–34; leadership and, 131–32,
    139–40; Marxism and, 113; middle-
    class Blacks and, 271n.44; organizing
    manual, 110–11, 116–17, 233–48,
    267n.7; patriarchal structures of, 136–
    37; police brutality and, 70–71, 111,
    122–23, 127–30; police surveillance
    and, 119–22, 269n.14; political
    alliances, 219–22, 267n.1; political
    education and, 111–17, 177; relation-
    ship with Black Panther Party, 219–
    20, 255n.33; women and, 131–33,
    136–37; Zinzun and, 109, 112, 120,
    127–29, 127–30
coalition building: Black/Jewish
    relationships, 43, 44, 170, 258n.27;
    blackness and, 217–19, 220; Bradley
    administration, 43–44, 258n.24;
    CAPA and, 130, 219–20; class and,
    135, 258n.27; coalition politics,

253nn.20–21; diasporic consciousness and, 220, 222, 253nn.20–21; electoral politics and, 43, 53, 258n.24; elitism and, 43–44, 258n.24; inter-ethnic relations and, 140, 219–20, 258n.27; popular mobilization and, 28–29; social movements and, 28–29, 184–85, 209–10; social transformation and, 22–23; solidarity and, 159–60, 165; women and, 218–19, 221–22

Coalition of Brothers and Sisters Unlimited, 283n.30

code switching, 16

Cohen, Cathy, 174–76

COINTELPRO (FBI Counter-Intelligence Program), 120, 121, 131, 133, 134

Coleman, Ornette, 161

Coleman, Wanda, 161

collective responsibility: blackness and, 221; collective existence and, 148; collective problem solving, 266n.6; CSGT and, 198; emotionalism and, 201–3; ethic of openness and, 174–76; expressive culture and, 145–48, 153, 172–73; individualism vs., 139, 199–208, 201–3; Islam and, 159–60; self-help strategies and, 200–203, 204, 207–8; structural inequities and, 17–18; women and, 266n.6

Collins, Patricia Hill, 253n.20

Coltrane, John: "A Love Supreme" (1964), 149, 273n.6; "Ascenscion," 155, 156, 273n.6; emotionalism and, 275n.9; *Kulu Se Mama,* 166, 279n.28; legacy of, 148–50, 155–56, 273n.6; spirituality and, 148–50, 167–68; "The Coltrane Quartet," 148–49, 273n.6, 276n.12

Community Alert Patrol, 179

community-based organizations: blackness and, 219–24; class diversity and, 133–34, 136; gangs and, 129–30, 179,

283n.30; gender and, 22, 30, 131–33, 136–37, 212; individualism vs. mutuality, 139; leadership and, 131–33, 136–37, 139–40, 271n.39, 271n.41, 284n.33; male-centered perspectives and, 132; membership organizations, 133–34; mutuality and, 135–37; residential stability and, 252n.13; resistance to, 136; social inequalities and, 28–31; women and, 70–71, 131–33, 136–37. *See also* Coalition Against Police Abuse (CAPA); Community in Support of the Gang Truce (CSGT)

Community in Support of the Gang Truce (CSGT): Amer-I-Can program, 177, 204–5, 206–8, 221, 285n.57; boundaries of blackness and, 220–22; CAPA influences, 189, 190–91, 284n.37; Civilian Police Review Board, 190–91; collective responsibility and, 198; gender issues and, 30–31, 212–13, 223; generational issues, 209–10, 219–22; history of gang truce, 28–29, 177, 184–89; interethnic relations and, 198–99; Latinas/os, 198–99, 209–10; male-centered perspectives, 198–99, 212–13, 223; organizational leadership, 284n.33; programs of, 188–91, 195–99; social critiques of, 191–95; social transformation and, 193; women and, 198–99, 212–13

Comprehensive Employment and Training Act (CETA), 37

consumption, 139, 178, 221, 256n.4, 284n.34

controlling images, 23–24, 254n.22

cooperative economics, 68, 80–81, 82–84

Corona (Queens), 250n.7

Cose, Ellis, 255n.32

Counter-Intelligence Program, FBI (COINTELPRO), 120, 121, 131, 133, 134

Cox, Courtland, 224

crack cocaine: babies and, 249n.3; CIA and, 129–30; crack houses, 2, 21, 31, 67, 87–88, 90–91, 98–99, 266n.4; drug dependence and, 4, 8–9, 21–22, 24, 67–68, 70, 77–79, 85, 87, 89, 91, 105, 174–75, 218; drug economy and, 249n.2, 266n.4, 282n.12; gangs and, 282n.12; pregnancy and, 249n.3; women and, 67–68

criminalization: arrest rates, 282n.15; controlling images and, 254n.22; of gang members, 287n.9; three strikes law, 3, 284n.37; of women, 85–86; young men and, 284n.37; of youth, 14, 189–90, 282n.10, 287n.9

criminal justice system: domestic violence and, 263n.2; incarceration rates of youth, 14, 59, 250n.5; substance abuse and, 263n.2; three strikes law, 3, 284n.37; women and, 85–86

CSGT. See Community in Support of the Gang Truce

Daood, Kamau, 29, 161, 162–63, 222

Davis, Mike, 42, 47, 60, 282n.10, 284n.34, 287n.9

deindustrialization: income inequality and, 36, 256n.2; social mobility and, 27–28; suburbanization and, 47–48; unemployment and, 56; working class people and, 35–36; work opportunities and, 27–28, 44, 56

diasporic consciousness, 31–33, 164–65, 167, 168–69, 220, 251n.11, 280n.31

discrimination: affirmative action and, 37; employment, 37, 46, 50–57; gender, 54–56, 263n.2; housing, 42–44; racial, 50–57; social mobility and, 37, 208

Dolphy, Eric, 161

domestic sphere, 22, 64–65, 68–69, 84, 263n.2, 263n.4

domestic violence, 68–69, 217–18, 263n.2

drug dependence: alternate views on, 21–22; drug economy and, 8–9; drug rehabilitation, 22, 44, 65, 67, 70. 73, 77–78, 79, 87–88; fast foods as, 21–22; men and, 8–9; poverty and, 78–79, 85–86; women and, 8, 21–22, 67–68. See also crack cocaine

drug economy: drug wars and, 184; gangs and, 5–8, 182–83, 184, 282n.12; homicides and, 282n.13; income inequality and, 5–6, 12–14; residential segregation and, 59–60; violence and, 183; work opportunities and, 59–60. See also crack cocaine; drug dependence

drug rehabilitation, 22, 44, 65, 67, 70. 73, 77–78, 79, 87–88

Du Bois, W. E. B., 251n.11

Dymally, Mervin, 128

economic development: CSGT and, 196–98; Economic Recovery Act (1981), 257n.9; Rebuild Los Angeles (RLA), 191–93, 194, 284nn.41–42, 285n.45

Economic Recovery Act (1981), 257n.9

educational achievement: BPP and, 272n.45; CSGT on, 191; employment and, 56–57, 261n.62; high school completion rates, 261n.59; income inequality and, 38–39; Latinas/os and, 55–56; Los Angeles Unified School District, 261n.59; manufacturing/construction and, 261n.62; men vs. women, 55–56, 261n.59, 261n.62; race and, 38–39; structural inequities and, 261n.59; unemployment and, 35, 55–56; women and, 44–45, 55–56, 261n.59; work opportunities and, 44–45, 55–57, 261n.62

Edwards, Harry, 282n.10
electoral politics: accountability and, 126; coalition building and, 43, 53, 258n.24; ethnic particularism and, 258n.24; race and, 42–44, 47; segregation and, 42–44, 47; social class and, 258n.24; social mobility and, 43; social transformation and, 43; suburbanization and, 42–43, 60, 262n.73; urban spaces and, 42–44; vote dilution and, 43, 262n.74; voter turnout and, 262n.74; war on welfare and, 37–38
elitism, 43–44, 258n.24, 258n.27
El Salvador/Salvadorans, 48
emotionalism: blackness and, 118–19, 268n.11; blues performance and, 277n.17; collective responsibility and, 201–3; expressive culture and, 149–53, 168, 172–73, 275n.9, 276n.11, 277n.17; jazz performance and, 149–51, 152–53, 172–73, 275n.9, 276n.11; kinship and, 4, 76–77, 85; men and, 277n.17. 201–3; myth of, 118–19, 268n.11; police brutality and, 118–19; popular mobilization and, 118–19; self-help strategies and, 201–3; social transformation and, 201–3
entrepreneurs, 15–16, 165, 175, 192, 285n.45
Erie, Steven, 258n.24
essentialism, 29–30, 169–72, 175
establishmentarian, 116, 267n.7
ethic of openness, 137, 151–52, 169, 170–71, 174–75, 222
ethics of caring, 24–25, 66–79, 84–85
Evans, Emory, 161
exclusion: blackness and, 217–19; popular mobilization and, 170–71; poverty and, 22; solidarity and, 170–75
Exodus (community organization), 283n.30

expressive culture: achievement and, 149–51, 153, 155–56, 161, 172–73; artistic innovation and, 148–49, 153, 155–56, 161–62, 172–73; blackness and, 151–52, 153, 222; the blues, 160–61; class diversity and, 145; collective responsibility and, 145–48, 153, 172–73; emotionalism and, 149–53, 168, 172–73, 275n.9, 276n.11, 277n.17; essentialism and, 29–30, 169–72, 175; ethic of openness, 137, 151–52, 169, 170–71, 174–75, 222; gendered critiques of, 30–31; healing nature of, 167, 173; individualism and, 153; intellectual complexity and, 160–61; Islamic religion and, 159–60; patriarchal structures and, 145, 150–51; playing cute, 149–50, 151; as political education tool, 195–96; popular mobilization and, 211; in primarily White venues, 153; public space and, 144–45; spirituality and, 167; spoken word, 161, 162–63, 168–69; writers, 161. See also jazz

Fair Housing Act (1968), 42
family structures, 24–25, 90–91, 103–5. See also kinship networks; social networks
Fanon, Frantz, 111
Fard, W. D. (Wali Fard Muhammed), 157–58
Farrakhan, Louis, 157–58, 185, 277n.15, 280n. 30
FBI Counter-Intelligence Program (COINTELPRO), 120, 121, 131, 133, 134
feminists of color, 223–24. See also Black feminist thought
Fielder, Dale, 142
Fifth Street Dick's, 141–43, 145–46, 155, 158–59, 226, 272n.2
Fighting Words (Collins), 253n.20

Filipinos, 48
Final Vinyl, 162
Fokus (community organization), 283n.30
Freeman, Charles, 112
Fulton, Richard, 141, 159, 266, 272n.2. *See also* Fifth Street Dick's

gangs: antigang laws, 184; BPP and, 179; CAPA and, 129–30; Clinton administration and, 129; community organizing and, 129–30, 179; consumerism and, 284n.34; crack and, 282n.12; criminalization of gang members and, 3, 287n.9; CRIPS, 179–80; drug economy and, 5–8, 182–83, 184, 282n.12; gang wars and, 281n.10, 285n.52; generational issues and, 163–64, 183, 281n.7, 283n.24; hip-hop and, 160; histories of, 178–81; homicide rates and, 3, 184, 185–86, 188; interethnic relations and, 178; within LAPD, 129; lynching and, 267n.5; middle-class people and, 183–84, 190, 287n.9; networks of support and, 181–82; NOI and, 185; O.G.s, 179, 202, 281n.7, 285n.52; popular mobilization and, 181, 191; Reagan administration and, 121, 284n.34; social networks and, 3–7, 11; women and, 7, 285n.52; work opportunities and, 3; young members of, 12–14, 186–87, 283n.24
gang truce (1992): Amer-I-Can program and, 177, 204–5, 221, 285n.57; annual celebration of, 208–12; drug economy and, 182–83; generational issues and, 283n.24; history of, 177, 184–89; homicide rates and, 188; Latinas/os and, 209–10; media coverage of, 283n.29; Million Man March and, 283n.22; NOI and, 187–88, 211; personal responsibility

and, 283n.22; popular mobilization and, 211–13; resistance to, 136; social transformation, 193–95; truce documents, 187–88; youth response to, 283n.24. *See also* Community in Support of the Gang Truce
Garrett, Donald, 279n.28
Garrett, Kenny, 273n.6
Garrison, Jimmy, 148, 279n.28
Gates, Darryl (Police Chief), 123, 124, 125, 126, 127, 128, 269n.25
gender: blackness and, 145, 151–52, 169–71, 173–74, 217–20, 223–24; citizenship and, 55; community-based organizations and, 22, 30, 131–33, 136–37, 212; controlling images and, 23–24; ethics of caring and, 219; income inequality and, 54–56; leadership and, 131–33, 136–37; male-centered perspectives and, 30–31, 253n.21; playing cute and, 149–50; racialization and, 22, 29, 254n.22; resistance and, 79, 136–37; sexuality and, 22, 151–52; social transformation and, 107, 219, 223–24; solidarity and, 217; structural inequities and, 85–86, 266n.6; women and, 164, 199, 254n.22; work opportunities and, 44–45, 55; youth and, 12–13
generational issues: blackness and, 219–22, 222–23; in BPP, 219, 268n.8; in CAPA, 219–22; in CSGT, 209–10, 219–22; gangs and, 163–64, 183, 281n.7, 283n.24; hip-hop and, 160, 163–64; leadership and, 134–35, 222; occupational status and, 39–41; senior citizens, 191; wealth and, 39–41; youth and, 222
genocide, 17–18, 19, 30, 131, 251n.11, 262n.71
Getz, Stan, 275n.9
ghetto, the: definitions of, 252n.13, 268n.11; electoral politics and, 42–44;

"ghetto pathology," 268n.11; residential segregation and, 42, 252n.13; social isolation and, 42–44; South Central as, 35
"ghetto pathology," 268n.11
Gilroy, Paul, 280n.31
Golden Hill snobs, 217
Gordon, Don (Playmate), 185–86, 199, 283n.26
Gordon, Walter, 130
Gregory, Steven, 253n.19
group survival, 107, 267n.7. *See also* genocide

Halliday, George, 126
Hallin, Daniel, 268n.9
Hanlon, Stuart, 270n.36
Harlin, Latasha, 126
Harris, Barry, 276n.11
Hawkins, Odie, 161
healing, 167, 173. *See also* spirituality
health care, 71–75, 77
Heckman, Don, 276n.11
heteronormativity, 150–51, 152
Higgins, Billy: Coltrane and, 155; community recognition of, 279n. 29; death of, 272n.2; drum technique of, 276nn.12–13, 279n.29; Islam and, 158, 171; spirituality and, 167–68; World Stage and, 29, 141
hip-hop, 145, 159–60, 161, 162, 163–64, 222, 279n.23
Holden, Christopher, 123
homophobia, 150–51, 223
hooks, bell, 107, 223, 253n.20, 277n.17
Hope (community organization), 283n.30
House, Mary (deputy city attorney), 124–25
housing: affordable housing, 60–61, 97–107; crack houses and, 2, 21, 31, 67, 87–88, 90–91, 98–99, 266n.4; discrimination and, 42–44; home ownership, 96–97, 99, 250n.7; income stability and, 44, 97–99; interethnic conflict and, 93–94, 105–6, 216; landlord/tenant relationships, 81–82, 93, 94, 96–97, 99; middle-class people and, 250n.7; real estate discrimination and, 258n.23; safety and, 4, 60–61, 97–98; stability of, 44, 84–85, 96–107; tenant pride and, 90, 96–97, 106. *See also* residential segregation
Huggins, Jon, 179
Hutchinson, Bobby, 155

Ice-T, 181
identity construction, 219–24
identity politics, 215–17
immigration: Asian, 47–48, 50, 126–27, 269n.50; impact on Blacks, 47–48, 50–53; Latinas/os, 27–28, 35, 47, 48, 49, 50–53, 262n.72; structural inequities and, 50–53, 260n.50; undocumented, 59, 262n.72; unemployment and, 50–53, 60; women and, 54–55, 54–56; work opportunities and, 47, 50–53, 56
income inequality: affirmative action and, 37; drug economy and, 5–6, 12–14; educational achievement and, 38–39; formerly incarcerated people and, 3; by gender, 54–56; income decline and, 256n.3; membership organizations and, 133–34; race and, 38–39, 47; residential segregation and, 48, 54, 259n.44; residential stability and, 97–99; Social Security Act (1935), 257n.17; structural inequities and, 44–45; wealth and, 36, 39, 256n.3, 257n.17; women and, 9, 54–56, 79–80, 266n.6; work opportunities and, 256n.2

individualism: Amer-I-Can program, 177, 204–5, 206–8, 221, 285n.57; blackness and, 221; expressive cultures and, 153; mutuality vs., 107, 139, 218; poverty and, 46; social mobility and, 177, 204–5, 221, 285n.57; social transformation and, 139, 201–3, 207–8; structural inequities and, 14, 17–18; women and, 217, 218. *See also* collective responsibility; mutuality; networks of support

interethnic relations: blackness and, 217; Blacks and Latinas/os, 93–94, 217, 221–22, 260n.54; citizenship and, 53, 55; coalition building and, 140, 219–20, 258n.27; CSGT and, 198–99, 209–10; gangs and, 178; interethnic conflict, 93–94, 105–6, 126–27, 216, 260n.54

internalized oppression, 23, 223, 253n.21, 268n.11

Iran/Iranians, 48

Islamic religion: Al-Islam, 157–58; collective responsibility and, 159–60; culture of dignity and, 144–45, 147; expressive culture and, 159–60; internationalism of, 165, 170–71; in Leimert Park, 156–57, 159; mutuality and, 145; Nation of Islam (NOI), 157–58, 170–71, 187, 211, 277nn.14–16; religious practice, 147

Jackson, Jesse, 126

James, Joy, 253n.21

jazz: the blues and, 277n.17; blues vs., 145, 160–61; emotionalism and, 149–51, 152–53, 172–73, 275n.9, 276n.11; gendered critiques and, 30–31; hip-hop vs., 145, 160–61, 163–64, 222; homophobia and, 150–51, 223; patriarchal structures of, 150–51, 223; paying dues, 172–73; process of

performance and, 280n.31; sexism and, 150–51; social awareness and, 279n.23, 279n. 28; spirituality and, 148–50

Jazz Caravan (1997), 155–56

John Coltrane Quartet, 148–49, 273n.6, 276n.12

Johnson-Powell, Gloria, 125–26

Jones, Elvin, 148, 154, 273n.6, 276n.12, 279n.28

Jones, Leroi (Amiri Baraka), 277n.17

Keil, Charles, 278n.18

Khalilullah, Rizza M., 268n.11, 277n.16

King, Rodney G., 124–25, 126, 127, 138, 195, 269n.25, 270n.27

kinship: emotionalism and, 4, 76–77, 85

kinship networks, 24–25, 65, 181–82

Klein, Malcom: and Cheryl L. Maxon and Lea C. Cunningham, 282n.12

Kofsky, Frank, 279n. 28

Koon, Stacy, 138

Korean Americans, 126–27, 220, 258n.27, 260n.50

Koreans, 48, 50, 126–27, 260n.50

Kroc, Ray A., 204

Kulu Se Mama (1965), 166, 279n.28

Kwaanza, 266n.2

Lacy, Steve, 161

Latinas/os: Asian immigration and, 269n.50; blackness and, 217; CSGT and, 198–99, 209–10; educational achievement and, 55–56; immigration and, 27–28, 35, 47, 48, 49, 50–53, 262n.72; income inequality and, 38–39; interethnic relations, 93–94, 217, 221–22, 260n.54; migration to South Central, 59; poverty levels and, 48; racial identity and, 31–33; residential segregation and, 48, 49–50, 59, 259nn.42–44; sweatshops and, 47–48,

56; work opportunities, 2–3, 11, 53, 55–56

Lawrence, Charles III, 286n.1

leadership: class differences and, 135; community-based organizations and, 131–33, 136–37, 139–40, 271n.39, 271n.41, 284n.33; gender and, 131–33, 136–37; generational issues and, 134–35, 222; membership organizations and, 133–34; popular mobilization and, 113, 123; social mobility and, 123; women and, 131–33, 136–37; youth, 134–35

Lee, General Robert, 285n.52

Lee, Lee Lew, 271n.41

Leimert Park: boundaries of blackness and, 174–76; class structures and, 174–76; as cultural center, 141, 162, 272n.1, 272n.2; diversity of, 57, 259n.42; ethic of openness and, 174; hip-hop and, 160, 161, 162, 163–64, 222; influences of Islam on, 159, 165, 171–72; normativity and, 29, 144–45, 156–57, 159, 164, 168–69; Saturday rallies, 170

Lewis, Earl, 66

Lewis, Juno Se Mama, 165–68, 222, 272n.2, 279nn.28–29

liberatory politics, 23, 30–31, 107, 140, 215–17, 224, 253n.20, 267n.7, 286n.8

Liebman, Dave, 273n.6

Lipsitz, George, 262n.74, 269n.46, 279n. 28

Lock, Graham, 176

Los Angeles: black residential population, 58–59; civic work opportunities and, 43; electoral politics of, 43–44; racial diversity within, 48–51; residential segregation within, 48, 49–50; South Central, 249n.4; suburbs and, 57–59

Los Angeles Police Department (LAPD): Committee for a Civilian Police Review Board and, 126–29; police brutality of, 270n.36; Rodney King incident, 124–25, 126, 127, 138, 195; spy lawsuit, 119–22

Los Angeles Unified School District, 261n.59

Los Angeles uprising (1992), 27, 35, 179, 180, 255n.31

Louis Harris poll (1988), 258n.23

Lowe, Frank, 273n.6

Lowndes County Freedom Organization, 255n.33

Lyle, K. Curtis, 161

lynching, 251n.11, 267n.5

M.A.D.D. (community organization), 283n.30

Mahogany, Kevin, 273n.6

Malcolm X, 109–10, 134, 158, 277n.15

Malcolm X Grassroots Movement (community organization), 283n.30

male-centered perspectives: blackness and, 223; blues and, 277n.17; CAPA and, 136–37, 223; controlling images and, 23–24; CSGT and, 198–99, 212–13, 223; ethic of openness and, 175; expressive culture and, 145, 150–51; gendered critiques and, 30–31, 253n.21; jazz and, 150–51, 223; women and, 85–86, 223–24; World Stage and, 22, 30–31

Mandel, Howard, 273n.6

Marxism, Black, 113, 252n.14, 253n.20, 267n.7

masculinity, 150–51, 275n.8

McLeod, Jay, 253n.19

media: Black-owned, 126–27; doctrine of objectivity and, 267n.7; establishmentarian tone of, 116, 267n.7; as ideological medium, 268n.9; mainstream media coverage, 116; as political education tool, 195–96;

popular mobilization and, 111–12, 114–16, 118, 122, 126–27

Media Monopoly (Bagdikian), 267n.7

membership organizations, 133–34. *See also* community-based organizations; popular mobilization

men: arrest rates of, 282n.15; controlling images and, 254n.22; criminal justice system and, 282n.15, 284n.37; domestic violence and, 217–18; educational achievement and, 55–56, 261n.59, 283n.26; emotionalism and, 201–3, 277n.17; ethic of openness and, 137, 174; poverty and, 24, 217; profeminist men, 253n.21; solidarity and, 217–18; unemployment of, 35–36; work opportunities and, 44

mental health, 3, 6–7, 8, 10

methodology, 18–19, 29, 31–33, 31–36, 272n.3

Mexican American Political Association, 128

Mexican Americans, 47, 48, 128

Mexicans, 27–28, 35, 51

middle-class people: BPP and, 272n.45; CAPA and, 271n.44; civil rights era and, 250n.7; community organizations and, 271n.44; criminalization of youth and, 287n.9; definitions of, 251n.10; educational achievement and, 57, 251n.10; gangs and, 183–84, 190, 287n.9; hip-hop and, 159–60; home ownership and, 250n.7; income and, 251n.10; Million Man March and, 283n.22; Queens (New York City) and, 250n.7; social mobility and, 39–41; social status and, 16; suburban migration of, 57–59; support for criminal justice system, 287n.9; work opportunities and, 57, 251n.10

Middle Easterners, 48

Miller, Jerome G., 59, 184, 250n.5

Million Man March, 157, 184–85, 280n. 30, 283n.22

Minor Parent Program, 265n.1

Mitchell, Marsha, 283n.29

Mohammed, W. D., 158

moon watching, 63–64

Morrison, Toni, 257n.13, 263n.3

Mothers Reclaiming Our Children/Mothers ROC (community organization), 283n.30

Muhammad, Don, 146–47

Muhammad, Elijah (Elijah Poole), 158

Muhammad, Wali Fard (W. D. Fard), 157–58

Mulgrow, Roy, 142

Murray, Sean, 262n.67

Museum in Black (art gallery), 162

mutuality, 107, 135–37, 139, 163–64, 217–18, 218, 222–23, 267n.7

National Welfare Rights Organization, 263n.4

Nation of Islam (NOI), 157–58, 170–71, 185, 187, 211, 277nn.14–16, 280n. 30

Native Americans, 48

networks of support, 63–64, 89–96, 103–5, 181–82

New African Vanguard Movement (community organization), 283n.30

Newton, Huey, 112, 132, 133, 195, 255n.33, 271n.39, 271n.41, 272n.45, 286n.8

No Guns (community organization), 283n.30

O.G.s (Original Gangsters), 179, 202, 281n.7, 285n.52

Ojenke, 161

Oliver, Melvin L.: and James H. Johnson, 260n.54; and Thomas Shapiro, 39, 40, 41, 58, 258n.17

Omni-Spheres, 196

Ong, Paul: and Abel Valenzuela, 50–51, 52
oppressor within, the, 23, 253n.21
Orange County, 49
Original Gangsters (O.G.s), 179, 202, 281n.7, 285n.52

Palms, 259n.43
Palos Verdes (LA), 49
Pan-Afrikan Peoples Arkestra, 161, 278n.19
Parker, Charlie, 162, 273n.6
Pasadena Police Department lawsuit, 122–23
Perry, Anthony (Brother Tony X), 187, 199
personal responsibility, 17, 29, 170, 202, 283n.22
Personal Responsibility and Work Opportunity Reconciliation Act (1996), 265n.1
Playmate (Don Gordon), 185–86, 199, 283n.26
police brutality: CAPA and, 111–12, 122–23, 127–30; Civilian Police Review Board, 126–29; criminalization and, 282n.15; emotionalism and, 118–19; gangs and, 6; interethnic conflicts and, 126–27; jury awards, 269n.18; patterns of abuse, 269n.25, 270n.27; photographs of, 111–112; police surveillance and, 119–22; race relations and, 126–27; Rodney King incident, 124–25, 126, 127, 138, 195, 269n.25, 270n.27; U.S. Commission on Civil Rights and, 129–30; women and, 69–70
political education, 111–17, 177, 195–96, 203
Poole, Elijah (Elijah Muhammed), 158
popular mobilization: agency and, 171–72; audiovisual media and, 111–12, 114–16, 118; Civilian Police Review Board, 126–29; class differences and, 133–34, 135, 136; coalition building and, 28–29; community meetings and, 117–18, 209–12; emotionalism and, 118–19; exclusivism and, 170–71; expressive culture and, 211; gangs and, 181, 191, 211–13; history as a tool for, 112; leadership issues and, 113, 123; legal action and, 117–18, 118; media coverage and, 111–12, 114–16, 118, 122, 126–27; mutuality and, 135–37, 217–18; political education and, 111–17, 177, 195–96, 203; racial essentialism and, 169–71; structural inequities and, 17–18. See also community-based organizations; liberatory politics; social movements
Porter, Lewis, 273n.6
poverty: AFDC and, 263n.4; Carter administration and, 257n.12; as clients, 250n.7; drug dependence and, 78–79, 85–86; electoral politics and, 38; ethics of caring and, 216–17; exclusion and, 22; families and, 85–86; government intervention and, 37–38; health care and, 71–75, 79; home ownership and, 252n.13; hunger and, 256n.8; individualism and, 46; men and, 24, 217; mental health and, 3; poverty-level income, 251n.10; race and, 46; residential segregation and, 48, 259n.44; residential stability and, 252n.13; sexual violence and, 263n.2; structural inequities and, 46, 260n.50; War on Poverty, 37, 178–81; welfare programs and, 37–38, 250n.7; women and, 21–22, 24–25, 54–56, 64–66, 79, 85–86, 216–17
Pratt, Geronimo, 131, 133, 138, 270n.36, 272n.46
Priestly, Eric, 161

Prima Materia, 273n.6
profeminist men, 253n.21
public space: agency and, 171–72;
    expressive culture and, 144–45;
    Islamic religion and, 157, 158, 159;
    normativity and, 29, 144–45, 156–57,
    159, 164, 168–69; rights and, 194,
    270n.31; social mobility and, 16–17;
    social movements and, 111

Q-Bone, 181

race: citizenship and, 55; educational
    achievement and, 38–39; electoral
    politics and, 42–44, 47; employment
    discrimination and, 46; income
    inequality and, 38–39, 47; organiza-
    tion of society and, 257n.13; poverty
    and, 46; racial identity and, 31–33;
    residential segregation and, 41–42,
    48–51; social mobility and, 27–28,
    39–41; urban spaces and, 41–44;
    wealth and, 39–41
radical social transformation, 253n.21,
    286n.1
rainbow rhetoric, 258n.24
Rainbow's End (Erie), 258n.24
Ransby, Barbara, 266n.6
Reagan administration (1981–1989):
    civil rights legislation and, 37;
    economic policies of, 47, 257n.9;
    electoral politics and, 37–38; gang
    membership and, 121, 284n.34;
    income inequality under, 28, 36–37;
    income taxes, 257n.9; popular
    support for, 37–38; residential
    segregation and, 42–43, 46–47;
    welfare and, 263n.4
Rebuild Los Angeles (RLA), 191–93, 194,
    284nn.41–42, 285n.45
Redman, Dewey, 161
Reed, Ishmael, 282n.10
Reid, Richard, 155

religion, 156–57. See also Islamic religion
reproductive health and rights, 11,
    76–77, 79, 80, 263n.4, 265n.1,
    265n.5
residential segregation: discrimination
    and, 45–46; drug economy and,
    59–60; Fair Housing Act (1968), 42;
    as genocide, 251n.11; ghettos and, 42,
    252n.13; household income and,
    259n.44; income inequality and, 48,
    54, 259n.44; Latinas/os and, 48,
    49–50, 59, 105–6, 259nn.42–44;
    within Los Angeles, 48, 49–50;
    poverty and, 48, 252n.13, 259n.44;
    race and, 41–42, 48–51, 259nn.42–44;
    residential stability and, 252n.13;
    social inequalities and, 27–28;
    social mobility and, 45–46, 57–59;
    social networks and, 44; spatial
    arrangements and, 41–44; structural
    inequities and, 27–28; unemploy-
    ment and, 44–45, 48, 259n.44;
    urban spaces and, 252n.13; women
    and, 44–45; work opportunities
    and, 44–48
resistance: everyday survival and, 17–18,
    22, 66, 79, 218–19, 253n.20; gender
    and, 79, 136–37; rent withholding,
    99–103, 104; social movements and,
    17–18. 136–137; structural, 218–19;
    temporary, 76–77, 218–19. See
    also liberatory politics; popular
    mobilization; social movements
Reynolds, Gerald, 270n.32
Ridley-Thomas, Mark, 128
Rise (community organization),
    283n.30
RLA (Rebuild Los Angeles), 191–93, 194,
    284nn.41–42, 285n.45
Roach, Max, 279n.23
Robeson, Paul, 251n.11
Robinson, Cedric J., 253n.20
ROVA Saxophone Quartet, 273n.6

Sanders, Pharaoh, 161, 279n. 28
Seale, Bobby, 132, 195, 255n.33, 271n.41,
    272n.45
segregation. *See* residential segregation
self-help strategies: Amer-I-Can
    program, 177, 204–5, 206–8, 221,
    285n.57; collective responsibility and,
    200–203, 204, 207–8; emotionalism
    and, 201–3; social critique and, 177–
    78, 191–95, 283n.22; social movements
    and, 283n.22; structural inequities
    and, 17–18; work opportunities and,
    205, 207–8; youth and, 177–78. *See
    also* individualism
sex industry, 263n.2
sexual expression, 76–77, 263n.4, 265n.1
sexual health, 76–77, 263n.4
sexuality, 45–46, 84, 151–52
sexual violence, 263n.2
Shadowboxing (James), 253n.21
Shepp, Archie, 161
Sherrils, Daude, 187, 199
Snipes, Wesley, 269n.25
social isolation, 26–27, 42–44
social mobility: Amer-I-Can program,
    177, 204–5, 206–8, 221, 285n.57;
    blackness and, 16–17, 221–22;
    deindustrialization and, 27–28;
    discrimination and, 37, 208; ethic of
    openness and, 174–76; individualism
    and, 177, 204–5, 221, 285n.57;
    leadership and, 123; public space
    and, 16–17; race and, 27–28, 39–41;
    residential segregation and, 45–46,
    57–59; social inequities and, 27–28;
    structural inequities and, 27–28;
    work opportunities and, 27–28, 45
social movements: blackness and,
    216–17; coalition building and,
    28–29, 184–85, 209–10; government
    accountability and, 283n.22; libera-
    tory politics and, 18, 23, 30–31, 107,
    140, 215–17, 224, 253n.20, 267n.7,

286n.8; personal responsibility and,
    201, 221, 283n.22; public space and,
    111; residential stability and, 252n.13;
    resistance and, 17–18, 136–37; self-
    help and, 283n.22; structural
    inequities and, 17–18. *See also*
    community-based organizations;
    popular mobilization
social networks: of gangs, 3–7, 11;
    residential segregation and, 44; social
    isolation and, 26–27; women and,
    87–96, 217–18; work ethic and, 25;
    work opportunities and, 25, 26–27,
    44–45
social transformation: Black feminist
    thought and, 223–24, 267n.7;
    blackness and, 22, 176, 215–17, 221–
    24; economic development and,
    193–95; electoral politics and, 43;
    emotionalism and, 201–3; ethic of
    openness and, 137, 151–52, 169, 170–
    71, 174–75, 222; gang truce and, 193–
    95; gendered critiques and, 107, 219,
    223–24; individualism and, 139,
    201–3, 207–8; liberatory politics and,
    23, 30–31, 107, 140, 215–17, 224,
    253n.20, 267n.7, 286n.8
Sohigan, Ronald M. (judge), 124
solidarity: blackness and, 16–17, 66, 83,
    215–17, 217–19; coalition building
    and, 159–60, 165; exclusion and,
    170–75; gender and, 217; kinship
    networks and, 24–25; men and, 217–
    18; social class and, 16, 217; women
    and, 63–66, 83–84, 92–93, 107,
    217–19, 253n.20
Solomon Group (community
    organization), 283n.30
South Central Los Angeles: as a Black
    ghetto, 35; danger of, 60; diversity of,
    53; geographic definition of, 249n.4;
    Latinas/os migration to, 59; middle-
    and working-class people migration

from, 262n.67; neighborhood map, 13; residential segregation within, 50

spatial arrangements: public policy and, 46–47; residential segregation and, 41–44; social distance and, 16; spatial mobility and, 41–44; suburbs and, 47–50

spirituality, 149–51, 167–68

spoken word, 162–63

Stormer, Dan, 125

Streetwise (Anderson), 24–25

structural inequities: blackness and, 15–18; class structures and, 15–18, 37, 44–45; collective responsibility and, 17–18; discrimination and, 17–18; educational achievement, 261n.59; ethnographic approaches to, 18–19, 19–21; gender and, 85–86, 266n.6; historicity and, 19–21, 29, 208, 253n.19; immigration and, 50–53, 260n.50; income inequality and, 44–45; individualism and, 14, 17–18; popular mobilization and, 17–18; poverty and, 46, 260n.50; residential segregation and, 27–28; self-help strategies and, 17–18; social mobility and, 27–28; social movements and, 17–18; work opportunities and, 45–46, 50, 88–89

suburbanization: Black migration to, 57–58, 60; deindustrialization and, 47–48; electoral politics and, 42–43, 60, 262n.73; immigrants and, 48; urban migration and, 57–58; urban spaces and, 262n.73; Whites and, 60; work opportunities and, 47

Sula (Morrison), 263n.3

support networks: ethics of caring and, 92, 107; mutuality and, 92–96, 107, 217

surveillance, 10, 65, 78, 119–22, 171, 287n.9

sweatshops, 47–48, 56

TANC (Temporary Assistance for Needy Families), 265n.1

Tapscott, Horace, 155, 161, 163, 222, 278n.19

Taylor, Cecil, 161

Temporary Assistance for Needy Families, 265n.1

Thomas, J. C., 275n.9

Thomas, Kenneth, 139

Tillmon, Johnnie, 263n.4

Toney, A. K., 163–64

transformative power of mutuality, 107, 163–64, 222–23, 267n.7

Troupe, Quincy, 161

Ture, Kwame (Stokely Carmichael), 224, 255n.33

Tyner, McCoy, 148, 149, 279n. 28

Ueberroth, Peter, 191–92, 284nn.41–42

UMAA (Underground Musicians and Artists Association), 161

unemployment: deindustrialization and, 56; educational achievement and, 35, 55–56; immigration and, 50–53; residential segregation and, 44–45, 48, 259n.44; times of greatest, 256n.7; women and, 55–56. *See also* work opportunities

Union of God's Musicians and Artists Ascension (UGMAA), 278n.19

Unity One (community organization), 283n.30

Urban Blues (Keil), 278n.18

urban spaces: electoral politics and, 42–44; migration to suburbs, 57–58; race and, 41–44; suburbanization and, 262n.73

U.S. Commission on Civil Rights, 129–30

Vernon, Robert L., 123, 124–25

Vieux, Phil, 155

War on Poverty, 37, 178–81
Washington, Raymond, 180
Waters, Maxine, 126
Watson, Bobby, 155
Watson, Diane (state senator), 269n.25
Watts, 49, 60, 177, 179, 262n.65
Watts Happening Coffee House, 162
Watts rebellion (1965), 27, 35, 161, 162, 179, 180, 255n.31
Watts Writers Workshop, 161, 164
wealth, 36, 39–41, 45, 256nn.3–4, 257n.17
We Keep America on Top of the World (Hallin), 268n.9
welfare programs: Aid to Families with Dependent Children (AFDC), 8, 9, 89, 263n.4; drug rehabilitation and, 77–78, 88; marriage and, 265n.1; networks of support, 89–96; Personal Responsibility and Work Opportunity Reconciliation Act (1996), 265n.1; reproductive rights and, 265n.1; screening processes, 265n.1; social workers and, 75–76, 77–78, 87–89; war on welfare, 37–38; women and, 4, 263n.4. *See also* welfare reform
welfare reform: Clinton administration and, 42, 88, 257n.12, 265n.1; electoral politics and, 38; Personal Responsibility and Work Opportunity Reconciliation Act (1996), 265n.1; poverty and, 37–38; public housing and, 257n.12; Temporary Assistance for Needy Families, 265n.1; women and, 87–89; work ethic and, 37, 88–89; workfare and, 257n.12, 265n.1; work opportunities and, 88, 257n.12, 265n.1
We Real Cool (hooks), 277n.17
White: definitions of, 249n.1
Whiteman Made Me Do It, The (Khalilullah), 268n.11
Wilkes, Jamaal, 126
Wilkins, Ron, 179

Williams, Tookie, 180
Wilmer, Valerie, 273n.6
Wilson, Peter (governor), 88, 265n.1
Wilson, William Julius, 25, 27, 254n.29
Wilson administration (1991–1999), 265n.1
women: addiction and, 87–88; blackness and, 217–18, 221–22; Black Panther Party and, 271n.39; CAPA and, 131–33, 136–37; childcare and, 76, 82; circles of sorrow and, 65–66, 83, 263n.3; class conflict and, 82–84; coalition building and, 218–19, 221–22; collective problem solving and, 266n.6; community-based organizations and, 70–71, 131–33, 136–37; cooperative economics and, 68, 82–84; CSGT and, 198–99; domestic sphere and, 21–22, 64–65, 68–69, 84, 263n.2, 263n.4; domestic violence and, 68–69, 217–18, 263n.2; drug dependence and, 8, 67–68, 77–78, 85, 87, 89, 91, 105, 174–75, 263n.2; drug rehabilitation, 22, 44, 65, 67, 70, 73, 77–78, 79, 87–88; educational achievement and, 44–45, 55–56, 261n.59; ethics of caring and, 64–79, 84–85, 107, 216–17; gangs and, 7, 285n.52; gender roles and, 164, 199, 254n.22; health care and, 71–75, 79, 80; homelessness and, 263n.2; household work and, 54–55; housing and, 64–66; immigration and, 54–56; income inequality and, 47, 54–56, 79–80, 266n.6; individualism vs. mutuality, 217; kinship networks, 65–66; leadership and, 131–33, 136–37; male-centered perspectives and, 85–86, 223–24; networks of support, 89–96, 103–5, 217–18; "playing cute" and, 149–50; police brutality and, 69–70; poverty and, 21–22, 24–25, 54–56, 64–66, 79, 85–86,

216–17; reproductive health and rights and, 11, 76–77, 79, 80, 263n.4, 265n.1, 265n.5; residential segregation and, 44–45; resistance and, 79, 217–19; sex industry and, 263n.2; social networks of, 87–96, 217–18; solidarity and, 63–66, 83–84, 92–93, 107, 217–19, 253n.20; welfare and, 8, 69–70, 87–89, 263n.4, 265n.1; work opportunities for, 44–45, 54–56, 82–83

work ethics, 25–26, 37, 45–46, 263n.4

work opportunities: African American vs. Latino, 2–3, 11, 53, 55–56; CETA and, 37; childcare, 76, 82; citizenship and, 55; CSGT and, 196–97; deindustrialization and, 27–28, 44, 56; drug economy and, 59–60; educational achievement and, 44–45, 55–57, 261n.62; formerly incarcer-+ated people and, 2–3, 9–10; gang affiliation and, 3; gender and, 44–45, 55; household work, 54–55; illegal economy and, 45; immigration and, 47, 50–53, 56; impact on mental health and, 3, 10; income inequality and, 256n.2; informal economy and, 45; membership organizations and, 133–34; middle-class people and, 56–57; residential segregation and, 44–48; self-help strategies and, 205, 207–8; service economy and, 55, 80–81; social mobility and, 27–28, 45; social networks and, 25, 26–27, 44–45; structural inequities and, 45–46, 50, 88–89; suburbanization and, 47; sweatshops, 47–48, 56; wealth accumulation and, 45; welfare and, 88, 257n.12, 265n.1; women and, 44–45, 54–56; work ethic and, 45–46; for youth, 12–14, 178

World Stage: alcohol policy, 158; amateurs/professionals and, 145–47, 273n.4; blackness and, 145, 223; class diversity at, 144; Coltrane legacy at, 148–50, 154; Fifth Street Dick's and, 141–42, 273n.5; gender and, 22, 144, 222–23, 272n.3; Higgins and, 141; jam sessions, 141, 142–44, 145–48, 172–73, 273n.5; Jazz Caravan (1997), 155–56; male-centered community of, 22, 30–31; public space and, 144–45; racial diversity at, 144; singers at, 272n.3; social interaction at, 145–48; women and, 22, 144, 222–23, 272n.3

Wretched of the Earth (Fanon), 111

Yaroslavsky, Zev, 124

youth: consumption and, 139, 178, 221, 256n.4, 284n.34; criminalization of, 14, 189–90, 282n.10, 287n.9; criminal justice system and, 14, 59, 250n.5; gangs and, 12–14, 186–87, 283n.24; gender and, 12–13; generational issues, 222; hip-hop and, 160, 163–64; homicide rates, 184; incarceration rates of, 59, 250n.5; leadership and, 134–35; self-help strategies and, 177–78; work opportunities and, 12–14, 178

Zimmerman, Paul, 273n.6

Zinzun, Michael: CAPA and, 109, 112, 120, 127–30; Civilian Police Review Board, 127–29; defamation lawsuit, 123–26; leadership of, 139–40; media messages, 116, 127, 137–38; spying lawsuit, 121–27

João H. Costa Vargas is assistant professor of anthropology and is affiliated with the Center for African and African American Studies at the University of Texas at Austin. He has collaborated with the Coalition Against Police Abuse of Los Angeles since 1996 and works with Afro-Brazilian grassroots organizations.

Robin D. G. Kelley is the William B. Ransford Professor of Cultural and Historical Studies at Columbia University. He is the author of numerous books, including *Freedom Dreams: The Black Radical Imagination* and *Yo Mama's Disfunktional: Fighting the Culture Wars in Urban America.*